THE
FOREST
SERVICE

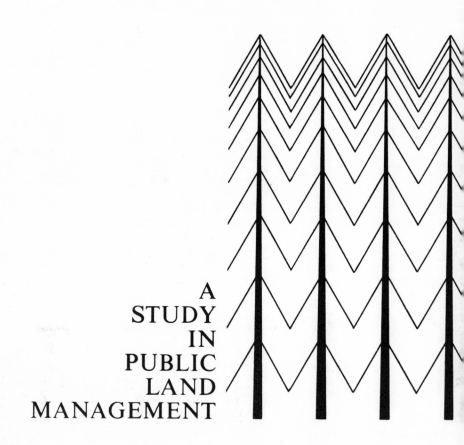

A
STUDY
IN
PUBLIC
LAND
MANAGEMENT

Glen O. Robinson

THE
FOREST
SERVICE

Published for RESOURCES FOR THE FUTURE, INC.
by The Johns Hopkins University Press, Baltimore and London

Resources for the Future is a nonprofit corporation for research and education in the development, conservation, and use of natural resources and the improvement of the quality of the environment. It was established in 1952 with the cooperation of the Ford Foundation. Part of the work of Resources for the Future is carried out by its resident staff; part is supported by grants to universities and other non-profit organizations. Unless otherwise stated, interpretations and conclusions in RFF publications are those of the authors; the organization takes responsibility for the selection of significant subjects for study, the competence of the researchers, and their freedom of inquiry.

The figures for this book were drawn by Frank and Clare Ford. The book was edited by Jo Hinkel.

RFF editors: Herbert C. Morton, Joan R. Tron, Ruth B. Haas, Jo Hinkel

Copyright © 1975 by The Johns Hopkins University Press
All rights reserved
Manufactured in the United States of America

Library of Congress Catalog Card Number 75-11352

ISBN 0-8018-1723-4

ISBN 0-8018-1768-4 *paper*

Library of Congress Cataloging in Publication Data will be found on the last printed page of this book.

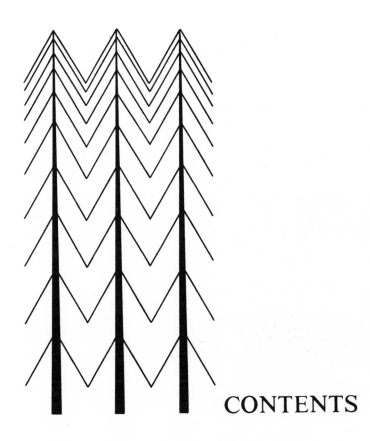

CONTENTS

PREFACE

Although the title of this book gives due notice of its content, anyone asked to read beyond the title of a book this length is entitled to some further explanation of what it is about and perhaps how it came to be written.

In its initial conception, this was to be a study of the Forest Service alone—its organization and processes. That conception had its origin in a rather casual suggestion put to me by the then-head of the U.S. Administrative Conference, whose primary activity is sponsoring research on, and proposals for improvements in, the organization and procedure of federal administrative agencies. The idea of studying the Forest Service was an appealing one, since the organization has all the important attractions for serious investigation. It is large (among the largest subdepartmental bureaus in the federal government); it is old with tradition; it has an important and an increasingly controversial mission (it is clearly foremost among the federal land-managing bureaus even though it is only the second-largest landowner); and it is multifaceted (its functions covering nearly the full range of federal land-management).

To be sure, the proposed study was not a novel idea. The Forest Service has been the subject of several books and many shorter monographs: Herbert Kaufman's *The Forest Ranger* (1960), is still regarded as a classic of its genre—a kind of broad sociological study of the agency. More recently, the agency has been briefly surveyed by Michael Frome in *The Forest Service* (1971). And most recently, it has been critically examined by the ubiquitous Nader's Raiders (Daniel R. Barney) in *The Last Stand* (1974). However, the fact that I would not be harvesting virgin timber was not discouraging, for the subject was large, and its allowable cut had not yet been reached.

My only reservation about a study of the Forest Service's organization and administrative processes was that it seemed too narrow to tap the most interesting attributes of the subject, or the most important. Doubtless a careful examination of the administrative process would have some usefulness, and certainly it would best fit my capabilities as an administrative lawyer. That is what administrative law, so-called, is. So, at least, it has been traditionally taught in law schools, where most legal subjects are labeled for the profession. But clearly in this case a limited approach runs the danger of exhausting itself quickly, for little return, unless one can examine it within the context of the particular functions, problems, and controversies which give life to the administrative process.

Hence the subtitle—*A Study in Public Land Management*—was added to fit the Forest Service within the larger framework of public (federal) land management. The object of the study then became not merely the Forest Service as an administrative institution, but the institution as a focal point for looking at the general processes, problems, and controversies of public land management.

The larger study was undertaken with some anxiety. Quite apart from the ambition involved in attempting to canvass the subject of federal lands, there is the fact that this has been a much-visited wood. Counting major studies alone, from Clawson's and Held's important survey, *The Federal Lands* (1957), to the monumental work of the Public Land Law Review Commission (completed in 1970), the literature is extensive, if not exhaustive. In spite of these other studies I concluded that there were yet things to be said, and perhaps new perspectives to be explored.

But what perspectives? As an administrative lawyer, I felt confident I was suitably trained to deal with the assorted legal aspects of agency procedure, with questions of adjudicatory procedures, rulemaking, public involvement, judical review, and the like. To venture into the many different problems of land-management policy required caution insofar as it called for an excursion into ecology, economics, and many other disciplines for which I make no claim of special expertise. This caused some uneasiness, but obviously not enough to deter the study. If war is too important to be left to generals, managing the environment is too vital to be left to professional land managers, be they economists, ecologists, or foresters. It should not be left to lawyers either, although the increasing resort to litigation has certainly created a real risk of that rather frightening prospect.

In a spirit of eclecticism I have attempted to blend something from each of the different professional perspectives into a general survey of the Forest Service and forest resource policy. If any one perspective tends to dominate, it is that of economics, broadly defined as the study of resource allocation under conditions of scarcity. I am mindful that such a viewpoint puts this study at odds with the trend of much popular thinking on the subject, a trend most evident in the writings of many modern environmentalists. In their writings and speeches the ecological conscience is pitted against the economic conscience. The former embraces, in Aldo Leopold's phrase, "a land ethic," while the latter is, variously, an ethic of money, commercial exploitation, and so on.

I believe such a view reflects a serious misunderstanding of the economic approach in its broader application. Contrary to quite common supposition, economics is not simply the science of commerce, nor even the science of market exchange. It is partly those, to be sure, but in the broader application economic evaluation is the study of choice and allocation under conditions of scarcity. It is with reference to that broad definition that I choose to characterize the dominant perspective of this study as an economic one.

The study has essentially a twofold structure. The first is essentially descriptive of the history, organization, decision-making processes, and major management responsibilities of the Forest Service. Chapters I and II are devoted to the first three of these aspects while the fourth is taken up in chapters III through IX, each dealing with a distinctive land use function. The second task of the study is a critical analysis of some of the major land-management problems and controversies, and of Forest Service policies. For the most part, the approach here has been to treat these distinctively by major land-management function (see chapters IV through IX). Finally, in chapter X, I return to the Forest Service as an institution, offering general comments on some of the administrative problems of organization, procedure, and related concerns.

My critical comments, regarding both the Forest Service and relevant aspects of land use policy, are perhaps somewhat impressionistic. Certainly they are not fully and reliably scientific. Though I have spent some two years gathering information from oral interviews as well as written sources, I have not conducted a complete empirical investigation of the agency or its work. And as will be quickly evident, this study lacks the kind of analytical rigor one would expect of a scientific study. Even in terms of the rather unscientific standards of legal commentary, this work is somewhat out of the mainstream.

In fact, throughout the entire effort I have been guided by conflicting standards: the standard of popular narrative exposition on the one hand and the more specialized requirements of academic scholarship on the other. These are infrequent companions and the attempt to mix the two together successfully has been most challenging. It is hoped the result is a book that can be of some value to all those who know enough about the problems of resource management to be concerned but not enough so they cannot learn more from an nonprofessional observer.

A final word of explanation is necessary about the time perspective of this study, which has proved even more troublesome than the problem of the professional viewpoint. In an earlier era the problem of timing would not be cause for great concern. The pace of events, if not exactly slow, was at least more leisurely, and one could be confident that major change would not render one's work obsolete before the ink was dry. The present age offers no such comforts. As concern over the environment has moved to the center of public attention, the pace of events has quickened. In response to events the Forest Service, too, has stirred. Whether it has done so sufficiently to keep pace with events, many critics doubt; but it is hard to dispute that in the past decade the agency has increased its motion for change over that of prior decades. And there are indications of greater change in the decade ahead. To attempt to depict events in motion is a hazardous venture. A slow lens can photograph a subject in motion sharply, but the resulting picture is of a past event. A fast lens may catch the motion but show only a blur. Obviously, what one wants is a motion picture camera. That is hard to match in print unless one produces a loose-leaf service. Thus, I have more or less alternated between a blur and a picture of yesterday's events. For the most part, the book speaks to matters as they stood on or about June 1974.

My debts to others for their help are many. The study was primarily supported by a grant from Resources for the Future, Inc., and I am particularly grateful to Acting President Marion Clawson for his assistance and encouragement. Not the least of his contributions were his many fine writings in the field of public land management. From them, and from several excellent monographs of the Public Land Law Review Commission, I have not only learned, but have often borrowed shamelessly. To my dean, Carl Auerbach, I am indebted for generous financial support and encouragement. Grants from the University of Minnesota Law School, as well as from the University's Graduate School and from the U.S. Administrative Conference, assisted my research over a two-year period.

Others who contributed ideas and information are too numerous to list completely, but a few should be mentioned specially. Many students at the law school contributed importantly to this study, both as research assistants and as members of my seminar in public land management. A special debt is owed to my father-in-law R. J. Costley. His versatile career in the Forest

Service provided a wealth of insights which he shared with me, even before I began this study.

The Forest Service itself contributed extensively. To mention all the individuals who cooperated and assisted would be impossible, but I must acknowledge particularly the singular aid and warm encouragement of Chester A. Shields. It is not fashionable to say kind things about the Forest Service; it seems to have critics behind every tree. I, too, have criticisms to offer, but none have altered my deep respect for the agency and its professionals. In the course of my two-year study I found agency officials remarkably cooperative, helpful, and well-informed. I expected to encounter from the agency some defensiveness in view of the many criticisms leveled upon it in recent years. There was surprisingly little. The great majority with whom I had contact were not only friendly but were also quite candid about the agency and its policies and problems. It was not my aim to write an exposé or an inside story of the Forest Service. I have doubts about the utility of such an enterprise; in any event, I leave this task to Nader's Raiders. Nor was my study particularly focused on the lower echelons within the agency, as was Kaufman's *The Forest Ranger*. I was more interested in obtaining the perspective of policy makers within the agency than that of the "man on the ground." (Even here my contacts were highly selective and limited—enough for impressions, but not adequate for a statistical survey.) At this policy-making level one does not expect to see many dissidents; not many make it to the higher echelons. Those who have done so I did not personally meet. This is not an important omission, however, for there is not much within the agency to criticize that has escaped the notice of those outside.

I have also benefited from discussions and, particularly, from the writings of outside critics, ranging from conservationists to timber interests, who are identified in the many footnotes with which the book is decorated.

Minneapolis, Minnesota   G. O. R.

THE
FOREST
SERVICE

A SHORT HISTORY OF THE FOREST SERVICE

By the standards of public institutions in the United States the Forest Service is an old agency. Few modern agencies can trace their ancestry in a straight and unbroken line of tradition from 1905 when the Bureau of Forestry assumed administration of the forest reserves and became the Forest Service; fewer still can go back to 1876 when the service was conceived, with the appointment of a special agent for forestry research for the commissioner of agriculture. And yet, from a different perspective, the service is younger than many of the trees in its forests. When the seed of the Forest Service was planted in 1876, most of the fir trees now standing in western and Pacific northwestern forests were already mature. For public institutions, of course, age itself is not as important as the process of aging. There are some critics today who would object to any analogy between the service and living trees, on the ground that in the former the sap has ceased to flow. Whether this is so or not, we can gain perspective by looking at the service's evolution.

At the outset I should emphasize that my purpose here is not to provide an extensively detailed history of the agency or of the public land laws (from which the agency's own history cannot be separated). My only purpose is briefly to sketch the historic events that are pertinent to later explorations of the agency and its policies. For some agencies and for many areas of admininstrative policy history is an ornament of only passing interest to any but the historian. This cannot, I think, be said of the Forest Service; its history and tradition continue to be an important influence on the agency, and no commentary on the agency or its policies would be complete without some brief acquaintance with this history.

We can begin with 1876 when a little-noticed rider to an appropriations act authorized the commissioner of agriculture to expend the grand sum of $2,000 to hire a man of "approved attainments" to investigate ". . . the annual amount of consumption, importation, and exportation of timber and other forest products, the probable supply for future wants, the best means adapted to their preservation and renewal, the influence of forests upon climate, and . . . measures . . . for the preservation and restoration or planting of forests. . . ."[1] Dr. Franklin Hough, a physician and naturalist, was appointed to conduct the study. It was a modest beginning, for both the Forest Service and professional forestry. Hough's report provided the first scientific basis for forest management. His position as special agent for forestry, which was elevated to the status of a separate Division of Forestry in 1881, provided the first foundation for an agency to perform that management task. However, before following further the subsequent growth of seed to sapling and sapling to tree, it will be helpful to make a brief survey of the general environment in which this division developed, beginning first with the emergence of the federal government as landowner. This could be a rather ambitious undertaking, for the history of the federal lands is an intimate part of the whole socioeconomic history of the nation. It will serve our purpose here to consider merely the barest outline of the growth and early disposition of the public domain.[2]

THE FEDERAL LANDS—
THE FORMATIVE YEARS

At the close of the American Revolution the original territorial boundaries of the United States included all land east of the Mississippi River, south of the Great Lakes, and north of the thirty-first parallel (the present northern boundary of Florida). The lands west of the present boundaries of the original thirteen states were claimed by Massachusetts, Connecticut, New York, Virginia, North Carolina, South Carolina, and Georgia under the terms of their colonial charters. Under the leadership of Maryland, the six states which did not have western claims demanded that the others cede theirs to the federal government. The cessions by the seven claimants to western lands, beginning in 1781 and ending in 1802, gave 236.8 million acres to the public domain of the young government. Included were Ohio, Indiana, Illinois, Michigan, Wisconsin, that portion of Minnesota lying east of the Mississippi, and the portions of Alabama and Mississippi located north of the thirty-first parallel. The remainder of the public domain was acquired through a series of purchases, annexation, and foreign cessions during 1803–67.

For nearly a century after the formation of the Union, public land policy was dominated by efforts to dispose of the public domain to states and private owners. Some of the initial motivation for disposition arose from the simple fact that the Confederation was land rich and money poor, but the underlying reasons for disposition go deeper than this. Until near the end of the nineteenth century, ownership and management of extensive public lands by the federal government was perceived as merely temporary, pending disposition to states and private settlers for the purpose of developing the country. The early cessions of land by the Colonies to the Confederation had been premised on this idea, as was the Continental Congress' Land Ordinance of 1785, providing for auction sales of public land to private individuals. From the perspective of present political philosophy and knowledge of what has happened to much of the public land thus disposed, one might be tempted to question the overriding emphasis put upon disposal rather than public ownership and management. But considering the then-prevalent philosophy that the federal government would play a limited role in the political and economic affairs of the nation, it would have been incongruous to conceive of the federal government as anything but a temporary custodian of the vast lands which were to become the public domain. Too, it must be remembered that the need for public land ownership generally was considered a limited one—to provide a land base for roads or other public facilities such as schools. Apart from this, the land grants to the states were made in the expectation that the land would be reconveyed (possibly after some development) to individuals. The idea that public, particularly federal, ownership was needed to conserve the land and its resources and ensure its proper management, was not to appear until after nearly a hundred years of experience with private and state development.

The means of disposal over this early period of public land history varied greatly. The homestead laws were probably the most important land-disposal laws.[3] Under the various homestead laws some 287.5 million acres, one-fifth of the original public domain, have been disposed of to date. This accounts for about one-fourth of the total area disposed of since 1781. Today, most of the public domain outside Alaska is closed to homestead entry, although some entries are still made in Alaska and in western lands classified by the secretary of the interior as suitable for agriculture and not needed for public purpose.[4]

The mining laws of 1866, 1870, and 1872[5] have also been a significant means of disposal to private landowners, as well as the subject of some abuse and fraud and a source of frustration to the public land agencies. The mining patent generally conveys title not only to minerals but to the surface area as well. Although the total acreage transferred is not large relative to other disposal measures, mining patents have provided the basis for many private landholdings that are frequently more important and valuable than the minerals themselves—particularly in areas strategically situated within a national forest or park.

The end of this "disposal era" is difficult to fix. The creation of extensive reservations from the public domain after 1891 might be a convenient bench mark insofar as it signaled a major shift toward a policy of reserving public lands for permanent ownership by the federal government. Another bench mark might be 1910 when Congress enacted the Pickett Act,[6] empowering the president to withdraw temporarily any public lands from settlement, sale, or entry for classification or other public purposes. However, the most decisive event marking the end of the disposal era was undoubtedly the Taylor Grazing Act in 1934.[7] Under this act, the secretary of the interior was empowered to establish grazing districts from vacant, unappropriated, and unreserved lands; the effect of this was to withdraw such lands from entry and settlement except as the secretary may thereafter classify such lands as suitable for uses other than those contemplated by the act. Shortly after its passage, President Roosevelt—under authority of the Pickett Act—withdrew from entry virtually all public domain lands outside Alaska, pending their classification and determination as to permanent use.[8] While there have been some problems and disputes over continued federal ownership of certain lands (primarily rangelands which were within the unreserved public domain at the time of the Taylor Grazing Act), the federal government's role as a major, permanent landowner has been accepted since the turn of the century when extensive forest reservations were carved from the public domain.

TRANSITION TO FEDERAL MANAGEMENT

The first century of American independence passed without any general forest land legislation being enacted. Land was an asset to be converted to cash. Forests were plentiful and were regarded as an obstacle to progress. Land had to be cleared for settlements, farms, and the raising of livestock. Through most of the nineteenth century the public forests were plundered. Settlers, commercial enterprises, railroads, and riverboats all contributed to the plunder. A number of acts were passed to protect public lands against extensive trespass. These were generally ineffective in that they were poorly enforced and easily evaded. In part this resulted from public apathy toward conservation, but it was also attributable to congressional failure to provide for the disposition of such timber. Although Congress devised many ways for giving land away or selling it, no thought had been given to selling the timber from the land. Theft was thus an expectable response,[9] particularly given the widespread assumption that the timber supply was inexhaustible.

CREATION OF RESERVES

By the late nineteenth century a growing awareness of the need for conservation was emerging. Public concern over the importance of forest cover for flood prevention and public interest in maintaining the forests for recreational and aesthetic purposes led to a number of private and local government efforts. The American Forestry Association, founded in 1875, was one of the early private conservation groups.[10] It was followed by a large number of state forestry boards and other public and private conservation groups. Through their efforts, the public became increasingly aware of European forest-management policies and the need for a forest-management program in the United States.

The response of the federal government to the conservation movement was sporadic. Political considerations played a large role in congressional action or inaction. Congress, in response to the growing conservation sentiment of easterners, did take several important steps to meet demands for action, despite opposition from western interests concerned about the growing shortage of suitable farmland. In 1872, Congress made its first important reservation of public land by creating Yellowstone Park.[11] Some 2 million acres were withdrawn from settlement and sale and dedicated as a public park "for the pleasure and recreation of the people." In 1875, public lands in Mackinac Island in Michigan were also set aside as a national park; however, this park did not survive. In 1890 three more national parks—Yosemite, Sequoia, and General Grant—were added to the reserves.

In addition to these first steps in a program of reservation, the federal government began its involvement in forestry with the appointment, in 1876, of Dr. Franklin Hough, special agent for the commissioner of agriculture, and the establishment of the Division of Forestry in 1881. When Bernard Fernow, was appointed head of the division in 1886, the foundations of professional forestry were laid. Under Fernow, the division became more professional, applying scientific research to forestry. The scope of division activities was expanded from primary emphasis on reforestation to much broader aspects of the needs, problems, and objectives of professional forestry.

As a consequence of governmental efforts, support grew for the proposition that some of the public lands should be reserved for public purposes such as parks and monuments. From this it was only a step further to recognize reservation as a means for protecting forest lands and watersheds. This step was taken in 1891 with an obscure rider to an act designed mainly to make various revisions in the public land laws. The last provision of the act, added by a conference committee, authorized the president to set apart "public lands wholly or in part covered with timber or undergrowth, whether of commercial value or not, as public reservations."[12] What was probably the "most important legislation in the history of forestry in America"[13] was enacted not merely without fanfare but without any evident realization by Congress of the far-reaching character of the power it conferred on the president to remove land from the public domain.

The 1891 act, while authorizing the establishment of forest reserves, made no provision for their management and use—for timber cutting, grazing, mining, or any other use. The act did not provide for active management, nor did it provide for even the most limited administration. Fires raged uncontrolled, and trespassers helped themselves to timber. But the act was an important beginning to an organized system of national public forests. Before leaving office in 1893, President Harrison created reserves of more than 13 million acres. In 1893, President Cleveland created two additional forest reserves in Oregon totaling 4.5 million acres. However, Cleveland refused to withdraw more land until Congress made provision for the administration of the already-existing forests.

In 1896, the secretary of the interior appointed a National Forest Commission of seven experts. This commission recommended, among other things, the establishment of thirteen additional reserves, and advised the establishment of an administrative agency to oversee the reserves, to create fire prevention programs, and to regulate grazing, mining, and removal of timber. Impressed with these recommendations, Cleveland promptly established the proposed reserves, covering over 21 million acres. Cleveland's proclamations precipitated a storm of protest in the West where mining and lumbering interests alleged their activities would be completely halted by the withdrawal of such huge parcels of land.

The commission's report, coupled with the furor caused by the Cleveland proclamations, set the stage for adoption of the Forest Management Act of 1897 (often referred to as the Organic Administration Act of the Forest Service).[14] The act was essentially a compromise between the strong advocates of conservation and the western interests who feared a strong reservation policy would threaten their very livelihood. The act suspended the proclamation of 1897 until March 1, 1898. Thus, the withdrawn lands were temporarily restored to the public (though they later reverted to reserve status). The president was given the authority to reduce or modify the area of the reserves and could vacate them entirely. The classification of land within the reserves could be changed, and the land better suited for agricultural or mining uses could be returned to the public domain. The policy of permitting miners, settlers, residents, and prospectors the use of timber for firewood, fencing, building, mining, and other domestic purposes was continued. More important than these provisions, however, were those relating to the administration of the forest reserves which remain today as the basic authority for forest management. The act directed that the reserves were to be administered to improve and protect the reservations, aid in water flow, and assist in furnishing timber. The secretary of the interior was authorized to make regulations which would govern the occupancy and use of the forest reserves as well as protect them. The secretary was also authorized to appraise and sell "dead, matured or large growth of trees." Perhaps the most unfortunate provision of the act was the forest lieu section which allowed settlers or owners of unperfected or patented land to abandon their tracts within the reserves. In lieu of their abandoned tracts they could select vacant land open to settlement which equaled the acreage of their abandoned land. Because the section, as adopted, applied to landowners as well as homesteaders, many scandals would arise in the application of this section as railroads and other large landowners traded their valueless or near-valueless land within the reserves for valuable land elsewhere.

Despite its numerous shortcomings, the 1897 act was a seminal step in the development of a reserve policy. With the 1891 act the foundation was laid for a radical change in U.S. land policy. After a century of public land disposal, the federal government was now committed to the policy of withdrawing some lands from the public domain so that they could be reserved for purposes which served the public interest.

EARLY ADMINISTRATION OF
THE FOREST RESERVES

Although the General Land Office was given responsibility for the administration of the forest reserves under the 1897 act, it was ill-prepared for this new duty. Its major obligations were related to disposal of the public domain rather than the administration of reserved land. It had no trained foresters. At the time of the transfer all the government foresters, "the whole two of them,"[15] were in the Department of Agriculture. Moreover, the integrity of the Land Office had been compromised by some questionable practices in the administration of the land laws. Nevertheless, the task fell to the Land Office as an almost casual addition to its general responsibilities for land administration. In 1897, the commissioner of the Land Office assigned a corps of agents to the job of administration. By 1901, a Division of Forestry within the Land Office had been created and had acquired a staff of over 400. One of the major problems encountered by the Land Office in its administration of the forest reserves was the widespread abuse of the forest in lieu provision of the 1897 act. Under the in lieu provisions, landowners were able to trade large cutover or otherwise low-valued lands for valuable timberlands. Others searched out and acquired valueless state lands within an area considered for a reserve in order to trade for valuable land elsewhere. Railroads, which held large areas of the land under land grants, were particularly benefited by the in lieu bonanza, as were several major lumber companies (Weyerhaeuser most notably) which subsequently acquired some of the valuable timberland.

By 1900, the Land Office itself was under attack for aiding and abetting this abuse by planning for additional reserves in areas where railroads had large holdings. Whether this particular charge was accurate, it was only part of a broader realization that the reserves were not being effectively administered and that the Land Office was, to an important degree, to blame. Whether, in retrospect, the Land Office was as culpable as it was made to appear at the time is debatable.

The most vocal critic was Gifford Pinchot, who in 1898 succeeded Bernard Fernow as head of the Division of Forestry (later the Bureau of Forestry) in the Department of Agriculture. As head of a rival agency, with ambitions to displace the Land Office as manager of the federal reserve, Pinchot was not an unbiased observer of the Land Office's performance. Still, Pinchot's view was not without credibility.[16] In any event, it gained increasingly wide acceptance because of his attacks on the Land Office.

As the Land Office fell in public estimation, Pinchot's new Division of Forestry rose yearly. Pinchot was a man for the times. The seeds of conservation had been planted; what was wanted was someone to nourish and cultivate them. In his own mind, Pinchot was that man, and he soon persuaded others of this, though not, by any means, everyone. His first task was to establish the division as the corps of professional experts in forestry. Initially without any land of its own, the division involved itself in numerous projects designed to provide technical assistance for private lumbermen in the management of their forests. Pinchot, however, had from the beginning set his sights beyond these minor tasks. He wanted the reserves and worked persistently to have them transferred from the Land Office to his division. In this he had the support not only of President Theodore Roosevelt, but that of Secretary of the Interior Ethan Hitchcock—gaining the latter's support in unique contradiction to all known laws of bureaucratic behavior.[17]

Still, the transfer was not a certain, simple thing. It faced opposition from many in Congress—western representatives especially—who were opposed to the reserves in general and to Pinchot in particular. After several years of effort, and several abortive efforts to gain control of the Land Office's forestry division, Pinchot finally succeeded. In 1905, Congress transferred some 85.6 million acres of forest reserves to the Department of Agriculture's Bureau of Forestry,[18] which Pinchot later renamed the Forest Service.

Theodore Roosevelt's Administration marked the high point in the growth of the reserves. Both Roosevelt and Pinchot were convinced that the timberlands could be saved only by the withdrawal of as much choice forest land as possible. By this standard they succeeded. During Roosevelt's Administration 148 million acres were added to the forest reserves (including 109 million acres after the Transfer Act), bringing the gross acreage of forest reserves to some 194.5 million acres at the close of his term.

The inclusion of such large areas, mostly in western states, could scarcely go unnoticed—nor uncriticized. Congressmen from these areas, accurately reflecting local public sentiment, were understandably disturbed at the large concentration of national forests in their states (39 percent of Idaho and 28 percent of Washington and California were now composed of forest reserves). As a consequence, Congress, in 1907, revoked the authority of the president to create new reserves in Oregon, Washington, Idaho, Montana, Colorado, and Wyoming without congressional approval. Subsequent amendments extended this to California, New Mexico, and Arizona, and reinstated the original authority as to Montana.[19] By the same act Congress also adopted a revenue-sharing procedure which provided that 10 percent of Forest Service revenue derived from fees and lumber sales would be given to the states in which the reserves were located, to be used for roads and schools. This amount was raised to 25 percent in 1908.[20] Related to the revenue-sharing provisions is a further provision, added in 1913, which allocates 10 percent of all receipts to a fund for roads and trails within the national forests in the states from which the receipts are derived.[21]

The Roosevelt Administration is significant not only for the rapid expansion of the reserves, it is equally important for establishing the beginnings of active federal management of the reserves. Pinchot's guiding philosophy was that the reserves were to be actively managed for use. His little "Use Book," the precursor of the present Forest Service Manual, declared, "The timber, water, pasture, mineral and other resources of the forest reserves are for the use of the people. They may be obtained under reasonable conditions, without delay. Legitimate improvements and business enterprises will be encouraged."[22]

Although not without an appreciation of the aesthetics of the forest, Pinchot was singularly unromantic about conservation and forest management. He saw forestry as a practical agricultural science, "Forestry is tree farming. . . . To grow trees as a crop is Forestry. Trees may be grown as a crop just as corn may be grown as a crop. The farmer gets crop after crop of corn, oats, wheat, cotton, tobacco, and hay from his farm. The forester gets crop after crop of logs, cordwood, shingles, poles, or railroad ties from his forest, and even some return from regulated grazing."[23]

While Pinchot's concept of forestry as "tree farming" will no doubt grate upon the sensitivities of modern conservationists, this is not ground for disputing his reputation as the outstanding leader of the early conservation movement in America. If modern aesthetic tastes tend to run more toward Thoreau, it bears remembering that the origins of modern land use conservation owe more to Pinchot's work on the Biltmore estate than to Thoreau's meditations at Walden Pond.

It is probably a testament to Pinchot's personal charisma as much as his ideas that his philosophy was so deeply and lastingly etched in the Forest Service within such a short period of time. But his accomplishment was not less notable on that account. In 1910, only five years after he began to implement his philosophy on the national forests (as they were now called), Pinchot was dismissed by President Taft for his public criticism of Secretary of the Interior Richard Ballinger.[24] To succeed Pinchot, Taft appointed Henry Graves, dean of the Yale School of Forestry, a choice Pinchot himself applauded.[25] Yet despite his dismissal—and despite his own later criticism of Taft for failing to adhere to Roosevelt's policies—forest conservation and management continued to advance.

THE YEARS OF GROWTH

Although it was not until Franklin D. Roosevelt took office that the ardor of the first Roosevelt's Administration in conservation was to be matched; nevertheless, conservation made important strides forward. Probably the most noteworthy legislative achievement was the Weeks Forest Purchase Act in 1911.[26] The Weeks Act broadened the forestry activities of both the federal government and the states. States were authorized to enter into compacts with other states. The secretary of agriculture was authorized to enter into agreement with states to protect against fire those forest lands situated on the watershed of navigable rivers. Matching-fund programs for this purpose were also authorized. The act gave the federal government, for the first time, the power to expand the national forest system by acquisition. The act established a National Forest Reservation Commission, composed of the secretary of war (now the secretary of the army or the chief of the Corps of Engineers), the secretaries of agriculture and the interior, and two members of each house of Congress (selected by the President of the Senate and the Speaker of the House) to purchase "forested, cutover or denuded lands within the watersheds of navigable streams," as recommended by the secretary of agriculture. (The act also requires the assent of the states to acquisitions within their boundaries.) Originally limited to acquistions for the purpose of protecting streamflow, the purpose was extended by the Clarke–McNary Act of 1924 to acquire lands valuable for timber production as well as watershed protection.[27]

Perhaps to a degree even greater than the acts of 1891 or 1897, the Weeks Act signaled the end of the era of public land disposal. It meant more than a mere end to the disposal policies of the prior decades, however; it meant the very reversal of the prior process. The federal government was now, more than ever before, in the land-management business and for its own sake. The Weeks Act provided the primary means for extending the national forest system to the East. Heretofore the system, dependent on reservations from the public domain, was primarily composed of lands west of the hundredth meridian. With few exceptions, most of the public domain in the East had been disposed of prior to the act of 1891; the national forest system was thus necessarily confined pretty much to the West. Since 1911, approximately 20.5 million acres have been acquired, primarily under authority of the Weeks Act; about 98 percent of this is in states east of the hundredth meridian.[28]

In contrast to the earlier reservations from the public domain, however, the land acquired under the Weeks Act has mostly been in a deteriorated condition. Indeed, that was the basic purpose of the act: to buy and restore timberlands severely damaged by excessive cutting, fire, disease, or farming (many of the lands included abandoned farms). Some of these were private lands, some were public (many private lands that were cutover were taken by the state for tax delinquencies), but nearly all were lands that had been abused, poorly protected, or ignored whose owners were happy to unload on the federal government. Thus, the Weeks Act might be viewed as a kind of modified in lieu law—the main distinction being that this time it was the government that could choose what it wanted.

The conditions that produced the Weeks Act also called public attention to the fact that private and state timberlands outside the national forest system were being poorly managed. Many lands were being excessively cut. Fire, disease, and insect controls were inadequate, and reforestation was ignored. Added to this was the growing demand for timber. The Weeks Act offered one solution to the problem—the extension of federal ownership. That was the course of action proposed in 1933 by the Copeland report, a landmark congressional report on forest management.[29] It recommended the acquistion of some 224 million acres over a period of twenty years—a program that would have more than doubled the size of the national forest system. Not surprisingly this idea never took hold. Even setting aside the prohibitive cost of the program, such a dramatic expansion of federal ownership was politically implausible.

There were other approaches to the problem besides federal ownership, and these provided the bones of contention in the 1920s and 1930s which have not yet been fully buried even today. Led by Gifford Pinchot—who, even after his departure from the service, continued to be an active and influential conservation leader —one group of conservationists urged enactment of federal legislation regulating private forestry practices. The model, naturally, was the Forest Service. The Forest Service, in what was probably its first significant break with Pinchot's philosophy, opposed regulation and urged federal cooperation with and support of state and private forestry.[30]

Congress adopted the latter alternative. In 1924 it enacted the Clarke–McNary Act,[31] establishing the foundations of Cooperative Forestry, which became the second major branch of the Forest Service. As mentioned earlier, the act amended the Weeks Act to permit the federal government to acquire land for the purpose of timber production as well as watershed protection. The main thrust of the act, however, was to provide authorization for federal assistance to state and private forestry. Building on an earlier provision of the Weeks Act which authorized matching federal funds to states for fire protection activity, the 1924 act extended these matching funds to private owners as well. It also provided matching funds to assist in the distribution of seedlings for reforestation and assistance to farmers in developing small woodlots through the utilization of modern forestry practices. The act did not forever end efforts to regulate private forestry to secure more efficient private management.[32] In fact, as timber needs have risen, private timberland management continues to be among the most vexing problems of forestry.

With Clarke–McNary the Forest Service's role expanded beyond federal land management. Later its nonmanagement responsibilities were further expanded with the McSweeney–McNary Act of 1928, which established the foundation of the third major branch of the Forest Service, Experimental Forestry.[33] Among other things, the act provided for establishment of experimental stations and programs for the study of subjects related to forest management, ranging from animal histories to the chemical properties of wood and the economic aspects of wood-product production.

While the second-score years of the Forest Service—the 1930s and 1940s—produced nothing comparable to the first, either in terms of organizational growth of the service or the geographic growth of the national forest system, they were noteworthy for two things: first, a significant expansion of conservation management occurred, and, second, a prolonged struggle took place between the Department of the Interior and the Forest Service over reorganization of forest-management responsibility.

The conservation effort of the 1930s was in part an outgrowth of the Copeland report's recommendations for expanded programs of reforestation and other conservation and forest-management activities. It was equally— perhaps even preeminently—a by-product of the New Deal programs to combat the effects of the Depression. But whatever the primary objective, it was effective conservation. The Civilian Conservation Corps (CCC) who swarmed over the forests, parks, and other public lands (over 500,000 workers at the height of the CCC) fought forest fires, built trails, planted trees, and constructed campgrounds and other recreational facilities. The same period saw substantial additions to the national forest system. Between 1930–50 some 15.3 million acres were added to the system by acquisitions and exchanges.[34] These were complemented by the later transfer to the system of more than 3.8 million acres of land originally acquired in the 1930s by the Soil Conservation Service.[35]

Considering all known laws of bureaucratic behavior, it would have been surprising if the growth of the Forest Service and of the national forest system had gone unnoticed or unenvied by the Department of the Interior, and, in fact, it did not. Secretary of the Interior Ethan Hitchcock may not have foreseen what he was voluntarily relinquishing in 1905, but FDR's secretary, Harold Ickes, knew very well, and he avidly sought to get it back by proposing to merge the Forest Service with the Department of the Interior into a so-called Department of Conservation (headed by Ickes).[36]

Ickes was not the first to propose such a merger. In fact, the Forest Service had scarcely taken title to the reserves before efforts were made to return them to Interior. While these early efforts were supported by Secretary of the Interior Franklin Lane (under Taft) and his successor, Albert Fall (under Harding), they undoubtedly reflected more than simple bureaucratic empire building by the Interior Department. The efforts also reflected substantial animosity toward the Forest Service and its conservation efforts. Indeed, it is evident some of the support for the transfer was really support for curtailing federal ownership and management of the reserves.[37]

Needless to say, Harold Ickes had more going for him than did either Franklin Lane or Albert Fall. First, the Forest Service had not grown alone in the field of public land management. When the reserves were transferred to the Forest Service most of Interior's land-management responsibilities went with them. The General Land Office retained its responsibilities for administering the homestead and mining laws, but these did not significantly involve the agency in active resource management. In the three decades after the transfer this was changed; Interior acquired important management responsibilities which duplicated and competed with those of the Forest Service. The creation of the National Park Service in 1916[38] gave it a leading responsibility in outdoor recreation. Enactment of the Taylor Grazing Act in 1934 gave to Interior (and a newly created Grazing Service) responsibility for permanent management of the unreserved public domain for grazing and other purposes.[39] Even in the area of timber, which had been preeminently a function of the national forests, Interior had jurisdiction over unreserved timberlands in Alaska, and more important, it fell heir (by historic curiosity) to very rich timberlands in Oregon.[40] In short, the Department of the Interior was now an important land-management agency and a significant rival of the Forest Service.[41] For the first time, a persuasive case could be made that the overlap of responsibilities—not to mention the bureaucratic rivalry—between the two agencies was wasteful, inefficient, and should be eliminated by merger. On the strength of the efficiency argument a presidential commission on government reorganization—the

Brownlow Commission—recommended, in 1938, the creation of a Department of Conservation. Although it did not specifically recommend the transfer to it of the service (leaving the exact composition of the new department to the Executive), such was the logical thrust of the proposal.[42]

Second, Ickes' proposal (and that of the Brownlow Commission) had the support of a powerful president—at least so Ickes had been led to believe.[43]

Finally, Ickes' reputation as an active conservationist gave credibility to his claim that reorganization would promote conservation. Thus, unlike his early predecessors Lane and Fall, he was not vulnerable on this score.

Nevertheless, despite these advantages and a passionate, unrelenting effort, Ickes was unable to obtain his reorganization. The Brownlow Commission, as it turned out, had little impact. FDR's support proved weaker than Ickes had first supposed, and anyway he had other worries. As for Ickes' standing as a conservationist, this was countered by the dogged opposition of another conservationist and practiced politician, Gifford Pinchot.[44] When World War II came, any lingering interest in domestic reorganization plans faded away.

Ickes' failure did not end the reorganization efforts, however. What it did do was set a tone for the rivalry between Interior and the Forest Service, prompting further consolidation proposals, which we shall examine later.

INTENSIVE MANAGEMENT—
THE MODERN ERA

The era of *intensive* management is characterized by two things: increased use of forest resources and increased conflict among users. Inasmuch as this period of history is what the remainder of this book is all about, only a few words of introduction to it are necessary here.

World War II and its aftermath brought great new demands for forest resources. The demand for timber and timber products and the demand for recreation in particular have almost literally exploded. In turn, these have created pressures on the other resources, on wildlife, on soil and water conditions, and, finally, it has led to pressures for a new kind of withdrawal—a preservation of wilderness. These two conflicting forces: the ineluctable growth in demand for productive resources and exploitive uses (timber, forage, minerals, recreation) versus the rising concern for the quality of the environment and correlative emphasis on protection, preservation, and nonexploitive uses have dominated the history of intensive management to date.

Illustrative of the former is the growth in domestic consumption of timber products. Between 1940–71, for example, lumber consumption rose 49 percent; pulp products, 235 percent; and veneer and plywood, 475 percent. Current projections indicate a continued demand increase, in response to population increases, from a present consumption of 13 billion ft.[3] in 1970 to nearly 23 billion ft.[3] by the year 2000.[45] Of course, not all of this increased demand can or will be met from the federal lands; currently, only about one-fifth comes from federal lands. However, there have been strong pressures from timber interests and others to increase not only the absolute contribution of the public lands, but their relative contribution as well—greatly increasing the intensity of public land management, particularly on national forests.[46]

A second, equally dramatic example of the increased demand for public land resources is the enormous growth of outdoor recreation in recent years. From 1956–70, visits to the national parks, forests, and wildlife refuges alone grew from 115 million to more than 367 million.[47] Outdoor recreation, until recently largely ignored as a use of the federal lands, has become one of the dominant uses. In the late 1950s, recognition of this development led to major competitive planning efforts by the two largest recreation agencies, the Forest Service and the National Park Service,[48] and, in 1962, to a massive study by a presidentially appointed commission—the Outdoor Recreation Resources Review Commission. Its research and recommendations provided a foundation for two important developments in the ensuing decade: the first was enactment of the Land and Water Conservation Fund Act of 1965,[49] which authorized federal recreation agencies to acquire land for outdoor recreation and provided an aid fund for both federeal and state land purchases and development. (In the case of federal agencies, the fund is available only for land acquisition, not for planning or maintenance.) The fund is supported in part by a structure of user fees for federal recreation areas. The second development was the creation of a Bureau of Outdoor Recreation (BOR) to administer the fund and also to promote coordination among land agencies and to formulate a comprehensive nationwide plan for outdoor recreation. (The plan is for the general guidance of Congress, the Executive, and the various land agencies: BOR itself administers no land.[50])

Needless to say, the explosive growth in the demand for these and other land resources has not been accepted with equanimity by many conservationists. Increased timber production on the federal lands has been resisted as being unnecessary and too costly in terms of the harm to the other resources (including, but not limited to, the scenic character of the land). Opposition has particularly focused on one by-product of intensive timber management, the practice of "clear-cutting," i.e., the cutting of all trees in a particular area, as opposed to partial or selective cutting.[51] To date these conservation forces have led to reduction in the use of clear-cutting and have partly held in check, temporarily at least, other attempts to increase the timber harvest. However, the pressures continue for more-intensive timber management and greater productive output.

The controversy over timber management is only part of the concern which has produced agitation and controversy. The rising tide of recreationists visiting public lands and the accompanying development of mass recreational facilities to accommodate them has engendered much the same kind of opposition from the same quarter.[52]

Much of the controversy that has arisen over use of public land resources concerns not merely the intensity of management of public lands but whether the lands should be managed or "used" at all. An important segment of the conservationist cause is now oriented toward "preservation" of some lands in a primitive, wilderness state in which the natural resources would not be subject to "exploitive" (or "consumptive") use.

The Wilderness Act of 1964[53] created a statutory wilderness system out of 9.1 million acres within the national forests, supplemented with lands from national parks and wildlife refuges to be added where future review shows appropriate. However, the wilderness concept and classification predated the 1964 act. The Forest Service first established such areas by administrative classification in the 1920s and 1930s. As timber harvesting on national forests increased in the 1950s, wilderness proponents, fearing that the administrative classification would be withdrawn, pressed for a statutory preservation. The Forest Service, at first opposed to an inflexible statutory system, dropped its opposition in exchange for congressional ratification of its longstanding multiple-use philosophy in the Multiple-Use and Sustained Yield Act of 1960.[54] But while it has supported wilderness preservation, the service has been far more cautious about it than most preservationists have desired. The result has been an intensive dispute which incorporates and illustrates the broader controversy over intensive land use policy. Curiously, all of the protagonists in the controversy claim support of the multiple-use principle. In fact, the principle is sufficiently vague to accommodate nearly anything, as we shall see.

Against the background of this historic sketch, we will turn for a closer look at the Forest Service itself in the chapters which follow.

NOTES

1. Quoted in Henry Clepper, *Professional Forestry in the United States* (Baltimore: Johns Hopkins University Press for Resources for the Future, 1971), p. 18.

2. In the following sketch I have relied primarily on several excellent accounts: Marion Clawson and Burnell R. Held, *The Federal Lands: Their Use and Management* (Baltimore: Johns Hopkins University Press for Resources for the Future, 1957); Samuel T. Dana, *Forest and Range Policy: Its Development in the United States* (New York: McGraw-Hill, 1956); Paul Gates, *History of the Public Land Law Development* (Washington, D.C.: GPO, 1968); and Benjamin Hibbard, *A History of the Public Land Policies* (Madison: University of Wisconsin Press, 1965). For the most part, I have avoided repeated references to these general sources, limiting myself to other specific references. Data on land acquisitions is taken from the U.S. Department of the Interior/Bureau of Land Management, *Public Land Statistics* (1973), except where otherwise noted.

3. There are a considerable number. For a short description, see Clawson and Held, *The Federal Lands*, p. 391; statistical data are given in *Public Land Statistics*.

4. See U.S. Department of the Interior/Bureau of Land Management, *Public Land Statistics,* p. 6. Lands reserved or withdrawn from the public domain—such as the national forests, parks, and wildlife reservations—are not open to homestead entry or public sale. Also, since 1934 virtually all of the remainder of the public domain, outside of Alaska, has been closed to homestead entry or public sale, pending classification by the secretary of the interior as to its permanent disposition. Entry on or sale of lands is thus restricted to those lands classified by the secretary as suitable for agriculture and not needed for public purpose. In Alaska no such prior classification is required (see Clawson and Held, *The Federal Lands,* p. 391). In 1973, homestead patents were issued for some 5,499 acres, all but a small part of which were in Alaska (*Public Land Statistics,* p. 41). Related to homesteads are desert land grants under the Carey Act, 43 U.S.C., § 643 (the grants are made to states for disposition to settlers). In 1973, desert land patents were issued for 26,143 acres, mostly in Idaho (ibid.). The total area patented in 1973 under all disposition laws was 566,338 acres, four-fifths of which was granted to states, most notably Alaska and Washington (ibid., p. 43).

5. 14 Stat. 251 (1866); 16 Stat. 217 (1870); 17 Stat. 91 (1872), 30 U.S.C., § 21 *et seq.*

6. 36 Stat. 847 (1910), 43 U.S.C., §§ 141–142. The authority was delegated to the secretary of the interior in 1952 by Executive Order 10355, 17 Fed. Reg. 4831 (1952). Withdrawal under this act does not affect "exploration, discovery, occupation and purchase" under the mining laws, with regard to metalliferous minerals, 43 U.S.C., § 142.

7. 48 Stat. 1269 (1934), *as amended,* 43 U.S.C., §§ 315 *et seq.*

8. Executive Order 6910 (Nov. 26, 1934) withdrew from entry all federal lands in twelve western states (excluding Alaska), pending classification or disposition under the Taylor Grazing Act. Subsequently, Executive Order 6964 withdrew the remainder of unappropriated public domain in twelve other states pending classification or disposition under the Federal Emergency Relief Act. The Taylor Grazing Act, as amended, after these withdrawals, specifically authorizes the secretary of the interior to classify and open for entry all such lands. In 1964 this authority was temporarily supplemented by the Classification and Multiple-Use Act [78 Stat. 986 (1964), 43 U.S.C., § 1412], which directed the secretary of the interior to develop criteria to determine which of the federal public lands (including those in Alaska) managed by the Bureau of Land Management (BLM) shall be disposed of and which retained, with those retained being managed under a multiple-use mandate similar to that of the Forest Service. The 1964 act expired in 1970; congressional proposals to provide a new statutory mandate to fill the place of the 1964 act are still pending as this is written.

9. Pinchot's comment on this situation [Gifford Pinchot, *Breaking New Ground* (New York: Harcourt, Brace, 1947), p. 83.] was typically trenchant:

If the public-land laws and their administration had been less soaked in politics that stank to Heaven, and therefore more workable, much of this orgy of stealing could, and perhaps would, have been avoided. Under the law government timber, for example, could not be brought apart from the land. A settler without timber on his claim must nevertheless build a house for his family, put up his fences, and keep his fire burning. Timber he had to have, but usually there was no legal way he could get it. More often than not he had to steal it or let his family suffer. So of course he did steal it.

Pinchot, however, was quick to add that this justification did not extend to those who wanted the timber for "profit." That seems a curious distinction. Presumably, the timber interests made a profit because someone needed the timber, and in the absence of practicable legal ways to obtain the lumber the theft of the timber seems equally understandable, even perhaps justified.

10. On the development of the profession generally, see Clepper, *Professional Forestry.*

11. As early as 1817, Congress granted authority to the president to set aside lands for particular functions such as military posts, wagon roads, etc. In 1832, Congress set aside four sections of land in Hot Springs, Arkansas, for future disposal because of the land's extraordinary beauty and value. In 1864, lands in California, where the giant sequoia grew, were granted to the state of California to be held for all time for the use and recreation of the public. The state park in Yosemite Valley was later receded to the United States and became

part of Yosemite National Park. For an extensive history of the national parks, see John Ise, *Our National Park Policy: A Critical History* (Baltimore: Johns Hopkins University Press for Resources for the Future, 1961).

12.   26 Stat. 1103, § 24 (1891), *as amended*, 16 U.S.C., § 471.

13.   Pinchot, *Breaking New Ground*, p. 85.

14.   30 Stat. 34–36, 43, 44 (1897), *as amended*, 16 U.S.C., §§ 424, *et seq.*

15.   Pinchot, *Breaking New Ground*, p. 140.

16.   Ibid., pp. 161–177. Pinchot, not an unbiased witness, seems to have ample corroborating evidence to support his charges. Among the evidence is a scandal involving Land Commissioner Binger Hermann, which Pinchot curiously does not cite. See Gates, *History*, pp. 579 and 591.

17.   See Gates, *History*, pp. 577–579. Pinchot did not have the support of Land Commissioner Binger Hermann. However, Hermann's successor, after 1903, W. A. Richards, was an active supporter of the transfer.

18.   33 Stat., part I, 628 (1905), 16 U.S.C., § 472.

19.   The restriction, first imposed in 1907 (34 Stat. 1271), was reenacted in 1910 (36 Stat. 847). In 1912 it was extended to California (37 Stat. 497, 16 U.S.C., § 471). In 1926 the restriction was extended to New Mexico and Arizona (44 Stat. 745, 16 U.S.C., § 471a). In 1939 the president's power to reserve land in Montana was reinstated (53 Stat. 1071, 16 U.S.C., § 471b).

20.   35 Stat. 259, 260, 267 (1908), *as amended*, 16 U.S.C., § 500, 671; 31 U.S.C., § 534.

21.   37 Stat. 843 (1913), *as amended*, 16 U.S.C., § 501.

22.   Pinchot, *Breaking New Ground*, p. 263.

23.   Ibid., p. 31.

24.   The dismissal grew out of a dispute between Pinchot and Secretary of the Interior Richard Ballinger (formerly head of the Land Office where he first incurred Pinchot's enmity). The dispute developed when a subordinate official in the Land Office, Louis Glavis, reported his suspicions that fraud had been committed in connection with certain mining claims in Alaska. When Glavis's report received no response from Ballinger (then head of the Land Office), he turned to the Forest Service. Pinchot, who had no use for Ballinger to begin with, gave his support to Glavis. Even after Glavis was fired for making unsubstantiated charges, he continued to press his accusations, and Pinchot continued to support them despite a warning from the president not to join in Glavis's cause. When the controversy evoked a congressional investigation, Pinchot wrote to Senator Dolliver a defense of his and the Forest Service's involvement in it. The letter was the triggering cause of Pinchot's dismissal. A full account of the episode is given in Nelson M. McGeary, *Gifford Pinchot: Forester Politician* (Princeton, N.J.: Princeton University Press, 1960), pp. 112–189.

25.   Pinchot, *Breaking New Ground*, p. 460. Pinchot thought Graves, who had once worked with him, to be "a man of the highest character, the best trained forester in America, with no little executive experience."

26.   36 Stat. 961 (1911), *as amended*, 16 U.S.C., §§ 513–21.

27.   43 Stat. 653 (1924), 16 U.S.C., § 515.

28.   See *National Forest Reservation Commission, 62nd Annual Report*, S. Doc. 93-17, 93 Cong., 1 sess., 1973, pp. 5, and 10–14. The figures given in this report show some inconsistencies between totals tabulated by time of acquisition and those by location; I have used the higher figure for the total acquisition figure.

29.   *The National Plan for American Forestry*, S. Doc. 12, 73 Cong., 1 sess., 1933, called the Copeland report after Senator Copeland of New York, who sponsored the resolution establishing the study. In addition to recommending extension of federal ownership of forest lands by some 224 million acres (177 million in the East and 47 million in the West), it recommended other programs such as assistance to states for regulating private forestry practices. Finally, it made recommendations for more intensive management of federal lands, including more intensive fire, insect, and disease protection and greater reforestation. It also urged increased planning for recreational use of the forests—a recommendation ahead of its time.

30.   The opposition was led by Chief Forester William B. Greeley, who succeeded Henry Graves in 1920. Greeley, a great admirer of Pinchot under whom he had worked, was

adamantly opposed to Pinchot's views on regulation, as is made very evident in his book *Forests and Men* (Garden City, N.Y.: Doubleday, 1951).

31. 43 Stat. 653 (1924), *as amended,* 16 U.S.C., §§ 471, 499, 505, 515, 564–567, 568, 569, 570. The cooperative assistance programs of Clarke–McNary were significantly expanded by the Cooperative Forest Management Act of 1950 [64 Stat. 473 (1950), 16 U.S.C., §§ 568c–568d], which authorizes the secretary of agriculture to cooperate with the states to provide technical services to private forest landowners and authorizes federal matching funds to states allocating money for this purpose.

32. Former Chief Forester Greeley gives a short account of subsequent regulation proposals in *Forests and Men,* pp. 209–225. Current efforts center not on regulation but on creation of special incentives for private forestation and cultivation. As we will note in Chapter IV, the problem is not, as it was once thought to be, that private lands are being overcut. Though there is still some concern over excess cutting of industry lands, the main problem is inadequate forestation and cultivation of private, nonindustry lands. Thus, government's recent efforts have been toward providing economic incentives for private woodlot development.

33. 45 Stat. 699 (1928), *as amended,* 16 U.S.C., §§ 581.581i.

34. National Forest Reservation Commission, *62nd Annual Report,* p. 5.

35. U.S. Department of Agriculture/Forest Service, *The National Grasslands* (1960), p. 3.

36. Testifying on proposed legislation in 1937 to create a Department of Conservation, Ickes declined to comment on whether the Forest Service should be transferred to such a department on the ground that "we have not yet reached that bridge" [U.S. Congress, Senate Select Committee on Government Organization, *Hearings on S.2700,* 75 Cong., 1 sess., 1937, p. 355]. However, he elsewhere made clear that such a transfer—in order to consolidate all conservation activities—was what was ultimately intended. See, for example, *Why a Department of Conservation,* S. Doc. 75–142, 75 Cong., 3 sess., 1938, prepared by the Department of Interior. For a good short account of his efforts, and of the resistance to them, see McGeary, *Gifford Pinchot,* pp. 408–413. Ickes' own account of the campaign is recorded in *The Secret Diary of Harold Ickes* (New York: Simon & Schuster, 1953 and 1954).

37. See Clepper, *Professional Forestry,* pp. 59–60; and John Ise, *The United States Forest Policy* (New Haven: Yale University Press, 1920). On the antireserve motive it is pertinent to note that Fall, as a senator before becoming secretary of the interior in 1921, had advocated transferring the national forests to the states—a proposal which had some significant support at the time (Clepper, pp. 56–59). In addition to the efforts under the Taft and Harding administrations to transfer the national forests to Interior, there were other proposals before Ickes to consolidate land-management functions. See Clawson and Held, *The Federal Lands,* p. 367, for a brief account. Interestingly, one of the proposals, advocated by the Hoover Administration in 1932, called for a transfer of parts of Interior to Agriculture. This was subsequently endorsed by the Hoover Commission in 1949—but by no one since.

38. 39 Stat. 535 (1916), *as amended,* 16 U.S.C., §§ 1–18f.

39. 48 Stat. 1269 (1934), *as amended,* 34 U.S.C., §§ 315–315o-L.

40. These are the so-called O & C lands—the Oregon and California Railroad lands—and the Coos Bay Wagon Road lands. The lands—comprising about 2.6 million acres—were originally granted to the Oregon and California Railroad and another company to construct a rail and telegraph line between Portland, Oregon, the California border and an Oregon wagon road. The grants were subject to the condition that lands not used for right-of-way would be sold to bona fide settlers at $2.50 an acre. When subsequent investigation revealed that the condition had been violated, an action was brought in 1908 to forfeit the grant and repossess the lands. After a Supreme Court decision which left the matter for congressional action, Congress revoked the grant and revested all unsold lands in the United States [39 Stat. 218 (1916)]. Jurisdiction was given to the Department of the Interior to classify the lands as to potential use for power sites, timberlands, and agricultural lands. The last two were open to entry. However, in the case of timberlands, the timber was to be sold first. The proceeds of all timber and land disposal was subject to a unique revenue-sharing arrangement, 50 percent going to Oregon, 40 percent to the Reclamation Fund (established by the Reclamation Act of 1902), and 10 percent to the federal treasury. In 1937 Interior was given permanent authority to manage the lands for

timber and grazing; see 50 Stat. 874 (1937), 43 U.S.C., § 1181a–e. The terms of the 1937 law were even more generous to Oregon—increasing its share to 75 percent of all receipts. One consequence of this generous revenue-sharing provision has been to cement state support for continued Interior management, making any transfer to the national forest system politically impossible. The Forest Service does—as a consequence of historic practice antedating 1916—manage about 400,000 acres of these lands which Ickes unsuccessfully sought to have transferred to Interior. Since 1954 these have been subject to the same revenue sharing as the other O & C lands.

41. As a consequence of executive reorganization in 1940 which shifted the Biological Survey from Agriculture to Interior, the latter also acquired a major role in wildlife management.

42. See the President's Committee on Administrative Management, *Administrative Management in the Government of the United States* (1937), pp. 34–35.

43. Ickes, *Secret Diary of Harold Ickes,* vol. 1, p. 151. It is interesting to note that Ickes gave a different report to Congress: in 1937 he reported that the president had not indicated whether he would transfer the Forest Service to a Department of Conservation if given authority. See *Hearings on S. 2700,* pp. 355 and 356.

44. On Pinchot's efforts, see McGeary, *Gifford Pinchot.* Interestingly, Ickes and Pinchot had been good friends, and the latter warmly applauded Ickes' appointment to Interior, even though he could not abide the thought of having the Forest Service put under the same roof with Interior. According to Ickes (*Secret Diary,* vol. 2, p. 412), FDR blamed the ultimate defeat of the reorganization proposal on the "Forest Service lobby." This included Earle Clapp who became acting chief of the Forest Service in 1939. Clapp never received a permanent appointment as chief, I am told, because of Ickes' opposition.

45. U.S. Department of Agriculture/Forest Service, *The Outlook for Timber in the United States,* Forest Research Report 20 (1973), p. 1.

46. See, for example, U.S. Congress, House Subcommittee on Forests of the Committee on Agriculture, *Hearings on the National Timber Supply Act of 1969,* 91 Cong., 1 sess., 1969.

47. U.S. Department of the Interior/Bureau of Outdoor Recreation, *Selected Outdoor Recreation Statistics* (1971). This does not take account of other major recreational lands under the jurisdiction of the Bureau of Reclamation, the Corps of Engineers, and TVA, which in 1969 accommodated some 360 million visits. Nor does it reflect the more than 90 million visits annually to BLM lands; see *Public Land Statistics,* p. 82.

48. The rivalry of these two agencies goes back to the beginning of the latter—Pinchot being an opponent of both national parks and the National Park Service. It has fed on a jurisdictional competition arising from the fact that many of the national parks and monuments continue to be created from national forests. However, there have long been significant differences in recreational philosophy which have sharpened the competition between those agencies.

49. 78 Stat. 897 (1964), *as amended,* 16 U.S.C., §§ 460L-4 to L-11.

50. See generally, Edwin Fitch and John Shanklin, *The Bureau of Outdoor Recreation* (New York: Praeger, 1970).

51. See *Izaak Walton League* v. *Butz,* 367 F. Supp. 422 (N.D. W. Va. 1973), appeal pending. For a comprehensive review and critique, see U.S. Congress, Senate Public Lands Subcommittee of the Committee on Interior and Insular Affairs, *Hearings on "Clear-cutting" Practices on National Timber Lands,* 92 Cong., 1 sess., 1971, 3 vol.

52. The celebrated Mineral King controversy, *Sierra Club* v. *Morton,* 405 U.S. 727 (1972), discussed below, has become both the symbol of the cause and harbinger of things to come.

53. 78 Stat. 890 (1964), 16 U.S.C., §§ 1131–36.

54. 74 Stat. 215 (1960), 16 U.S.C., §§ 528–31.

II

THE
FOREST
SERVICE
BUREAUCRACY

THE DEPARTMENT OF AGRICULTURE

Historic political circumstances placed the Forest Service within the Department of Agriculture, where it is now one of several bureaus under the aegis of the assistant secretary of agriculture for conservation, research, and education. As part of the Department of Agriculture it is the only important federal land-management agency outside the Department of the Interior which exercises parallel responsibility in each of the major areas of land management. Although there is some policy coordination between the service and its sister agencies within the Department of the Interior, primarily the Bureau of Land Management (BLM), the National Park Service, the Bureau of Sport Fisheries and Wildlife (BSFW), and the Bureau of Outdoor Recreation (BOR), there is no organizational structure for routine coordination of functional policy.

Although the Forest Service is formally responsible to the secretary and the assistant secretary of agriculture, in practice the service has traditionally functioned as a largely autonomous, independent agency. While its management discretion is bounded by fiscal limits and major policy directives set by departmental and higher executive levels—by the Office of Management and Budget (OMB) or the White House—typically these provide only very broad authority and independence of action. To some degree, of course, all large bureaus, particularly those with highly specialized missions, enjoy considerable autonomy from the departments of which they are part. This simply reflects the practical limits of top-executive control and the fact that such bureaus generally have some political support outside the agency.

But the Forest Service does seem to enjoy an autonomy unique in the federal bureaucracy. Its independence is closely related to the insulation of the service from political control of its top-level executives. Even the position of the chief has traditionally been insulated from political control in the Forest Service. Except for Pinchot, who was dismissed by President Taft under extraordinary circumstances and for reasons other than political convenience,[1] no chief has been removed from office; and except for Pinchot's successor, Henry Graves, only Forest Service professionals have been appointed to the position.[2] This phenomenon, rare in any agency, is particularly remarkable considering the highly political milieu in which the Department of Agriculture itself functions and the highly political and controversial issues with which the Forest Service has been involved. Various explanations can be offered. One is the image of nonpolitical professionalism the agency has successfully cultivated into a tradition of independence. Another is the relative balance of power, in matters of land-management policy, between the Executive and Congress. Perhaps even more it is ultimately a consequence of the balance of pressures from the many different interests to which the Forest Service multiple-use mandate exposes the agency:

> [T]he Forest Service does not stand alone in the face of pressures from one direction. One Chief of the Forest Service is alleged to have said, "I am supported by the pressures which surround me." With skillful manipulation, the various clientele groups tend to cancel out each others' efforts. To the extent that this occurs, the administrator is given greater discretion to make decisions which he considers to be in the public interest.[3]

Before taking a closer look at the agency we need to examine briefly some of its surrounding landscape.

THE IMMEDIATE ENVIRONS

The Congress and the Executive

The main focus of attention must be the House and Senate Committees on Interior and Insular Affairs, the Senate Committee on Agriculture and Forestry, and the House Committee on Agriculture, which oversee the activities of all of the land-management agencies. There are also other pertinent committees: two Appropriations Committees which execute fiscal control also exercise a more or less routine jurisdiction over forest management. Additional committees with occasional interests in specific problems affecting the Forest Service and forest management include the House and Senate Committees on Public Works, which are concerned with Forest Service road construction; the House and Senate Committees on Government Operations, concerned with governmental reorganization plans involving the service and others; the Senate Committee on Banking, Housing, and Urban Affairs, recently involved extensively in the subject of timber supply; the House Committee on Merchant Marine and Fisheries routinely considers wildlife matters—as does the Senate Commerce Committee (and its House counterpart). And so on. In short, there is scarcely a committee in Congress that does not at least have a subcommittee which is, from time to time, directly concerned with forest resource management.

Among this small army of committees, the Interior and Insular Affairs committees have been publicly the most visible in recent years, not only as sources of most of the major legislation in the field, but also as continuing watchdogs of the Forest Service and its management policies. The two Agriculture committees also exercise an important role in forestry, but their role has been less pervasive than that of the Interior and Insular Affairs committees, which to a rather exceptional degree are involved in the detail of management policy. Their impact has seemingly been augmented with the rising interest in environment, but it is not simply that the environment has become the cause of the day; these particular committees have a more direct interest in forest and other public land-management matters. Both are largely comprised of congressmen and senators from western states whose economic livelihood is heavily dependent upon (in some cases totally dominated by) the federal lands, of which the national forests are generally the most important economically and environmentally. By contrast, western representation on the two Agriculture committees has been relatively slight; both have been dominated by Southerners. Though forestry is important in the southern states—which have become large suppliers of timber—the federal lands do not contribute the major share of forest resources as they do in the West.

It should not be inferred, however, that the congressional and executive authorities are monolithic. Although there are occasions when major issues crystallize in terms of congressional versus executive authority, or national versus regional/local interest, on most of the major issues the interests and the source of political power do not so nearly divide. Within each sector—particularly within the congressional—are represented several divergent socioeconomic interests and corresponding political influences. There is not much point in identifying these, the important organized groups are well known—from the Sierra Club or the Wilderness Society at one end of the spectrum to the National Forest Products Association or the American National Cattlemen at the other.[4] On any given issue several of these groups may surface as vocal advocates for or against a particular policy. Each will secure some spokesman, more or less influential, within one of the major committees or within the executive branch. As mentioned earlier, the clash of interests can result in something of a standoff, or at most a kind of vague and ambiguous compromise, which permits the Forest Service a broad latitude to pursue its own policy inclinations.

Sister Agencies

No tour of this bureaucratic forest would be complete without some notice of the Forest Service's sister agencies with whom it shares responsibilities for public land policies. While there are many federal agencies that own land, only four have land management as their primary responsibility: the BLM, the National Park Service, the BSFW (all in the Department of the Interior) and, of course, the Forest Service. These four own about 94 percent of the total federal land.[5] The first three have functions which parallel at least one of the functions of the Forest Service.

The Bureau of Land Management. With more than 450 million acres (almost two-thirds in Alaska, with virtually all of the remainder in the eleven contiguous western states),[6] the BLM is the nation's largest land-owner.[7] The BLM was created in 1946 by consolidating the General Land Office (whose origin in 1812 made it one of the earliest federal agencies) and the Grazing Service (created in 1934). Although the BLM is the largest landowner,[8] nearly all of its lands are relatively poor in productive natural resources. Most of these BLM lands were public domain lands not reserved for national parks, forests, or other federal reserves (e.g., wildlife refuges, military reservations, Indian reservations, reclamation lands). The best areas were either selected for reservation and withdrawal, or were homesteaded; what remained thus tended to be land of limited economic value. However, the BLM does own valuable timberland in Oregon and Alaska, and some other areas possess valuable mineral wealth (the Outer Continental Shelf lands are leased for mineral exploration, and valuable oil lands exist in the Intermountain West and in Alaska). The third major use of BLM lands is grazing. Although revenues from grazing are only a small fraction of those from timber sales and a tiny fraction of revenues from mineral leases,[9] grazing has traditionally been the most widespread use of BLM lands. Outside of Alaska almost 90 percent of the BLM land is incorporated into grazing districts.[10]

The National Park Service. Of all the Interior agencies the National Park Service is today the best known to the public.[11] And of all the Interior agencies, it is doubtless the closest rival of the Forest Service, partially reflecting the fact that a substantial part of the 30 million-acre national park system has been acquired from national forests.[12] The Park Service was established in 1916 within the Department of the Interior. Prior to 1916, each national park and monument was administered as a separate unit; there was no central management of what had become, even then, an extensive system of parklands. The National Park Service Act of 1916 continues to provide the primary general directive for that service which is "to promote and regulate the use" of the park areas and to "conserve the scenery and natural and historic objectives and the wildlife therein," and further to provide for the enjoyment of these "in such manner and by such means as will leave them unimpaired for the enjoyment of future generations."[13] This directive has been supplemented by other statutes, but these do not significantly modify the primary mission of the Park Service or the character of its policies.

The Bureau of Sport Fisheries and Wildlife. This agency administers over 300 wildlife refuges (consisting of migratory waterfowl, migratory bird, big-game, and game refuges) on over 30 million acres, of which 28 million are owned by the bureau (some refuge lands are on holdings of other federal and various state and local agencies; the bureau is responsible for fish and wildlife on these lands but not for other resources).[14]

Refuges first came into existence through the activities of conservation groups early in this century, prior to the existence of any administrative agency. The first was established on Florida's Pelican Island. Additions were made in a similar manner and often patrolled by volunteers, until 1924, when Congress first appropriated funds for refuges along the upper Mississippi. In 1929, the Migratory Bird Conservation Act,[15] based on the 1916 Migratory Bird Treaty with Canada (and later with Mexico), authorized and funded development of a refuge system administered by a Migratory Bird Conservation Commission and assisted by the Biological Survey. As predecessor of the present BSFW, the Biological Survey was first established in the Department of Agriculture. In 1940 it was transferred by executive reorganization to a newly formed Fish and Wildlife Service in the Department of the Interior. The present bureau was established as a part of the Fish and Wildlife Service by the Fish and Wildlife Act of 1956.[16] The bureau has a limited mission—the conservation of wildlife and management of its habitat. The Fish and Wildlife Act of 1956, which established this bureau, directs it to develop, manage, conserve and protect "wildlife resources" through research, acquisition of refuge lands, development of existing facilities, "and [by] other means." More specific resposibilities are contained in several enactments before and since the 1956 act.[17]

Interagency Relations. Obviously, the parallel responsibilities of the Forest Service and its sister agencies in Interior create occasions for competition or cooperation in land use policy. The relationships among the agencies is a mixture of both. In the absence of a single departmental structure for all of the agencies, unified land use policy is generally left to cooperative arrangements between the individual bureaus (or, occasionally between the two departments) on individual issues. In some cases, coordination of policy may be mandated by statute or executive directive[18] or by giving special policy-making functions to one departmental secretary (typically Interior),[19] but even here the practical reality is that coordination is left to the discretion of the bureaus (or departments), and only rarely will Congress or the White House intervene to direct what the agencies themselves do not accomplish. We shall have occasion later to note some of the processes of policy coordination and the cooperative arrangements between the Forest Service and other agencies in regard to particular land use functions. We shall also observe some instances of inconsistency and conflict which have prompted recurrent proposals for unification of the agencies.

INTERNAL ORGANIZATION
OF THE FOREST SERVICE

Organizationally the Forest Service, like Gaul, is divided into three parts: the National Forest System, Forestry Research, and State and Private Forestry. Geographically, the agency presides over an area larger than Gaul, dispersed over a nation larger than the Roman Empire and managed by an army of administrators that even Caesar would envy (Figure 1).[20]

The main focus of this study is the National Forest System, the dominant part of the organization. It is largest in size, accounting, in 1973, for approximately 85 percent of the total permanent staff of the agency and more than 83 percent of Forest Service appropriations. It is also the most centrally related to the main mission of the Forest Service—management of the national forests. Forestry Research is second in size, accounting for some 13 percent of the permanent staff and less than 11 percent of Forest Service appropriations. It provides basic and applied research on all aspects of forestry and forestry management, including forest-product economics. The State and Private Forestry branch is the smallest in the service, having less than 2 percent of the permanent staff and receiving about 6 percent of Forest Service appropriations.[21] Essentially the compromise product of several abortive efforts to obtain federal regulation of private forestry, State and Private Forestry was established to provide a variety of aids, such as assistance in fire, insect, and disease control, tree planting, etc., to state and private forest owners.

There are four main levels of organization for the National Forest System.[22] At the top is the relatively small Washington office, with less than 3 percent of the total permanent staff of the agency—in 1973 about 700 employees. It is not much larger than most regional offices and is actually smaller than some. This office is headed by the chief of the Forest Service.

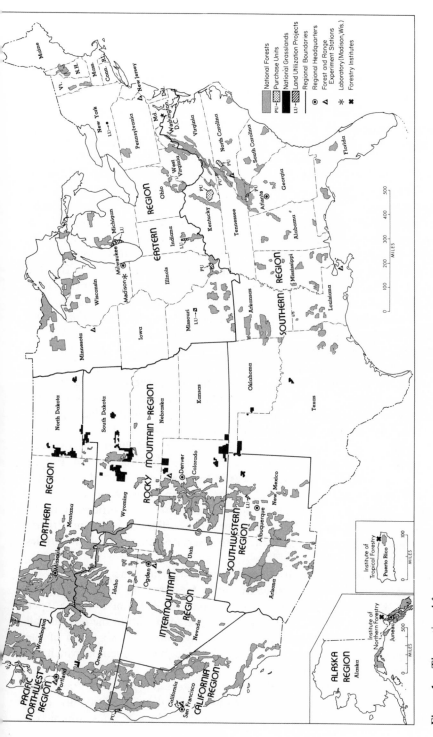

Figure 1. The national forest system.

27

Since 1905, when the Bureau of Forestry (formerly the Division of Forestry) became the Forest Service, there have been ten chief foresters. All have been professional foresters, and seven were career Forest Service officials before their appointment.[23] Most have served until retirement from the service or until death. Pinchot is the only chief forester ever removed, either for cause or political convenience.[24]

Below the chief are five major offices, each headed by a deputy chief: (1) Programs and Legislation, (2) Administration, (3) Research, (4) the National Forest System, and (5) State and Private Forestry. Each of these has several subdivisions, but only those of the National Forest System need be noted here. There are nine functional divisions in the National Forest System: timber, range, wildlife, watershed, recreation, engineering, fire control, lands, and land classifications. Each of these divisions is headed by a director. As a staff specialist the division director has no direct authority over either line officers or staff at subordinate levels. However, as an advisor and assistant to the chief and the deputy chief, he is responsible for formulation and implementation of policy guidelines within his functional area. Because of his position at the top of the organizational hierarchy and his proximity to the chief, each divisional director has considerable influence over the actions of subordinate officers in the field, with regard to the particular functional areas they supervise (Figure 2).

While the Washington office is responsible for general policy directives, most Forest Service operations—including a broad policy-making authority—are delegated to the field offices. For Research, the field organization consists of eight experimental stations, a separate Forest Products Laboratory, and an Institute of Tropical Forestry (in Puerto Rico), each headed by a director reporting directly to the chief. State and Private Forestry currently has two area offices in the East, each headed by a director reporting directly to the chief. In the western states, state and private forestry work is organized as a division within the regional offices. With the exception of Research and the two eastern field offices of State and Private Forestry, the regional offices of the Forest Service administer all the affairs of their respective regions.

There are nine such regions across the country. Since the geographic, environmental, and sociopolitical character of these regions varies greatly, so too does the management emphasis put upon the different Forest Service functions. However, although the different characteristics of the regions call for a difference in management emphasis and program mix, each of the regions is sufficiently large to embrace all of the major functions which the Forest Service has identified for itself.

Each regional office is headed by a regional forester (generally grade level GS-16), having a staff of varying size and organization. Traditionally, most regional offices were organized into functional divisions (various administra-

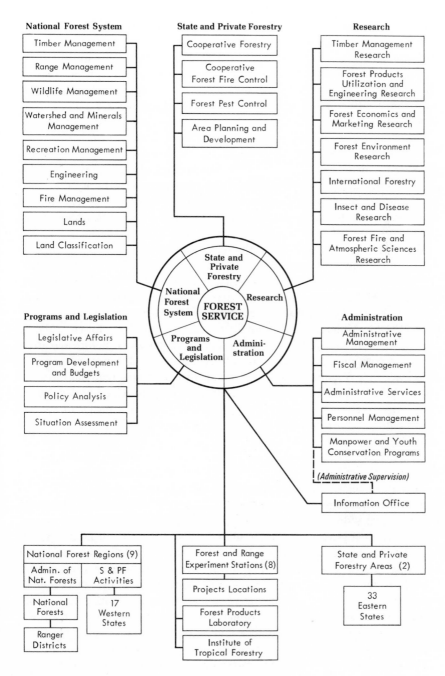

National Forest System

- Timber Management
- Range Management
- Wildlife Management
- Watershed and Minerals Management
- Recreation Management
- Engineering
- Fire Management
- Lands
- Land Classification

State and Private Forestry

- Cooperative Forestry
- Cooperative Forest Fire Control
- Forest Pest Control
- Area Planning and Development

Research

- Timber Management Research
- Forest Products Utilization and Engineering Research
- Forest Economics and Marketing Research
- Forest Environment Research
- International Forestry
- Insect and Disease Research
- Forest Fire and Atmospheric Sciences Research

Programs and Legislation

- Legislative Affairs
- Program Development and Budgets
- Policy Analysis
- Situation Assessment

Administration

- Administrative Management
- Fiscal Management
- Administrative Services
- Personnel Management
- Manpower and Youth Conservation Programs
- (Administrative Supervision)
- Information Office

State and Private Forestry

National Forest System

FOREST SERVICE

Research

Programs and Legislation

Administration

National Forest Regions (9)	
Admin. of Nat. Forests	S & PF Activities
National Forests	17 Western States
Ranger Districts	

Forest and Range Experiment Stations (8)
Projects Locations
Forest Products Laboratory
Institute of Tropical Forestry

State and Private Forestry Areas (2)
33 Eastern States

Figure 2. Organizational chart of the Forest Service.

tive support divisions and separate divisions for most of the functional components of the National Forest System headed by assistant regional foresters/division chiefs reporting directly to the regional forester. Recently the regional organizations have undergone some changes: Resource management divisions now have been consolidated under a deputy regional forester for resources; administrative divisions are under a deputy regional forester for administration; and state and private forestry functions are under a third deputy forester.

The Regional Forester

As director for all activities within his region, the regional forester is delegated broad authority. Indeed, such is the extent of his authority that only modest exaggeration is required to describe the Forest Service as a collection of regional organizations coordinated through a central Washington office.

The experience and training of the regional forester varies, but it does so within predictable boundaries. The regional foresters in office in 1973 all had at least one college degree, and with but one exception that degree was in forestry.[25] All joined the Forest Service at the lowest echelon (GS-5) and progressed through the ranks to become a regional forester—at ages varying from 44 to 54. All but one had been district rangers (de rigeur for virtually all career foresters), and all but one had been forest supervisors. Before and after these line positions each held various staff positions. All but one had some experience in a Washington staff position before becoming regional forester, and all held at least one position outside of the region which he headed in 1973. However (somewhat surprising in view of the frequency of moves within regions), most of them spent the major part of their careers within a single region.

The Forest Supervisor

Immediately below the regional level is the national forest, headed by a forest supervisor. Presently there are 155 separately named national forests in the system (146 administrative units),[26] aggregating some 183.7 million acres (excluding grasslands, purchase units, and other special units). Apart from Alaska, which is exceptional in having only two national forests (aggregating, however, nearly 21 million acres), the number of forests in a particular region ranges from thirteen in the southwestern region (Region 3) to thirty-three (thirty administrative units) in the southeastern region (Region 8). In addition to the national forests there are some nineteen national grasslands (3.9 million acres), administered by the supervisors of the several forests to which they are assigned.[27]

The national forest is regarded as the central functional planning level of the field organization. The supervisor (the present median grade level of supervisors is between GS-13 and GS-14) is given broad authority and responsibility for functional planning; while some functional planning is conducted at the district level, the supervisor's office either prepares or closely controls the planning effort for all of the major resource functions. In addition, it is responsible for supervising the operations of the various ranger districts.

The profile of the supervisor is rather similar to that of the regional forester through the early years of career development. He has invariably progressed through the ranks of forester, ranger, staff officer, being appointed supervisor in his late thirties or early forties.[28]

The supervisor's office is organized generally on a functional staff basis similar to that of the region, with specialists in one or more related functions providing assistance to the supervisor. The staff is responsible for forest planning, coordinating, reviewing, and directing the technical aspects of their individual functions. As in the case of senior staff they are policy planners and advisors; they are not in charge of the execution of resource-management work, and they do not have direct authority over subordinate line officers.

As one would expect, the administrative as well as the geographic size of the forest varies greatly across the national forest system. Some idea of the spread is conveyed by the budget figures which, for fiscal 1973, ranged between $900,000 and $10.7 million. The average in that year was $3.9 million.[29]

The Forest Ranger

The lowest administrative unit within the Forest Service is the ranger district. There are currently 692 districts; the number has been reduced over the past decade and is expected to be reduced somewhat more. The district is headed by a ranger (the median grade of ranger currently is between GS-11 and GS-12), the primary line officer responsible for the routine work of forest management. Whereas the forest supervisor's office is typically located in a principal city near the forest, the ranger's office is generally found in the small town nearest the area in which the work is done. The ranger may have some direct planning responsibilities—most notably the responsibility for preparing multiple-use plans for coordinating the various functional management plans. He also participates in the preparation of forestwide management plans. However, he is not primarily a policy-planning officer but an operating officer. The ranger district is not extensively staffed. To perform any particular project, laborers (typically part-time summer employees) will be assigned to the ranger as needed. Professional technicians such as wildlife biologists, landscape architects, or engineers will also be assigned for project or program work (e.g., timber sales), but there are few professional staff members permanently assigned to the ranger district level. For most of the routine work, the ranger is expected to be his own specialist. Some exceptions still exist. In some of the larger districts a ranger may have a major staff, one rivaling that of a small forest. The most notable examples are the timber-rich districts in the Pacific Northwest region. In some of these districts the annual volume of timber sales and harvest equals or exceeds that of entire forests elsewhere, and, of course, the district budget corresponds directly to that work (among other work), as does the size of the permanent staff. Again, the range in budgets gives an indication of administrative size. In fiscal 1973, the smallest ranger district budget was $34,000, the largest was $1,155,000, and the average was $334,000.[30]

THE FOREST SERVICE
PROFESSIONAL

In the early years of the Forest Service it would have sufficed to describe the handful of field employees—forest inspectors, supervisors, rangers, and forest guides—as amateur woodsmen and the Washington staff as amateur bureaucrats. Neither group had any special training skills or professional background. After Pinchot molded the Forest Service into a professional organization one could no longer fairly describe the forester as an amateur (woodsman or bureaucrat); but the professional was still very much of a generalist.

Today that has changed. Within a total agency work force of over 20,000 permanent full-time employees, some 10,000 (8,200 within the National Forest System) are professionally trained in specialties ranging from mathematics to meteorology, from botany to business management analysis. Not all of these professional specialties are represented in the National Forest System; many of the scientific specialties are within the research arm of the Forest Service, and many of these specialized business management analysts will be found in administration. But even within the National Forest System, in which we are primarily interested, the range of professional backgrounds and diversity of professional roles is very broad. Given this diversity, any attempt to paint a single portrait of the modern Forest Service professional requires artistic license. However, for all the diversity that does exist, the service, especially the National Forest System, is still dominated by the generalist forester whose professional background is broader than it is deep. And, quite apart from professional training or occupational role, some common features of the professional forester do stand out, permitting a reasonable likeness to be achieved by a single, composite portrait.[31]

To begin with, the professional forester is white. Under pressure from minority groups and from civil rights organizations, efforts have been made to increase hiring of minorities, but success in this venture so far is still largely confined to administrative and clerical positions. The number of minority persons in the professional groups is still very small (these are Indians and Chicanos; for blacks, the number is near zero), just as the number of minorities being trained in forestry schools is small.

Typically, the forester comes from a small town and the middle class. His education includes college; over 90 percent of the Forest Service professionals have at least one university degree, and of these, 11 percent have advanced degrees, most often in natural science specialities such as biology or hydrology. Most of the professionals within the National Forest System decided upon their career before graduating from high school and most chose the Forest Service before graduating from college. The majority of the foresters worked for the Forest Service one or more summers during college.[32] As of December 1969, there were fifty-four colleges and universities offering instruction in forestry and related curricula leading to a degree, of which thirty-five were accredited by the Society of American Foresters[33] However, some 60 percent of all Forest Service professionals come from only twenty schools.[34]

The Forest Service professional is a settled family man with two or three children—still relatively young. Within the forestry and engineering career fields the mean age is thirty-eight but with more than 60 percent under that age (the mean age of the business administrators is forty). The age structure varies significantly among regions. For example, in the Pacific Northwest region, only 31.6 percent of the profession sampled in 1970 were under thirty-eight, in contrast to the eastern region where some 72.4 percent were under that age.[35]

The occupational interests of the professional vary greatly, as is suggested by the range of specialties represented in the Forest Service. Within the National Forest System the three major career fields are forestry, engineering, and business administration.[36] Each of these fields contains several occupational specialties. For example, in forestry there are eleven different specialties, ranging from general forester to wildlife biologist.[37] Traditionally, occupational specialties within the forestry career field have dominated the three main career fields within the National Forest System. This follows from the basic mission of the agency itself. Forestry is concerned more or less with ultimate management objectives, whereas engineering and business administration have been viewed as merely support functions. Within the forestry career field the dominant occupational specialties have tended to coincide with the traditional production functions of the Forest Service, for example, timber or range management. In recent years, however, there is evidence of some significant shifts in career interests and occupational specialties. For one thing, there has been a substantial shift of the general career interests away from forestry to engineering and business administration. In 1958 it was reported that over 90 percent of all Forest Service professionals were foresters; in 1970 65 percent were foresters; in January 1973, the figure was 52.5 percent in the National Forest System and only 50 percent in the agency overall.[38] At the same time there appears to be a significant shift in specialties in functional roles within the general forester career field away from the traditional production functions to areas such as outdoor recreation and wildlife. Of course, the choice of specialties is highly influenced by the importance assigned to it in terms of advancement; for this reason, general administration is the first choice of foresters. Discounting this concern, however, a strong interest is shown in recreation and wildlife, particularly among those under age thirty-eight.[39]

Though these shifts in professional and occupational interests might suggest a shift in attitude toward forest management, one must be cautious not to read too much into this. Forest professionals surveyed in 1970 indicated, by a large margin, a continued belief in *active* management of the forest. This is particularly true of the foresters surveyed. Of these, 71 percent believed that making resources available to users was the most important mission of the Forest Service. Only 2 percent thought maintaining natural beauty took precedence over active management, and only 15 percent believed preservation of natural resources took preference over active use. Those in engineering and business administration career fields indicated greater support for preservationist mission than foresters, but the majority of such professional groups still agreed with the foresters in supporting active—even intensified—use and management of the forest resources as distinct from preservation or preservation-oriented use.[40] While no breakdown of these attitudes has been made by age, the fact that over 60 percent of the foresters are under thirty-eight suggests that the above reflects substantially the attitudes of the younger as well as the older foresters.[41] In any event, there is no evidence which suggests the changes in professional interests occurring today necessarily presage a change in the basic philosophy of land use management. While such changes in attitude suggest an interest in a more balanced multiple-use management of *all* forest resources, this appears still to be very much within the traditional framework of a utilitarian ethic of productive use of forest resources.[42]

The Forest Service professional, particularly the forester, is active socially and professionally—probably more so than the typical university graduate. For an agency of such size the Forest Service is rather remarkable, even virtually unique, in the strong ties of sociability and professional kinship that bind the agency together. Frequently transferred, among forests and among regions and sometimes to Washington and back again, the forester in particular develops a wide array of social acquaintances and friends. And quite independent of permanent transfer,

Forest Service personnel generally—at least those at higher grade levels—travel often and widely to meetings, inspections, and ceremonies.

Beyond the personal ties among individuals there is a still broader kinship among the Forest Service personnel. In part it is born of common professional training and interests, but that is by no means the entire basis of it. As already mentioned, the Forest Service professional has become increasingly specialized. A wildlife biologist and a hydrologist may both be foresters (i.e., both within the forestry career pattern), but they could not be said to have a common professional background except insofar as both are members of a single organization.

The latter consideration appears to be the most important: the specialist within the Forest Service is very likely to have somewhat closer ties to his colleagues in the Forest Service, regardless of occupational specialty, than to his professional counterpart in another organization, such as the National Park Service. The "school tie" of the agency is at least as important, if not more so, than the color of the academic cowl. Identification with the organization is strengthened by the fact that, for most, work in the Forest Service is typically a long-term career. The number of departures by professionals from the Forest Service is remarkably low, and most of these occur within either the first-year probationary period or a few years thereafter. Of those who remain, most are well-satisfied with the Forest Service: over 85 percent of those surveyed in 1970 indicated they would likely choose the Forest Service again, and most would approve of a son working for the service[43] (no question was asked about daughters).

Identification with the agency is also strengthened by the practice (for which the service has been roundly criticized in recent years) of promoting to higher levels almost exclusively those from within its own ranks.[44] This is seen most clearly at the top echelons of the service. As mentioned earlier, since Henry Graves, every chief of the Forest Service has been appointed to the position from within the organization, except for Silcox, who spent most of his career in the service, even though he left before being appointed chief. The same pattern has prevailed in selection of regional foresters, supervisors, and even rangers—the lowest line officer in the National Forest System. For the vast majority of Forest Service professionals, entry into the organization is as an apprentice forester, a position he will hold for one year until promotion to forester. Lateral entry into senior positions (those above entering grade for the career specialty) is not prohibited, and not unknown. In fact, a number of positions are filled by outsiders. However, in the National Forest System these are almost invariably specialists in junior staff positions—for example, wildlife biologists or computer technicians—and not line or senior staff positions. Moreover, even in junior staff positions, lateral entry into senior positions is clearly the exception to the rule of promotion or advancement from within.[45]

We shall have occasion to discuss some of the implications of this rule later: for now, it is enough to identify it as one of the strongest influences toward identification of the professional with the Forest Service. It means not only that the senior professionals will have the perspective of one with experience within the Forest Service (in the case of a senior line officer, a typically varied experience in different line and staff positions), it means also that the junior professional has the security of knowing his promotion to senior positions will not be impeded by outside competition. This does not mean, of course, that promotion is automatic or based on tenure only. But seniority (time and grade) in experience in a particular position is probably the single most important factor in making promotions among at least the lower echelons. Beyond the minimum requirements proposed by civil service regulations, the length of time in any one position or grade classification varies significantly. For example, it may take from three to ten years to become a ranger. In general, however, the promotion path in the National Forest System tends to be stable and relatively slow, particularly for those in the traditional forestry career series (as distinguished from engineers and business administrators). Apart from the simple time and grade criteria, the determining factors in promotion are difficult to fix in a clear and uniform pattern. However, casual observation suggests a few generalizations.

One rule that clearly holds is that promotion to higher grades and senior line and staff positions is strongly related to the breadth of one's professional background and experience. This means that, among the major career fields, there are more senior positions—line and staff—open to the forester than to the engineer or business administrator; and within a particular career field, such as the forester, more positions are open to the forester–administrative generalist than to, say, the wildlife biologist.[46]

More is involved than a professional role; for promotion to advance position, it is generally recognized that exposure to different line and staff positions within the agency is essential. Most senior staff professionals, especially those at regional levels and above, have held at least one line position as ranger, and many at the regional or Washington level will also have served as supervisors. Senior line officers will invariably have held one or more staff positions in addition to having served as rangers.[47] All of this requires frequent transfers.[48] Transfers are not always mandatory; if a particular position is not one needed for placement of other personnel and the incumbent's performance is reasonably competent, he may be permitted to extend his tour (in some cases for an indefinite period until he retires). But a long extension in one position is obtained at a sacrifice to future career advancement. Forest Service policy is to make frequent transfers, to broaden the experience of its personnel and to reinforce their identification with the service. Without such broad exposure the Forest Service professional is unlikely to make it very far to the top.[49]

MAINTENANCE OF CONTROL
AND DIRECTION

For an agency as large and diversified in its functions as the Forest Service, maintaining control and direction is obviously a problem of the first magnitude. Authority, like energy, dissipates over space. The decentralized character of the organization adds a special dimension to the problem. For one thing, the diffusion of field-level discretion and responsibility adds to the distance, geographic and personal, over which control and direction must be exercised; with each level of bureaucracy the problems of communication and accurate reporting are multiplied. Decentralization also enhances the influence of local interests, which often pull in directions that do not serve, and may even frustrate, overall agency objectives. These problems are not, of course, unique to the Forest Service; they are endemic to all large bureaucracies—a phenomenon widely noted. But the Forest Service does present an excellent model of these bureaucratic problems, and the structure of controls it has created to overcome them appears elaborate to a unique degree in any nonmilitary agency. Since these have been superbly discussed in Kaufman's *The Forest Ranger,* we need only review them generally here.

Official decisions are controlled and directed—or in Kaufman's term, *preformed*[50]—in many different ways. Most of these are techniques carefully and deliberately designed by the agency leadership, but some are largely the result of the traditional character and orientation of the agency and of its professionals. The first measure of direct control, of course, is the definition of delegated authority, but we need not pause to examine this inasmuch as the various organizational levels of respective authority and responsibility have been outlined earlier. It need only be noted that because of the broad delegated authority given to regional foresters and the broad discretion given to them to redelegate authority to lower levels, the degree of responsibility in authority of line officers varies considerably throughout the system.

Within the scope of the general power delegated to line officers, decisions are authorized and constrained by statutes, executive orders, and departmental regulations, as well as by service regulations and directives. The first three are of slight importance or interest here. Even at the Washington level the directions and the constraints set by statute are for the most part broad, enabling acts conferring a range of power and authority that describe relatively few constraints. This is also true, though to a lesser extent, of departmental regulations and executive orders. Occasionally, the Executive will direct a particular policy emphasis,[51] but usually these provide only occasional direction and are of such a general nature as to be more hortatory than compelling.[52] As for departmental regulations, these too are very general—typically adding little beyond that provided by statute or what is already prescribed by the Forest Service itself.

The heart of the directives system and the basis of agency policy is the Forest Service Manual, the *vade mecum* of the agency. Within more than twenty tedious but carefully designed and generally useful volumes, the manual incorporates and interprets virtually all of the relevant legal documents, statutes, executive orders, departmental regulations, results of judicial decisions and, within the scope of these, prescribes the management policy for the agency.[53] The manual gives the detailed breakdown of the organization of the agency, the authority delegated and broad management directives for each activity within each of the three main branches of the agency. The main body of the manual, as it affects overall service policy, is prepared by the Washington office. To these policies are added regional policy directives in the form of supplements to the manual. Further supplementation may also be provided by the forest supervisors within the scope of their authority. Finally, the ranger will add a fourth layer of directives through the addition of multiple-use plans which appear as supplements to the manual.

The manual describes the legal and administrative structure and administrative policy; a second set of directives tied to the manual by common classification are the Forest Service Handbooks, which provide detailed direction on how to perform a variety of functions—road construction, timber surveys and valuation, fire reporting, range analysis, improvement of wildlife habitat and many other functions.

Compliance with agency policy is determined through several means.[54] One of these is simply through information obtained in formal reports. Generally these are routine statistical or business reports designed for accounting or general planning purposes; they are neither intended to serve as compliance checks nor regarded as important surveillance measures. On the other hand, the reports do contain information which provide the basis for any (surveillance) system in control. At the very least, the information provides data on the achievements of the various officials, enabling senior officers to determine whether specified target objectives have been made. Beyond this, reports may also disclose actions that do not conform to management prescription. Aside from routine reporting, information pertinent to compliance may be derived from countless sources outside the organization—from the public generally, or more commonly, from organizational groups. Information gleaned through these channels may develop in the course of a formal appeal procedure, from an informal complaint, or through other informal contacts. The channels are as many and diverse as the number of persons and groups whose interests are affected by Forest Service decisions.

The most direct means for ensuring compliance is inspection. Since the time of Pinchot, who established a special core of inspectors operating directly out of his office, the Forest Service has had a highly developed inspection system. Now, however, each level of the Forest Service is responsible for inspecting the level below it.

All of these techniques are designed, more or less directly, for the purpose of surveillance and control of official action and decision making by subordinate officers. But assurance of conformity to agency norms rests more upon confidence in the officers and staff themselves. In the long run, therefore, control and guidance takes the direction of developing what Herbert Kaufman calls "the will and capacity to conform."[55] There is no process one can describe for forming the will and capacity to conform.

This is rather the function of the entire environment which the Forest Service creates for its professionals. It begins with the initial training of the forester in school, training the Forest Service influences by its leadership in professional forestry generally, as well as by its position as one of the major employers of forestry graduates. Thereafter, the attitudes which prevail are influenced by the selection process of forestry graduates and then by the process of promotion and career assignments. While the Forest Service can and does tolerate a variety of views on particular issues and on particular subjects, it does attempt through its hiring, assignments, and promotions to develop loyalty to traditional policies of land use and management. While the agency does not consciously attempt to discourage innovation or new ideas, the incentives created by its emphasis on internal promotion and loyalty to institutional values favor a fairly conservative and stable policy of land use management. This may now be changing somewhat as the agency shows signs of being more receptive to major changes in policy; however, even with a new change in management emphasis of the Forest Service as a whole, the agency will continue to place a very high premium on loyalty to the organization and the established policy orientation and philosophy of the Forest Service. Whatever incentives are created for reform or innovation, the Forest Service will undoubtedly continue its past insistence that all members of the organization be "team players."

PLANNING AND
DECISION MAKING

Within the broad directives of the Forest Service Manual, the design of individual management activities is further drawn by management planning.[56] The source of planning and decision-making responsibility is often vague. As one recent study noted, "The web of decision-making events is so intertwined that in most cases it is more reasonable to say *decisions emerge* from the Forest Service rather than that they are made in some definable office."[57] Moreover, the lines which set planning apart as a distinct activity are inevitably blurred—at both ends of the planning/decision-making spectrum. At one end, where the planning process is most general, the planning becomes indistinguishable from the general agency policy. Thus, the manual is not merely a general directive for controlling agency action, it can also be regarded as an overall policy plan for all of the activities of the Forest Service. At the other end of the spectrum, as the planning process becomes more specific, it ultimately merges into particular management activities and work projects.

If we cannot sharply identify the boundaries of planning, it will suffice to say that it lies somewhere between broad agency objectives on the one hand and particular management work on the other. Within that realm are two major components of the planning system. (Later we shall consider whether it can accurately be called a *system* with the usual connotation that term carries.) The first major component of the planning process is functionally oriented. It comprises a series of long-range plans for individual land-management opportunities and for general multiple-use management. The second component is essentially an activity-planning and a budget-planning process; it is designed to translate long-term management objectives (as outlined in the functional plans) into annual work plans, within the framework of specific budget constraints.

Functional Planning
Functional planning takes place to some degree at each of the three field levels. At the regional level broad planning guidelines are prepared in the form of "multiple-use" (the traditional designation) or "land use" (the preferred current designation) guides. In addition, the regional staff may plan for particular management functions. However, generally the role of the regional office is to provide planning guidelines and priorities and to approve particular management plans. The primary administrative level for planning in the National Forest System is the forest, and it is the forest supervisor who has responsibility for most functional management planning. The district ranger does not typically have a major role in long-range planning, although he is responsible for multiple-use plans and, in some cases, for planning individual functions or their short-term action plan component.

Traditionally, the heart of functional planning has been the individual management plan for resource-management functions such as timber, recreation, wildlife, range and watershed, and for other supporting activities such as fire control, transportation (road construction), land adjustment (acquisition or transfer of lands), and others. The number, scope, and detail of such plans varies among the regions and forests, depending upon the kinds of activities prominent in the local area as well as upon current planning priorities. Typically, these plans are prepared at the national forest level and contain a long-term management program, from which short-term action plans are prepared to implement the long-term objectives (some, such as the timber-management plan, are prepared for a fixed time period; others are for an indefinite period).

Under the traditional planning scheme these individual functional plans are subject to the coordinating directives of multiple-use plans. Though the multiple-use planning system is currently being replaced by a new, so-called, land use planning system, the new system is essentially an extension of the old; it is necessary therefore to describe briefly the older system.

Although the multiple-use concept is as old as the Forest Service, multiple-use planning as a formalized process is a relatively recent phenomenon. In fact, as the early national forests were managed they served multiple uses. The service had some general idea of coordinating these different uses, but for the most part each of the respective management functions tended to be performed independently of the other, with little formal effort being made to integrate or coordinate them. There was relatively little need for this during most of the early period of forest management. So long as the demand for the various resources could be met without intensive management, the various uses of the forest could be substantially accommodated without extensive coordination or integrated planning. Many of the uses were effected with almost no planning and, indeed, with very little management. As the demands for all forest resources have increased, so the corresponding need for more intensive management has compelled increasing attention to the problem of coordination within the management of various resources. In the late 1950s increased attention was given to the need for more formal recognition of multiple-use objectives and to more specific directives to coordinate individual resource uses into a multiple-use framework.

In 1960, Congress enacted the Multiple-Use and Sustained Yield Act, which, for the first time, embodied the multiple-use concept in statutory language. The act signaled the need for a greater effort in the direction of multiple-use planning. The Forest Service could hardly ignore that implication. The act had been passed at its urging, to ratify the agency's multiple-use philosophy in the face of the rising demand for what was considered to be single or dominant land uses (most notably, wilderness preservation). Having obtained a congressional ratification of its multiple-use philosophy, it was incumbent on the agency to reorient its planning to give greater attention to multiple-use objectives. Accordingly, it established a system of multiple-use planning through regional multiple-use guides and ranger district multiple-use plans to provide a coordinating framework for the various functional resource use plans (such as timber, range) and activity-management plans (such as fire protection and transportation).

To implement multiple-use objectives a multiple-use survey and report was required for all major environmental impact-type activities such as timber sales, range allotment, management, recreation, development, etc. As the name indicates, the major purpose of the survey is to provide an analysis of the environmental impact of one particular management activity on the various other multiple uses and resources of the forest. In recent years it has become common to refer to the multiple-use surveys as "environmental analysis" or "impact" surveys. The names are somewhat misleading insofar as they suggest some relationship to the environmental impact statements required by the National Environmental Policy Act of 1969 (NEPA).[58] The multiple-use surveys, however, antedate NEPA and thus were not intended to fulfill the function of environmental impact statements. And it is clear the typical multiple-use survey does not satisfy the requirements of a NEPA impact statement.[59] In any event, the multiple-use survey is not the agency's surrogate for NEPA; it is employed routinely in planning situations which (by reasonable interpretation) are probably not "major federal actions significantly affecting the quality of the human environment," for which NEPA prescribes an impact statement.[60]

In 1971 the Forest Service instituted a new system of resource and multiple-use planning designed to replace the present functional planning system. This new approach recognizes a need for more completely integrated forms of planning resource uses, particularly in light of the increased public consciousness of the environment reflected, for example, in the enactment of the NEPA and in the expanded role of public participation in administrative decision making as well as by such new techniques in resource management as the growing use of computers and the increased attention to interdisciplinary planning.[61]

While some details of the new planning scheme are still being developed as this is written, the general character of the system can be outlined.[62]

Under the new system, functional planning begins at the regional level, where broad planning guides somewhat similar in purpose, although not necessarily similar in content to the existing multiple-use guide, are developed. Within the broad framework established by the guides, individual land use plans are developed, by special interdisciplinary planning teams appointed by forest supervisors, for natural ecological units within the district or forest.

The important contribution of the new land use planning scheme lies in the more substantial, more direct involvement of interdisciplinary skills. The planning team is comprised of different specialties drawn from the supervisor's and the regional forester's staffs. The plan is designed to be comprehensive for all functional activities, supplanting the traditional multiple-use plan with an integrated resource use and with an integrated resource and functional plan. How it will affect individual functional management plans is not at this time clear. Some Forest Service officials have expressed the view that the new plans will not alter the present functional outlines but will simply provide a kind of new multiple-use plan. Others, however, think the new unit plans will, at least ultimately, replace individual functional management planning altogether. For the immediate future, it is apparent that the individual functional management plans for such major functions as timber management, range management, recreation, fire control, transportation, and others will continue. However, the land use plans possibly will reduce their importance and shift emphasis to integrated planning with the ultimate objective of making functional plans merely component parts of the comprehensive unit plans; or they will be simply excerpted from the unit plans for all of the units of the forest. Thus, the aim is to reduce the importance of functional designs to the point where ultimately the unit plans become the operative plans and the functional outlines little more than informational guides for the use of the forest supervisor and higher echelons.

Perhaps the most important aspect of the "new" planning is the increased use of more sophisticated analytic techniques for measuring and evaluating the relative costs and benefits of particular programs or work activities.[63] Particularly notable is the development of computer program models for evaluating conflicting uses. The Forest Service is currently developing and implementing several computer-based, linear program systems which will allow the planner to examine the effect of various decisions on the resource base (the forest) and on the product output levels (e.g., timber, wildlife, and recreation).[64] Current systems include the Timber Resource Allocation Method (Timber RAM), the Resource Capability System (RCS), and the Wildlands Resource Information System (WRIS). Of the three major planning systems, Timber RAM[65] is the most fully advanced. It is already being utilized on most western national forests for the preparation of new timber-management plans.

Work Load and Fiscal Planning
The second major component of the planning and decision-making process, work load and fiscal planning, overlaps the periodic functional planning process, but is more directly oriented to the budget and appropriations. Until recently, work load and fiscal planning was broken down into three principal processes: project work inventory, annual work planning, and work load analysis.[66]

The *project work inventory* provided a comprehensive list of projects which served as the basis for developing agency programs. However, because of the cost of maintaining an annual inventory of projects, this phase of planning was recently abandoned. Now projects are inventoried only under individual functional plans.

Annual planning consists of identifying objectives in major programs to be accomplished by the various administrative units within specified periods. Work plans are prepared by each major echelon under the district ranger. The chief's work program is prepared annually, setting principal objectives and jobs for the fiscal year. It may include some major assignments for a period longer than one year, but it is essentially an annual program. The program includes objectives and jobs for the service as a whole, as well as specific jobs for the chief's office in Washington. The chief's annual work program then becomes the basis for similar work programs prepared by the regional foresters, the experimental station directors, the state and private area directors, and finally provides the basis for the national forest uniform work-planning system, which identifies, describes, and assigns time and priorities to specific jobs.

At the ranger district level, the annual work plan provides a comprehensive list of "doing" and "supervising" tasks and specific job assignments for the ranger and his personnel. The ranger district plan becomes fully integrated into that of the forest supervisor, thus comprising a total forest plan of work. The culmination of all annual planning under the uniform work-planning system is, of course, implementation of the projects and programs by specific on-the-ground action. The annual plan is therefore the immediate guide for on-site management; before it can be implemented all the work covered by the functional and other periodic plans is incorporated into the annual work plan for a particular fiscal year.

The third traditional component of work load planning is an analysis of each program activity (timber management, range management, etc.) to determine the time, manpower, and, consequentially, the budget requirements for each activity. In recent years *work load analysis* has fallen victim to budget constraints and has not been kept current; however, I am informed that efforts are now being made to update the work load analysis. Briefly the process of work load analysis is as follows: each activity is broken down into component jobs which must be performed to accomplish the management goals set for each of them; standards of quality and intensity, and the time requirements needed to perform a particular unit of work, are determined and applied to each job; these data, together with other information, are then used to determine the number of work units to be accomplished during a year, and the work units are subsequently used to determine the total job requirements in terms of man-hours per activity or per function.

Annual planning and work load analysis is integrated with the budget cycle and budget-planning process. The budget-planning process is thus not an independent planning process but rather a central component of annual work planning, and, in turn, work planning and analysis are the basis upon which budget requests and allocation of appropriations are made.

The traditional process of appropriating funds annually has constrained fiscal planning to a very short term. Though the agency does engage extensively in long-term program and functional planning, the absence of long-term budgetary support (or any assurance of it) has tended to undermine the practical utility of long-term functional planning. To meet the need for stable, long-term fiscal planning—particularly in key resource areas such as timber—from time to time it has been suggested that a trust fund approach be used, in which the revenues collected by the agency would be earmarked either for specific forest management activities or for all agency operations. As will be discussed later, a number of such funds have been established in particular areas for special purposes, but proposals to extend this to other activities (such as timber mangement) or to the agency generally have failed.

However, Congress did take a step toward providing for long-term fiscal planning with enactment of the Forest and Rangeland Renewable Resources Planning Act of 1974.[67] The act provides for periodic assessment, by the secretary of agriculture, of present and future uses, demand for and supply of forest and rangeland resources, and for the subsequent development of a "renewable resource program." The first assessment and program are to be prepared not later than December 31,1975, and it is thereafter to be updated in 1979 and each tenth year thereafter. The assessment and proposed program, together with a statement of policy, are to be sent to Congress for its use in framing budget requests for the following five- or ten-year program period. (The statement of policy also serves as the basis for agency action except as it may be disapproved or otherwise changed by Congress.)

The essential purpose of the act is to provide a basis for assessment of budgetary requests in light of long-term resource needs and management programs. Though it does not alter the annual budgetary process, it enables the annual budgetary process to be more responsive to longer-term fiscal needs. As this is written, the Forest Service has begun to implement its survey and analysis obligations under the act. However, it is difficult even to speculate what effect, if any, this will have on Congress in meeting its more amorphous responsibilities.

Public Participation

Mention has yet to be made of public involvement in the planning process. Here as elsewhere in discussing the planning and decision-making processes, generalizations are made difficult by the large variation and wide range of planning situations. Later, in the context of individual mangement functions, we shall have occasion to take another, closer look at the role of various private groups. For now, we need only consider the larger outline of public participation.

Traditionally, participation in the Forest Service processes by public groups has been quite circumscribed. Since matters "relating to public property" are exempt from the rulemaking provisions of the Administrative Procedure Act, land use plans are not subject to the provisions of that act[68] requiring public notice and opportunity for public comment on proposed plans and policies. In some areas, those directly affected by the management decisions have participated extensively in the planning and decision-making processes. Illustrative is range-management planning where those permitted to use the range for grazing are closely involved in the management process. However, the degree of outside participation in range management is somewhat exceptional. It is the legacy of an historic concept of quasi-partnership between the range users and the stockmen on the one hand and the government on the other, a concept based partly on the fact that grazing was an extensive use of the forests before the creation of the forest reserves. Thus, it does not reflect any deliberately formulated general policy of encouraging public participation and management planning and decision making. Traditionally, there are few general public hearings held in conjunction with management planning in any area of management activity. At most, outside involvement has tended to be an occasional and very informal matter. Formal proceedings are held in the context of individual adjudication under the appeals procedure. This is a rather complex process providing appeal through various levels of the agency by persons complaining of an agency decision or action. Although the procedure is primarily designed for those to whom the service has some form of written obligation, for example, a range permittee or a timber contractor, it can also be used to challenge Forest Service decisions by individuals or groups who have no such relationship.[69] However, it is a rather cumbersome vehicle for airing general public complaints, and, of course, it does not really achieve the objective of providing a means for general public input into the planning and decision-making process itself, but is only a means of challenging the process after it has been completed. Moreover, except where the appellant has some relationship with the Forest Service (typically under lease or contract), he is not entitled to a full oral hearing.

Although the Forest Service has traditionally avoided formal public hearings and formal public participation in its management-planning and decision-making processes, it has actively promoted informal contracts with the public and special interest groups. Some of these contracts are more or less formalized through the establishment of official public advisory councils or committees, and in some instances these may be required by statue or departmental regulation. For example, in the case of range mangement, livestock advisory boards are mandated by statute and departmental regulation for each forest or grassland whenever a majority of grazing permittees petition for such a board. While not required by statute or departmental regulations either at the regional or at the forest level, such groups may be established at the discretion of the regional forester and forest supervisor, respectively. Most of the officially constituted advisory councils are established at the forest level, but less than half the forests have such councils; others rely on *ad hoc* or informal advisory groups or contacts with various segments of the public and affected industry groups.

Official advisory groups are probably not as important as more informal contacts with the community which Forest Service officers are expected to maintain. Typically, the forest supervisor and the district ranger will be among the leaders of their respective communities; they and others are invariably active in community affairs, with membership in a wide variety of civil, social, and professional groups.

Despite the many informal avenues of communications existing between the Forest Service and the community, in recent years there has been considerable resentment, particularly among a number of conservation groups, over the absence of a more direct and formalized role for such groups to participate in the policy-planning and decision-making processes of the service. This is reflected by a concern and demand for greater public awareness of and involvement in all administrative processes affecting the environment. This in turn is part of a yet-broader movement toward public involvement in administrative processes generally, something which requires a major study in its own right.[70] But whether it is viewed as part of a larger movement or as a distinctive concern special to forest management, the complaint of insufficient public involvement has had its impact. Although the Forest Service, following its traditional style, has resisted being *mandated* to expand public involvement, it has itself taken steps to do so.

Most significant in this regard is the role for public involvement created by its new planning system. Under this system, public involvement is formally sought at two main stages. First, when the preparation of the planning area guides occurs, at which time the public is invited to contribute orally through informal conferences and "listening sessions," or in writing. Occasions for such public input are planned for at the beginning of the initial development of the guides and again prior to the preparation of a final draft plan for approval by the regional forester. The second and more important stage for public input is the preparation of greater detailed unit plans at the forest level. Again, the public is invited to participate except at this point, of course, the particular activities, and correspondingly, the planning and decisions, are better focused and particularized. This procedure parallels that used in cases subject to the requirements of a NEPA statement.[71]

As mentioned earlier, there is much that is not yet known about the operation of the new system, even assuming it is fully implemented along the lines of its present design. Consequently, there is little more that can be said descriptively about greater public participation in the planning and decision-making processes. Some speculations and critical comments on this and on other aspects of the Forest Service bureaucracy will be offered later. Here it seems best to defer comment until after we have examined specific land use functions and policies.

NOTES

1. Formally he was dismissed for insubordination. The background of the dismissal was noted earlier (see p. 10).

2. Besides Graves the only chief not appointed from a position within the agency, Ferdinand Silcox, had previously been a long-time Forest Service professional.

3. Outdoor Recreation Resources Review Commission Study Report, *Federal Land Management Agencies and Outdoor Recreation*, vol. 13 (1962), p. 28.

4. For a list of the various organized interest groups and professional associations (still reasonably inclusive although compiled nearly two decades ago), see Marion Clawson and Burnell R. Held, *The Federal Lands: Their Use and Management* (Baltimore: Johns Hopkins University Press for Resources for the Future, 1957), pp. 136–139.

5. See U.S. Department of Interior/Bureau of Land Management, *Public Land Statistics* (1973), pp. 11–13. Passing mention should also be made of the Bureau of Reclamation (in Interior) and the Corps of Engineers (in Defense) which own approximately 7.6 and 7.5 million acres, respectively. These lands (and waters) are managed primarily for water development and associated benefits such as outdoor recreation. The Forest Service and its sister agencies manage much of the recreation use under special agreements.

6. As of June 30, 1972, total landholdings were reported as 474 million acres, but only 451 million acres are administered under nonmineral public land laws. See U.S. Department of the Interior/Bureau of Land Management, *Public Land Statistics*, pp. 12 and 31.

7. Marion Clawson, *The Bureau of Land Management* (New York: Praeger, 1971), gives an excellent survey of the agency, its history, and functions to which the following discussion is indebted. See also Herman D. Ruth and Associates, *Regional and Local Land Use Planning*, Study for the Public Land Law Review Commission (Springfield, Ill.: Clearinghouse for Federal Scientific and Technical Information, 1970), vol. II, ch. IV.

8. The BLM also administers mineral leases on all federal lands—a function inherited from the General Land Office. (The overseeing of mining operations rests with the Geological Survey.)

9. In fiscal 1973 the BLM received some $104.6 million from timber sales, $4.1 billion from mineral leasing, and $9.3 million from grazing (U.S. Department of the Interior/Bureau of Land Management, *Public Land Statistics*, p. 168).

10. Grazing districts cover some 157.5 million acres (some of the area within the external boundaries of grazing districts is managed by others but owned by the BLM). Outside of the districts, grazing leases in the western states and Alaska cover about 15 million acres (Ibid., p. 89). Administration of grazing has also been the subject of bitter controversy, at one time becoming so intense as virtually to threaten the continued existence of the BLM's predecessor, the Grazing Service. For a detailed account, see Philip Foss, *Politics and Grass: The Administration of Grazing on the Public Domain* (Westport, Conn.: Greenwood Press, 1960); and E. Louise Peffer, *The Closing of the Public Domain* (Stanford, Calif.: Stanford University Press, 1951).

11. On the history and functions of the Park Service, see William C. Everhart, *The National Park Service* (New York: Praeger, 1972); John Ise, *Our National Park Service Policy: A Critical History* (Baltimore: Johns Hopkins University Press for Resources for the Future, 1961); and Ruth, *Regional and Local Land Use Planning*, vol. II, ch. V.

12. The Park Service reports total net area as approximately 29 million acres and gross area as 30.5 million (excluding private and other publicly owned lands within the external boundaries of park land). See U.S. Department of the Interior/National Park Service, *Areas Administered by the National Park Service* (1974), mimeographed. Inexplicably these figures differ from those given in U.S. Department of the Interior/Bureau of Land Management, *Public Land Statistics*, p. 12, which reports a figure of 24.5 million acres owned by the Park Service.

13. 39 Stat. 535 (1916), *as amended*, 16 U.S.C., §§ 1-18f. One original statutory directive, charging the Park Service with nationwide recreational planning, has now been taken over by the Bureau of Outdoor Recreation. See generally, Edwin M. Fitch and John Shanklin, *The Bureau of Outdoor Recreation* (New York: Praeger, 1970).

14. On the history and functions of the agency, see Ruth, *Regional and Local Land Use Planning*, vol. II, ch. VI. Owned acreage figures are from U.S. Department of the Interior/Bureau of Land Management, *Public Land Statistics*, p. 12.

15. 45 Stat. 1222 (1929), 16 U.S.C., § 715 *et seq.*

16. 70 Stat. 1119 (1956), 16 U.S.C., § 742a–k.

17. The first of these, the Migratory Bird Treaty Act of 1918 [40 Stat. 755 (1918), 16 U.S.C., § 703–711], provides for the protection of migratory birds by the secretary of the in-

terior. This program of protection was extended by the Migratory Bird Conservation Act, noted above. Other important legislation includes the Fish and Wildlife Coordination Act [72 Stat. 563 (1958), *as amended,* 16 U.S.C., § 661–666cc] and the Endangered Species Act of 1973 [87 Stat. 884 (1973)]. The former authorizes a broad range of BSFW activities, to "provide assistance to, and cooperate with, federal, state, or private agencies and organizations in the development, protection, rearing and stocking of all species of wildlife. . . ." The latter recently supplanted the Endangered Species Act of 1966, which gave substantial responsibilities to the secretary of the interior (and thereby the bureau) to use land acquisition and other authorities of the Migratory Bird Conservation Act, the Fish and Wildlife Act of 1956, and the Fish and Wildlife Coordination Act to conserve, protect, restore, and propagate selected species of fish and wildlife threatened with extinction. That authority is expanded by the 1973 legislation which, as will be discussed later, extends federal protection for endangered (and threatened) species on nonfederal as well as federal lands and provides for cooperative assistance to states in protecting such species.

18. See, for example, the Endangered Species Act of 1973 which gives to the secretary of the interior the general responsibility for coordinating endangered species protection.

19. For example, both the Outdoor Recreation Programs Act [77 Stat. 49 (1963), 16 U.S.C., § 460L] and the Land and Water Conservation Fund Act [73 Stat. 897 (1964), *as amended,* 16 U.S.C., § 460L] give special responsibilities for setting national policy in outdoor recreation.

20. A detailed geographic breakdown of the national forest system is given in Appendix A. The 187.3 million acres (net acreage) constitutes about 8 percent of the surface area of the United States and accounts for about 24 percent of all federal lands. As of January 1973, it employed more than 20,000 permanent, full-time employees and more than 9,000 temporary or part-time employees (unpublished data from the Forest Service).

21. The percentages on staffing are taken from an unpublished monograph prepared for the Administrative Conference of the United States [Michael Klimpl, "The Forest Service" (1971), p. 11]. The figures on appropriations are very rough estimates derived from 1973 budget data; appropriations are made by function and not broken down specifically by organizational division, my extrapolations are made by treating all Forest Research items under research (although some of the funds are under the National Forest System); state and private funds are specifically identified in the budget; all other appropriated funds are treated as National Forest System funds.

22. On organizational structure I have drawn substantially on the Forest Service Manual, Title 1200 and *Organization and Management Systems in the Forest Service* (1970), a useful summary of the manual provisions that is designed to instruct (and to some degree indoctrinate) new Forest Service employees. Some up-dating of these sources has been made on the basis of unpublished materials supplied by the Forest Service.

23. The exceptions are Pinchot, Henry Graves, dean of Forestry at Yale, and Ferdinand Silcox, who had been in the service but resigned to become a labor relations advisor.

24. Graves left the service to return to his former position as dean of forestry at Yale; his successor William Greeley resigned from the service at an early age (forty-nine); the next two chiefs, Robert Stuart and F. A. Silcox, died in office; following them, Earle Clapp served only as acting chief; the last three chiefs—Lyle Watts, Richard McCardle, and Edward Cliff retired from office. The present chief, John McGuire, was appointed in 1972. Eliminating the two who died in office and the one temporary appointment, the typical tenure has been eight to ten years.

25. One of the regional foresters had a B.S. in engineering and an M.P.A. in public administration, another had a B.A. in chemistry as well as a B.S. and M.S. in forest management.

26. See Appendix A for a complete breakdown of areas. In several instances, two separately named forests comprise a single administrative unit under a single supervisor. In some cases this is the result of a consolidation of previously separate administrative units. In others it is the consequence of having a particular area named in honor of some great person or event (I am told the Forest Service is besieged with requests from politicians to name special areas, or rename existing forests, in honor of a notable person).

27. The grasslands—most of them in the Great Plains area—were created in 1960 from some twenty-two land utilization projects. The land was acquired in the 1930s (first under an

emergency submarginal land acquisitions program, later under the Bankhead–Jones Farm Tenant Act of 1937 [50 Stat. 525 (1937), *as amended,* 7 U.S.C., §§ 1010, 1012, 1013a] for the purpose of restoring the condition of the land. The grasslands are primarily managed for grazing livestock, wildlife habitat, and outdoor recreation. Some of the grasslands are administered as part of forest ranger districts, others as independent districts. See generally, U.S. Department of Agriculture/Forest Service, *The National Grasslands* (1960). In addition to the grasslands there are nineteen land utilization projects (151,754 acres as of June 1972) (U.S. Department of Agriculture/Forest Service, *National Forest System Areas*). These are the residue of the land acquired in the 1930s, which has not been transferred to national forests, grasslands, or to other federal agencies (as much of the original purchase was). The projects are administered by ranger districts. There are also some twenty-six areas (120,495 acres) designated as research and experimental areas outside the national forests; and some twenty-six (229,944 acres) "purchase units"—areas acquired but not included in formal forest boundaries.

28. Precise data on all of the supervisors is unavailable; the above is extrapolated mainly from regional forester profiles and is, of course, subject to bias since these are obviously somewhat atypical.

29. Data supplied by the Forest Service. The smallest budget is that of the Roosevelt National Forest in Colorado; the largest is that of the Mt. Hood National Forest in Oregon.

30. Data supplied by the Forest Service. The smallest budget is that of the Rita Blanca District, Cibola National Forest in New Mexico. The largest, the Tiller District of the Umpqua National Forest in Oregon.

31. Much of the following data is taken from a study of the three major professional groups within the National Forest System, conducted for the Forest Service in 1970. William McWhinney, *The National Forest Service: Its Organization and Its Professionals* (Los Angeles: UCLA Graduate School of Business Administration, 1970). As a sample survey it bears all the infirmities of partial data, and there are a considerable number of ambiguities in the survey itself. It also suffers somewhat from age in an area undergoing considerable change. Nevertheless, it is still a reasonably good and current likeness. Other sources of data are personal interviews and references, as specifically noted.

32. A detailed profile of the forester's background appears in McWhinney, ibid., pp. 64–77.

33. Henry Clepper, *Professional Forestry in the United States* (Baltimore: Johns Hopkins University Press for Resources for the Future, 1971). For a critical study of professional education, see Samuel T. Dana and Evert Johnson, *Forestry Education in America: Today and Tomorrow* (Washington, D.C.: Society of American Foresters, 1963).

34. McWhinney, *The National Forest Service,* p. 85.

35. The following is a percentage breakdown of career fields as of January 1973: forester, 52.5 percent; engineer, 13.2 percent; business administrator, 11.6 percent; other (social services, recreation, computer, mathematics and statistics, etc.), 22.7 percent. This corresponds roughly to the breakdown for the entire agency (as one would expect from the fact that the National Forest System accounts for over 80 percent of its professional staff).

36. The specialities include wildlife biologist, range conservationist, and nine forester specialties—administrative, general forester, watershed management, land uses, fire control, timber management, range management, recreation, and wildlife management. The two largest groups are timber management and administrative.

37. McWhinney, *The National Forest Service,* pp. 70–71. One possible explanation here is the different management emphasis in these regions which may affect age selection. As the dominant timber-producing region, the Pacific Northwest has a relatively higher demand for persons in timber management, and indications are that this specialty currently attracts fewer of the young generation of professionals.

38. The 1958 figure is taken from Herbert Kaufman, *The Forest Ranger* (Baltimore: Johns Hopkins University Press, 1960). The 1970 figure is that of McWhinney, ibid. The 1973 figures are from unpublished data supplied by the Forest Service.

39. See McWhinney, *The National Forest Service,* pp. 99–105.

40. Ibid., p. 41.

41. Ibid., p. 71.

42. Some officials in the service expressed surprise at this conclusion; it was their *impression* that the philosophy of the younger, emergent generation of service professionals is at

least somewhat less commodity-use oriented. Such too was *my* first impression. On reflection, however, it seems to me really impossible to draw hard conclusions one way or another. The McWhinney sampling is woefully inadequate for this purpose. What one needs to survey is not simply different age groups within career groups, but within different occupation specialities in the service and differences in attitudes among professionals at different line and staff positions (and at different levels).

43. McWhinney, *The National Forest Service*, p. 72.

44. See Kaufman, *The Forest Ranger*, pp. 176–183. (Kaufman is *not* critical of the practice.)

45. The Forest Service's personnel office estimates that in the past ten years fewer than ten persons have been appointed from outside the agency to any of the line officer positions (ranger, supervisor, regional forester) or senior staff positions (division directors at the regional or Washington office level). It is also estimated that not more than a hundred individuals entered other staff positions from outside the agency, in the past ten years. It should be noted that, in the research arm of the agency, a substantial number of scientists do enter the agency at senior levels. However, inasmuch as such personnel do not have a direct policy-making role that fact does not, I believe, significantly qualify the point which is made here.

46. See McWhinney, *The National Forest Service*, pp. 78–99. This phenomenon is, of course, not unique to the Forest Service, or even to governmental agencies. For most large, diversified organizations, it is the generalist who rises to the top.

47. For example, the current regional foresters served in an average of twelve positions before being appointed to regional forester.

48. The transfers tend to be predominantly within a region until higher-level positions are reached; however, for larger regions this may still involve considerable change.

49. See Kaufman, *The Forest Ranger*, pp. 176–178, for an excellent discussion of the service's transfer policy.

50. Kaufman, *The Forest Ranger*, p. 91.

51. The case of timber supply is a current illustration. See President Nixon's 1970 statement directing development of programs for increasing timber yield, following the recommendations of a special cabinet committee, both printed in U.S. Congress, Senate Public Lands Subcommittee of the Committee on Interior and Insular Affairs, *Hearings on "Clearcutting" Practices on the National Timberlands,* 92 Cong., 1 sess., 1971, pp. 1044–1051.

52. The above-noted case of timber supply is again illustrative. It is, I think, accurate to say that President Nixon's directive to increase yield had little tangible impact on management practices; the service has continued to insist that it will not increase the allowable cut without additional funds, enabling it to increase long-term productivity. This is not inconsistent with the president's directive, which was so broad and qualified as to leave full discretion to the Forest Service.

53. Gifford Pinchot would no doubt be stunned to see how his little "Use Book" (*The Use of the National Forest Reserves*) has grown. A small volume, which was designed to be carried in a ranger's pocket, the Use Book contained less than a hundred pages of "general information, directions, regulations, and special instructions." See Gifford Pinchot, *Breaking New Ground* (New York: Harcourt, Brace, 1947), pp. 264–265.

54. For a thorough discussion, see Kaufman, *The Forest Ranger*, pp. 126–160.

55. Ibid., pp. 161–200.

56. For an excellent, detailed survey of planning procedures, see Ruth, *Regional and Local Land-Use Planning*, vol. I, ch. III. Although the Ruth survey does not reflect recent developments in planning, it is still useful. I have also relied heavily on discussions with Forest Service officials and a variety of Forest Service documents, including selected management plans, planning guides, and, of course, the Forest Service Manual.

57. McWhinney, *The National Forest Service*, p. 43.

58. 42 U.S.C., §§ 1857 *et seq.*

59. The act itself [§ 102(2) (c)] lists five required elements of a NEPA statement: (1) the environmental impact of the proposed action; (2) any adverse environmental effect which cannot be avoided should the proposal be implemented; (3) alternatives to the proposed action; (4) the relationship between local short-term uses of man's environment and the maintenance and enhancement of long-term productivity; (5) any irreversible and irretrievable commitments of resources which would be involved in the proposed action should it be implemented. Judicial in-

terpretation of the act has added a sixth element, a cost–benefit analysis. See, for example, *Calvert Cliffs' Coord. Comm.* v. *AEC,* 449 F. 2d 1109 (D.C. Cir. 1971), *cert. denied,* 404 U.S. 942 (1972). The multiple-use survey would not satisfy either the third or the sixth requirements. In fact, it might not satisfy any in view of the quite rigorous standards of compliance which some courts have set. See, for example, the *Calvert Cliffs* case; see generally, Frederick Anderson, *NEPA in the Courts, A Legal Analysis of the National Environmental Policy Act* (Baltimore: Johns Hopkins University Press for Resources for the Future, 1973), pp. 200–271.

The multiple-use survey procedure also would not comply with NEPA's requirements that the agency shall consult with other federal agencies with pertinent expertise, and that copies of the environmental statement with comments of such other federal agencies be "made available to the President, the Council on Environmental Quality [CEQ] and to the public" (the latter according to Section 3 of the Administrative Procedure Act, 5 U.S.C., § 552). Nor would the multiple-use survey comply with the requirement for public involvement and public hearing "when appropriate" which Executive Order No. 11514 [35 Fed. Reg. 4247 (1970)] and CEQ Guidelines [38 Fed. Reg. 20550 (1973)] have added to NEPA.

60. This may seem a bold statement to those aware of the liberal interpretation of NEPA by the CEQ Guidelines [38 Fed. Reg. 20550 (1973)] and judicial decisions. See, for example, *Students Challenging Regulatory Agency Procedures (SCRAP)* v. *United States,* 346 F. Supp. 189 (D.D.C. 1972) *reversed,* 93 U.S. 2405 (1973), which held that an impact statement was a prerequisite to effectuating a tariff increase on scrap metal; the reversal was based on interpretation of Interstate Commerce Act, not on NEPA. There are a couple of straws in the wind indicating that NEPA statements may be required in situations not heretofore contemplated by the service, such as timber sales. However, to date, these have involved sales in wilderness or potential wilderness areas. See *Minnesota Public Interest Research Group* v. *Butz,* No. 4-72-Civil-598 (D. Minn., Sept. 18, 1974), and *Minnesota Public Interest Research Group* v. *Butz,* 498 F.2d 1314 (8th Cir. 1974), concerning certain timber sales in portal zone of Boundary Waters Canoe Area.

61. Since the new planning procedure seems designed to comply with at least most of the requisites laid down by NEPA for "major Federal action significantly affecting the quality of the human environment," it appears that each land use plan will, in effect, be the equivalent of an environmental impact statement.

62. On land use planning, see Forest Service Manual, Title 8200 and 8300. I have also relied in part upon an earlier description contained in U.S. Department of Agriculture/Forest Service, *System for Managing the National Forests in the East* (1970), a pamphlet prepared by the two eastern regions, and on discussions with service officials both in Washington and in several regions.

63. The Forest Service's current cost–benefit program—called Invest III—is designed for use at all levels, for calculating benefit–cost ratios, using four different discount rates, and for calculating an alternative internal rate of return.

64. For an introductory treatment, see Robert Dorfman, "Mathematical or 'Linear' Programming: A Nonmathematical Exposition," *American Economic Review,* vol. 43 (1953), p. 797.

65. For a full description, see Daniel I. Navon, *Timber RAM,* U.S. Department of Agriculture/Forest Service Research Paper PSW-70 (1971); LeRoy C. Hennes, Michael J. Irving, and Daniel I. Navon, *Forest Control and Regulation,* U.S. Department of Agriculture/Forest Service Research Paper PSW-231 (1971).

66. I have here relied primarily on U.S. Department of Agriculture/Forest Service, *Organization and Management Systems in the Forest Service,* FS-35 (rev. 1970), pp. 20–23; and on discussions with Forest Service officials.

67. 88 Stat. 476 (1974).

68. See 5 U.S.C., § 553. This exemption has been criticized and proposals have been made to change it. See "Recommendation 16," in *Recommendations and Reports of the Administrative Conference of the United States* (1970), p. 305; and Arthur Bonfield, "Public Participation in Federal Rulemaking Relating to Public Property, Loans, Grants, Benefits, or Contracts," *University of Pennsylvania Law Review,* vol. 118 (1970), p. 540. It is not clear whether these proposals would subject *all* land use plans to the rulemaking requirements, but presumably major national forest plans would be so subject. In light of the Forest Service's new procedures, coupled with the mandated procedures of NEPA, I doubt it would much

matter to the Forest Service if it were amended to make *major* land use plans subject to the Administrative Procedure Act (APA).

69. 36 C.F.R., § 211.20-211.119. Appeals are divided into three classes. Class-one appeals are from initial decisions which raise issues relating to a "breach" of the terms of written instruments—leases, contracts, etc.—to which the appellant is a party. Class-two appeals are from decisions not involving a breach but having, "an effect on the enjoyment of use under a written instrument" to which the appellant is a party. For example, an order to a grazing permittee to remove his livestock before the normal end of the grazing season would be a Class-two appeal. Class three covers all appeals other than those in Classes one and two. Class three requires no relationship between the appellant and the agency and thus provides a procedure for airing general grievances by the public—for example, a Sierra Club challenge to a timber sale or management plan. The class designation governs two things; first, the avenue of appeal and, second, the character of the hearing. The process is essentially as follows:

A person may appeal an adverse decision of a supervisor to the regional forester who reviews appellant's complaint and a responsive statement by the supervisor. Before ruling, however, the forester classifies the appeal for purposes of further possible appeal.

The forester's classification, and his decision on the merits, may be further appealed to the Board of Forest Appeals. The board is comprised of five members designated by the secretary of agriculture. Three are regular employees of the department but from agencies other than the Forest Service (one must be from the General Counsel's office). The other two are persons not employed by the government for at least the prior two years.

Before the board appellants in Classes one and two are entitled to oral hearings. In Class-one appeals a board decision on the merits is final (a decision on classification may be further appealed to the secretary of agriculture). In Class two the board merely submits recommendations to the chief forester for his decision. In Class three the board transmits the appeal directly to the chief without recommendations or comment. In Class-two and -three appeals the chief's decision may be further appealed to the secretary.

It should be noted that, at whatever point the appeal process ends, the decision becomes a "final" decision of the agency and subject to judicial review in a federal district court (an action for injunction or declaratory judgment). Prior to that time, however, a suit is subject to dismissal for failure to exhaust administrative remedies.

70. There are three main legal aspects of public awareness and involvement: (1) public notice of agency decisions and disclosures of agency information; (2) participation in agency proceedings by "interested" (but not distinctively affected) members of the public; and (3) private standing to seek judicial review of agency decisions. Each of these is treated at some length in Glen O. Robinson and Ernest Gellhorn, *The Administrative Process* (St. Paul: West, 1973), chs. 3, 4, and 12; and Kenneth C. Davis, *Administrative Law Treatise* (St. Paul: West, 1958 and 1970 Suppl.), chs. 3, 6, 8, and 22.

71. NEPA does not itself specifically prescribe solicitation of public comment; it does provide that environmental impact statements should be available to the public in accordance with Section 3 of the APA, 5 U.S.C., § 552. The APA provides for publication in the federal register of, among other things, "statements of general policy or interpretations of general applicability," and it provides that statements of policy not so published shall be available for public inspection. Section 3 of the APA does not provide for public comment. However, Executive Order No. 11514, 35 Fed. Reg. 4247 (1970), directs agencies to develop procedures to "obtain the views of interested parties" which procedures are to include "whenever appropriate, provision for public hearings." CEQ Guidelines also call for public comment. See 38 Fed. Reg. 20550, 20555 (1973); (40 C.F.R., § 1500.9). On the basis of these directives several cases have mandated hearings, although they have recognized that some lesser form of public involvement may generally suffice. See, for example, *Hanley v. Kleindienst*, 471 F. 2d 823, 835 (2d Cir. 1972), *cert. denied*, 93 S. Ct. 313 (1973); *Calvert Cliffs' Coord. Comm. v. AEC*, 449 F. 2d 1109 (D.C. Cir. 1971), *cert. denied*, 404 U.S. 942 (1972). It would appear that public notice and opportunity to file written comments will generally suffice, unless a threshold showing is made that a full hearing is required. See Roger Cramton and Richard Berg, "On Leading a Horse to Water: NEPA and the Federal Bureaucracy," *Michigan Law Review*, vol. 511 (1971), p. 526.

III

RESOURCES AND USES— A PREFATORY NOTE

Traditional classification identifies several major natural resources (or uses) of the public lands: timber, outdoor recreation, wilderness, minerals, forage, water, and wildlife. This order is not necessarily an accurate reflection of relative social importance of these resources. In the absence of some clear criterion for measuring social value, any such ranking would be enormously difficult. Even an economic gauge is difficult (though not impossible), for the normal vehicle for measuring economic value is the market; and for many of the resources on public lands, we have either no market or at least a very limited market. Water and recreation are excellent examples. Both have enormous economic value, but for the former, we have virtually no market for evaluating federal management activity, and for the latter, only a very limited market. One consequence of this is that we have no clear, objective criteria for land-mangement planning or for allocation of scarce resources among the various uses.

The problem of allocation is a crucial one and becoming more so. Increased demand for resources has led to increased intensification of land management to meet those demands. With intensified management, conflict among uses grows and so, correspondingly, does the need for choice among uses. Environmentalists may argue in some cases that a particular allocation they favor does not involve any *significant* sacrifice of other uses (see page 176). That may be true in some very few instances, but they are hardly worth our notice, for if there truly are no competing uses to be sacrificed, there is really no conflict—and no problem. Unfortunately, even casual observation demonstrates that the range of situations in which this holds is exceedingly small and becoming smaller all the time.

I would expect this simple point would provoke little dissent among reasoning minds. How the problem is to be resolved—even how it should be approached—is another matter. If there is a philosopher's stone by which the different conflicting interests can be brought into a golden harmony, it has not been found. Some, steeped in classic economics, have thought it lay in the marketplace. Others have rejected the alchemy of the marketplace and have put their faith in governmental decision making.

The suggested antithesis between these approaches can be overdrawn. In public resource allocation today no market operates unregulated by legislative, administrative, and judicial power. Few think that it should. On the other hand, there is virtually no aspect of public resource management in which administrative or legislative decisions are not in some measure influenced by private market choices. Again, there are few who would argue that *all* such influence should be purged. Those who emphasize the principle of market choice may be content, for example, with administrative planning, provided the administrator uses economic criteria (not necessarily purely private market criteria). On the other hand, the administrator, as administrator, is predisposed to rely on his own professional judgment independent of market criteria, just as the legislator is predisposed to rely on his political instinct. As labels for this taxonomy of perspectives we might choose the terms *economic, bureaucratic,* and *political.* Use of these labels is, of course, oversimplification, but they are still useful shorthand for differentiating the various approaches to land use management. In the main, the bureaucratic and political perspectives have tended to dominate national forest land use policy and public discourse about that policy. While economic considerations have certainly had an influence, these have tended to be subordinate to political and bureaucratic attitudes.

Examples of each of the three approaches will be seen in the chapters which follow. However, one particular aspect, characteristic of the bureaucratic approach to land use management, does call for brief notice here. This is the scheme of land use classification which is the foundation of forest land management, as well as the central issue in public debate about management policies.

By established convention federal lands are classified into three categories, forming a continuum of: (1) single use, (2) dominant use, and (3) multiple use.[1] It is almost trite to note there are virtually no tracts of land of significant size that have only a single use, since all lands on which rain falls can be regarded as having at least a passive watershed use in addition to some other use for which the land is generally managed actively. Too, most large tracts of rural lands produce wildlife and—to the extent either hunting or fishing is permitted—that use in turn produces recreation. Although there are few lands with *no* multiple use or resources, one could say there are some that are only actively *managed* for a single use—military reservations, for example, or other lands specially reserved for a restricted purpose. However, it seems reasonable to ignore these uses as not really involving *any* active land management: land is held, and it is used in support of activities not related to what we commonly regard as the "natural resources" of the land.

Lands which have, and are managed for, a dominant use are more easily found. National parks, including related areas such as national recreational areas, wildlife refuges, and primitive and wilderness areas (some of which are found within the former two areas, but most of which are carved out of multiple-use lands) are examples of this. The dominant-use concept implies several uses, all of which may (and generally do) receive some active management attention, but with one use (or in the case of wilderness, one might say "nonuse") predominating in terms of management policy.

Lands *formally* subject to multiple-use management comprise the largest acreage in public landholdings. The Multiple-Use and Sustained Yield Act of 1960 prescribes multiple use as the general management policy for national forests. However, setting apart formal classification and broad policy directives, the distinction between multiple and dominant use is, in practical fact, difficult to define—a difficulty which has aided and abetted a considerable controversy about public land management and contributed no small confusion to the ongoing debate over land use policies.

Section 4 of the Multiple-Use and Sustained Yield Act defines use as follows:

"Multiple use" means: The management of all the various renewable surface resources of the national forests so that they are utilized in the combination that will best meet the needs of the American people; making the most judicious use of the land for some or all of these resources or related services over areas large enough to provide sufficient latitude for periodic adjustments in use to conform to changing needs and conditions; that some land will be used for less than all the resources; and harmonious and coordinated management of the various resources, each with the other, without impairment of the productivity of the land, with consideration being given to the relative values of the various resources, and not necessarily the combination of uses that will give the greatest dollar return or the greatest unit output.[2]

As with any definition, the important question is whether it is meaningful and useful for the purposes offered. Does the above description clearly distinguish between dominant and multiple use? More to the real point, does it really provide a useful directive for land-management policy or a basis for judging the performance of land managers? One recent commentary answered this bluntly, calling the statutory definition of multiple use a "vacuous collection of platitudes," one which in practice gives the agencies "nearly unlimited discretion in the allocation of land to particular uses."[3] Herein lies the basis of an involved and somewhat tedious dispute between the Forest Service and its critics. I add to the tedium of debate only a few elementary points by way of introduction to the treatment of the particular land use functions which follows.

Concerning unlimited agency discretion under the Multiple-Use Act, it must be emphasized that the act is not the sole, nor the primary, source of statutory authority or responsibility for the Forest Service. Indeed, the act did not actually alter in any material way the agency's specific authority or its responsibilities under prior statutes, such as the Organic Act of 1897. Nor has it preempted later statutes—such as the Land and Water Conservation Fund Act, the Endangered Species Act, the National Environmental Policy Act, or the Wilderness Act—which have conferred further specific authority and responsibilities. To single out the Multiple-Use Act for giving unlimited delegation of discretion thus seems a little pointless—rather like saying the Preamble to the Constitution is unduly vague for not specifying how the government will "promote the general welfare."

Of course, it can still be questioned whether statutes other than the Multiple-Use Act put sufficient constraints on agency discretion. As to this, conclusions are premature until we have inspected the Forest Service's particular resource functions more closely. However, apropos of the assertion that Forest Service discretion is "nearly unlimited," one point should be made: a casual glance at the statutes noted above should suffice to show that this supposed discretion is exaggerated, but if it does not, a reading of recent court decisions enjoining Forest Service action does.[4]

The question of discretion aside, other points about the multiple-use concept warrant mention. The first is the rather obvious fact that multiple use as a guideline for policy has meaningful application only when applied to large tracts of land, as the 1960 act explicitly states. For multiple use to be meaningful, it must be practicable. To attempt to manage each 40-acre plot of land by giving full consideration to every possible use of that land, would not achieve an effective multiple-use policy. In practical effect the multiple-use constraints imposed by the more sensitive uses, such as recreation, would foreclose the more intensive uses, such as timber. The second point, equally obvious but worth mentioning, is that as a guideline for management policy—as opposed to mere description of land uses—designation of the land for either multiple or dominant use is meaningful only where there are conflicts among uses. If within the parameters of the management decision to be made there are no important conflicts among uses (between, say, timber and recreation), then there is no important choice to be made and no particular point to a classification of multiple or dominant use. On the other hand, given a particular conflict (between, say, timber and recreation), neither the multiple-use nor the dominant-use rubric furnishes a useful policy prescription for resolving that conflict. To the extent of conflict in that particular instance, multiple use is not possible; whichever use is favored becomes, to that extent, dominant.

It follows then that the most one can claim for the terms *multiple use* and *dominant use* is that they denote, in very broad and amorphous terms, land use philosophies applicable to large areas of land. Multiple use has come to mean an emphasis on balanced use: all uses will be attentively considered and an effort made to reach some kind of optimal output of all major uses.[5] Dominant use has come to mean emphasis on maximizing, over a wide area, a designated use, subject perhaps to minimal constraints imposed by certain other resources: for example, maximizing timber output subject to such constraints that watershed or wildlife values are not needlessly destroyed.

Unfortunately, given the generality with which these terms can be used, they have become mere battle slogans in controversies over land management. Among many conservationists and their supporters, dominant use has become an emotionally loaded epithet associated with commercial "exploitation" by timber interests and others, while multiple use is commonly employed to denote a "true" conservationist ethic.[6] These are certainly not necessary connotations. Dominant use, for example, does *not* necessarily imply greater commercial use, as should be evident from the fact that wilderness areas, wildlife refuges, and national parks are all instances of dominant use. However, the pejorative connotation has stuck, partly because it is the commercial interests—the timber and livestock industries particularly—that have been the primary advocates of dominant use, as a means of obtaining greater commercial use of the lands. That the Public Land Law Review Commission advocated a dominant-use concept[7] has not allayed fears that the only uses which would, in fact, be dominant are timber and livestock (and perhaps mining), inasmuch as the commission membership was weighted in this direction.

In the final analysis, framing the problems of resource allocation and use in terms of a conflict between dominant versus multiple use has served mostly to obscure the complex economic and social issues involved in the different functional areas of land use management. Thus, the kind of economic and social "tradeoffs" (to use the economists' jargon) between, say, wilderness and timber values is only hidden by resort to such labels. The problem of deciding whether to invest in wildlife conservation for a particular area is not aided by considering whether an area is designated for multiple or dominant use.

With these general comments in mind, in the following chapters we will take a more detailed look at each of the major resource functions of the Forest Service, and the particular processes of policy formation and major policy issues with respect to each of these resources.

NOTES

1. See generally, Marion Clawson and Burnell R. Held, *The Federal Lands: Their Use and Management* (Baltimore: Johns Hopkins University Press for Resources for the Future, 1957), ch. 2; and Kenneth P. Davis et al., *Federal Public Land Laws and Policies Relating to Multiple-Use of Public Lands,* Study for the Public Land Law Review Commission (rev. ed., Springfield, Ill.: Clearinghouse for Federal Scientific and Technical Information, 1970).

2. 47 Stat. 215 (1960), 16 U.S.C., §§ 528-31.

3. Note, "Managing Federal Lands: Replacing the Multiple Use System," *Yale Law Journal,* vol. 82 (1973), pp. 787 and 788.

4. See, for example, *Parker v. United States,* 448 F. 2d 793 (10th Cir. 1971), *cert. denied,* 405 U.S. 989 (1972), concerning a refusal to consider area for inclusion in wilderness system; and *Izaak Walton League v. Butz,* 367 F. Supp. 422 (N.D.W. Va. 1973); appeal pending, concerning clear-cutting.

5. Cf. Davis, *Federal Public Land Laws,* p. 9.

6. See, for example, Michael Frome, *The Forest Service* (New York: Praeger, 1971), pp. 167-175.

7. See Public Land Law Review Commission, *One-Third of the Nation's Lands* (1970).

IV

THE
TIMBER
RESOURCE

One-third of the land surface of the United States, 754 million acres, is forest land. Of that total, about 500 million acres are classified as commercial forest land, suitable and available for continually growing crops of timber (this does not include land, otherwise suitable, withdrawn for parks or wilderness areas in which harvest is precluded).[1]

The commercial forest land is divided, by ownership as follows[2]:

Owners	%	Millions of acres
National forests	18	91.9
Federal government owned		
Bureau of Land Management	1	4.8
Other federal landowners		
(e.g., Department of Defense)	2	10.4
State and local governments	6	29
Forest industry	14	67.3
Farm and miscellaneous ownership	59	296.2

As was noted earlier, the production of timber was not the earliest concern of national forest conservation; indeed, it was not until the 1920s that it became the most prominent economic function (prior to that time revenues from grazing permits returned the largest amount to the Treasury). However, since that time (and most notably since World War II), it has become increasingly important; today it is clearly the foremost activity of the Forest Service. One commonly cited illustration of its prominence is the amount of congressional appropriations.[3] Appropriations for forest land management (not including research and many other allied activities) totaled approximately $306.1 million in 1975. Of that, some $134 million went directly for timber-resource management. This was more than double the amount for the second-highest appropriation, outdoor recreation ($46.8 million), and more than six times that for range management ($17.4 million), third highest among resources. Looking to other allied functions, timber's share is even larger. For example, in forest research, nearly half of the appropriations in 1975 went for timber-management research.[4]

Admittedly, these figures are far from a precise measurement of the prominence of timber management in national forest administration. For one thing, at least some of the money appropriated to timber management also benefits other resources; there are many "spillover" benefits to other resources from proper timber management—for example, wildlife and recreation. Nevertheless, the above figures are reasonably indicative of the central position of timber management. It is an importance which, despite the growing demand for competitive forest uses (recreation, wilderness preservation), is unlikely to diminish in the near future, for timber is one of the most versatile of all natural resources. The hundreds of uses to which timber can be put are typically divided into four general categories: (1) lumber, (2) plywood and veneer, (3) pulp and paper products, and (4) miscellaneous uses, such as fuelwood, posts, etc.

In each of the first three categories the demand for timber products has increased dramatically in the post-World War II decades, increased to a point which many conservationists have come to regard with alarm, as it pushes for more extensive and more intensive forest timber management.

THE TIMBER-MANAGEMENT SCHEME

The Long-Term Outlook

As timber has traditionally been a dominant management concern for most forests, so the planning of timber-resource management and sales has been a major focus of national forest planning.[5] This process is the most well developed and regularized of all resource-management planning. To the outsider, it is also a bewildering and complex process, primarily because of the many highly technical components—for example, the techniques of inventory and allowable-cut determination, to name just two of the early steps in a long sequence of processes. The difficulty in understanding and describing the process is compounded by the fact that it is not uniform throughout all of the national forests. The divergences in planning among different regions—particularly between western and eastern regions—was mentioned earlier. These are not peculiar to timber management, although in some respects the differences may be more pronounced than in other areas of common resource management. Inasmuch as the western regions are the primary timber producers, they are the main models for this outline. Major differences between eastern and western regions will be noted, however.

As in other functional areas, long-term timber-management planning is primarily the responsibility of the forest supervisor and his staff, with the active participation of the district rangers. The regional forester must approve the basic management plan, and his staff will be called upon to provide expert assistance (e.g., the aid of soil scientists where they are not staffed at the supervisor level) or technical services (such as computer programming or statistical calculations). But the primary responsibility for planning is normally placed on the supervisor.

The Working Circle.   The geographic unit for timber-management planning has traditionally been the working circle, a somewhat arbitrarily defined area of the forest designed to be large enough to support local forest-based industries. It is within this area that the allowable cut is determined, consistent with sustained yield over the circle area. Traditionally, the working circle did not correspond to the administrative boundaries of either the national forest or the ranger district: a particular national forest would have several such circles, and each could be administered in turn by several districts. However, the desire for greater flexibility (and efficient management planning at the forest level) led over the past score years to a consolidation of working circles by expanding circle boundaries to coincide with the national forest boundaries (a development which has engendered criticism from some conservationists). Today most national forests (virtually all in the eastern and southern regions) have a single working circle, and the circle concept has ceased to have any importance. Since 1972 Forest Service regulations have provided that the national forest, not the working circle, is the planning unit for timber management.[6]

The Timber-Management Plan.   Long-term management planning is organized on a ten-year cycle governed by a timber-management plan, prepared by the forest supervisor's office with the aid of the district ranger. Every national forest has such a plan, and as would be expected, they differ in detail among forests although their basic features are similar. The objective of the plan is to provide comprehensive information on timber and other resources and to prescribe policy for the protection, management, and disposal of timber over the ten-year period. The plan includes a general history of management (i.e., of previous planning and harvesting in the forest), a description of the forest and its resources—with primary attention focused on the type, volume, and condition of timber. Following the information section, a broad statement of multiple-use management principles is de rigeur. As do all functional management plans, the timber plan incorporates multiple-use constraints and coordination requirements, as set forth in multiple-use plans and related directives. In some cases these constraints may impose special limitations or conditions for harvesting.[7] On most commercial forest lands managed for timber production, the constraints typically consist of generalized directives or cautions: for example, a directive to leave open natural meadows for livestock or wildlife use, to take precautions against erosion, to maintain aesthetic values, and so on.

The activity part of the management plan deals with particular management prescriptions over a ten-year period, which provide the basis for shorter-term timber-sale action plans and annual programs. Management prescriptions include an outline of silvicultural treatments (i.e., cutting, reforestation, and stand improvement), road construction, and protection (i.e., prevention and control of fire, insect, and disease damage). Of these management prescriptions, cutting is, of course, the central activity. Or perhaps we should say, cutting is the central *class* of activities, for there are different types of cutting which serve distinct objectives—for example, timber supply, regeneration, stand improvement, and multiple-use objectives other than timber management.

Traditionally, timber-management plans (indeed, virtually all functional plans) have been in-house affairs seldom seen by outsiders other than a handful of specially interested groups or individuals. Largely as a consequence of the National Environmental Protection Act (NEPA) this is now changing. Current practice is to prepare a NEPA impact statement for each new or revised timber plan. This relatively new practice will add a further dimension to timber-management planning. For one thing, such impact statements require an evaluation of alternatives and (in conformity to judicial interpretation) a cost–benefit analysis of planned actions. For another, they require public participation (again, an interpretation engrafted upon the act by executive and judicial interpretation) to the extent of inviting public comment.[8]

The Inventory. Basic to every management plan is the inventory and the allowable cut which is derived from it. The inventory—prepared by statistical derivations from field examinations of sample plots and stands and aerial photomaps—is made every ten years at the outset of each new management plan. The service is working in the direction of establishing a more or less continuous inventory in which the basic data on timber (type, volume, growth, condition) could be collected, maintained on computer tapes, and adjusted annually. Whether this will eliminate the need for some periodic reinventory is not known; if so, it would presumably also affect the entire planning cycle. For the near future, however, most forests will continue with the periodic inventory and planning process.

The Allowable Cut. The inventory of volume and growth rate provides the basis for determination of an allowable annual cut which is both an outer limit on cutting and a general target objective for planned harvest.[9] Recently the Forest Service has altered somewhat its traditional allowable-cut concept. Instead of a single calculation, Forest Service regulations now call for two—a potential yield calculation and an annual programmed harvest.[10]

Potential yield is the maximum potential annual harvest consistent with sustained yield, considering existing site conditions, current logging technology, multiple-use constraints, and current standard cultural treatments. The concept of *sustained yield* as a constraint on harvest levels requires explanation. In its strict literal sense the concept simply means a yield of forest products that can be sustained in perpetuity. In that sense sustained yield is not a significant constraint on annual harvest levels. The most that it signifies is that the forest be managed in such a way as to protect the soil conditions to the extent necessary to ensure renewal of the forest (more particularly, the timber resource). Assuming this condition were met, a harvest of all of the trees in the forest in a single year would not be inconsistent with sustained yield, if the forest were replanted. Ultimately—somewhere between thirty and one hundred years—the timber would grow back and would be harvested again. Admittedly, the yield would be sporadic, but it would be "perpetual." The example is extreme but nevertheless illustrates an important point often overlooked: sustained yield does not necessarily imply uniform annual yield; it does not necessarily imply an annual yield at all. The implication of a *uniform annual yield* has, however, been added to the sustained-yield requirement under the Forest Service's policy of "even-flow" management. Under this policy, allowable-cut levels are designed to secure, on a sustained basis, an annual yield that is more or less even from year to year. This does not mean that the yield is perfectly uniform. In fact, allowable-cut levels have substantially risen over the past score years. The policy prescribes merely that such increases are permitted only when the new harvest level can be sustained. In short, the even-flow policy is designed to avoid marked fluctuations in harvesting, at least over short periods of time.

The programmed harvest is that part of the potential yield scheduled for a specific year. In contrast to the potential yield, the program cut is based on current demand situations and funding. Where the program cut is less than potential yield, for example, because it is uneconomic to employ necessary techniques to increase harvest to the potential yield, the objective is to work toward bringing the program cut up to full potential yield.[11] Except where it is necessary to focus specifically on the differences between potential yield and program cut, we can continue to use the traditional term *allowable cut* to refer to both calculations.

The allowable cut is calculated for each forest. From the aggregation of forests a regional figure is derived, and by further aggregation a figure for the system as a whole is obtained. It should be emphasized, however, that only the calculation for the forest has direct operational significance. Within the forest the allowable cut is apportioned to districts. In allocating the cut to the blocks, consideration is given to commercial timber area, volume, and other factors such as road access and proximity to markets. While it is possible (though unusual) to allocate all of an allowable cut to one block (ranger district), the allowable cut cannot be reallocated between working circles (forests). Thus, there are now no tradeoffs between working circles to permit one to exceed its allowable cut to the extent another falls short of its cut.[12]

Various methods are used for calculating the allowable cut in different circumstances. In western forests, the allowable cut has generally been regulated by volume. A variety of formulas are used. A traditional and commonly used formula calculates allowable cut by the volume of mature (and overmature) timber, divided by the rotation age or cutting cycle for the species, plus the average annual growth.[13] A different formula is often used in cases where it is desired to adjust the growing stock of timber (e.g., to liquidate overmature timber),[14] and there are other variations as well.[15] The use of formulas for calculating allowable cut is now diminishing. New volume allowable-cut calculations are derived from tabular methods or computer models. Most regions are now in the process of recalculating allowable cuts, using computer program models (e.g., the Timber RAM model noted on page 43), by which various harvest programs can be prescribed for varying objectives (e.g., maximize harvest volume over X period of time), subject to specified constraints (e.g., sustained yield and even flow, with specified limits on variation in yield over X period of time).[16]

All of the volume-regulation methods are aimed at establishing a "regulated" cycle for commercial timberlands. In somewhat oversimplified terms this means a desirable level of inventory, comprised of even-aged stands, and a balanced distribution of age classes. In a well-regulated forest harvesting becomes essentially a function of the growth rate, with adjustments for changes in rotation age to reflect changes in growth rate or changes in standards of utilization.

Once established on a regulated cycle, volume allowable-cut calculations lose much of their significance as a means of controlling the harvest rate. Instead, harvesting is governed predominantly by area control. In its simplest form, area control would be practiced by subdividing the planning area (an area of even-aged stands and balanced distribution of age classes is assumed) into a number of units corresponding to the rotation age and by cutting one unit each year. Thus, if the rotation cycle were 100 years, $\frac{1}{100}$th of the total area would be cut each year.[17] An annual allowable cut can be calculated simply by multiplying the area to be cut each year by the volume of timber in the stands to be cut; however, volume allowable cut as a regulatory device ceases to have much effect because the harvest is regulated by area, not volume. Area regulation is being increasingly used on the national forests. In eastern and southern forests, most of which are in their second cycle (many in the South are in their third), area control is predominant now; in western forests it will take some time before a regulated cycle has been established which permits area control, although it has been introduced in a few forests.[18]

An important variable in allowable-cut calculations is the *rotation age*. By determining the harvest rate or cycle, the rotation age essentially determines the character of the forest. The rotation age varies greatly, depending on type of species, growth conditions (soil and climate), the commercial use for which the timber is needed, and other circumstances (e.g., multiple-use considerations). Presently the Forest Service recognizes two major standard rotations, one for sawtimber and the other for cordwood.[19] The former is defined very generally in terms of the number of years required for a tree of average basal area on an average site to reach a diameter of the size "desired for new crops." No uniform size is specified, although the new regulations note that 17–20 in. "will be suitable for many species and types." Within this general directive each region prescribes its own size limits. For commercial areas not capable of producing timber crops of sawtimber size and quality (within 120 years), a cordwood rotation is prescribed. This is defined as the "number of years to culmination of mean annual cubic foot increment." At this point the physical volume of timber *yield* in a given area is maximized.

To be distinguished from rotation age is the conversion period of liquidating overmature timber and establishing a uniform age among species in a particular stand. Under present Forest Service practice the two appear generally to be set at the same age: that is, the overage timber is to be liquidated over the period of one rotation (in some cases longer conversion periods are being set in order to avoid a decline of timber at the end of the conversion period). However, there is no necessary correlation between the two. Old-growth timber could be liquidated in a fraction of the rotation period—say, twenty years as opposed to a hundred years.

Sale Planning. The timber-management plan prescribes the general policy and long-term objectives for timber sales and management; these are translated into shorter-term plans and programs for each district by a *sales action plan*. This is the district ranger's plan for implementing the management prescriptions of the forest timber-management plan. Essentially, it is a schedule of planned sales, road construction, and silvicultural treatment (principally the kind of cut needed) for the district over a relatively short-term period—normally an ongoing five-year period.

The silvicultural treatment prescribed will vary greatly with environmental conditions.[20] Silvicultural prescriptions are guided by a number of objectives. Providing an adequate sustained supply of timber is, of course, one objective—and in terms of long-range general objectives it may be dominant—at least in forests with major commercial timberland. As mentioned earlier, this economic objective is subject to multiple-use constraints which are of variable practical importance, depending on whether the competing use precludes cutting (as in wilderness or areas where recreation is a dominant use) or merely limits it.[21] Quite apart from the multiple-use aspect, however, the supply objective itself does not dictate any single prescription. To produce a high and sustained timber yield, even without any consideration for other uses, a mix of silvicultural practices is required. Most of these consist of various types of cutting and removal. Other techniques are also used; controlled burning, for example, but the dominant treatment is cutting, and this in turn is accomplished through timber sales of some kind. However, while virtually all cutting is accomplished through timber sales, commercial timber supply is not always the paramount short-term objective. A sale may be designed primarily as a vehicle for removal of a stand of trees burned, windblown, or affected with disease. That the salvage timber has commercial value makes possible the use of commercial sales for removal of the stand to facilitate its regeneration, but that value may or may not be a significant incentive for planning the sale. The need to remove the timber to facilitate regeneration may dictate a sale in which the sale costs equal or exceed the revenues; the sale proceeds not only offset part of the necessary costs of removal or burning, but they also typically provide special, additional funds for reforestation which would not be available out of appropriated funds. Quite apart from the multiple-use aspect, however, even the objective of timber supply itself does not lead to any single or uniform prescription for meeting that objective. In economic terms alone wise policy requires management of the forest to produce a high sustained yield, and this in turn dictates conservation and management practices which only incidentally serve an *immediate* supply function. In a broad sense one can think of most timber harvests as serving the dual purposes of selling inventory and producing future supply. In short, successful planning requires a balancing of short- and long-term objectives.

Harvest practices are classified by the service into two broad categories: *regeneration cutting*, which includes all cuts for which immediate regeneration (artificial or natural) is planned, and *intermediate cutting*, which is any cut prior to a regeneration cut, principally including salvage and various types of stand-improvement work. The former category is broken down into four types of cut: selective cut, seed tree, shelterwood, and clear-cut. *Selective cutting* involves removal of individual trees at repeated intervals—yielding an all-aged stand. *Seed tree cutting* calls for successive cuts, with the first cut leaving enough trees to provide seed for the cut area and the second removing the seed trees after regeneration has been established. *Shelterwood cutting* is essentially similar to seed tree cutting except that it leaves sufficient trees to provide shade for a part of the area as well as a future seed source. *Clear-cutting* calls for a one-cut removal of all trees in a defined patch, strip, or block of varying size. The cut area is either prepared for natural regeneration, artificial seeding, or planting. The result is an even-aged stand.

The choice of regeneration cut (along with such intermediate cuts as may be prescribed) in a particular sale area is made within a relatively limited range set by silvicultural and economic considerations and, more recently, by administrative directives. For regeneration cuts, the choice is nearly always confined to some form of the even-aged method. Selective cutting, once quite common, is infrequently used except where aesthetic or other multiple-use demands require a very limited partial cut and an all-aged stand. Since World War II clear-cutting has been increasingly favored for economic and silvicultural reasons, since it is the most efficient and least expensive form of logging per volume unit harvested and it facilitates the regeneration of commercially valuable species. In the face of growing public criticism of the practice, and acknowledged adverse environmental consequences in a number of instances, the service is now retrenching on clear-cutting in many areas (mainly in favor of shelterwood).

The economic design of individual sales varies greatly in volume, dollar amount, and duration.[22] The volume size of a sale and its term are functions of several variables. First, silvicultural factors may play a role insofar as a certain treatment (e.g., insect control) dictates a particular area to be cut; however, these factors work mainly through their influence on the program cut. Second, the unit's program cut will influence the size and term of sale. Other things being equal, larger cuts will dictate larger-volume sales, and this will dictate a longer term. Third, road construction and other costs are major influences; the volume must be large enough to make logging practicable and to cover all assorted sale costs. Particularly in areas where access is limited, a large-volume, long-term sale may be required to support construction of roads. Fourth, local industry structure and conditions influence sale size and term. Generally this tends to keep sales relatively small, numerous, and short term in order to enable all local mills to participate effectively.[23] On the other hand, where new or increased industry investment is desired, a larger, longer-period sale is called for. Contrary to those who contend the service makes sales of such size that small mills are excluded, the agency has generally favored small or medium-sized, short-term sales that are within the capability of the very smallest mills. For example, a typical sale would be under 5 million bd.-ft. over a period of five years or less. Relatively small sales are favored, not simply to facilitate full participation, however. Such sales also involve fewer risks to the purchaser (chiefly, those of rising costs or changes in market price affecting the operability of the timber) and correspondingly less chance that the Forest Service will be required to declare the contract to be forfeit for nonperformance.[24] This does not, of course, preclude large-volume, longer-term sales—over 15 million bd.-ft. and more than five years in duration.[25] Indeed, in order to induce development of a local timber industry in Alaska, contracts have been made for as much as 8 billion bd.-ft., to be cut over a fifty-year period.[26] But this is a rare situation, not even remotely approached by sales outside of Alaska.[27]

Presale Preparation. The sale action plan for the district contains an annual schedule of proposed timber sales based on the allocation of allowable cut among the districts and silvicultural or other management prescriptions. Consistent with general budget planning, the planned sales for the year will become part of the work program. If final appropriations allow, the sale may then be advertised. Before advertising, however, two major steps must be completed: first, a *multiple-use survey* is made (for most, but not all sales) and a report prepared. Second, the sale area's boundaries are defined and marked, the timber is "cruised" (i.e., surveyed for volume and quality) and appraised as to market value. This information is the basis for a *timber report and appraisal.*

The multiple-use survey report (or *environmental analysis report* as it is now officially styled) is designed to implement the district multiple-use plan in the planning of the sale. As mentioned earlier, the multiple-use survey is not unique to timber sales but is part of a general planning requirement applicable to all management programs. However, because timber harvesting is the dominant activity in terms of routine planning and requires multiple-use coordination, the multiple-use survey is most prominently seen in the context of timber-sale planning. The survey and resulting report is the responsibility of the district ranger, although the assistance of specialists from the supervisor's staff is generally required. The detail of the multiple-use survey will vary, depending on the size and the circumstance of the sale and on the staff available to the ranger. The multiple-use survey itself will frequently involve some special investigation of the proposed sale area by specialists: biologists will review the impact on fish and wildlife, soil scientists will evaluate the impact on soils, landscape architects will determine the aesthetic impact, and so on. However, much of the pertinent information is known and can be evaluated without special on-site investigation by experienced district foresters familiar with the area from having participated in the initial sale design. Indeed, in a well-designed sale most of the multiple-use aspects will already have been considered. They are an integral part of the management prescription for the stand and should be accounted for in the initial design of the sale. Thus, the multiple-use survey report serves largely as a formal review and record of what has been (and what has not been) considered.

Within the basic multiple-use constraints, the particular sale boundaries are defined and marked,[28] cutting techniques specified (type of cut—clearcut, shelterwood, or other), and logging and grading methods and other management measures, such as slash disposal and regeneration, are outlined. These are detailed in the *timber sale report,* normally prepared prior to advertising for bids. Much of the information and the prescriptions set forth will have been completed in preparing the initial sale action plan. The sale report also contains a calculation of the timber volume and quality on the basis of which an appraisal of the value of the stumpage is made. The calculation is based on a cruise of the stand, involving a systematic examination of trees in sample plots. Total volume is then determined by statistical analysis (with the aid of computers). The volume estimates provide the basic foundation for calculating the appraised value of the timber.

Under the Organic Act of 1897, timber may not be sold for less than the appraised value. The appraisal process attempts to construct a market value for the stumpage (uncut timber) by working backward from the selling prices of the final timber products. From this final value is subtracted all estimated operating costs for an operator of average efficiency—including the costs of road construction, cutting and removal of timber, milling and manufacturing—and a margin for "profit and risk," one which is "adequate to maintain stable operations and a stable market for timber." The "residual" value remaining is the stumpage value.[29]

Administration of Sales, Harvest, and Reforestation

The Sale. Once the timber sale report and appraisal are made, the sale is advertised for bids. A thirty-day, formal public advertisement must be given for all sales except those under $2,000 in appraised value (for which it is discretionary). The notice includes, among other things, the location and volume of timber, the appraised value, and the time and place when initial bids will be opened and subsequent oral bids, if any, will be received. More detailed information is contained in a sales prospectus which, together with the formal advertisement, is mailed to prospective bidders on the service's mailing list (those who have previously expressed interest in sales).

Bidding is generally closed only to those who have been formally disbarred for prior misconduct (e.g., collusion in bidding or breach of contract) or those unable to show financial ability adequate to sustain the logging, manufacturing, and marketing of the timber products.[30] Exception to open bidding is made in the case of "small-business set-aside sales," in which only businesses with 500 or fewer employees are permitted to bid. (However, within the confines of the set-aside the award is normally made to the highest bidder.) One other exception to general open bidding is the sustained-yield unit established under the Cooperative and Sustained-Yield Act of 1944.[31] There are two types of sustained-yield units: federal and cooperative. The former are established entirely on national forest lands where it was thought necessary to exclude outside competition in order to protect the local economy and community. A cooperative unit is a management unit consisting of private land and intermingled, adjacent (or functionally interrelated) national forest land placed under unified management, the timber from which is sold to the private landowner. There is only one cooperative unit[32] and but five federal units.[33] The creation of new sustained-yield units was suspended in 1957, and none have been since created. They were always a dubious measure, never enthusiastically accepted by the Forest Service.

For advertised sales, the service employs two methods of bidding: sealed bid and oral auction following sealed bids. In the former, the sale is based on sealed bids only; in the latter, the sealed bids are followed by an oral auction among bidders who meet the appraised value.[34] Choice of the particular method depends on local sale conditions. For eastern and southern forests, sealed bids are predominantly used. However, in the West, the service has favored oral auction because it enables local mills dependent on public timberlands to meet outside competition.[35]

Although the contract is normally awarded to the high bidder, the high bidder must offer proof of his financial ability.[36] The high bid may also be rejected on the strength of poor past performance (or breach of contract) by the bidder, or it may be rejected for economic reasons. For example, the emergency need of a local bidder might warrant an award of all or some part of the sale volume to him. A low bidder also might be favored over a high bidder in order to prevent monopoly or to avoid local unemployment.[37] However, emergency awards have been rare, and, I am told, none have been made in recent years.

Virtually all commercial timber is priced by volume, with the appraised value and bid expressed in terms of dollars per 1,000 bd.-ft. of sawtimber or in cords or 100 ft.^{3} of pulpwood.[38] There are two bases for measuring volume for purposes of determining total payment—tree measurement and log scale. In the case of tree-measurement sales, the purchaser pays a lump sum based on a calculation of utilizable timber made by the Forest Service's presale cruise of the standing timber.[39] In log-scale sales, the calculation is made after cutting by scaling the logs.[40] Scaling is done at stations near the forest or at the purchaser's mill. Most often, scaling is done by the Forest Service, though in parts of the Pacific Northwest an independent scaling bureau is used.

Both types of sales are employed by the service; in the eastern and southern forests tree-measurement sales have become dominant, while in the western forests log scale is the most prominent.[41] This reflects the different character of the forests. In the eastern forests the second growth (and some third growth) is much more uniform in volume and quality and can be more reliably calculated by tree measurement. However, in the old-growth stands of western forests, timber volume and quality is subject to wide variation and is difficult to determine by tree measurement. The amount of defective, "cull" timber can be reliably determined only after the tree is cut and the individual logs scaled. Reliance on tree measurement in such cases adds a significant risk for the operator in that the actual volume of utilizable timber might be less than that estimated and paid for. The risk is not necessarily unilateral, for the service runs the risk that conservative tree measurement will underestimate the volume and quality of the timber. It appears to be a fact, however, that the major risk tends to run against the purchaser. This is, I believe, one reason the industry supports log scale and has strongly resisted proposals to convert to tree measurement.[42] The main impetus for such a change has come from the criticism that log scale encourages waste and inadequate cleanup of the forest after cutting.[43] The assumption is that, since the purchaser pays only for what he removes from the forest (to the scaling station), there is an incentive to leave logs of poor quality in the forest. But where payment is made in a lump sum on the basis of tree measurements, the incentive for removal is greater, since the operator will remove any log with a value exceeding the marginal cost of removal.[44] Without attempting to examine this controversy in detail, several points should be noted here to clarify the practice. Under log-scale sales the purchaser is obligated by contract to pay for all utilizable timber. There has been some uncertainty as to whether this also requires its *removal*.[45] Of course, it might be thought that, if the contractor had to pay for it, he would remove it, at least where the value exceeded removal cost. However, contractors in log-scale sales could avoid payment for felled but unremoved timber if service enforcement were lax because the material would never be presented for scaling. In recent years the service has taken steps to obtain greater removal by requiring removal of utilizable material (or in some cases, payment to cover the cost of removal).[46] The service has also altered its contracts to provide economic incentives to remove low-grade logs: the purchaser pays the bid price for every log meeting the volume and grade standards for a minimum merchantable product, not for every log removed; for logs below this standard a charge is made, but it is a much smaller amount.[47] When these facts are taken into account it is not clear that the incentives to remove poor-quality logs are too much different under the two types of sales. What *can* be said is that log-scale sales cost more to administer than do tree-measurement sales, not only because of the cost of scaling,[48] but because of the cost of surveillance to ensure that all timber is taken to the scaling point.[49]

Contracts extending over a period of several years present significant risk to the purchaser in that a subsequent, *unforeseen* decline in timber-product prices could impair the profitability of his purchase. (Correspondingly, we could say that the Forest Service bears the opposite risk.) Obviously, this risk is not unique to timber sales, although the duration of many of the contracts (and also the uncertainties arising from the fact that the demand for timber is derived from the demand for other products) may make it somewhat more troublesome. In any event, as is typical with long-term sales contracts generally, timber-sale contracts frequently include provision either for subsequent redetermination of the rates, or for an adjustment in the rates by a prescribed amount, or both. Departmental regulation requires a rate-redetermination provision in all contracts for periods longer than seven years (a special provision for long-term Alaskan sales permits a period of ten years before redetermination); for lesser periods, this is optional with the contracting officer. In substance, the rate-redetermination provision permits the Forest Service periodically (at intervals of not less than twelve months) to redetermine the rate by adjusting the initial appraisal data in accordance with current market data (e.g., as reflected in the current marketing of timber from the sale area).[50] Stumpage rate-adjustment clauses may be included in contracts where a selling price index has been established that reasonably indicates changes in market prices. In substance, stumpage rate adjustment makes allowance for rises in market prices by raising the rate by 50 percent of the price rise, but for decline in market price by lowering the rate to the index (subject to a base rate below which it will not be adjusted under usual sales). In effect, the government shares half of a price rise but bears all of a price decline.[51]

The Harvest. In implementing the prior plans governing the sale, the sale contract, of course, specifies the roads to be constructed, the area to be cut, and the type of cut as prescribed in the sale plan. The sale contract goes well beyond these general specifications,[52] however, in prescribing the details of road design and construction, logging methods,[53] and provision for removal of residues. The performance of these requirements by the operator is subject to inspection and general supervision by the service. Noncompliance is the basis for a fine, or for egregious malperformance, a declaration by the service of a breach of contract and suspension of operations. Occasionally such sanctions are required, but from all evidence not often enough to ensure reliably adequate performance. Some of the fault, of course, lies with the plans and design of the sale, the type of cut or the road design, and not with the execution by the operator. But even the best, most carefully designed road, harvest plan, or logging method cannot prevent careless execution by an operator. Since his short-term incentive induces him to cut the costs imposed by management constraints, a systematic supervision and rigorous enforcement of contract specifications is required—and it has not been always forthcoming, as we will see.

Cleanup and Reforestation. After a particular area has been cut, the unutilized residue or *slash* must be removed (or burned) and the site prepared for regeneration. As noted earlier, current contracts call for removal of all utilizable timber; nonutilizable residue is provided for either by requiring removal by the contractor or a payment in lieu of removal.

Of course, for some types of timber disposal, the cut is an integral part of the process of regrowth. Selected cuts for thinning or removal of overstory, for example, may be made as much for purposes of facilitating regeneration as for commercial sale. In other words, the cut is itself a part of the process of regrowth. In a broad sense this can be said of all timber harvest, particularly inasmuch as old, diseased, or windblown stands are the first singled out for sale. Unaided nature eventually removes old timber through fire, disease, and decay. Man does it faster (and generally with less grace) by cutting and removing the timber before it is destroyed by these natural methods. Therefore, it is perhaps somewhat arbitrary to single out any particular stage of timber management and call it regeneration or reforestation: in a well-managed forest it is part of continuous treatment. However, having made that obvious point, we can pass it by for the purpose of describing artificial regeneration of cutover forests.

The plan for reforestation or stand-improvement work is determined for each sale area as part of the presale planning and total stand prescription. The cost of this work is recognized as part of the cost of the sale which normally will be covered by timber sale receipts. Under the Knutson–Vandenberg Act of 1930,[54] the service may require the purchaser to make cash deposits, in addition to the payments for the timber, to cover the cost of planting, seeding, or removal of undesirable competitive growth, in order to improve the future timber stand on the cutover land. This money is earmarked for stand improvement and reforestation work.[55]

Provision for "KV funds," as they are commonly called (after the Knutson–Vandenberg Act), is discretionary with the officer planning the sale; however, for most sales where significant reforestation work is desired, a KV deposit will be required. KV funds are limited to sale areas from which they are collected[56]; they cannot be used for timber stand improvement or reforestation of burned or blowndown areas, or for other areas in need of reforestation or improvement. Reforestation of nonsale areas must be paid for with general appropriations, which have been anything but generous in this regard, leading to a backlog of nearly 5 million acres in need of reforestation.[57] This backlog of reforestation work does not, it should be noted, include recent sale areas. Though a sale area might go for several years before it is seeded or planted, this is not included in the above figure which consists of burned or blowndown areas, cutover areas not part of a recent sale area where regeneration failed, or other areas which are inadequately forested. Within sale areas, KV funds are used for a variety of work including planting and seeding (along with preparation of the site for planting and seeding) and stand-improvement work, such as thinning and pruning of young stands.[58]

Increasingly, the Forest Service has come to rely on artificial reforestation by seeding or planting. Cutover areas will regenerate naturally, over some period of time. This is true even of large clear-cut areas, though, of course, the larger the area, the less seed naturally available and the longer the period of time required for nature to seed the area. Other variables such as soil conditions, climate, and competing growth obviously affect the natural regeneration process. However, for large areas, natural regeneration is too indefinite in its results to be relied on for commercial management. Under some conditions it could require decades for successful regeneration of a large cutover area; and even then the particular species desired might not be established. However, artificial regeneration is not confined to large-area cuts. It is now common to seed or plant small areas where natural regeneration could be reasonably expected in a matter of a few years. In fact, even for areas where shelterwood or seed tree cuts (both specifically designed for natural regeneration) are used, it is common to seed artificially or to plant.[59] In this way, regeneration can be established more quickly and more reliably, and genetically improved, faster-growing species can be introduced. The additional cost of artificial regeneration[60] is generally more than recouped by the earlier establishment of a new stand and its faster growth (though, as we shall see, this is not invariably the case).

PROBLEMS
AND
CONTROVERSIES

Clear-cutting

Among the many environmental controversies confronting the Forest Service in recent years few have burned so fiercely as the clear-cut controversy.[61] In itself the clear-cut controversy is interesting and important, but it is especially so for reasons going beyond the immediate issues raised. The controversy touches on and dramatizes a spectrum of environmental issues almost as broad as the field of public land management.

The silvicultural benefits of clear-cutting were recognized in central Europe as long ago as the sixteenth century. However, in the early years of harvesting in the national forests selection cutting was the dominant harvest technique. The shift from selection cutting to clear-cutting (and variant forms of even-aged management such as shelterwood) was initially the consequence of recognizing that selection cutting had substantial silvicultural drawbacks: many of the largest and most valuable commercial species such as Douglas fir are shade intolerant and thus will not reproduce under selection-cutting conditions but will be replaced by less desirable, shade-tolerant species (e.g., hemlock). Perhaps a more important factor was the recognition that some species such as the Douglas fir tend to be shallow rooted and especially susceptible to windthrow when partial cutting removes only some of the stand. Other factors as well influenced the choice of clear-cutting—for example, the need to clear an area of disease or to facilitate slash disposal, and for other considerations which will be noted.

Although clear-cutting was used substantially in the Douglas fir region of the Pacific Northwest as early as the 1920s, it did not become the dominant mode throughout the national forest until the post-World War II period, when it corresponded with a substantial increase in harvesting generally. By the mid 1960s, clear-cutting established itself as the foremost harvest method on federal timberlands (it had long since been the dominant form of harvesting on private lands). By 1969, 61 percent of the volume of timber on western national forests was clear-cut; on eastern forests, some 50 percent of the volume was clear-cut.[62]

To say this growth of clear-cutting, and, more generally, the increases in harvesting itself, aroused public ire is to note the obvious. It was inevitable there should be a confrontation over increased timber cutting generally, and clear-cutting in particular. The same developments that brought increased demand for timber products produced conflicting demands for other uses of the forests. The demand for outdoor recreation soon transformed the national forests into potential national playgrounds. This rising recreational use of the forests brought into public view vast expanses of forest, heretofore the exclusive domain of the logger, just as the logger's axe was being swung with increased vigor. Coincident with the rising conflict has been increased public sensitivity to environmental conditions generally. Finally, with the formal, legal recognition of the right of public groups to participate in decision-making processes and to challenge them in the courts, the elements for effective public clamor were ripe for questioning the increased, intensified cutting of federal timberlands. Clear-cutting, though not the sole (nor ultimately even the most important) concern, became the focal point of public discontent. The public, by now well-educated to protest, reacted sharply when clear-cuts impaired scenic vistas, and appeared to destroy fishing streams, to harm wildlife, and even to reduce chances for forest regeneration. The most vocal opposition to clear-cutting was triggered by charges of mismanagement of the Monongahela National Forest of West Virginia and of the Bitterroot in Montana.[63] These forests were not the only targets of criticism and controversy—national forests in Wyoming and the Tongass National Forest in Alaska were also prominently identified.[64] But the first two have received the most attention and have become symbols of the controversy. No useful purpose would be served in recounting the details of these cases, but a summary outline may highlight some of the substance of the more general controversy.

The Monongahela National Forest. This forest was established in 1920. Prior to its acquisition as a national forest, the Monongahela had been the victim of more than a century of neglect and abuse. Once known as the Great Burn and the Great Brush Patch, the Monongahela, under Forest Service auspices, had become a valuable commercial forest property. Though the overall revenue from timber sales is relatively modest, for some of the depressed communities in this area it is an important part of the local economy.[65] On the other hand, because of its proximity to several large eastern cities (Washington, D.C., and Pittsburgh), the forest had become a major recreation area. Attracting about 1 million visitor-days' use per year, the forest accounts for a significant portion of West Virginia's yearly $1 billion tourist industry. These two demands have become increasingly competitive, producing conflict not only over how timber should be cut but whether it should be cut at all, with several areas being actively promoted for wilderness classification.

The forest was managed under an all-age management system (selective cutting) until 1964, when an even-age management system was adopted. The outcry against this shift by forest users was immediate. Fears that clear-cutting might imperil West Virginia's tourist industry seemed quickly affirmed as improperly designed and located clear-cuts threatened scenic vistas, wildlife habitat, and water quality. Aroused to opposition, concerned citizens caused passage by the West Virginia Legislature of three resolutions in 1964, 1967, and 1970, calling for an investigation into Forest Service management practices. In response to such public criticism, the Forest Service appointed a special review committee to investigate charges of mismanagement on the Monongahela National Forest. The committee's findings confirmed the existence of substantial abuse in the application of clear-cutting to the forest.

Generally, these abuses were the direct consequence of deficient multiple-use management. In part the problem lay in the absence of effective planning. The controversial clear-cuts on the Monongahela, with their great potential impact on other forest resources, were commenced five years prior to the formulation of multiple-use plans. Also deficient was the forest's inventory of forest resources. The Forest Service study found inadequate inventories of the location, age, and acreage of forest types; population, range and habitat requirements of wildlife species; location and requirements of recreational areas; and a cataloging of visual resources. Moreover, no assessments had been made of long-term public need regarding timber, wildlife, recreation, and water requirements; nor had there been any public discussions of these needs. Aside from this, there was substantial evidence of managerial negligence in implementing existing guidelines: erosion from improperly planned logging and road construction, inattention to wildlife needs, and unnecessary visual blight from inadequate landscape design.

The Bitterroot National Forest. The Bitterroot, though a different kind of forest, presented similar circumstances. As in the Monongahela, the controversial clear-cuts marked the introduction of clear-cutting in this forest; this corresponded to the introduction of important commercial harvesting to some parts of the area for the first time.[66] Although the Bitterroot, unlike the Monongahela, is not so heavily used by recreationists, it is nevertheless very sensitive to aesthetic impact. Part of the forest is located in the Selway–Bitterroot Primitive Area, and demands have been made for additional wilderness inclusions. In general, then, the Bitterroot Valley was not one where extensive logging was either common, or accepted. And it was not well received. Criticisms by local conservationists in 1968 led again to creation of a special Forest Service study team. In very general terms the findings were parallel to those for the Monongahela: inadequate long-term, multiple-use planning as well as negligent planning and administration of particular sales, resulted in overintensive cutting, careless road construction and site preparation. This, in turn, created both aesthetic damage and real or potential harm to the watershed (soil erosion and stream sedimentation).

Efforts to Eliminate Clear-cutting. For most of the deficiencies, both the Monongahela and the Bitterroot study reports recommended (in varying detail) greater emphasis on multiple-use planning and more careful timber management. As to be expected, this did not satisfy nor silence the critics, who continued to press for more extensive reforms—either elimination of clear-cutting or at least a moratorium on it to permit further study.

After extensive congressional hearings on clear-cutting in 1971, the controversy abated somewhat. The Forest Service made some significant changes in its policy toward clear-cutting, taking steps to reduce the incidence of clear-cutting and the size of clear-cut areas. The reduced emphasis on clear-cutting has been sufficiently substantial as to invoke criticism from those on the other side of the conservation fence. Nevertheless, the original critics were not satisfied; they continued to press for a moratorium on clear-cutting while its effects were further studied. When no such relief was forthcoming from Congress, several conservation groups turned to the courts, seeking to enjoin clear-cutting as a violation of the Organic Act of 1897. This time the opposition succeeded. In late 1973 the U.S. District Court for West Virginia ruled[68] that the Organic Act of 1897 permitted only the harvesting of "dead, matured or large-growth" trees and required the agency to mark each individual tree to be cut. Since clear-cutting necessarily involves cutting of green, nonmature trees, and moreover violates the requirement of individual tree marking, it violates the 1897 act. While the decision at this point directly controls only the reach of the court's jurisdiction—West Virginia (the Monongahela is the only national forest in the state)—its rationale is obviously not confined to any forest or region. If upheld on appeal (and as this is written appeal is pending) and if accepted by other federal circuits (a similar suit has been filed in Oregon), this ruling would have an almost incalculable impact on timber management in the national forests, for it would not merely eliminate clear-cutting but all forms of even-aged management which predominate in both eastern and western national forests.

The remarkable aspect of the decision is not merely its potentially far-reaching impact on forest management (such a major change in timber-harvest practices would, of course, have major impacts on the management of the entire forest), but the fact that it should be the consequence of interpreting a basic forest administration more than seventy-five years old. In the United States, clear-cutting itself is not so old, but it has been practiced for at least one-third of the time the Organic Act has been in effect. One might suppose that on matters so basic as this the authority of the agency would not have gone so long unnoticed or unchallenged. Such a point could be argued as a basis for construing the statute to permit clear-cutting under the "rule" of statutory construction, and that administrative interpretation, particularly where known to Congress, should be given substantial weight in construing the statute.[69] However, it is not so much as a rule of statutory construction that the administrative practice should be weighted (it is a rather weak and unreliable rule of construing legislative intent anyway[70]), but rather as a matter of appreciating the practical consequences of the decision. A practice so prevalent—and, some conservationists notwithstanding, widely accepted in forest management—ought not to be cast aside lightly by a fussy parsing of language in an 1897 statute. And one can hardly refrain from noting the latitudinarian interpretation which courts have given to other statutes when it has suited the court's view of what the times required. The broad judicial interpretations given to the National Environmental Policy Act are illustrative.[71]

Nevertheless, these considerations at most argue for a hospitable approach to the question of authority; they plainly cannot supplant the statute itself. The district court in the clear-cutting case refused to be drawn into a consideration of the pros and cons of the agency's practice, or of the practical consequences of its ruling, on the ground the statute was clear on its face in not permitting clear-cutting or even-age cutting of any kind. It is difficult to fault the court for this; the statute does very clearly specify the sale and cutting of dead, matured, or large-growth trees.[72] While it does not say in exact terms this is all that can be cut, that is its obvious meaning. And while the court declined to consider legislative history, this seems clearly to support the court's reading.[73] Further support for this interpretation is provided by a provision of the act that, before being sold, the timber "shall be marked and designated," the former being understood by contemporaneous administrative interpretation to mean individual tree marking.[74]

Nothing so far said touches on the merits of clear-cutting as a management practice. Congressional views on conservation in 1897, or, indeed, those of the Department of the Interior or the fledgling Division of Forestry, may affect the question of the legal authority given in an 1897 statute, but they are of no importance to the question of the proper role of clear-cutting, if any, in modern forest management. Whether or not the Monongahela decision is sustained and prevails throughout the National Forest System, the merits of clear-cutting must be considered. Clear-cutting and its effects raise many particular problems and questions, some of which are not yet fully understood. However, in general terms the basic elements of controversy can be at least identified, even if not fully explored here.

Advantages and Disadvantages of Clear-cutting.   The rationales for clear-cutting are, broadly, three:

1. Clear-cutting is necessary for reliable regeneration of shade-intolerant species of high commercial value and is virtually the only practical means by which stocking in superior species can be achieved.
2. Clear-cutting is often the only effective means of controlling disease and insect infestation.
3. Clear-cutting is generally the cheapest and most efficient method for harvesting.

On the silvicultural aspects there seems to be general agreement, at least on the basic biological phenomena.[75] As mentioned earlier, the clear-cutting on the national forests began in the Douglas fir region of the Pacific Northwest after studies showed the Douglas fir would not regenerate itself in its own shade. Under selective cutting, therefore, the Douglas fir would eventually be succeeded by shade-tolerant species such as hemlock and spruce, both commercially inferior species. In other regions too, the most highly valued species is shade intolerant. In Alaska, for example, the Sitka spruce, a commercially valuable species, is intolerant. In the South, southern pine; in the East, yellow poplar, black cherry, red oak, paper birch, and ash are intolerant. Untouched by man, these species would eventually be supplanted by shade-tolerant trees; the ultimate "climax forest" (rarely found) would be composed of the most tolerant species. Of course, the steady succession of species is naturally disrupted by fire and disease accounting for the current extensive stocking of Douglas fir in the Northwest and pine in the South. But given the premise the forest should be managed for use, these natural alternatives to clear-cutting are not attractive. If the premise is not one of use, then the focus of the controversy shifts away from clear-cutting to the broader question of whether to harvest timber at all. But for now, we will concentrate solely on clear-cutting.

Clear-cutting is not an invariable prescription, of course. Much depends on the species of a stand and which of the species is to regenerate. Shelterwood, where part of the stand is to provide seed and partial shade for the cut area, is frequently used, even for species such as Douglas fir. However, even where such a partial cut yields acceptable regeneration, it may be unsound because of disease and insect infestation. Dwarf mistletoe, for example, a disease very common to ponderosa pine, Douglas fir, and lodgepole pine, can be effectively controlled only by clear-cutting the diseased area to prevent the spread of disease. Any form of partial cut will leave the disease in the uncut overstory, from which it will fall and infect new growth. Moreover, even where partial cuts achieve satisfactory results, they may be far from optimal in achieving swift regeneration of a vigorous new stand.[76] With clear-cutting the site can be prepared to promote new growth, and it can be artificially reseeded or planted, a process which, however delayed, is often swifter and more reliable than natural reseeding and which also permits superior new species to be planted in the area. These reasons are only partly silvicultural; in significant part they involve the economics of reforestation, part of a larger economic rationale for clear-cutting.

Clear-cutting may offer some economies in harvesting. On a timber-volume basis, significant cost savings can be realized in road construction, logging, and increased utilization.[77] Clear-cutting may also offer some economic advantages in regeneration. Clear-cutting in relatively large areas (of, say, 40 acres or more) requires artificial seeding or planting for successful regeneration, a cost that can generally be avoided under partial cutting.[78] However, this cost will generally be more than recouped through faster, more complete stocking and more rapid growth, as well as the ability to generate superior stock.[79] These latter savings may be qualified by particular forest conditions. In some areas artificial seeding or planting may be uneconomic in that the yield may not cover the cost invested in artificial regeneration. Under such conditions it is questionable whether clear-cutting is economically justified, at least where it would require artificial regeneration. This was one of the central contentions of the so-called Bolle report on clear-cutting in the Bitterroot.[80] In any event it is apparent that, as the Bolle report indicates, there is need for more systematic cost–benefit studies of clear-cutting on the basis of each area's economic factors.

We can list most of the disadvantages to clear-cutting under the label of environmental damage, but it must be recognized they are not merely that. Most of the more important environmental impacts also have a corresponding economic impact. Soil erosion, stream damage, and even aesthetic injury have significant economic content. Not that this is important to most of the critics, but it ought to be remembered by those who advocate the economic justifications for clear-cutting.

Silviculture aside, the full environmental effects of clear-cutting are far from apparent, and what is known of the effects has been very muddled by the rhetoric of debate. For some undiscriminating critics, clear-cutting is not distinguished from the early rape of eastern forests in the "cut-and-get-out era."[81] If that is an extreme position, it nevertheless cannot be denied that clear-cutting can leave ugly scars on the landscape. With clear-cutting it is difficult not to damage the scenery of a forest. As one service official remarked sadly, "Some things just cannot be made beautiful." The forest, of course, returns, but this takes time, and time for human satisfaction is short.

Yet the aesthetic damage can certainly be mitigated by judicious planning and restraint. Many of the cases attracting critical attention are instances of managerial negligence that could and should have been avoided. Examples include cutting along travel-influence and water-influence zones in violation of the service's own multiple-use guides, which explicitly require that special consideration be given to scenic values and exposure of the forest to visitors. In many instances, no effort has been made to design the clear-cut to conform to natural contours and openings in the forest, resulting in an effect like that of a poodle cut on an English sheepdog.[82] In the main, destructive scenic effects are avoidable by advance planning, and it appears likely such mismanagement will be avoided now that the Forest Service's attention has been focused on the problems. The increased staffing of landscape architects is a worthwhile step in alleviating such an effect.

The effects of clear-cutting on wildlife are so variable as to defy easy generalization.[83] The destruction of cover and the disturbance of the forest that occurs with large clear-cuts can have an adverse effect on all wildlife. In hardwoods, clear-cutting removes a significant source of food for species such as squirrels and turkeys. On the other hand, by opening up clearings in the forest canopy, thereby promoting the growth of new trees, plants, and grasses, clear-cutting plainly benefits many wildlife species such as deer, elk, grouse, and rabbits, which depend on this new growth for browse and for cover.[84] And it plainly benefits predators[85] who prey on these species. Experimental studies have shown clear-cutting benefits some species of songbirds, a consequence of the fact that clear-cut openings promote insect life.[86] None of these commonly recognized effects on wildlife can be reliably generalized to all circumstances however. Even for particular species, the effects are difficult to determine in the absence of some concrete specifications, such as the size of the cut area. For example, while it is universally acknowledged that clear-cutting can benefit many wildlife species by opening up clearings in the forest (increasing the "edge effect"), these benefits are fully obtained by openings smaller than many clear-cuts; large openings needlessly destroy cover.[87] Probably the most notable adverse impact on wildlife, for which clear-cutting is blamed, is the harm done to fish habitat. The destruction of cover and the disturbance of the forest are part of a larger environmental impact which goes beyond injury to wildlife.

Clear-cutting has been indicted for a variety of ecological impacts. The most prominent is erosion caused by accelerated water runoff in the harvest area. The erosion removes or leaches nutrients from the soil. This also causes excessive sedimentation in stream channels. In turn, natural stream vegetation and food organisms are destroyed. Sediment reduces fish propagation by silting up spawning gravels and smothering fish eggs and fry.[88] Suspended sediment increases the cost of water treatment for municipal water supplies and causes excessive wear on turbines, pumps, irrigation sprinklers, and other equipment at increased expense to water users. The deposit of sediment in rivers and estuaries increases the need for the costs of dredging to maintain channels for navigation. The effects could probably be extended much further (the lawyer will instantly recognize the "proximate cause" chain of events). Erosion is not the only impact. Slash left in or adjacent to streams decomposes, increasing the amount of dissolved chemicals and plant nutrients in the water. Direct evidence of such water-quality degradation is the growth of bacterial slime and algae which thrive on the materials released by organic decomposition. Extensive bacteria and algae growth can reduce the amount of dissolved oxygen in the stream to levels lethal for fish. Thermal pollution is also a hazard. Stream temperatures can rise by four to fourteen degrees during passage through a clear-cut area, which may put it above the tolerance level for trout and salmon.

Although these adverse impacts are widely identified with clear-cutting, not all stem from clear-cutting itself. Studies of the notable cases of erosion in the Bitterroot and Monongahela indicate a significant part of the erosion was caused by road construction, not by cutting.[89] To the extent roads are the problem, since clear-cutting reduces the need for road construction, it would actually lessen the impact of cutting. Insofar as clear-cutting involves fewer entries into a harvest area than any of the other logging methods the adverse impact caused by heavy logging trucks and equipment should also be reduced, other things being equal. Whether this would be the case depends on whether other things would, in fact, be equal. It might be that if clear-cutting were eliminated, some areas would not be worth cutting at all. In areas especially sensitive to erosion, that may be the appropriate solution. The Forest Service, however, views erosion, and most other significantly adverse impacts, as controllable with better planning and better supervision, without elimination of clear-cutting. It can readily be conceded that for much of the damage, careful planning and supervision would have eliminated the source of complaint. Excess and poorly designed roads, poor logging techniques (e.g., tractors skidding on slopes with fragile soil), clear-cutting in travel- or water-influence zones—all these could be eliminated without eliminating clear-cutting. Even if this could be assured, it would still not satisfy all critics of clear-cutting who regard the practice as inherently damaging to the environment.

It has been argued that clear-cutting is directly and indirectly stripping the soils of their nutrients so fast that permanent soil sterility of western forests will be reached in less than 200 years.[90] In another age such forebodings of doom were largely limited to a handful of fanatics, armed with religious scripture. Today, the Jeremiahs are often well-trained scientists and the scripture, an ecology treatise. The differences may be more apparent than real. In this particular instance the evidence to support the prediction that American forests are on their way to becoming another Dalmatian Coast is not likely to convince anyone who does not already believe this without evidence.[91]

If the grim forebodings of some environmentalists seem excessive, it is not reason for ignoring legitimate criticism of clear-cutting excesses. That they have been largely excesses suggests they can be eliminated by changes in harvest practices, short of an abandonment of the practice altogether. Such is the assumption of the Forest Service, which adopted a number of measures designed to modify both the extent and the impact of clear-cutting. Reporting on its hearings on the clear-cut controversy, the Senate Subcommittee on Public Lands, in a rather captious aside, notes that these changes were more a defensive response to environmentalist pressures than the product of Forest Service initiative.[92] As an observation on administrative behavior, this is interesting if true (and I think it is), though scarcely a revelation. As a criticism of administrative behavior it seems disingenuous: the same criticism could be addressed with equal strength to virtually every large governmental institution, not excluding the subcommittee itself. The criticism, in any event, obscures the more important point which is not whether the service has been defensive but whether it has been responsive—and to whom it has responded, and how.

That the Forest Service has responded to the conservationist critics in the face of competing demands from industry cannot be, I think, reasonably debated. Whether the response has been adequate is more debatable, in the absence of any obvious standard of agency responsibility in this matter. It has not abandoned clear-cutting. Few thought it should, as a general policy. Even the Bolle report, among the most critical of clear-cutting on the Bitterroot and elsewhere, appears to concede it is an acceptable practice for some areas, though not all areas where it is now practiced. (The Bolle report's major claim was that the Forest Service was practicing uneconomic—as well as environmentally damaging—forestry by intensively harvesting only marginally productive areas.[93])

Revision of Clear-cutting Practices.   Although the Forest Service has not abandoned clear-cutting, it has adopted a number of policies in line with recommendations of the Senate Subcommittee on Public Lands, which promise a more cautious, and in many areas a significantly reduced, use of clear-cutting.[94] The most far-reaching, at least in *intended* scope, is the redesign of the multiple-use planning system which looks in the direction of integration of individual resource-management planning and multiple-use planning. The thrust of the new planning system has been discussed earlier and requires only brief further comment here. This new system is not, of course, aimed simply at the problem of clear-cutting, or even timber harvesting generally. However, if implemented as now designed (and it is, as noted earlier, far from being fully implemented especially outside the eastern and southern regions), the new planning concepts could help to eliminate *some* of the problems noted in connection with clear-cutting.

As indicated by the recent Monongahela case, the reforms have neither satisfied the more vocal critics nor resolved the controversies over timber-management policies. In fact, it is doubtful clear-cutting was ever the major bone of contention. The clear-cutting controversy is but a small part of a larger problem of timber supply with which both the Forest Service and its critics must contend.

Timber Supply—
Meeting Future Needs
As with other subjects on which this study touches, the problem of timber supply leads us into matters beyond the narrow realm of national forest management. Unfortunately, the problem of timber supply cannot be neatly fragmented into separate parts with only so much as concerns the national

forests being treated here. The fact is that all aspects of timber supply have a direct and important bearing on national forest management policy—just as it, in turn, vitally affects all those other aspects. So it is necessary to survey the general problems in order to understand both the context and the ultimate consequences of national forest policy.

Defining the Problem.   U.S. consumption of the timber resource for uses other than fuelwood has been increasing steadily since World War II. The following figures from 1950–72 (the latter being the latest date for which official statistics are available) are illustrative of the trends in timber consumption.[95] Consumption of industrial timber products from roundwood increased from 9.9 billion ft.^{3} in 1950 to 13.7 billion ft.^{3} in 1972. Plywood and veneer consumption increased almost fivefold in that same period, with a 1950 consumption of 350 million ft.^{3} and a 1972 consumption of 1.6 billion ft.^{3}. Pulpwood consumption almost doubled from a 1950 level of 2.4 billion ft.^{3} to a 1972 level of 4.2 billion ft.^{3}. Lumber consumption increased from a 1950 consumption of 6.4 billion ft.^{3} to a 1972 consumption of 7.3 billion ft.^{3}. Hardwood lumber use—mainly in the furniture, pallet, and railroad industries—actually decreased from a 1950 level of 1.2 billion ft.^{3} to a 1972 use of 1.1 billion ft.^{3}; but softwood lumber consumption edged up from 5.2 billion ft.^{3} in 1950 to a 1972 level of 6.2 billion ft.^{3}. The decrease in hardwood lumber consumption was due to a growing substitution of nontimber products, primarily for construction uses; but that substitution appears to have run its course, and increased softwood and hardwood lumber use is predicted in the next three decades.

Estimates of consumption in 1973–74 show some drop in consumption of softwood lumber and plywood, as a consequence of the downturn in housing starts.[96] However, despite the current distress in the residential construction industry and the general economic recession, the trend in timber products demand is still predicted generally to rise over the next thirty years.

The projected demand for timber products is dependent on assumptions as to price, particularly increases in prices relative to the prices of other commodities. The Forest Service has projected future demands on three alternative price assumptions: constant-1970 relative prices; relative prices above 1970 averages (30 percent above 1970 prices for lumber/plywood, 15 percent for miscellaneous products and fuelwood, and 10 percent for paper and board), and annually rising relative prices (*annual* relative price increases for the above three categories of 1.5, 1.0, and 0.5 percent, respectively). Assuming a continuation of present levels (or trends) of management, the projected supply has also been estimated. For softwood the picture for the year 2000 is as follows[97]:

| | In millions of board-feet | | |
Demand	At 1970 relative prices	At increased relative price over 1970	At rising relative prices
Total demand	72.6	61.9	55
Exports	5.6	5.6	5.5
Imports	6.4	10.8	11.4
Demand on U.S. forests	71.8	56.7	49.1
Supply[a]	47.0	48.6	51
Balance	−24.8	−8.1	+1.9

[a] The assumptions on which supply from U.S. forests is projected are too detailed to discuss here (see U.S. Department of Agriculture/Forest Service, *Outlook for Timber*, ch. 2). In terms of the relative contributions of different ownership classes, the projections assume only a minor increase in national forest harvest levels (actually a declining percentage of the total supply), the increase coming from the South. They assume increases in farm and miscellaneous private harvest levels (assumed to be somewhat price elastic), and a decrease in supply from industry lands (reflecting a decline in inventory on the Pacific coast).

As is apparent, at 1970 price levels and even at the 30–15–10 percent price-increase level, there will be a serious "shortage" of timber, while there will be a modest surplus with annually rising relative prices.

There does not appear to be important controversy over the basic data, given the assumptions on which they are based.[98] There is an endless and increasingly strident dispute over the policy implications to be drawn from the data. At the outset a brief and elementary point about the nature of the problem may be useful. Although it has become a commonplace to refer to the timber *shortage* problem, that term is incomplete at best and misleading in its implied suggestion that demand for timber products represents some unyielding norm against which the adequacy of the supply must be measured. What the shortage means, of course, is that at a given price level, demand exceeds supply. Our elementary economics texts tell us when that happens prices will rise and demand will decline, resulting in the end of the shortage and an end to the problem. If that response seems cavalier and simplistic, it nevertheless does, by exaggeration, correct the implied bias inherent in the word *shortage,* which seems to take the demand as fixed and then seeks to adjust the supply to meet it. The point is illustrated by the data given above. If one accepts the relative price rise of 1.5 percent (for lumber/plywood), the shortage predicted for the year 2000 becomes a surplus. Under that assumption the shortage problem would be more aptly described as a problem of *excessively* high prices, causing a socially undesirable restriction on demand. To the sophisticate this rearrangement of words may seem pointless. Perhaps it is, but if it has focused attention more sharply on the problem, it has served a useful function. Certainly, this formulation does force us to ask a few questions we might otherwise overlook. For example, should a relative price increase, over 1970 prices, of less than 0.5–1.5 percent on timber products be deemed excessive?[99] It should also be noted that this is less than past relative price increases, which have averaged approximately 1.7 percent since 1800.[100]

This does not at all dispose of the problem, it merely suggests the next question, What are the consequences of allowing relative prices (and corresponding restrictions on demand) to continue to increase over the next two and a half decades? A number of important impacts are readily identifiable. Perhaps the most obvious is that the cost of housing will continue to rise, and the housing supply will be correspondingly constricted.[101] On the assumption our national policy continues not only to favor but actively to promote more and better residential housing,[102] this effect must be given very serious consideration. And, of course, housing is only one of the many necessitities and amenities of modern life that would be curtailed.[103]

In many cases wood substitutes are available and would become increasingly attractive at higher timber prices. Unfortunately, the pressure for substitution only compounds the more general problem of natural resource supply. Not only are the substitute products directly more expensive to produce, they are more costly in terms of environmental impact as well. Various calculations have been made to demonstrate the superiority of wood over substitute products in terms of energy consumed. One recent estimate indicates that wood structures require only about one-fifth of the energy to produce as steel and about one-twentieth as much as aluminum.[104] This obviously has special significance in view of the growing energy crisis. When it is further considered that wood is a renewable resource (as the raw materials of steel and aluminum are not) and also that its production requires less damage to the environment,[105] the environmental superiority of wood is undeniable. Furthermore, substantial increases in the use of wood substitutes would necessitate increased dependence on imports of raw materials (bauxite, iron ore, and petroleum), with corresponding aggravation of current balance-of-trade problems.[106] Finally, any increase in timber-product prices relative to other prices will add to the overall inflationary forces in the economy.[107]

On the other hand, a policy of increased timber supply is not without substantial costs of its own. The nature of these costs, and whether they are greater or less than the identified gains from increased supply, depends upon the measures chosen for achieving it. And, of course, it also depends on individual and social value judgments about such things as "progress," the "good life," and so forth. It is no doubt inevitable the latter should influence one's perspective on the former; however, the following review of the main alternative measures for increased timber supply will attempt merely to raise the major issues.

Export–Import Adjustments. Current studies of the timber-supply problem assume that most of it must come from increased domestic production. This is almost certainly correct, but in view of the substantial international trade in lumber, the assumption requires some explanation.

In recent years the rising export of logs from the United States in the face of rising domestic demand has raised a number of critical eyebrows among both conservationists and congressmen who have urged export controls as a first measure for increasing domestic supply.[108] U.S. export on a major scale is a relatively recent phenomenon: in 1950 the United States exported some 140 million ft.^{3} of timber products; by 1960 it had tripled this amount and by 1970 had tripled it again, to reach a level of about 1.4 billion ft.^{3}.[109] The largest portion of this increased export trade has been with Japan, which in the 1960s began an aggressive search for softwood timber-product material—most notably logs and pulpwood chips.[110]

When coupled with the rising domestic demand for lumber and other wood products in the late sixties, this export of raw material generated strong opposition. In 1968 this opposition led to an administrative export restriction. The secretaries of agriculture and the interior required that all timber harvested from federal lands in western Oregon and Washington (primarily national forest, but including some BLM lands) be given primary manufacture in the United States. This original limitation was to last from April 1968 until July 1969, and it included a general exception—350 million bd.-ft. of logs per year could be exported from federal lands. That figure was chosen because it was estimated to be the approximate level of exports of federal timber in 1966. Before this administrative restriction expired it was replaced by the Morse Amendment to the Foreign Assistance Act, which provided that only 350 million bd.-ft. of logs per year could be exported from federal lands in the West.[111] This statutory restriction has been extended; it is currently due to expire in June 1975.

To date, only in small measure have restrictions been "conservationist" in motive or effect. They do not restrict the export of lumber, only of logs. This reflects a primary rationale of the legislation not to preserve lumber for domestic consumption but to protect local sawmills unable to compete for the raw material. Whether their plight is a proper subject for public concern is a question we can pass over for now; suffice it to say that this concern does not, in any event, go to the heart of our present problem.

Apart from protection of local sawmills, the argument is made that it is incongruous for the United States to export timber to Japan at the same time it is importing it from Canada for eastern U.S. markets. In fact it does make sense, for inefficiencies in our transportation system make it cheaper to import Canadian timber than to transport it to eastern markets from the Pacific Northwest.[112] However, reducing imports is hardly a solution to the basic problem of meeting increased timber demands.

In terms of our present concern, the real point of curbing log exports is to preserve supply for domestic consumption, lessening the pressure on national forests and private lands for increased harvesting. For export restrictions to make any sense from this point of view, at least three major assumptions must be made: (1) that restricting log exports would not be offset by export of processed lumber; (2) that the logs or lumber saved from export would find a domestic market; and (3) that reduction in exports would *not* be offset by reduced imports. (I am ignoring the adverse balance of trade and other general international trade effects, not because they are unimportant, but because it is unnecessarily complicating to consider them in the present brief discussion.)

Regarding the first assumption, it is likely Japan will not import substantial amounts of processed wood products from the United States because of the impact on Japanese mills. It is more likely they will simply increase their imports from Russia and Canada.[113] Of course, that is not an unmixed blessing: while it leaves the lumber available for domestic consumption, it also deprives many Pacific northwestern and Alaskan sellers of their present markets. However, this would be a short-term loss, because they could then sell to domestic markets. Unfortunately, this will not necessarily occur; for one thing, some of the species preferred by the Japanese, such as hemlock and cedar, have traditionally had little market in the United States. Also, some of the products are not domestically utilizable—at least at present prices. If they were not exported, some of these species would not be sold domestically; they would either not be harvested or would be left behind or disposed of as slash.[114] Even those species considered commercially utilizable would be difficult to market domestically under present circumstances. The same transport inefficiencies which currently favor Canadian producers over domestic suppliers in selling to eastern markets would limit domestic use of much of the timber now being exported. This is especially true of Alaskan timber.[115] Finally, we turn to the third assumption, that reduced exports would not reduce imports. It is not inconceivable that, if a domestic market is found for currently exported logs, it would add to rather than displace imports. On the other hand, a curtailment of exports to Japan is almost certain to cause them to turn to Canada and to compete with the United States for Canadian timber. Just how much this *could* reduce U.S. imports is difficult to say in the absence of a clearer picture of the future availability of Canadian timber.

This, in turn, introduces us to the other half of the international aspect of timber supply. Quite apart from the practicability or desirability of export restrictions, one alternative source of increased supply is imports. There is little doubt timber imports will play an important role in future supply; in fact, they already do. In 1972, imports of timber products exceeded 2.9 billion ft.^{3}, accounting for about one-fifth of the total U.S. supply.[116] This was almost double the level of 1950.

Although current estimates indicate that imports—most notably of softwood—will continue to rise, a number of factors make it difficult to assume increased imports can by themselves meet projected future needs. Currently, most softwood imports come from Canada, also looked to as the likely source of additional foreign supply in the future.[118] While Canadian forests are capable of supporting a considerably larger yield than at present, much of this yield only will become available at considerably higher prices. In part this reflects increased development costs to gain access to the timber; it also reflects the almost certain increase in competition for Canadian timber from other nations (including Canada herself), as well as increased environmental constraints on the use of existing commercial timberland for timber production.[119]

Increased Yield from National Forests. The limited promise which adjustments in foreign trade hold for meeting increased timber demands leaves us with our own public and private lands. Current Forest Service studies indicate that, in the long run, private lands will have to bear the lion's share of this burden; indeed, they already do.[120] However, this has not prevented the timber industry and others—most notably the Public Land Law Review Commission (PLLRC), and the recent President's Advisory Panel on Timber and the Environment—from insisting on increased production from the national forests.[121] The industry in particular has emphasized that, while the national forests produce only about 17 percent of the nation's total harvest (from a commercial forest base of some 18 percent of the commercial forest land), they contain some 34 percent of the total growing stock and 46 percent of the softwood—the most important commercial timber.[122] From this it is inferred that the national forests contain a large, as yet untapped inventory of timber (particularly in the West) which could and should be harvested at a rate more rapid than is presently occurring. Needless to say, the conservationists (including but by no means limited to wilderness preservationists) have resisted *any* effort to increase cutting on the national forests. The Forest Service is somewhere in the middle. It has favored increased cutting and other practices designed to increase timber productivity, but it has refused to accede to the full demands of industry and other critical observers, such as the President's Advisory Panel and the PLLRC, for dramatic increases in harvest levels.

The issues are too complicated to be fully examined here. About all that can be done is to outline some of the main elements of this increasingly acrimonious controversy, which in recent years has outstripped the national forests in growth, if not in productive yield.

We can start with what appears to be the simplest measure for increasing timber yield, that is, planning and implementing more sales in order to bring actual cutting up to full allowable cut (potential yield). Although most of the concern about meeting long-run supply needs is directed at increasing productivity (and hence allowable cut), it should be noted that the present allowable cut is not now being harvested.[123] The principal reason usually given is lack of funds to plan and administer sales and to build access roads.[124] However, while some modest increases in timber supply could be obtained by simply bringing current sales and cutting into line with allowable cut, this is not so simple a measure as might first appear. As emphasized earlier, the total allowable cut is not a single account on which the Forest Service can draw, but rather an aggregate of over a hundred individual forest accounts. Many of these forest accounts are already fully drawn (some overdrawn).[125] Those forests whose allowable-cut limits have not been reached are typically those with large areas which are only marginally productive or are subject to special multiple-use constraints. Under either circumstance the amount of timber that could be economically harvested consistent with environmental needs is less than current allowable-cut limits.[126] Indeed, a recent Forest Service study of six western forests indicates some of this timberland is misclassified and should be excluded altogether from commercial forest classification.[127] Finally, there is the matter of wilderness preservation. Many of the lands so far inaccessible for timber harvesting—through lack of roads—are for that very reason potential candidates for wilderness preservation, and are now under study for possible inclusion in the wilderness system. Obviously, cutting is restricted in areas under study, even though the timber yield in these areas has been included in the allowable cut.[128]

What all of this means is that the present total allowable-cut limits are not a reliable guide for sales and harvest levels. As this is written most of the western national forests are in the process of reinventorying or at least reevaluating their timber resources and revising their forest lands and allowable-cut determinations in accordance with the agency's new classifications. To date, the effect of this effort has been generally to reduce the number of forest areas classified as primary or standard commercial lands where timber is the key value and is not subject to special constraints based on multiple-use or environmemtal considerations.[129] All of these will have the effect of reducing, not only the economically practicable yield (programmed harvest), but also the maximum possible yield (potential yield).

Setting aside the question of wilderness preservation, at least some of the lands not now economically productive could be made so with an adequate program of reforestation. The problem evokes playwright George S.

Kaufman's comment on his partner's lavish efforts in surrounding his yard with fully grown trees: "It's beautiful, Moss—just what God would do if he had the money." But not, evidently, what Congress or the Office of Management and Budget (OMB) would do. Though every study in recent years has called attention to the need to reforest some 4.8 million acres of national forest land, little progress is being made to do so: in 1973, only some 130,000 acres of this land were planted.[130] Since this particular reforestation cannot be financed by current sales (or KV receipts), it is entirely dependent on appropriations. These have continued to be modest by any reasonable measure of present need.[131] New planting is only the most obvious example of an array of silvicultural practices which influence productivity and which could substantially increase yield.[132] It seems curious that the OMB and Congress should be so reluctant to appropriate adequate funds for this purpose; and as the demand for timber increases, it becomes, as Alice expressed in Wonderland, "curiouser and curiouser." In defense of this parsimony it is often noted that timber supply needs must compete with other social demands. An economically rational allocation of government investment must consider the relative return from alternative investments. Only if the returns equal an acceptable rate of interest can the investment be justified economically. That response, however, is incomplete. The government is not being asked to give away the money, but merely to invest it for a reasonable rate of return. Of course, not all the possibilities for reforestation or other measures will produce satisfactory rates of return in economic terms—which is a major reason for the refusal of OMB to request or Congress to appropriate funds for reforestation. Whether "uneconomic" investment should be made must therefore turn on the possibility of other benefits. However, we can overlook this latter reason, for relying on economic returns alone would appear to justify considerably greater investment, for some lands at least, than is presently evident.[133]

The current system of annual appropriations is a significant impediment to increasing investments. In such a system every budget request must compete with every other, in the process of which tradeoffs are made for political as often as economic reasons. Also, requests which promise reasonable rates of return for individual investments beyond present appropriations levels are nevertheless restricted because of general spending limits on government as a whole. To eliminate such restrictions in this area and to ensure proper levels of funding, it has been proposed to establish a trust fund which would finance the agency's timber management (and other activities) from timber receipts.[134] Such proposals have been opposed by conservationists who have argued this would increase the incentive to overcut the forests, or would at least tend to reinforce the already large emphasis on timber management to the detriment of other resource uses.[135] Budget makers in the administration and Congress have also opposed the trust fund approach on the ground that earmarking of funds would eliminate budgetary flexibility.[136] It is not possible to examine the relative merits of trust fund-versus-appropriations financing, but some comments are in order so far as the controversy here is concerned.

Clearly, earmarking would deprive budget makers of discretion. This is the whole basis for trust fund financing. The question is whether eliminating such discretion (to the extent of the trust fund) would impede achievement of sound political and social objectives. This is hard to answer categorically. There are many instances of trust fund financing within as well as outside of the field of natural resources.[137] Since the purpose (and effect) of these schemes has been to ensure a higher level of funding than that obtainable from annual appropriations,[138] one's view of the financing scheme tends to be influenced by one's view of the social merits of the activity in question. Thus, conservationists have applauded such schemes as the Land and Water Conservation Fund, which supports public outdoor recreation facilities, and have complained about the Federal Highway Trust Fund because it supports construction of highways. There is no inconsistency here once one realizes that since *both* kinds of financing have good and bad social effects, the choice between them should properly be influenced by one's view of particular effects and particular activities.

In the case of timber, conservationists have vigorously opposed trust fund financing for partly the same reasons that timber interests have favored it: it would increase emphasis on timber supply to the inevitable detriment of other considerations. This seems to me a plausible but somewhat exaggerated concern. Making a large part of the agency dependent on timber receipts would perhaps increase incentives for greater emphasis on timber. On the other hand, under recent proposals, the earmarked funds would not be devoted merely to timber management but to other resource uses. Thus, the fund does to some extent provide a partial counterpart to timber emphasis by securing funds for other resources, which under current appropriations tend to be underrepresented vis-à-vis timber.

Proposals for trust fund financing for timber management have so far shown little likelihood of being adopted in the face of opposition by both budget makers and conservationists. What this portends for the level of future appropriations is unclear, but it appears doubtful they will be dramatically increased.

There are some who have urged that increased appropriations need not be made to obtain substantial increased timber supplies. Both the timber industry and other observers have argued that quite apart from such measures as reforestation and timber stand-improvement work, the Forest Service could substantially increase yields immediately by changing its "conservative" harvest policies. Two major changes have been urged: first, accelerated liquidation of old-growth timber on western forests; and second, a reduction in the rotation age for commercial timber, particularly sawtimber.[139]

For some time, Forest Service policy has been to convert its commercial forests to fully "regulated" forests in which there is a balanced distribution of even-aged stands of different age classes, the oldest of which would generally be no older than that desired for commercial sawtimber. Such a policy involves a liquidation of old-growth timber (i.e., trees over the desired age for rotation) over some period of time. However, the Forest Service has opposed proposals urged by some outside critics to achieve this liquidation within some arbitrary, short period of time, say, twenty to thirty years. The service has no uniform, fixed period of time for converting old-growth stands. The general policy is to plan liquidation over a period of time long enough so that the increase in harvest required to liquidate old-growth timber is more or less offset by increased rates of growth, maintaining an even-flow yield, a more or less constant harvest level, over time.[140] Any shorter period of conversion would, the service argues, violate the even-flow principle. Although liquidation of old-growth timber does produce increased rates of growth,[141] it is not sufficient to offset the very large increases in harvest levels that would be produced by accelerated conversion.

Proponents of an accelerated conversion policy concede there would be some drop-off in yield after conversion, but they argue that with increased growth rates the yield would still be higher than it is at present.[142] The Forest Service nevertheless contends a violation of even flow would still have adverse consequences.[143] A main objection is the impact on industry stability. A rapid increase in sales, followed after a few years by a substantial decrease, would introduce undesirable instability in the industry and in related sectors of the economy. Mills and communities dependent on them would be rapidly expanded to absorb the increased supply, only to find within a few short years that the supply could not sustain the expanded level of productivity. This particular rationale for even flow seems very weak. First of all, the assumption that even flow itself will materially stabilize industry and promote local community well-being is tenuous. Even assuming the efficacy, it is a most dubious judgment to permit such a potentially important element of national well-being (in the form of more and cheaper timber products) to turn on the *possible* impact upon a bare handful of local industries and communities (realistically, only the smaller communities would experience much impact).[144]

However, if the local impact rationale of even flow is weak, there are other reasons for being uneasy about any sudden acceleration of yield. One concern is the immediate environmental impact any large increase in harvest would be likely to have. More roads, more intensive cutting, and larger-area cuts (more and larger clear-cuts) would all very probably cause impacts far worse than any witnessed in the past decade—even if Congress were generous in providing increased funds to apply needed environmental constraints.[145] A more serious concern is the possible long-term impact. Any large increase in the flow of timber, leading to lower prices and increased consumption, could create enormous pressure to avoid subsequent cutbacks in supply (even to levels above the present) after conversion. Pressures to make the temporarily inflated harvest levels permanent would emphasize the relaxation of multiple-use constraints and the opening up of wilderness or other areas.

Even flow would not necessarily be affected by proposals calling for permanent reduction in the rotation age for commerical timber, particularly sawtimber. Instead of the 100–120-year sawlog rotation, which is now standard for national forest softwoods, it has been proposed to reduce rotation to sixty or seventy years.[146] It appears such a reduced rotation age would significantly increase the volume yield, even though reductions of this magnitude would produce a significantly smaller tree.[147] Under one set of proposals it is not particularly important whether the reduced rotation would increase volume yield since the aim of the proposal is not to maximize yield but to maximize economic value. There are variations in the economic value approach,[148] but the most widely accepted one aims at maximizing present net worth. This is simply an application of standard capital budgeting analysis; timber is grown to an age at which the value added by growth is at least equal to a specified interest rate—the interest rate representing the opportunity cost of the timber investment.[149] Put in other terms, the tree is allowed to grow to the point of diminishing marginal value.

Although this economic approach has the support of recent professional studies,[150] the Forest Service has resisted applying this economic, or "financial maturity," model to determining rotations.[151] It has instead generally adhered to a silvicultural standard of maturity, defined as the culmination of mean annual growth. This silvicultural model is designed to maximize the volume yield from a given area, in contrast to the economic model which maximizes economic benefit. It appears that the service is backing away from any rigid adherence to this silvicultural standard. As noted earlier, the revised national guidelines for sawtimber rotation prescribe only that the rotation age be sufficient to produce utilizable sawtimber, although this is subject to a general guide that timber on national forests ought usually to be larger than that on private lands, and it is subject further to modified rotation for special multiple-use considerations. It is noteworthy that the Forest Service Manual now gives as a "suitable size" tree-width measurements that were a few years ago considered too small.[152] On the other hand, it is not clear that this has affected actual practice on the forests, at least some of which are apparently still applying older standards.[153]

Once again the Forest Service finds itself between extremes. Conservationists criticize the Forest Service for reducing the rotation age—harvesting trees before they are biologically "mature." The industry criticizes it for not reducing the rotation age more—in accordance with an economic standard of "financial maturity" (or at least a closer approximation of it). Just how wide the gap is between these extremes can be illustrated by reference to the Douglas fir, the dominant softwood species of the Pacific Northwest. Applying a biological maturity approach, the rotation age would be set around 100 to 120 years, depending on site conditions and climate. Applying a strict financial maturity standard could lead to rotations as short as thirty years.[154]

For the immediate future, the choice of rotation age would appear to have limited significance for most western forests which are characterized by old-growth stands consisting of trees that have passed their biological maturity. For overmature stands, the chief question now is how fast the old growth will be liquidated and the forest converted to a regulated forest. Here again, the Forest Service has been conservative in choosing a conversion period which ensures a more or less even flow of timber over the growth cycle. However, in forest areas where the overmature stands have been converted to a regulated cycle the problem of selecting an appropriate rotation age is a critical one and must be faced.

From a purely economic point of view it is difficult to dispute the contention of resource economists that the Forest Service's current standard for rotation (and for converting old growth to a regulated cycle) is inefficient in that it fails to account adequately for the opportunity cost of holding a large inventory of timber beyond the age of economic maturity. On the other hand, there are clearly noneconomic, or perhaps more precisely, nonmarket considerations as well. A commercial forest of Douglas fir where the oldest tree is thirty or even sixty years of age may yield a higher return on timber investment, but it would certainly have diminished aesthetic, recreational, and wilderness values.

In response to this last concern, it has been argued that these other nontimber values need not be sacrificed if intensified timber management is concentrated on those few forest areas with the highest timber productivity, with only partial harvesting—or no harvesting at all—on the larger number of areas with relatively low timber productivity.[155] In essence this is a dominant-use concept, for in some areas timber would be the dominant (though not exclusive) use, while in others wilderness or various types of recreational use would be dominant.

Despite the intense criticism that conservationists have leveled at the dominant-use idea the concept deserves careful consideration. The advantages of specialization, which is the underlying aim of dominant use, are sufficiently obvious and require little elaboration here. This is already recognized throughout public land management. It is most evident in the many different areas—such as national parks, recreation areas, wildlife refuges, and wilderness areas that are set aside for limited, special uses. It is less obvious but still visible in commercial timberlands where some areas are in fact, if not in name, managed predominantly for timber value.

This is not to suggest that formal adoption of a dominant-use system would not significantly change present management practices in commercial timberlands. As mentioned earlier, there is still a significant difference in management emphasis between the present multiple use and dominant use as proposed by advocates of the latter. Indeed, if no difference existed it would be hard to see what all the controversy between the timber industry and conservationists on this point is all about. What is suggested is that the differences may be less deep than the ideological battle suggests.

Ideology aside, the chief barrier to greater emphasis in the direction of dominant-use specialization is the local orientation of forest land use and management. Every movement in the direction of greater specialization limits the uses to which any particular area can be put. Over large regions, or over the nation as a whole, these restrictions balance out. The recreational use which is restricted in one area by dedicating a forest to dominant timber use is offset in another area by restricting timber use in favor of recreational use. But these regional or national tradeoffs are less than satisfying for the local interests of the respective areas. From a national or regional perspective it may make little or no difference whether timber harvesting in a particular forest is restricted in favor of, say, wilderness preservation, for the timber sacrificed can be more than made up by intensified timber harvesting elsewhere. To the local community whose economic livelihood depends on local timber sales, however, this overall view is irrelevant. Similarly for wilderness preservation, the demand for locally accessible wilderness is the immediate and relevant reality.

As has been noted, Forest Service policy has traditionally been strongly oriented toward this local perspective, in timber management and in other areas of resource management as well. Whether this is fully consonant with national needs is debatable, but we shall pass over that issue for now. The principal point to be made here is simply that, so long as land use policy continues to be strongly attached to local needs and interests in the area of timber management it is unlikely that we can expect any major shift toward dominant-use specialization.

Private Lands and Timber Supply. Given the existing and foreseeable constraints on the national forests, the problem of securing an adequate timber supply inevitably focuses on private timberlands.

Some 73 percent of the nation's commercial forest land is in private ownership—about 14 percent in industry holdings, and the remainder in farm and miscellaneous private holdings. As a future source of increased timber yield, it is generally conceded that little more can be expected from the private industry lands whose current production already exceeds their relative share of commercial lands or current inventory. It is anticipated that industry's relative share of production will decline by the year 2000, a consequence of its eventual elimination of present inventories of old-growth timber.[156] Having just concluded that large, sustained increases in yield from national forests (or other federal lands) cannot be reasonably expected (at least under present conditions), we are left with farmland and miscellaneous private lands as sources for future increases in supply. Unfortunately, the present promise of these lands is not great—particularly with respect to supply of softwood sawtimber, which is where the present and future pinch will be most sharply felt. Generally these private lands, located mainly in the East and South, are poorly stocked. Historically they have been poor timber producers; in fact, their production actually declined by one-fourth between 1947–68,[157] period in which production on other lands was increasing to meet steadily rising demands. Whether this trend of private production can be reversed is conjectural. Since the enactment of the Clarke–McNary Act in 1924, several programs have been implemented, designed to promote private forestry timber management in particular.[158] However, the reach of these programs has not been broad nor their results impressive.[159]

The failure of steadily rising prices to produce greater private investment, even when coupled with modest government aids, seems at odds with what economic sense leads us to expect. The explanation lies largely in the long-range character of the investment and the substantial diseconomies of small woodlot management. The length of time needed to grow trees—particularly sawtimber which is in greatest short supply—means that individual owners cannot look to immediate returns from current investments. In fact, in many cases no return could be expected within the current lifetime of the owner (particularly since small woodlot owners tend to be elderly). Quite apart from the delay in returns, many of the areas are too small to make any significant investment worthwhile, at least the kind required for effective management.[160] To offset these disincentives will require a far greater level of federal assistance—including outright subsidy—than has so far been undertaken. A number of such proposals for extending federal assistance, primarily through cost-sharing arrangements, are currently pending.[161] Given the relatively low level of funding for management improvements for national forests and other federal lands, it seems unlikely Congress will be generous in subsidizing private land production. If so, it will be up to the market to create sufficient incentives.

Effective Utilization.   The invariable consequence of abundance is waste. Timber—wood fiber—is no exception. Under present typical harvesting conditions it has been estimated that between 5 and 15 percent of the volume of trees harvested remains in the forest as slash or logging residue.

Of the logs reaching the mill, between 14 and 24 percent of the volume is unused for any product.[162] The largest portion of unused residue is the result of logging (including slash). Recent estimates put the volume of this residue for all forests as high as 1.6 billion ft.[3] annually—more than one-tenth of the nation's total output of timber in 1970.[163] For logging residue on national forests, the Forest Service appears to be as much concerned about disposal as utilization. In addition to being unaesthetic, logging residue creates a serious fire hazard, a significant impediment to swift forest regeneration (which has economic as well as environmental effects), and adds to the administrative costs of management (most notably, fire prevention and reforestation).[164] Given present and predicted future limits on timber supply, it has become increasingly evident that logging residues are more than an environmental "mess"; they are potentially a significant addition to the supply of wood fiber. Although much of the residue is not economically utilizable by the contractor (given transportation, milling, and marketing costs),[165] the evidence indicates much of the waste could be effectively utilized with changes in harvest practices.

Various measures have been proposed and adopted to achieve its greater utilization or removal. As mentioned earlier, one proposal has been to emphasize lump sum tree-measurement sales to provide greater incentive for removal. In areas with substantial old growth (which is where the problem of residue commonly appears), the Forest Service has been resistent to tree-measurement sales. In part, this reflects the industry's dislike of log-scale sales in such areas, but there is also a credible explanation for it beyond that. Because of the variation in tree quality in old-growth stands, it is difficult to gauge fair market value by tree measurement. While it is not technically impossible to make accurate valuation by such measurement, it does require a fairly intensive timber cruise, and this could cost more than scaling the logs. In any event, it is not clear that tree-measurement sales would necessarily provide greater incentive to remove (and utilize) timber.

At some point under any kind of sale agreement the economic incentives for removal reach an end. Although much of the residue could be used for fiber products, even though not utilizable for lumber or plywood, local mills are unable to utilize it, or are unable to find a market for it in which the price covers the milling and transportation costs. This does not mean the service could not require removal by the contractor of nonutilizable material. However, in the face of past recalcitrance of contractors, coupled with the cost of adequate agency enforcement, it would seem preferable to have the Forest Service remove the material (or to contract the task to private enterprise), covering the cost of removal out of contract deposits or sale proceeds.

The final aspect of the utilization problem warrants brief mention here—that is, the need to develop a more effective milling technology. There seems to be no doubt that more efficient technology could increase utilization in ways which would increase not only the supply of wood products but supplies of lumber and plywood as well. For example, the Forest Service's Project STRETCH is designed to use computer decision making and automatic saw setting to increase lumber yield from small logs as much as 15 percent.[166] It has been claimed that other methods, including thinner saws, greater precision, and smoother cutting could result in 30 percent-greater lumber yields.[167] Part of the difficulty in implementing such improvements is the nature of the lumber milling industry, which consists of thousands of small sawmills, with only a relative handful of larger operations. Most of the smaller mills in the Pacific Northwest were built when timber was plentiful and cheap and when there was no premium on efficient sawing. Today many are marginal mills too small by today's standard, or located in areas with a dwindling supply of old-growth timber, or ones that cannot obtain the capital needed for modernization. Unfortunately, the Forest Service's timber policies have tended to protect many small, local mills whose marginal efficiency has only compounded the larger problem of timber supply.

CONCLUSIONS

In surveying the multifaceted aspects of timber management no simple concluding statements seem adequate. To bring all the problems together into a single focus—with or without suggested solutions—requires some fairly glib generalizations. Still, a few generalizations suggested by the foregoing discussion, bear stating here.

One of the most common generalizations made about the Forest Service is that it is a captive of industry interests, and foremost among these is the timber industry. There seems to be inadequate evidence in support of this charge. That the Forest Service is continually concerned with the timber industry is obvious, and so far as I know the agency does not deny it. The invidious interpretation of this fact is that the Forest Service has "sold out" to the industry. The innocent interpretation is that the agency perceives the interests of the industry as parallel to, if not quite coextensive with, the interests of the public. Of the two interpretations, I think the latter is the more reasonable. If fault is to be found it lies more with the agency's traditional emphasis on the timber resource vis-à-vis other, competing resources. Even here, however, there are many indications that this emphasis is changing in the face of insistent pressure from enviromentalists. Illustrative is the Forest Service's resistence to industry demands to alter management policies in order to permit greater increases in timber yield—its refusal to liquidate old-growth timber at a faster rate, its unwillingness to reduce rotation ages to accord more closely with economic investment criteria, its reduction in clear-cutting, and its withdrawal of some lands from timber harvesting. Environmentalists continue to insist that the agency is preoccupied with timber supply needs and is guilty of excessive, as well as environmentally damaging, harvesting of the national forests. Nevertheless, in the continuing conflict between timber interests and environmentalists, the latter seem to have the upper hand in terms of influencing Forest Service policy. Though present policy is clearly a compromise between the extremes of industry and environmentalist demands, the compromise looks more toward the latter than the former. The Forest Service has served notice that future increases in national forest timber supply can be obtained only through additional investment in intensive management, and even with such investment the national forests cannot be relied upon to meet the projected future demand for timber.

In general terms it is easy to accept the conclusion that the national forests cannot be expected to bear the full burden of the nation's increased demands for timber. That they should not be expected to bear more of the burden than at present is not so easy to accept. If we choose not to increase national forest yield then either dramatically greater yield must be obtained from private lands (nonindustry lands in the main), or the price of timber will have to rise to ration demand. The first effect is at present a doubtful one. Given the disincentives and inherent inefficiencies in current private landholdings, only a substantial rise in prices is likely to bring forth the necessary supply.

As was explained earlier, an increase in relative prices for timber products would not be an unthinkable tragedy. In general, rising prices are an efficient means of rationing scarce resources and signaling new production, through new technology or redirection of resources employed in other enterprises. From the perspective of resource conservation such effects are not, however, unambiguously desirable. Environmentalists talk of cutting back on "wasteful" consumption, as exemplified by modern paper packaging, but if the alternative to paper is plastic, which consumes far more resources to produce and to dispose of, the saving of the former is a poor economy measure. The same point can be made for the widely pedaled nostrum of recycling. Before embracing this as a solution we would do well to ensure that the environmental (and economic) costs of recycling a tree are not greater than those of growing another tree. Finally, there is that *deus ex machina,* new technology. One of the virtues of rising prices is that they can signal technological innovation to develop new and cheaper ways to meet demand. Mention was made of some recent innovations in milling technology which can increase timber utilization. Desirable as such innovation may be, the effects may again prove ambiguous. Improved utilization may serve to stretch existing supply, but it may also serve to create new product markets which produce new demand. That would appear to be the lesson of past innovations which led to the manufacture of plywood and, more recently, of fiberboard.

The short of the matter would seem to be that scarcity is a pervasive problem which cannot be met by devoting attention to any one resource in isolation from all others. This fact is a convenient excuse for my not pursuing the present problem any further: the care and conservation of the world is not within the scope of this study.

NOTES

1. U.S. Department of Agriculture/Forest Service, *Outlook for Timber in the United States,* Forest Research Report 20 (1973), p. 8. *Commercial forest* is variously defined. The Forest Service defines it as any land capable of producing an annual yield of 20 ft.[3] per acre which is not withdrawn from timber utilization by statute or administrative regulation (Forest Service Manual, § 2412.14). The BLM, on the other hand, has no such precise definition, but defines it as land "growing stands of forest trees which possess(es) present or potential merchantable value." The differences in definition cause disparity between the Forest Service and BLM calculations. See Banzhaf and Co., *Study of Public Land Timber Policy,* Study for the Public Land Law Review Commission (Springfield, Ill.: Clearinghouse for Federal Scientific and Technical Information, 1969), appendix G, table 4.4a.

2. U.S. Department of Agriculture/Forest Service, *Outlook for Timber,* p. 11. The last category, "farm and miscellaneous ownership," are lands held by an estimated 3 million persons. Most of the tracts are very small, between 5 and 50 acres; only a few are as large as 5,000 acres. Although this land comprises 59 percent of the nation's commercial forest land, it holds only 19 percent of the nation's softwood inventory. It is estimated that only 29 percent of the land is managed in any way for timber production, that 26 percent is in urgent need of planting, and 45 percent is in similar urgent need of stand improvement. See Report on H.R. 8817, Pub. Law 92–592.

3. See Appendix B, Table B-1 for a complete breakdown of 1975 appropriations.

4. Ibid., it should be noted too that many other items are directly or indirectly supportive of timber management. For example, fire protection and control, insect and disease control, and road construction and maintenance, among others, are supportive of timber management. They also support other resources; however, it seems reasonable to treat these as being *for* the benefit of the commercial timber resource management to the extent of the ratio which the latter bears to all other resource-management functions. What this means is that the ratio which timber-resource management bears to other resource-management functions (recreation, range, wildlife, water) is much the same for the entire appropriated funds. A glance at the items in Appendix B will show this to be a reasonable assumption.

5. I have drawn on many sources in the discussion which follows. In addition to the Forest Service Manual, § 2400, the PLLRC study by Banzhaf and Co., and the recent *Report of the President's Advisory Panel on Timber and the Environment* (1973) have been extensively relied upon. I have also drawn upon timber-management planning and sale documents and quite extensively upon discussions with Forest Service officials and others.

6. Forest Service Manual, § 2412.

7. Current regulations (Forest Service Manual, § 2412) establish a rather elaborate scheme of forest land classification. All land capable of producing industrial wood in excess of 20 ft.[3] per acre is classed as productive. This, in turn, is divided into three classes: (1) productive lands withdrawn from timber utilization (e.g., wilderness areas); (2) deferred forest land which is under study for possible withdrawal, e.g., potential wilderness areas; and (3) commercial land. Commercial land is subdivided into four categories: standard, special, marginal, and unregulated. The standard category includes all lands on which timber can be harvested, with adequate protection to the environment under normal contract procedures. Special areas are those where special treatment is required to protect other key values, such as recreation, watershed, and aesthetics. Marginal lands are those which, under current cost conditions or resource constraints, are economically marginal, such as areas in need of reforestation, or inac-

cessible areas that cannot be economically harvested at current market prices. Finally, unregulated areas are those where timber utilization is not an aim of management, although cutting may take place incidental to other purposes; for example, experimental forests or recreation areas. It is "unregulated," not in the sense of being random or uncontrolled, but in the sense that it is not part of the program of regular timber harvesting.

8. See *Report of the President's Advisory Panel,* p. 162, which is critical of formal public review insofar as it generally produces opposition to increases in allowable cuts.

9. As a limit on harvesting the allowable cut, although expressed in annual terms, is actually directed toward the ten-year period of the management plan. Thus, an allowed but uncut amount can be made up in succeeding years. However, this carry-over cannot be extended beyond the period of the current management plan (Forest Service Manual, § 2415.42).

10. Ibid., § 2415.41–46.

11. The objective may be unrealistic. A study of recent plans on several western forests found that potential yields were being calculated for some areas without recognition of multiple-use constraints which would reduce or preclude cutting. What this means is that the potential yield is unrealistically high because no investment (or change in economic conditions) would permit the full harvest of areas so included. See *Report of the President's Advisory Panel,* pp. 164–165, and 169 (report of consultant Carl Newport).

12. Ibid., p. 79. It has been recently suggested that in some cases the working circle could be expanded even beyond forest boundaries, which would, of course, permit just such transfers.

13. This is the so-called Hanzlik formula (see Kenneth P. Davis, *Forest Management,* (2d ed., New York: McGraw-Hill, 1967), pp. 137–138. Assume, for example, a total volume in mature Douglas fir stands is calculated from the inventory to be 2 billion bd.-ft. The net growth is 10 million bd.-ft. (traditionally estimated on the basis of yield tables, computer models are now being used to calculate yield under various conditions); the rotation age is set at 100 years. The allowable cut would be 30 million bd.-ft.

14. Ibid., pp. 135–136. This is the so-called Austrian formula. Under this formula, the allowable cut is determined by taking the current volume of the area, subtracting from it the volume desired to maintain in the forest, and dividing this total by the period desired to convert the forest to the preferred inventory level. The conversion period is arbitrary: it can be a full rotation period or some lesser period for conversion. Although the formula is commonly used to liquidate excessive inventories in national forests, it can also be used to adjust an inadequate inventory upward.

15. Ibid., pp. 138–144, and *Report of the President's Advisory Panel,* p. 166.

16. See *Report of the President's Advisory Panel,* pp. 167–168, for a useful, brief discussion.

17. See Davis, *Forest Management,* pp. 124–130.

18. *Report of the President's Advisory Panel,* p. 167.

19. Forest Service Manual, § 2415.21 and 2415.22. The Forest Service also recognizes modified rotations for special purposes: longer rotations for landscape, cut areas where aesthetic or other objectives dictate larger trees (ibid., § 2415.23), and shorter rotations where biological conditions dictate (ibid., § 2415.24).

20. Detailed silvicultural prescription is commonly based on presale examination of a particular area. In western forests this is done chiefly by individual stands. In eastern and southern forests this is done by "compartments," a subunit of varying size used for record keeping and for management control.

21. Of course, multiple-use considerations may support cutting as a means of promoting some other use such as wildlife or water yield; which is merely to say that multiple use is not always a *constraint* on the economic objective.

22. The greatest number of sales are small—a few thousand board feet—and are made under the district ranger's authority. Such sales are made for silvicultural reasons such as stand-improvement work and have no economic significance. Economically significant sales are divided into four classes: (1) up to 2 million bd.-ft. (2) 2–5 million bd.-ft., (3) 5 million bd.-ft., (4) over 15 million bd.-ft. (Forest Service Handbook, § 2409.13).

23. It should not be assumed, however, that there is necessarily a positive correlation between size of sale and size of mill. Forest Service officials report that large firms are as likely

to bid for 1 million as for 6 million bd.-ft.; and the data reported by Banzhaf and Co., *Study of Public Land Timber Policy,* pp. 7–36, also suggests that larger companies do not necessarily prefer larger sales.

24. It is in major part the administrative inconvenience and expense of terminating a contract, reappraising the timber, and planning a new sale for the area that accounts for the Forest Service's past practice of liberally granting extensions in the period of the contract. This, I am informed, is being changed in favor of making somewhat longer-term contracts, but with tighter standards for extensions. This apparently is based on the experience that extensions frequently do not achieve the purpose, since purchasers unable to harvest the timber within the contract period are frequently overcommitted and unable to market the timber economically even within the extended period.

25. Authority to make such sales is, however, quite restricted. Regional foresters may delegate to supervisors the authority to make large sales, but only a few supervisors in the heavy timber forests have been given such authority. Regional foresters themselves have sale authority for between 20 and 50 million bd.-ft., depending on the region. Above that, sale authority remains with the chief of the Forest Service. See Forest Service Manual, §§ 2404.13 and 2430.43.

26. The contracts have been severely criticized by the Sierra Club, whose chief forester asserted that the service has in some of the areas sold more timber than exists! U.S. Congress, Senate Public Lands Subcommittee of the Committee on Interior and Insular Affairs, *Hearings, "Clear-cutting" Practices on National Timberlands,* 92 Cong., 1 sess., 1971, pp. 100–101. The assertion is answered by the chief of the Forest Service (pp. 841–842). The dispute revolves around differences in estimates of volume measurements and growth calculations.

27. Illustrative of a very large sale outside of Alaska is the sale of some 150 million bd.-ft. in the Targhee National Forest in Idaho. I was informed by the Forest Service that the purpose of the sale was to attract to the area a mill with the capacity to handle some 25 million bd.-ft. per year; a cut of that size was deemed necessary because of extensive pine beetle damage. Unfortunately, as is often the risk with such large sales, the contractor was unable to perform according to contract, and a new sale had to be planned.

28. Area boundaries are typically marked by some kind of signal marker; in areas not clear-cut, individual trees must be marked with paint or axe.

29. 36 C.F.R., § 221.7; Forest Service Manual, § 2420.02.

30. Forest Service Manual, § 2431.79.

31. 58 Stat. 132 (1944); 16 U.S.C., § 583–583i; Forest Service Manual, § 2469.

32. The Shelton Cooperative Unit in Washington combines over 158,000 areas of private timberland with over 111,000 areas of national forest lands under a 100-year management agreement between the Forest Service and the Simpson Lumber Company.

33. The units, established between 1948–50, are in Arizona, California, New Mexico, Oregon, and Washington. They cover a total of over 1.5 million acres, but this is somewhat misleading as an indication of importance in that over 900,000 acres contained in Arizona and New Mexico are not large timber-producing regions.

34. Bidders whose sealed bids do not meet that minimum price are offered an opportunity to raise their sealed bids in order to qualify for oral auction. The bidding procedures are set forth in the Forest Service Manual, § 2431.

35. Walter Mead, *Competition and Oligopsony in the Douglas Fir Lumber Industry,* (Berkeley: University of California Press, 1966). The rationale for the different practice is that in the West local buyers are more dependent on federal timber than those in the East and South where alternative sources of supply exist. For the same reason, the BLM, under insistent demands from industry, has, since 1949, used predominantly oral auction for timber sales in the Pacific Northwest.

36. Forest Service Manual, §§ 2431.56 and 2431.79. Bids must be accompanied by a bond to guarantee the bid; the financial ability requirement is independent of this and is designed as a more general assurance of adequate capability to perform.

37. See 36 C.F.R., § 221.10; and the Forest Service Manual, § 2431.73. In the case of two or more equally high bids, the sale officer may reject all bids and readvertise or he may offer to divide the timber among the bidders in some mutually agreeable way or make the award by lot.

38. Cull timber is now frequently sold on a rate-per-acre basis.

39.   There are two distinct types of sales made under lump sum payment; in one, a single sum is bid and paid for all timber within an area, in the other separate sums are bid and paid for each species.

40.   In all sales, payment must be made or guaranteed by bond or pledge of securities in advance of cutting; in the case of log scale the payment or guarantee would be based on the presale, tree-measured volume, but final payment would be based on the scaled volume.

41.   I have made no effort to obtain complete and exact figures on use of these two types of sales in the different regions, but the rough estimates obtained in interviews illustrate the extremes. In the eastern region approximately 95 percent of all sales are tree measurement; in the Pacific Northwest the opposite extreme holds, with over 90 percent of sales volume being by log scale.

42.   Marion Clawson, *The Bureau of Land Management* (New York: Praeger, 1971), p. 100. The BLM, which employs tree measurement on its O & C lands, provides a model for such proposals.

43.   In passing it may be noted that the concern here is not simply more complete utilization of timber, but also postharvest cleanup. Inadequate cleanup of logging slash delays reforestation, thereby increasing both administrative costs (to have the work done and to take action against the operator for failure to perform the contract) and investment costs.

44.   See, for example, Clawson, *The BLM*, pp. 101–102; and *Report of the President's Advisory Panel*, p. 231. The advisory panel, it should be noted, does not urge a shift to lump sum sales as the necessary answer. Instead it urges the use of special contract provisions in scaled sales to provide special incentives to remove marginally utilizable material and special credit for removal of nonutilizable material.

45.   U.S. Department of Agriculture Forest Service, *Report of the Committee on Close Timber Utilization* (1972), p. 16.

46.   Comptroller General, *Report on Actions Needed to Increase the Use of Felled Trees on Federal Timber Sale Areas* (1973), p. 42 (reply of Forest Service).

47.   Recently, this incentive feature has been modified in Region 6 by a combination of scale and tree measurement where a purchaser pays for all merchantable logs, by log, but a separate charge is not made for culls; instead these are sold on the basis of a price per acre, for which a separate bid is made.

48.   In some areas, scaling is done by an independent scaling expert selected jointly by the service and industry, in others it is done by service personnel; either way the cost becomes a cost of the sale.

49.   Cf., Clawson, *The BLM*, p. 101. "Log accountability" has been a problem particularly where the scaling point is far removed from the forest (say, at the mill) and where there are multiple exits from the forest, enabling the operator to avoid the scaling point or to divert the logs to another mill. This may partly explain the BLM's reluctance to use scaling: because the O & C lands are intermingled with private lands, the costs of log accountability would be high. This is less a problem for the national forest, but it is still a real one. However, in response to criticism from the GAO, the service has put in effect a strict scheme of accountability involving the recording of logging trucks as they move off the forest and matching this record against what is presented for scaling. Also, Forest Service officials report that the practice of charging by the acre for cull timber has reduced the problem significantly.

50.   36 C.F.R., § 221.7; and Forest Service Manual, §§ 2423.8 and 2427.33. Purchasers may apply for an emergency rate redetermination under certain conditions.

51.   Forest Service Manual, § 2434.3.

52.   See generally Forest Service Manual, ch. 2450.

53.   Various logging systems are used to meet different circumstances: topography, the type of cut, the road system, and environmental factors such as soil stability. Among the methods commonly used are tractor-skidding, jammer-skidding, high-lead logging. Experimentally (under the so-called Falcon program) some forests employ aerial logging methods, using balloon and helicopters to remove logs in sensitive areas (such as slopes or alpine lands with fragile soils).

54.   46 Stat. 527 (1930), 16 U.S.C., §§ 576–576b.

55.   Though separately calculated, KV deposits are not included with the stumpage payment for the timber. However, as timber is harvested, the KV funds received are separated

from the rest of the sale payments and placed in a special account for "sale area betterment." While any excess of the funds over cost must be returned to the National Forest Fund (entered under "miscellaneous receipts" in the Treasury), KV funds are not considered part of the stumpage price. They are not therefore subject to revenue sharing with the states. See *State of Alabama* v. *United States,* 461 F. 2d 1324 (Ct. Cl. 1972).

56. Moreover, the amount of money withheld cannot exceed in terms of cutover acreage, the average cost of planting other comparable national forest lands during the prior three years.

57. For ten years, through fiscal 1970, appropriated funds for reforestation and stand improvement were only 39 percent of the total requested in that period, contrasted with an appropriation of 95.5 percent for sales. See testimony of Edward P. Cliff, former chief of the Forest Service, in U.S. Congress, Senate Public Lands Subcommittee, *Hearings on "Clear-cutting" Practices,* pp. 836–837.

58. Stand improvement work is limited by a general time limit for expenditure of KV funds. Except with prior approval by the regional forester, KV funds must be spent within five years of their receipt.

59. This is the common practice in the Pacific Northwest.

60. The word "additional" should be stressed, for even where natural reseeding is relied upon, there will generally be some need for site preparation to facilitate new growth. This involves such measures as burning or scarifying the area to remove competitive vegetation and sources of infection, as well as preparing the soil to facilitate new growth; it may also involve terracing or contouring steep slopes to prepare a proper bed. Later, after young growth is established, thinning of the area may be undertaken to promote growth.

61. The literature on clear-cutting is extensive. A substantial amount of it is included with testimony before the U.S. Congress, Senate Public Lands Subcommittee, *Hearings on "Clear-cutting" Practices,* I have drawn heavily on the materials in the three volumes of these hearings. See also *Report of the President's Advisory Panel,* appendices L and M, for recent reviews of clear-cutting.

62. See U.S. Senate, Public Lands Subcommittee, *Hearings on "Clear-cutting" Practices,* p. 449. The following gives the full breakdown:

In 1969: By percentage method	Eastern forests		Western forests	
	area cut	volume	area cut	volume
Group, patch, stand, clear-cut	39.6	50.2	30.1	60.8
Shelterwood, seed tree	9.8	14.6	46.9	28.7
Selection	2.5	1.3	5.9	1.3
Intermediate	48.1	33.9	17.1	8.4
Salvage	—	—	—	0.8

Notice that the percentage of volume is much larger than the percentage by area. Though the volume figure is most frequently cited to show how extensive clear-cutting has become, the area-figure seems the more reliable indicator in measuring the impact on the forest.

63. Each of these was the subject of special studies by Forest Service task forces, both producing critical reports. See U.S. Department of Agriculture/Forest Service, *Management Practices on the Bitterroot National Forest* (1970); and U.S. Department of Agriculture/Forest Service, *Even-Age Management on the Monongahela National Forest* (1970). The discussion which follows is based in large measure on these reports and on the Clear-cutting hearings. In passing it may be noted that while these reports provided the basis for subsequent changes in clear-cutting practices in western and eastern regions, somewhat ironically they have also provided the basis for much of the subsequent criticism of the service by conservationists.

64. See *Report of the President's Advisory Panel,* p. 397. On the Wyoming episode, see U.S. Department of Agriculture/Forest Service, *Forest Management in Wyoming* (1971).

65. See Kenneth P. Davis, *Federal Public Land Laws and Policies Relating to Multiple*

Use of Public Lands, Study for the Public Land Law Review Commission (Springfield, Ill.: Clearinghouse for Federal Scientific and Technical Information, 1970), pp. 32–37.

66. The shift toward more intensive management reflects changes in the merchantability of certain species prominent in this region. Thus as late as 1941, only the ponderosa pine was considered to have sufficient value to be included in the plan; not until after 1957 were major species such as lodgepole pine, Douglas fir, and Engelmann spruce included in the allowable cut. See U.S. Department of Agriculture/Forest Service, *Management Practices on the Bitterroot,* pp. 61–64.

67. See *Report of the President's Advisory Panel,* p. 171 (report of consultant Carl Newport); and Carl Newport, "Measuring the Impact of a Reduction," in Stuart U. Rich, ed., *Timber Supply and the Environment* (Eugene, Ore.: Forest Industries Management Center of the University of Oregon, 1972), pp. 4 and 9.

68. *Izaak Walton League* v. *Butz,* 367 F. Supp. 452 (N.D.W.Va. 1973), appeal pending.

69. See, for example, *Red Lion Broadcasting Co.* v. *FCC,* 395 U.S. 367, 381 (1969). In this case, Congress not only was aware of the agency's interpretation, but also amended the statute in such a manner as to imply, if not specific approval, at least not disapproval.

70. See J. G. Sutherland, *Statutory Construction* (C. Dallas Sands, ed. Chicago: Callaghan, 1973), vol. 2A, § 49.10.

71. See, for example, *Calvert Cliffs' Coord. Comm.* v. *AEC,* 449 F.2d 1109 (D.C. Cir. 1971), *cert. denied,* 404 U.S. 942 (1972).

72. See 16 U.S.C., § 476: "[F]or the purpose of preserving the living and growing timber and promoting the younger growth on the national forests, the Secretary of Agriculture [formerly Secretary of Interior] . . . may cause to be designated and appraised so much of the dead, matured or large growth of trees found upon such national forests . . . and may sell the same. . . ."

73. The language was substituted for that of an earlier bill which would have permitted the sale of "timber of commercial value" for the express purpose of restricting harvesting to dead or mature timber. See *Congressional Record,* vol. 25 (1893), p. 2371; vol. 86 (1894), pp. 110 and 367; and vol. 30 (1897), pp. 909, 917, and 1401.

74. Current agency interpretation is that the timber must be "marked or otherwise designated" (36 C.F.R., § 221.15). However, contemporary administrative interpretation, shortly after the statute was enacted, indicates that all trees were to be marked. See *Annual Report of the Secretary of Interior,* H. Doc. 22, 57 Cong., 1 sess., 1901; appendix Exh. B, CCXXXIII; U.S. Department of Agriculture/Forest Service, *The Uses of National Forests* (1907), p. 820. The latter reflects Pinchot's view that "timber could be cut on the area designated by the forest officer, and *no green trees could be cut unless they had first been marked for cutting.*" See Gifford Pinchot, *Breaking New Ground* (New York: Harcourt, Brace, 1947), p. 274.

75. The discussion which follows draws heavily on useful summaries in: U.S. Department of Agriculture/Forest Service, *Management Practices on the Bitterroot;* testimony of Professor K. P. Davis in U.S. Congress, Senate Public Lands Subcommittee, *Hearings on "Clear-cutting" Practices,* pp. 550–558; and *Report of the President's Advisory Panel,* pp. 391–396.

76. In passing it may be noted that most of the intolerant species regenerate best at between 50 and 100 percent full sunlight, but in most cases 30 percent is sufficient. Unfortunately, the amount of basal area that must be removed to achieve the above amounts of full sunlight is not linear. Thus, to obtain 30 percent full sunlight, about 60 percent of the basal area must be removed. To obtain 50 percent, 80 percent must be removed. The argument then runs that with so little of the old stand left the residual trees are subject to windthrow and a rapid decrease in quality, and should be removed. See David A. Marquis, "Effect of Forest Clearcutting on Ecological Balances," in *A Perspective on Clearcutting in a Changing World* (New York: Society of American Foresters, 1972), pp. 47, 55.

77. See *Report of the President's Advisory Panel,* pp. 393–394 (report of consultant David Smith). A study of these by Weyerhaeuser, set forth in U.S. Senate Public Lands Subcommitte, *Hearings on Clearcutting,* pp. 245–252, gives suggested figures. While the study cannot be regarded as fully authoritative, and it does not purport to consider all variables, I know of no convincing refutation of these particular economics. On road construction, the savings are achieved partly through less mileage required for large-area cuts and the fact that roads can be

built over a shorter period of time, requiring less investment over time in road building equipment for a particular sale. The Weyerhaeuser study reports the following costs:

Size of area (in acres)	Relative cost per 1,000 ft.[3] (%)
100	100
40	192
10	254
Selection	198

Increased logging costs result from inability to use more efficient mechanical equipment for cutting and log removal. The Weyerhaeuser study estimated these savings (exclusive of road costs) to be:

Size of area (in acres)	Relative logging costs per 1,000 ft.[3] (%)
100	100
40	108
10	119
Selection	166

Smaller harvest areas mean greater incidence of damage from both cutting and removal of timber. In very small areas it may be impossible to use large logging machinery without damage to the standing timber. Apart from the added costs incurred in attempting to reduce the losses considered above, the lost value in timber should be estimated. The Weyerhaeuser study estimated the relative yields as follows:

Size of area (in acres)	Relative yield (%)
100	100
40	98
10	95
Selection	80

Totaling all of the savings, Weyerhaeuser calculated the following relative value per acre:

Size of area (in acres)	Relative value per acre (%)
100	100
40	84
10	69
Selection	39

One of the main difficulties with the Weyerhaeuser study is that it provides only a cost comparison between clear-cutting and selection cutting. Presumably, the latter does not include shelterwood or seed tree methods, the main alternatives to clear-cutting.

78. Not invariably, as noted earlier. In the Pacific Northwest artificial regeneration is often employed, even for shelterwood cuts.

79. The Weyerhaeuser study (see U.S. Senate Public Lands Subcommittee, *Hearings*

on "Clear-cutting" Practices,) estimated relative costs of *per unit of wood grown* regeneration, thinning, fertilization, and supervision of these activities for four different-sized cuts as follows:

Size of area (in acres)	Relative cost (%)
100	100
40	122
10	169
Selection	326

80. *Report of the Select Committee of the University of Montana on the Bitterroot National Forest* (1970), reprinted as *A University View of the Forest Service,* S. Doc. 91-115, 91 Cong., 2 sess., 1970.

81. See *Report of the President's Advisory Panel,* p. 391 (report of consultant David Smith), which comments critically on this "ill-deserved and heavy burden of guilt by association." In view of this identification it should be noted that while some lands which are *now* national forests were victims of this rapacity, they were at the time private or state lands; many of the eastern forests—the Monongahela is a good example—were acquired by the federal government precisely for the purpose of restoring them.

82. Most commonly this appears in experimental watersheds where clear-cutting has been designed to increase water yield, which calls for large and artificially manicured openings.

83. For a short general survey of land management impacts, see National Academy of Sciences, *Land Use and Wildlife Resources* (Washington, D.C.: National Academy of Sciences, 1970), pp. 96–105. See also *Report of the President's Advisory Panel,* appendix N (report of consultant William Webb).

84. For statistics on the increased size of the deer and elk herd after clear-cutting, see U.S. Department of Agriculture/Forest Service, *Management Practices on the Bitterroot,* p. 71.

85. An example of predator relationships is seen in northern Minnesota where the timber wolf is faced with a declining prey population because the maturing forest is increasingly unfavorable to deer.

86. See *Report of the President's Advisory Panel,* pp. 475–477 (report of consultant William Webb).

87. U.S. Department of Agriculture/Forest Service, *Forest Management,* pp. 21–23. The Forest Service's own study concluded that openings larger than about 40 acres do not improve big-game habitat. See also National Academy of Science, *Land Use,* p. 105.

88. Here is a good example of an environmental impact with a direct, immediate economic effect insofar as it results in the loss to recreational and commercial fishing. The damage to Salmon spawning beds in Idaho is an often-cited example, see U.S. Senate, Public Lands Subcommittee, *Hearings on Clearcutting,* pp. 101 and 113 (siltation of the South Fork of the Salmon).

89. See *Report of the President's Advisory Panel,* Appendix M (report of consultant Earl Stone).

90. U.S. Senate, Public Lands Subcommittee, *Hearings on "Clear-cutting" Practices,* p. 173 (testimony of geologist Robert Curry).

91. The most obvious shortcoming of Curry's prediction is its heavy reliance on nutrient-loss data from an experimental program, by the Forest Service, the Geological Survey, Dartmouth, Yale, and Cornell, conducted on the Hubbard Brook Experimental Forest in New Hampshire. Here, in order to study water yield and nutrient cycling under extreme conditions, the study area was not only virtually denuded, but was also thereafter repeatedly treated with herbicides to continue the increased water yield. These were highly experimental conditions, not remotely approached on nonexperimental forests; even so, recent reports indicate that after herbicide treatments stopped, subsequent growth in two seasons restored much of the nutrient loss. For a Forest Service summary of the results from this and nine other studies of nutrient cycling, see ibid., pp. 1057–1067. A more extensive review of these other studies is given in the *Report of the President's Advisory Panel,* appendix M (report of consultant Earl Stone).

92.   *Report on Clear-cutting on Federal Timberlands*, Committee Print, Senate Subcommittee on Public Lands of the Committee on Interior and Insular Affairs, 92 Cong., 2 sess., 1972, pp. 5–6.

93.   Assuming a decision is made to cut an area, the Bolle report (*Report of the Select Committee of the University of Montana*) lists four major alternatives which may be economically justified depending on the circumstances of each particular area:

1.   Removal of large timber by highgrading, leaving a residual stand that could be re-cut on a long cutting cycle of perhaps 40 or 50 years.
2.   Cut the overstory but retain the understory for advanced regeneration, even if this means a timber species conversion or the necessity of accepting a low quality or low vigor second growth stand.
3.   Use an even-aged cutting system (clearcut, seed, tree, or shelterwood) *but depend on natural regeneration,* even if this means long regeneration periods and irregular stocking.
4.   Make a more drastic distinction between high quality and poor quality sites. On the most productive and accessible sites, manage as intensively as economic conditions allow (even clearcutting and artificial regeneration). On low quality sites minimize capital investments or postpone all cutting to some indefinite future date.

The report acknowledges that under its approach, greater use of items 1, 2, and 3 would reduce yield, but it argues that it would increase efficiency, as measured by return in investment. However, it is not clear just how much yield would be reduced under the Bolle approach, because it is not known how much commercial timber area would be affected. The report is concerned mainly with the Intermountain West where productivity is relatively low. In areas of low productivity, where a decision is made to cut, the Bolle report contends that the timber should be regarded as a "stock" and "mined" rather than managed as a "flow" resource. There has been some confusion among uncritical readers of the report, as to what was being said; some newspapers reported that Bolle was accusing the service of "timber mining." That is something of a misunderstanding; in popular conception "mining" implies some kind of total depredation of an area in order to remove a resource, but in the Bolle report "mining" refers to the fact that the timber, as a "stock" resource, would not be regarded as a renewable (or "flow") resource. Thus, it would not be treated as a crop to be periodically harvested, but as a nonrenewable resource which would be depleted. The rationale for the latter treatment rests on the argument that in areas of poor productivity, artificial or natural regeneration is so slow and unreliable that, for management purposes it should be regarded as nonexistent. Under such circumstances cutting is acceptable only on a limited, select-cut basis. As was later explained by one member of the Bolle committee, its criticism of the Forest Service was not simply that the service was mining, but that it was doing it badly by not recognizing that the productivity of the land was too low to warrant investment to reproduce the timber once it was cut. Had the agency recognized timber as a stock resource, it would have cut more cautiously and less extensively, without "wasting" capital on investment in unnecessary roads and reproduction—investments which are proper only for a "flow" resource. See R. W. Behan, "Timber Mining: Accusation or Prospect?" *American Forests,* vol. 77 (November 1971) p. 4.

94.   The Subcommittee on Public Lands in its *Report on Clear-cutting* made the following recommendations which have been adopted by the Forest Service:

1.   Clear-cutting should not be used where:
     a.   Soil, slope or other watershed conditions are fragile and subject to major injury.
     b.   There is no assurance that the area can be adequately restocked within five years after cutting.
     c.   Aesthetic values outweigh other considerations.
     d.   The method is preferred only because it will yield the greatest dollar return or the greatest unit output.

2. Clear-cutting should be used only where:
   a. The size of the clear-cuts are kept at the minimum necessary to accomplish silvicultural and other multiple-use forest-management objectives.
   b. A multidisciplinary review has first been made of the potential environmental, biological, aesthetic, engineering and economic impacts on each sale area.
   c. Clear-cuts are, in all cases, shaped and blended as much as possible with the natural terrain.

Actually, although the above are ostensibly the policy recommendations of the subcommittee, every one can be traced to the Forest Service's own prior staff studies, most notably a general review of timber management, U.S. Department of Agriculture/Forest Service, *National Forest Management in a Quality Environment* (1971), reprinted in *Hearings on "Clear-cutting" Practices*, pp. 423–487. See also the sequel, *Action Plan* (1972).

Several regions have crystallized these general policies into more particularized limitations on clear-cutting. This includes in some cases a maximum limit on the size of the area which can be clear-cut (e.g., since the Monongahela controversy, a 25-acre limit has been placed on the size of clear-cuts), a somewhat dubious measure insofar as it restricts flexibility in designing a cut area to suit both environmental and aesthetic needs.

95. The data which follows is from U.S. Department of Agriculture/Forest Service, *The Demand and Price Situation for Forest Products, 1972–73* (1973), pp. 40–43. It is interesting to note that, while *total* consumption has steadily risen, *per capita* use of timber has consistently declined—from a 1950 high of 80.6 ft.^{3}, to a 1972 consumption of 67.9 ft.^{3} (p. 59).

96. Ibid., p. 1. Data from the National Forest Products Association shows a decline in lumber consumption of some 2.2 billion bd.-ft. (about 340 million ft.^{3}) in 1973. Data for the first two quarters of 1974 show a continuation of this decline.

97. U.S. Department of Agriculture/Forest Service, *Outlook for Timber*, p. 216. Projections for hardwood (p. 217) indicate a modest shortage only at 1970 prices.

98. Basically, the same data form the basis of the projections of the *Report of the President's Advisory Panel* (appendix C). For reasons not clear to me, the advisory panel uses 1967 prices as a reference point, which has the effect of magnifying slightly future price increases (1970 prices were 103 percent of those in 1967).

It should be noted at this point that apparently different figures are frequently given by different sources. Most of these differences are attributable to different measurements and standards. For example, the above data are given in board-feet. Quite commonly, however, cubic feet is used for total product measurement. Also there are different measures even for calculating board-feet (e.g., Scribner or international log scale).

99. Ibid., p. 216. The path of future increases required to produce equilibrium is not calculable; the increased price level required for equilibrium in the year 2000 is between 50 and 60 percent over relative 1970 prices. The 0.5–1.5 percent increase represents a 62 percent increase.

100. *Report of the President's Advisory Panel*, p. 39.

101. Ibid., p. 71. Approximately 40 percent of softwood lumber and 56 percent of plywood is used in residential construction. Together these account for about 12 percent of the cost of a detached, single-family unit. It is noteworthy, however, that a single-family unit in a multifamily dwelling requires only about one-third of this volume. Testimony of acting deputy assistant secretary of Department of Commerce in U.S. Congress, Senate Subcommittee of the Committee on Banking, Housing and Urban Affairs, *Hearings on Shortages and Rising Prices of Softwood Lumber*, 93 Cong., 1 sess., 1973, p. 85.

102. See 42 U.S.C., § 1441. The full statement of policy is too lengthy to quote here. Broadly, the policy is to remedy the "serious housing shortage," to eliminate the "substandard and other inadequate housing," and to realize "as soon as feasible . . . the goal of a decent home and a suitable living environment for every American family." The policy, first stated in the Housing Act of 1949 (63 Stat. 413), was subsequently reaffirmed in the Housing and Urban Development Act of 1968 (82 Stat. 601), which quantified the policy by stating as a goal of the "next decade" the construction or rehabilitation of 26 million housing units, of which 6 million would be for low- and moderate-income families (42 U.S.C., § 1441a). See also the National Housing Act, 12 U.S.C., § 1701 *et seq.*, particularly § 1701t.

103. At the present time it is softwood sawtimber that is in shortest supply relative to current demands. However, to the extent that sawtimber (using this term to denote all timber that could be utilized for construction) is now being used for manufactured products, increased prices for sawtimber should logically result in shifts in this utilization toward construction and a consequent reduction in supplies available for paper and other products.

104. *Report of the President's Advisory Panel*, p. 354.

105. Ibid. The environmental damage point requires no assumption that timber harvesting is in fact done with greater care than mining (although a comparison of, say, clear-cutting with strip mining strongly suggests that such an assumption would be warranted). The point here is that, other things being equal, mining for the raw materials used to produce steel or aluminum *necessarily* involves greater environmental depradations than does timber cutting.

106. Sacman, *The Wood Resource and The Environment—Some National Options and Alternatives*, U.S. Department of Agriculture/Forest Service, Forest Products Laboratory (1972).

107. *Report of the President's Advisory Panel*, p. 72.

108. See testimony of Gordon Robinson of the Sierra Club in U.S. Congress, Senate Subcommittee of the Committee on Banking, Housing and Urban Affairs, *Hearings on Log Export Restrictions*, 93 Cong., 1 sess., 1973, pp. 72–90.

109. U.S. Department of Agriculture/Forest Service, *Outlook for Timber*, p. 326. The level in 1972 was down by some 25 million cubic ft.[3]. All but 200 million ft.[3] is softwood.

110. Ibid., p. 327. However, Japan's share is less than is implied in general statements about exports. Actually, less than 35 percent of the total U.S. exports in 1972 went to Japan. About 30 percent went to Canada and 20 percent went to Europe.

111. 16 U.S.C., § 617 (1968). Additional specific quantities and species of logs could be exported if they were declared surplus to domestic needs. This restriction covered the calendar years 1969–71 and was later extended through 1973. Legislation which would completely ban log exports was introduced in the Ninety-third Congress but failed; similar legislation has been introduced in the Ninety-fourth Congress.

112. One of the major inefficiencies is largely imposed by the Jones Act (46 U.S.C., § 889) which provides that domestic cargoes moving by water or by land and water to domestic ports must be transported only on vessels built in the United States and owned by U.S. citizens. Because shipping on U.S. bottoms is substantially more costly than on foreign bottoms, Canadian producers have a cost advantage over U.S. producers. Efforts to modify or eliminate the Jones Act to correct this disadvantage have so far failed. See U.S. Congress, Senate Subcommittee of the Senate Committee on Banking, Housing and Urban Affairs, *Hearings on Log Export Controls*, 92 Cong., 2 sess., 1972, pp. 335–337. The lesson of this failure seems to be that subsidies to the maritime industry take priority over the needs of the timber industry, the American consumer, and a national housing policy of providing low-cost housing.

113. *Report of the President's Advisory Panel*, p. 300.

114. Ibid., pp. 299–300. The argument is made by the advisory panel's consultant that to the extent the products saved have no current market in the United States, a restriction on exports would impair efficient timber utilization (such as low-valued logs now left in the forest or mill wastes) and would also reduce the attractiveness of private timber investment in western forests.

One difficulty with these conclusions is that they rest implicitly on an assumption of unchanged price levels. One would suppose, however, that rising relative prices for sawtimber and timber products would produce markets for species not currently used and would also provide incentives for increased utilization of timber products—low-valued logs and mill wastes.

115. Ibid., p. 301. Presumably a change in transport conditions and policies (e.g., elimination of the Jones Act restrictions) would warrant reconsideration of this conclusion. But given past difficulties in achieving transport efficiencies, it seems foolish to limit exports on the mere expectation that they will be changed.

116. U.S. Department of Agriculture/Forest Service, *Outlook for Timber*, p. 126. The net of imports over exports accounted for some 11.6 percent of U.S. supply.

117. That is, supply of softwood. Hardwood imports come from Asia and will continue to do so (*Report of the President's Advisory Panel*, pp. 302 and 323). Other possible sources of

imports are the USSR and China, but at this juncture substantial imports from either country seem unlikely to develop (Ibid., pp. 324–325).

119. Ibid., pp. 304–306. Also, U.S. Department of Agriculture/Forest Service, *Outlook for Timber*, pp. 135–136. It is noteworthy that Canadian exports to the United States currently account for 60 percent of Canada's production.

120. U.S. Department of Agriculture/Forest Service, *Outlook for Timber*, p. 51. Note the following percentage breakdown of domestic production of roundwood for 1970 and projected for the year 2000 (assuming no change in present management policies and trends):

Ownership	1970 (%)	2000 (%)
Forest Service	17	15
Other public	7	9
Industry	28	19
Farm and miscellaneous private	48	57

The respective percentages for sawtimber alone show a relatively larger contribution from the national forests (Ibid., p. 53).

121. *Report of the President's Advisory Panel*, p. 84; and Public Land Law Review Commission, *One-Third of the Nation's Lands* (1970).

122. U.S. Department of Agriculture/Forest Service, *Outlook for Timber*, pp. 11 and 32, gives the following breakdown:

Ownership	Area (%)	Growing stock (%)		
		Total	Softwood	Hardwood
Forest Service	18	34	46	8
Other public	9	10	11	9
Industry	14	15	17	12
Farm and miscellaneous private	59	41	26	71

123. U.S. Department of Agriculture/Forest Service, *National Forest Timber Sale Accomplishments for Fiscal Year 1972* (March 1973). In fiscal 1972 the harvest volume was 11.7 billion bd.-ft., about 85 percent of the programmed allowable harvest (on which budget requests were prepared). It should be noted that there is some ambiguity in the allowable-cut figure. Although it is indicated this is programmed allowable-cut under the Forest Service's new twofold classification, it would seem rather to indicate potential yield since it appears that some of this volume could not be economically cut under present conditions. See also U.S. Congress, Senate Subcommittee of the Senate Committee on Banking, Housing and Urban Affairs, *Hearings on Shortages and Rising Prices*, 93 Cong., 1 sess., 1973, p. 99. Actually, as pointed out below, it is uncertain what the *realistic* programmed allowable cut should be until current inventories and land reclassifications are completed.

124. Some access roads are constructed by the purchaser of individual sales (the cost being a credit against purchase payment). In many areas, however, the cost of access roads exceeds the value of any one sale of timber. Therefore, appropriations are needed if access roads are to be built into those areas. Appropriations for constructing and maintaining access roads have consistently provided for only slow growth of the national forest roads and trails system. In fiscal year 1973, for example, funding was about two-thirds the level considered optimum by the Forest Service, and 11 percent of that appropriated was impounded by the president. (U.S. Congress, Senate Subcommittee of the Committee on Banking, Housing and Urban Affairs, *Hearings on Shortages and Rising Prices*, pp. 63 and 100.) One estimate of the amount needed to complete most of the needed road construction would involve maintaining the roads and trails budget at a minimum of double its existing level for ten years (Banzhaf, *Study of Public Land Timber Policy*, ch. 10).

125. See U.S. Department of Agriculture/Forest Service, *National Forest Timber Sale.* Cutting in excess of allowable cut is frequently accounted for by the fact that thinning and salvage cuts are not included in the allowable cut. Recall also that, under current regulations the annual allowable-cut volume which is uncut may be carried forward to future years, within the period of the management plan.

126. Testimony of John McGuire, chief of the Forest Service, in U.S. Congress, Senate Subcommittee of the Committee on Banking, Housing and Urban Affairs, *Hearings on Shortages and Rising Prices,* p. 99. See also, *Report of the President's Advisory Panel,* pp. 164–165 (consultant report of Carl Newport).

127. See John H. Wikstrom and S. Blair Hutchison, *Stratification of Forest Land for Timber Management Planning on the Western National Forests,* U.S. Department of Agriculture/Forest Service, Research Paper Int. 108 (1971), who indicate that the area suitable for growing the crops on these forests is 22 percent less than what had been classified. The inferences to be drawn from this are unclear. First, there is no evidence one way or the other that the data are representative of the entire system. Second, it is not in any event apparent—as the authors stress—what this inflation of the base implies for allowable cut; it is evident that the 22 percent could not be simply transferred over to allowable cut because the lands to be excluded are those in the marginal or special class, and this would not have contributed to the allowable cut in proportion to land area.

It is also not clear what the impact of these findings will be. The Forest Service's outlook for timber study does not *specifically* advert to this study but does assume future reductions in commercial forest lands, *other than* withdrawals for wilderness, as a result of reclassifications (U.S. Department of Agriculture/Forest Service, *Outlook for Timber,* p. 70). It should be noted too that current inventories in western forests and the reclassification of commercial lands into subcategories of standard, marginal, or special has resulted in reducing the standard commercial land and correspondingly the allowable cut. *Report of the President's Advisory Panel,* pp. 160–164 (consultant report of Carl Newport).

128. U.S. Department of Agriculture/Forest Service, *Final Environmental Statement on Roadless and Undeveloped Areas* (1973), p. 77. This refers to the so-called new study areas (NSAs) currently being studied for possible wilderness preservation. (Timber in primitive areas being studied for permanent preservation as wilderness has never been calculated in the allowable cut.) The total annual allowable cut is estimated at 229 million bd.-ft. for the 274 acres (approximately 12.3 million acres) selected as NSAs. These are placed in the deferred category under allowable cut since, pending final disposition, no harvest can take place within these areas. It should be noted that this does not take into account nearly 44 million acres of roadless areas excluded from the NSAs; however, some of these other areas will be urged for wilderness by preservationists. Because much of this area is (by definition) presently inaccessible and because the Forest Service will face certain opposition when it seeks to open it to timber sales, realistic planning would recognize that much of the timber in these areas is not attractive at present market prices.

129. *Report of the President's Advisory Panel,* pp. 162–163 (consultant report of Carl Newport); U.S. Department of Agriculture/Forest Service, *Outlook for Timber,* pp. 43–44.

130. Testimony of John McGuire, the chief of Forest Service in U.S. Congress, Senate Subcommittee of the Committee on Banking, Housing and Urban Affairs, p. 99.

131. See Appendices B and C for current and past appropriations.

132. U.S. Department of Agriculture/Forest Service, *Outlook for Timber,* p. 105. Estimates of the increase vary, depending on what assumptions are made and who is making them. The latest and most complete estimate by the Forest Service calculated the yield based on (1) a number of practices such as fertilization, thinning, type-conversion of stands, increased salvage of burned, windblown or diseased timber, increased fire and disease protection; (2) when such application to those lands would yield at least 5 percent return on investment; and (3) on the assumption of a 30 percent price increase over 1970 prices. On these assumptions, the increase is estimated at 1.1 billion bd.-ft. by the fifteenth year of effort and by 4 billion by the forty-fifth year.

133. Depending, of course, on the interest rate, the "social rate of discount" as public sector economists call it. As noted above, the Forest Service applied a 5 percent rate for calculating the impact of measures to increase yield. The basis for selecting that rate is not clear, but

the calculation appears to exclude potential nonmonetary returns which would probably justify the expenditures even assuming a greater discount.

134. The most prominent recent earmarking proposal was the proposed Timber Supply Act of 1969 (S. 1832, 91 Cong., 1 sess.), introduced by Senator Sparkman and others in April 1969, at a time of extremely high lumber and plywood prices. This proposed act would have established a High Timber Yield Fund, consisting of all net receipts from the sale of timber. The fund was to be used "only for increasing timber yield." Funding for other uses would have continued through the regular appropriations process. The 1969 bill failed not only because of better opposition, but because the "crisis" of high prices which spawned it soon disappeared.

In 1973 Senator Sparkman and others tried again with a trust-fund proposal (see S. 1775 and S. 1996, 93 Cong., 1 sess.). Unlike that of 1969, this proposed fund would receive not only timber sale receipts but also all other sources of revenue from the national forests, such as recreation fees and other use permits. The funds would be spent for capital or basic investments—but not for current expenses—for *all* uses of the national forests, not just timber production.

A trust fund approach was endorsed by the Public Land Law Review Commission (*One-Third of the Nation's Land*, p. 95). The recent Advisory Panel on Timber and the Environment also hints in this general direction without making a specific recommendation to that effect. See *Report of the President's Advisory Panel*, pp. 85–86.

135. See, for example, U.S. Senate, Subcommittee of Senate Committee on Agriculture, *Hearings on S. 1832*, 91 Cong., 1 sess., pp. 63–74 (Sierra Club); pp. 95–97 (Wildlife Federation), p. 97 (Izaak Walton League).

136. Ibid., p. 12. For contrasting views on the economic consequences and desirability of trust fund financing, cf. James Buchanan, "Earmarked Taxes," *Journal of Political Economy*, vol. 71, 1963, p. 457; with Walter Heller, "CED's Stabilizing Policy After Ten Years," *American Economic Review*, vol. 47 (1957), p. 634.

137. The most well-known fund outside the natural resources field, which has provided something of a model for others, is the Federal Highway Trust Fund, but it is not unique. It has been estimated that there are more than a hundred such special trust funds. Bernard Herber, *Modern Public Finance: The Study of Public Sector Economics* (rev. ed., Homewood: Irwin, 1971), p. 267. There are several earmarking schemes in the natural resources area. Notable examples include the Migratory Bird Conservation Fund (16 U.S.C., § 718), which earmarks tax receipts from federal migratory bird hunting stamps to maintain migratory bird refuges, and the Land and Water Conservation Fund (16 U.S.C., § 400L-5), which earmarks recreation user fees and other receipts in support of outdoor recreation facilities.

138. See Banzhaf and Co., *Study of Public Land Timber Policy*, p. 27, which estimates that a timber supply fund could result in a 70 percent increase in funds for timber management. This, of course, assumes a scheme like that proposed by the Timber Supply Act of 1969, in which all timber receipts go exclusively to timber management.

139. See, for example, *Report of the President's Advisory Panel*, pp. 4 and 171–175; and Rickard, *The Action Forest: A Report to the Oregon Legislative Interim Committee on Public Lands*, reprinted in U.S. Congress, Senate Subcommittee of the Committee on Small Business, *Hearings on Timber Management Policies*, 90 Cong., 2 sess., 1968, pp. 413–528.

140. See, for example, *Report of the President's Advisory Panel*, p. 165. Although the Forest Service endorses even flow as a general policy, it is a policy not rigidly followed in practice, as indicated by past and prospective fluctuations in yield (ibid., p. 170). A 1969 Forest Service study of Pacific Coast Douglas fir forests showed that with then-current rotations, management practices, and utilization, the then-current harvest levels would drop after the first rotation (i.e., after liquidation of old growth). U.S. Department of Agriculture/Forest Service, *Douglas Fir Supply Study* (1969) and *Forest Regulation Study*, pp. 2–3 (preliminary draft, 1973). However, it should be noted that the yield could be maintained without such a drop-off if intensive management practices were applied. Also, as indicated earlier, allowable cut is being revised for these and other western forests with expected reductions in future yields.

141. Many of the old-growth stands have only slight growth. Trees not only grow slower past the age of maturity, but they impede other new growth. Because of this, coupled with the higher mortality rates in old-growth timber, some stands may even have negative net growth.

142. See Rickard, *The Action Forest*, pp. 43–47 (in U.S. Congress, Senate Subcommittee of the Committee on Small Business, *Hearings on Timber Management Policies*, pp. 460–464). The Rickard report also adjusted the rotation age downward from 100 years to 60 years. It should be noted that the study assumes a level of management practices beyond that being applied.

143. For the Forest Service view, see ibid., pp. 529–530.

144. For further elaboration of these criticisms, see for example, Banzhaf and Co., *Study of Public Land Timber Policy*, pp. 6-29–6-31; and John T. Keene, "Even Flow—Yes or No," *American Forests*, vol. 78 (June 1972), p. 32.

145. Another distinct but related consideration in liquidating old growth is the objective of establishing, after conversion, a balanced distribution of age classes. A rapid conversion of large areas of old-growth timber could produce a stock of young trees disproportionate to other age classes. It is not clear whether the Rickard report took this into account in proposing a conversion period of fifteen years. Present management plans prepared under the Timber RAM computer model do take this into account.

146. See, for example, Rickard, *The Action Forest*; and *Report of the President's Advisory Panel*, p. 172.

147. *Report of the President's Advisory Panel*, p. 172.

148. See generally Davis, *Forest Management*, pp. 234–242.

149. See William Bentley and Dennis E. Teeguarden, "Financial Maturity: A Theoretical Review," *Forest Science*, vol. 11 (1965), p. 76. See also E. J. Mishan, *Cost–Benefit Analysis* (1971), pp. 194–197, for a simple and lucid illustration of the general concept.

150. See, for example, the Rickard report (*The Action Forest*); and the Public Land Law Review Commission, *One-Third of the Nation's Land*, p. 96. See also, *Report of the President's Advisory Panel*, p. 174 (report of consultant Carl Newport; the panel itself made no recommendation on this).

151. For the Forest Service staff review of the Rickard report, see U.S. Congress, Senate Subcommittee of the Committee on Small Business, *Hearings on Timber Management Policies*, p. 532.

152. Cf. Forest Service Manual, § 2415.21 (17–20 in.) with testimony of former Chief of the Forest Service Edward P. Cliff in ibid., pp. 255–256, implying that 18- and even 20-in. trees were too small for national forests.

153. *Report of the President's Advisory Panel*, pp. 171–172.

154. U.S. Department of Agriculture/Forest Service, *Forest Regulation Study*, pp. 43–44. This is based on a 5 percent rate of discount. At thirty years the yield of merchantable timber falls to zero. I am informed that industry has adopted a thirty-year rotation for some of its Douglas fir lands.

155. This is fully developed in Marion Clawson, "Conflicts, Strategies, and Possibilities for Consensus in Forest Land Use and Management," in Marion Clawson, ed., *Forest Policy for the Future: Conflict, Compromise, Consensus* (Baltimore: Johns Hopkins University Press for Resources for the Future, 1974), pp. 101–191. See also Marion Clawson and William Hyde, "Managing the Forests of the Coastal Pacific Northwest for Maximum Social Returns," (Resources for the Future, 1973), mimeographed.

156. See U.S. Department of Agriculture/Forest Service, *Outlook for Timber*, p. 51.

157. James and Rudolph, *Clear-cutting in the Public Forests*, Report to the Council on Environmental Quality (1971), pp. 11–12.

158. Under Clarke–McNary and subsequent amendments, such as the Cooperative Forest Management Act, matching federal funds are provided for fire prevention, distribution of seedlings, and technical assistance to private owners. See 16 U.S.C., § 568.

159. In fiscal 1971, management assistance under the Cooperative Forest Management Program—the leading program for federal forestry assistance—was rendered to over 125 thousand woodland owners and nearly 8 million acres (*Report of the President's Advisory Panel*, p. 241). That means less than 3 percent of the private, nonindustrial forest land received federal assistance.

As to the results, it seems enough to note that some 59 percent of the nation's private and nonindustrial forest area contains only 41 percent of the growing stock (only 26 percent of the softwood stock). See U.S. Department of Agriculture/Forest Service, *Outlook for Timber*, pp. 11 and 32.

160. See Charles H. Stoddard, *The Small Private Forest in the United States* (Baltimore: Johns Hopkins University Press for Resources for the Future, 1961), pp. 29–30.

161. For a summary of recently proposed cost-sharing legislation, see *Report of the President's Advisory Panel*, pp. 245–246. Another proposal which has attracted attention calls for government-subsidized leases of private lands to forest industry owners. The essential purpose is to overcome the small-size diseconomies inherent in private, nonindustry ownership by aggregating small woodlots into large management units (ibid., pp. 271–282).

162. Gedney and Henley, U.S. Department of Agriculture/Forest Service, Pacific Northwest Experimental Station, *Utilization Estimates for Western Softwoods—Trees, Logs and Residue* (1971).

163. U.S. Department of Agriculture/Forest Service, *Report of the Committee on Close Timber Utilization* (1972), p. 29. This does not include materials from cull trees, dead trees, or from species classified as nonmerchantable so the total volume of residue is considerably higher.

164. Ibid., pp. 32–39; also see Comptroller General, *Report on Actions Needed to Increase the Use of Felled Trees in Federal Timber Sale Areas* (1973), pp. 16–22.

165. See U.S. Department of Agriculture/Forest Service, *Report of the Committee on Close Timber Utilization*, pp. 40–43; see also Comptroller General, *Report*, pp. 41–42 (reply of Forest Service to main report). It is interesting to note, however, that the Forest Service has not obtained concrete data as to just how much of the felled wood currently left in the forests could be economically utilized despite evidence that a significant volume does have market value (ibid., pp. 13–14).

166. U.S. Department of Agriculture/Forest Service, *Forest Service Response to Recommendations of Forestry Deans* (1972), p. 22.

167. Estimates of Thrasher Corporation, Ukiah, California, quoted in U.S. Senate Housing and Urban Affairs Subcommittee of the Committee on Banking, Housing and Urban Affairs, *Shortages and Rising Prices of Softwood Lumber*, 93 Cong., 1 sess., 1973, p. 700.

V

OUTDOOR RECREATION

Of outdoor recreation, Aldo Leopold once wrote, "Barring love and war few enterprises are undertaken with such abandon, or by such diverse individuals, or with so paradoxical a mixture of appetite and altruism, as that group of avocations known as outdoor recreation."[1] Writing in the 1940s, Leopold was plainly dismayed by what he then saw in the exodus from the cities of motorized recreationists seeking an ever-diminishing "ration of peace, solitude, wildlife and scenery." Dismayed then, Leopold would be stunned today: more people driving faster cars, hauling bigger trailers, and pushing farther and farther into the remotest corners of the countryside. In the fifteen years between 1956 and 1970, visits to the major federal recreation lands—the national parks, forests, and wildlife refuges—more than tripled. Even Leopold, with no fondness for statistical measurements in such matters, would doubtless be impressed (and depressed) by the fact that over 188 million visitor-days were spent within the national forest lands in 1973.[2] Every indication is that the demand will continue to increase as will the problems of meeting it. But before we discuss that we need to take a closer

119

look at outdoor recreation and at the role of the federal government—more particularly that of the Forest Service.

Outdoor recreation is not easy to define: it can include an almost endless list of activities—camping, picnicking, water sports, hunting and fishing, backpacking, use of all-terrain vehicles, bird-watching, sight-seeing, and even driving for pleasure. Outdoor recreational activities, in fact, seem limited only by the participant's imagination. We could, then, say that outdoor recreation is any activity done outdoors primarily for pleasure. If such a definition perhaps seems overly broad, it is only because we customarily think of outdoor recreation in conjunction with developed recreational facilities. However, any expanse of forest or section of a stream or a lake provides recreational opportunities by its mere existence. Indeed, the heavy demand and use of these resources led to the construction of recreation facilities as much for the protection of the environment as for the convenience of the users. Therein lies much of the problem of the land manager's responsibility.

The beginning of the federal government's active involvement in outdoor recreation, like most such enterprises, is difficult to pin down to a single date, or even decade.[3] A convenient date might be 1864, when Congress ceded lands in Yosemite Valley and Mariposa Grove to California to be held "inviolate for public use, resort and recreation."[4] A more auspicious date would be 1872, when Congress created the Yellowstone Park as a "public park or pleasuring ground for the benefit and enjoyment of the people,"[5] the first such national park in the United States (and reputedly the world). Clearly this was a beginning. In 1890, two more parks, Yosemite and Sequoia, were created; by 1900, there were five. Still, it was more a recognition of need than a management policy that the creation of the national parks exemplified. Little attention was given to any kind of active management role for several decades thereafter; not until 1916 did Congress respond to that need by creating the National Park Service to administer the national parks and, thereby, to assume a leadership role in outdoor recreation.[6]

The role of the Forest Service in managing its lands for recreation emerged in response to the same use pressures which produced the Park Service.[7] From the beginning, it was recognized that the national forests were used for recreation such as hunting and fishing, although these activities were not cited in the 1897 act. Pinchot's little "Use Book" notes, ". . . quite incidentally, also the National Forests serve a good purpose as playgrounds for the people . . . and their value in this respect is well worth considering."[8] Looking back, Pinchot's casual aside seems ironic in light of the current level of playground activity. But Pinchot's was a simpler era.

In 1915, Congress first recognized recreation in the national forests by giving the service authority to lease forest land to private persons or associations for the construction of summer homes, hotels, stores, or other recreation-related facilities.[9] For nearly a decade after, private initiative and financing remained the only source of developed recreational facilities (although roads built for general access and for timber also served a recreational purpose). Not until 1923 did the Forest Service receive an appropriation for recreational facilities ($10,000), and it was earmarked only for sanitation. If that seems a modest sum when measured by the demand for forest recreational facilities then beginning to develop,[10] it was probably not more inadequate than the $46.8 million appropriated for 1975, measured against current demands (and allowing for devaluation of the dollar). But that is a matter for later comment.

While the use of the forests for recreation grew significantly in the 1920s and 1930s, it was in the post-World War II years that boom times began.[11] Increased leisure time, greater mobility, and higher personal incomes all contributed to this greater use. Unfortunately for the recreationist, minimal appropriations for their upkeep during the war, overuse, and their increasing age contributed to the serious deterioration of the CCC-constructed facilities in our national parks and forests. By 1955 the situation had become so critical that immediate positive steps were necessary. Both agencies responded to this crisis in about the same way. In 1956, the National Park Service began Mission '66—a program for developing recreational facilities over the decade to follow. The Forest Service, spurred by the competition, followed suit in 1957 with Operation Outdoors, a five-year program to provide sufficient recreational facilities to accommodate projected use in 1962.[12]

The Forest Service, however, felt a need to go beyond the limits of Operation Outdoors, and in 1959 launched the National Forest Recreation Survey. Unquestionably a major impetus for this effort was the creation in the previous year of the Outdoor Recreation Resources Review Commission whose seminal studies, completed in 1962, provided an important foundation for outdoor recreation policy in the 1960s. The Forest Service in its efforts was particularly concerned about the need for specific quantitative and qualitative data about the recreational resources of the national forests that could be utilized to meet the recreational demands expected by the year 2000. Such an ambitious program, quite expectedly, was not an unqualified success and was never formally published as a completed plan.[13] Though the survey was inadequate in scope and insufficiently sophisticated to serve as a basis for long-term planning, it nevertheless did provide a basis for immediate planning which contributed significantly to the development of recreation management in the Forest Service.

Simultaneously with its survey, the Forest Service was lobbying for congressional approval of its emergent role in outdoor recreation, particularly to protect itself from being preempted by a rapidly growing (sometimes at the expense of the Forest Service) Park Service. The Multiple-Use Sustained Yield Act of 1960 gave the Forest Service, for the first time, this statutory recognition. Functionally more important than the Multiple-Use Act, however, was the Land and Water Conservation Fund Act of 1965,[14] which, among other things, gave the Forest Service (i.e., the secretary of agriculture) authority to purchase lands for purposes of outdoor recreation.

Prior to the Land and Water Conservation Fund Act of 1965, the Forest Service had no authority to purchase lands for purely recreational purposes.[15] Section 6 of the 1965 act,[16] gave the Forest Service (and the Park Service and Bureau of Sport Fisheries and Wildlife) authority to purchase private in-holdings in national forest wilderness areas or other areas within the boundaries of the national forests where the lands are primarily valuable for recreation. Outside lands adjacent to the forests may be acquired up to 500 acres. An overall limit on acquisitions under the act specified that not more than 15 percent of the land added to the national forest system may be west of the hundredth meridian.[17] In addition to authorizing and supporting federal land acquisition for recreation, the act provides for assistance to states for acquiring and developing recreational facilities. Sixty percent of the fund is allocated to the states for this purpose.[18]

To support federal land acquisitions and state recreational developments, the act, as amended, establishes a fund comprised of appropriations and various federal receipts, sufficient to provide an annual income of at least $200 million through 1970 and $300 million thereafter through June 1989. The act also provided specific statutory authorization for charging user fees for certain recreational lands and facilities, an authorization limited by further amendments, which we shall examine.

ADMINISTRATION OF THE RECREATIONAL AREA

The original role of the forest manager in outdoor recreation could be simply defined as providing access, opportunity, and perhaps some guidance on where to camp—even how to camp, etc. Beyond that, recreationists could forage for themselves (with a modest amount of herding perhaps). To a considerable degree the Forest Service still follows this original pattern, a reflection of the fact that the dominant use of the national forests is still a dispersed one. Of the 188 million visitor-days spent on the national forests in 1973, less than 40 percent were on developed sites.[19] The remaining 60 percent of visitor-days were dispersed throughout undeveloped forest areas (including travel on roads and trails).

Apart from providing roads and trails, or undeveloped campsites, the management task for such undeveloped areas should, at least in theory, be minimal. Generally, undeveloped areas of the national forest are available for public recreation use with minimum restrictions. Regulation is confined to that which is necessary to protect the resource and to safeguard public health, safety, welfare, or convenience.[20] However, the burgeoning use of the forests, and particularly their invasion by off-road motor vehicles ranging from snowmobiles to trailbikes) in recent years has greatly increased the burden of administration—of developing new restrictions on use, patrolling, and cleanup. Increased dispersed-site use has also magnified the need for modest camping and sanitation facilities. More and more, dispersed use is coming to resemble developed-site use.

Developed sites include a wide variety of sites and facilities, such as developed campgrounds (with sanitation facilities), observation sites, outdoor sports sites (ranging from swimming and boating facilities to ski resorts). For noncommercial facilities, such as campgrounds, picnic grounds, observation sites, or visitor centers, the Forest Service plans, develops and administers the site itself.[21] The general objective has been to provide sufficient basic facilities to accommodate, without overcrowding, the average peak-season weekend use.

However, the limited amount of appropriations has dictated some strict priorities restricting this objective.[22] The highest priority is given to the care, policing, and maintenance of existing developments and supervision of occupancy and use. Next is the rehabilitation and quality improvement of worn-out facilities or lands in existing developments. Finally, funds are expended for the expansion of existing developments or construction of new sites, as needed to accommodate the demand. Within the above categories the following priority applies: (1) sanitation, safety, and fire protection improvements; (2) site protection improvements; (3) public service and convenience improvements; and (4) improvements in information dispersal.

Long-established Forest Service policy permits only recreation facilities of a character suitable to the rural environment. Urban and suburban activities, such as golf and tennis are generally disfavored while nonrecreational pursuits such as nightclubs are excluded altogether from the national forests.[23]

Actual administration of the developed sites is the responsibility of the district ranger. Primarily, the ranger is concerned with the protection of public health and safety; the prevention of site deterioration caused by fire, overuse, or misuse; the maintenance of sites and facilities for public use and enjoyment; and preservation of the forest environment so as to maintain the recreational opportunities of the area.

Use and Admission Fees

One of the most controversial aspects of recreational management is that of user charges. Because of erratic legislation by Congress the subject of fees has also been one of the most confusing aspects of management.

Before the Land and Water Conservation Act of 1965, the Forest Service charged admission fees at designated areas, such as developed campsites, and user fees for providing special services, such as boat launching facilities. (At commercial sites, operated by private concessions, prices are charged for concession services.) Statutory authority for such charges rested on the agency's general power to regulate the use and occupancy of the national forests under the Organic Act of 1897—the same basis on which its imposition of grazing fees was upheld in 1911[24]—and also on Title V of the Independent Offices Appropriations Act of 1952.[25] The 1952 act authorized that any "work . . . services, benefits, privileges, authority, use, franchise, license . . . or similar thing of value" provided by the federal agencies should be self-sustaining to the fullest extent possible. To accomplish this, all federal agencies were authorized to impose "fair and equitable" charges on the recipients of these benefits. As subsequently interpreted by a Budget Bureau directive, the charges should be designed to cover the full cost of any "special benefits to an identifiable recipient above and beyond those which accrue to the public at large."[26] Use of natural resources, including recreational facilities, were specifically recognized as being within the class of benefits for which fees could be charged.

The Forest Service and some other recreation agencies did impose some fees primarily on authority of the 1952 act (and in the case of the service, the 1897 act also); however, there was neither uniformity of fees nor coordination of fee policy among the agencies. In an attempt to provide some unity, Congress provided in the Land and Water Conservation Fund Act of 1965 for the establishment of two categories of fees, admission fees and user fees (for the use of facilities within an area for which an admission fee may or may not be charged). Subject to certain general guidelines, the president was given the authority to designate fee areas and prescribe charges.[27] The act also provided for an annual permit—subsequently dubbed the "Golden Eagle Passport"—which for seven dollars admitted the purchaser and anyone in his automobile to any federally operated outdoor area. In 1968 the disappointing contributions of the fee system led Congress to reevaluate it.

The act was amended to provide for the expiration of the fee system and the Golden Eagle Passport, effective in 1970, at which time the agencies would then revert to whatever user-fee authority they earlier held.[28] (All of them had, of course, such authority as the 1952 Appropriations Act provided, which is somewhat vague on certain aspects.) In 1970 Congress extended the program for another year with the stipulation that the secretary of the interior study and make recommendations on the entire user-fee problem. His report recommended continuation of the Golden Eagle Passport and a coordinated scheme of user fees for specialized sites and services.[29] In 1972 Congress again amended the act on the question of fees; this time it was far more restrictive in that it limited collection of admission fees to designated units of the National Park System and national recreation areas.[30]

No recreation areas of the Forest Service have been so designated. Because of the open access to these areas from major highways, it has been found impractical to attempt to restrict entry in order to collect a fee.

The 1972 amendments to the act strictly limited admission fees, but they continued the prior authorization of user fees for specialized sites, facilities, equipment, or services provided by the agencies. These fees are not restricted to areas where admission fees are charged, since they were intended to be distinct charges for *special* services.[31] However, the intended distinction between admission fees and user fees was not clear. In particular, it was not clear from the 1972 amendments just what kinds of facilities in developed campsites would suffice to justify a user fee.

In 1973 the act was further amended to "clarify" the congressional intent to limit user fees only to the most highly developed campgrounds for specialized facilities which would not necessarily be used by all visitors. It, therefore, limited campground user fees to campgrounds with certain services or facilities, including such civilized conveniences as showers and designated tent or trailer spaces. Although the amendments were not evidently intended to impose further major restrictions on user fees for national forests, such was their temporary effect: since only a bare handful of forest campgrounds provide shower facilities, as contemplated by the 1973 amendments, the Forest Service was virtually put out of the user-fee business.[32] After it was apprised of what it had unwittingly done, Congress, in 1974, restored the authority to the Forest Service (and Interior agencies) to charge fees for campgrounds having simple facilities such as tent or trailer spaces, toilet facilities, drinking water, and other modest conveniences (which accounts for about two-fifths of national forest campgrounds).[33]

Commercial Use

Since 1915 the Forest Service has permitted privately owned recreational facilities on the national forests, under special-use permits.[34] Originally most such permits were for purely private uses such as summer homes, but present policy permits such uses only where land is not suitable or needed for public use. Though the term *public use* is a broad and flexible one, most permitted recreational facilities are commercial concessions providing general services to the public, such as gas stations, restaurants, motels, stores, or special recreational services such as outdoor sport facilities.[35]

Plans and designs for public service sites are prepared through collaboration of the district ranger and the permittee. These plans, however, must meet the standards established by the regional forester. Privately financed developments are subject to various terms and conditions; the general conditions require the permittee to protect public health and safety, to furnish satisfactory public service at reasonable rates, to resolve conflicts with other uses, and to preserve the forest character of the site. District rangers inspect concession-operated sites regularly to ensure that improvements are being maintained adequately and used as authorized and that public health and safety are protected.

Winter Sports Facilities. In view of their importance, winter sports facilities warrant special mention; they will serve to illustrate some of the basic features of the permit system. Winter sports—skiing in particular—have become one of the most prominent recreational uses of the national forests. Since 1936 when the first ski runs were constructed at Sun Valley, Idaho, skiing has mushroomed on the national forests. In 1973 some 218 ski areas were located wholly or partially on the national forests, accommodating nearly 8.5 million visitor-days of use.[36] Needless to say, winter sports are not only popular, they are big business. It is estimated, for example, that in the 1963–64 winter season, expenditures by skiers in the twelve western states alone (including Alaska) exceeded $115 million.[37] As a consequence of this the Forest Service, particularly in western states, has been under heavy economic pressure to develop winter sports sites—a pressure not without opposition by environmentalist groups, who view this new invasion of recreationists with understandable alarm.

As with most other commercial recreation facilities, the Forest Service relies primarily on private initiative in planning winter sports sites, although, of course, all such plans are subject to Forest Service approval. The principal initiative may come from local civic or business groups (interested in the contribution which a ski area would make to a local economy), from a local ski group, from a prospective permittee or from a combination of all. Approval of the site for development as a winter sports site is the responsibility of the regional forester. Essentially, approval requires a showing of suitability of the area and economic feasibility of the proposed operation. The former is mainly a determination of snow conditions, climate, character of the ski area, and general environmental acceptability; the latter involves estimates of probable demand and availability of other ski areas.

Once the suitability and feasibility of a development is determined, a special use permit can be issued to a qualified applicant.[38] Where circumstances allow, the policy here, as for other major commercial concessions,[39] is to seek multiple, competitive applications by issuing a prospectus containing a preliminary development plan, an outline of Forest Service preferences and conditions for development. Applicants then respond with their proposals: how the site would be developed, the services offered, and the amount they are willing to pay above the basic minimum fee. The competitive bids are then reviewed (generally by the regional forester) and the best overall proposal (considering the fee as only one of the variables) is selected.[40]

There are many important winter sports sites where it is not possible to obtain competitive applications. Where all of the site to be developed is located on government-owned land—as in most of the sites on the West Coast—the Forest Service has a free hand in seeking competitive applications; however, most of the important sites in the Intermountain West have been developed around private lands within the forest boundaries. Typically, these lands provide the base for lodging and other resort facilities, with the surrounding government land providing the area for the ski run, which is subject to a permit. In this case, the Forest Service's ownership of the latter gives it control over the planning and the operation of the entire site, but obviously not a choice of permittees.

After the applicant is approved, a permit is issued, subject to the approval of a final site-development plan prior to actual construction. There are two types of special-use permits, annual and term; both may be used in winter sports sites if the entire development is on government land.

Term permits may be issued for a period not exceeding thirty years, for an area not exceeding 80 acres,[41] in cases where development requires substantial capital outlays not amortizable within a short period, and when the business requires stability of tenure. In winter sports sites these permits are issued for the area used by the lodge and other related facilities and for uphill-lift equipment. Term permits may be revoked for reasons of public interest, or for failure on the part of the holder to pay fees or otherwise comply with permit requirements (or for "violation of law or regulation"). However, in the case of terminations in the public interest, the government is obligated to pay for the permittee's improvements. Notice of reasons, and the opportunity for a hearing in accordance with the service's appeal procedures, are prescribed.[42]

Annual permits are revocable on the same grounds as term permits or at the discretion of the service.[43] The annual permit is automatically renewed each year so long as the fee is paid (except in a few cases where free permits are issued) until it expires by its own terms or is otherwise terminated. Annual permits are issued for the ski trails within winter sports areas.

For most special-use permits, a fee is charged; in some cases the fee is nominal, but in most it is intended to be "commensurate" with the value of the use. Formerly, the fee was set as a flat percentage of sales; this has now been changed for all major concessions (with revenues above a specified minimum) including winter sports sites, by the so-called graduated *rate-fee system*.[44] The system operates by applying a selected rate from an established schedule of graduated rates to the concessioner's gross sales. The rate to be used is determined by the proportional relationship of the concessioner's sales to his gross fixed assets. As sales increase in relation to assets, a higher rate from the schedule of graduated rates is applied to the higher increment of sales, and the total fee increases. Conversely, if sales decrease in relation to assets or if assets increase in relation to sales, lower rates apply to larger portions of sales, and the total fee lowers. This means that the permittee and the government share in both increases and decreases in business.

When permits are awarded through competitive bidding, rival bidders are given the opportunity in their proposals to specify what surcharge, if any, they are willing to pay in addition to the fee provided in the established fee schedule. This surcharge, expressed as a percentage, will apply for a specified number of years, not exceeding ten, after sales are first generated, regardless of subsequent changes in ownership. In cases where nearby concessions are paying a surcharge or the ownership of key private land amounts to an unfair competitive advantage, a higher fee will be negotiated in the form of an equitable surcharge.

The rationale behind the graduated rate-fee system is to encourage investment, by basing the fee upon the ratio of sales to gross, fixed assets. Thus, during the period between the investment and the compensatory gain in sales, the permittee has a lower total fee obligation.

Management Planning

The Forest Plan.   In contrast to timber management with its sharply defined routine, recreational planning has been typically rather loose and amorphous.[45] In part this reflects the somewhat later development of recreation as a *major* function of forest management. It was not until the 1960s that functional recreation plans were developed at the forest level, and even then they tended to be mainly collections of information rather than particularized plans with concrete management objectives. Moreover, the rather vague character of recreational planning reflects the somewhat ill-defined role of the recreation manager. The timber manager has a set of clearly defined objectives and prescribed sequentially ordered steps by which they are accomplished. For the recreation manager, no such clarity or single-mindedness of purpose (or of ways to accomplish it) aids his task. At least this is how it appears to an outsider.

As recreation management has matured, so has the planning process in order to accomodate the demand for recreational facilities of every kind. Traditionally, the national forest recreation-management plan and the district multiple-use plans were the primary bases of recreational planning. The national forest recreation plans were inspired by the National Forest Recreation Survey, but were intended as a more detailed supplement of a regional recreation plan. When the regions failed to produce such a plan, the forest supervisor and the district rangers were left with nearly total responsibility for recreational planning.[46] The national forest plans establish objectives and policies for the management of the recreation resource in the national forest, showing how the coordination requirements and management decisions of district multiple-use plans are to be implemented; and they describe functional recreation-management problem areas requiring more specific planning. Management prescriptions for various areas follow the Forest Service classification scheme, which defines six classes of recreational areas in terms of intensity of use, each class calling for a distinct management emphasis appropriate to the characteristic type of use.[47]

The Composite Plan. For many recreational developments, a forest recreation plan has proved to be neither practical nor desirable. In recent years emphasis has shifted to what is described as a recreation "composite" plan, which appears to have largely supplanted the forest plan. The composite plan, the primary responsibility of the forest supervisor (subject to the regional forester's approval), is similar to a forest plan except that it is designed for a specific geographic area rather than an administrative one. The composite area is a complex of recreational development sites and dispersed recreation areas (existing or potential) with sufficiently strong interrelationships to be considered together rather than separately. The planning area generally includes all recreation areas which "compete" for use by visitors within the forest. The areas frequently cross districts; they may even cross forest boundaries, although normally the composite area would be smaller than, and contained within, a particular forest.[48]

Composite plans are also used for specially designated areas, for example, national recreation areas (NRAs) and wilderness areas. Although administration of wilderness areas is treated by the service as a recreational function, it is that only in part; in fact, it seems more appropriate to regard it as a separate resource function insofar as preservation, not use, is the paramount objective. NRAs by contrast are oriented toward a more *active* recreational use.

First proposed, in 1973, by the President's Recreation Advisory Council to provide special, additional recreational opportunities and facilities,[49] NRAs are established specifically by a congressional act setting forth the general uses permitted. Although these areas are managed primarily for their recreational potential, other uses are permitted, if they are compatible with recreation use. (They thus differ, at least in degree, from national parks.[50])

The Effect of Multiple-Use Plans. The impact of the new land use planning system on the existing schemes is yet unknown. The basic design of the new system would seem to be compatible with most current, up-to-date recreation plans. The composite plans look essentially in the same direction as do the new land use plans, insofar as both are oriented toward geographic rather than administrative planning areas. But, of course, the composite plan is a recreation plan, not an integrated land use plan. Like all management plans, the recreation plan incorporates the usual multiple-use constraints, in accordance with multiple-use guides and plans. But the new planning concept emphasizes the need for fully integrated multiple-use planning. Carried out logically as designed, this would imply that the recreation plans would become subordinate to the basic land use plan; of course, in cases where recreation is a dominant use (as in NRAs), presumably the recreation composite plan will continue to be the primary management plan.

However the formal accommodations are drawn between functional recreation plans and the new land use plans, the new planning system seems certain to change the planning process in one respect, by increasing public participation. Public involvement in planning, here as elsewhere in public land management, has been very limited—except perhaps for especially interested groups. In some instances, this reluctance to seek broad participation in *major* plans has brought the agency more grief than it has saved it trouble. But this seems to be changing substantially, particularly in cases involving major planning development where a full environmental impact analysis is made under the National Environmental Policy Act (NEPA) of 1969.

THE FOREST AS PLAYGROUND—
PROBLEMS AND CONTROVERSIES

The rush of recreationists to the forests has already been noted, as has the fact that the rushing is increasing. It is estimated that visitor-days on the national forests will increase from 172.6 million in 1970 to 250.6 million by 1980, a growth rate considerably greater than that projected for the population as a whole.[51] Some comfort may be taken in the fact that growth in the demand for outdoor recreation must eventually level off, becoming proportional to population. But with a continued rise in population, that is very small comfort. Even a zero population growth would be small solace for the forest-recreation planner who is given the task of satisfying this rising demand created, not by increased population alone, but also by increased affluence and leisure. Obviously, he must plan for more intensive recreational land use, as well as more extensive land use, a task fraught with peril.

Mineral King

One such peril is the certain fight with conservationists opposed to the environmental impairment attendant on such use. The celebrated, and seemingly endless, Mineral King controversy is illustrative. Though not unique (except perhaps in the magnitude and notoriety of the battle), Mineral King has become an important symbol of the contest over intensive recreational development of public lands. For this reason, it is worthwhile to consider this case in some detail before discussing the more general issues relating to the demand and supply of outdoor recreation facilities.

Mineral King is a small valley, about 2 miles long and a quarter of a mile wide, located in the High Sierras of south-central California, which consists of eight alpine basins surrounded by mountains up to 12,400 ft. above sea level.[52] The valley is bordered on three sides by the Sequoia National Park. When the park was established in 1890, the valley was excluded because of its mineral deposits and still-remnant developments from an earlier era of mining activity (in the 1870s and 1880s). Instead, the valley, together with surrounding lands, became the Sequoia National Forest. In 1926, the valley was declared a game refuge in which hunting and trapping of birds or game was prohibited except under regulations of the secretary of agriculture.[53] Following this, a plea was made by the secretary and the state of California for cooperative management.

Though the valley is scarcely a wilderness, it is still relatively undisturbed. Located nearly equidistant from Los Angeles (228 miles) and San Francisco (271 miles), the valley currently attracts some visitors, including a few skiers.[54] However, because its only access road is seasonal, winter use of the valley is very limited. But the valley's potential for winter sports development could not long go unnoticed. In response to inquiries, a forester, sent into Mineral King in 1945, reported the area would be desirable as both a summer and/or winter recreation area.

Though the Forest Service initially decided not to develop the valley, interest continued, and, in 1949, the service issued a prospectus inviting proposals from private developers. None were received. The cost of building a 25-mile, all-weather road through the mountains was too great for a private developer, and the state would not bear the cost. In 1953 the proposed development of the valley was considered in a public hearing held in Visalia, some 55 miles east of the valley. Support for the development was expressed by a wide range of groups and individuals, including local county officials and the superintendent of Sequoia National Park. Even the Sierra Club did not object, although its acquiescence merely reflected its concern that, if Mineral King were not developed, another area of greater wilderness value, the San Gorgionio area, would be. When the latter was safely locked into the wilderness system in 1964, the Sierra Club changed its stance on Mineral King.[55]

Thereafter, there was no action by the service on proposals for development until February 1965, when the Forest Service published a second prospectus, inviting interested parties to submit proposals for the development of Mineral King. The Forest Service received six bids, four of which met all the minimum qualifications. One of them was that of Walt Disney Productions. In June 1965, the Sierra Club requested a public hearing on the proposed development before any proposals were accepted. Its request was denied. The regional forester explained that recreational development was a major feature of the multiple-use plan for the Sequoia National Forest, that there was a public demand for additional ski areas in Southern California, that Mineral King could supply such a need, and that a public hearing at that stage would be inconsistent with the long-range plans and the issuance of the prospectus.[56]

When the state of California, in July 1965, approved the building of a road into Mineral King as part of its state highway system, the economic obstacle to development was cleared. In December 1965, the Forest Service accepted the proposal of Walt Disney Productions for a $35 million development. The development called for construction of an alpine-type village, with lodges, restaurants, and other commercial services, as well as extensive skiing facilities. In October 1966, a preliminary permit for planning was issued to Disney for a term of three years in order to make the necessary studies and prepare a master plan.

However, the project was contingent on a proper access road, and this remained a matter of uncertainty, for although the state of California had agreed to build the road, the only access was through the Sequoia National Park and its use required the approval of the Park Service and the secretary of the interior. This was opposed by the secretary, not only because of the possible impact of an all-season road through the national park, but also because of the development of Mineral King itself. After two years the opposition ended as a consequence of pressure from the secretary of agriculture and the Bureau of the Budget.[57] In December 1967, the secretary of the interior approved the road.[58]

In January 1969, the Forest Service accepted Disney's master plan for the development of Mineral King. In June 1969, before a thirty-year term permit was issued to Disney, the Sierra Club filed suit in a federal district court in San Francisco seeking preliminary and permanent injunctions to restrain all action toward the implementation of the development, on the grounds that Forest Service approval and issuance of a term permit for construction and operation of the resort were in violation of Mineral King's status as a game refuge and in excess of the Forest Service's statutory authority to grant term permits; it also sought an injunction against the secretary of the interior's approval of an access road and his approval of a power transmission line across the Sequoia National Park.

The Sierra Club obtained a temporary injunction in the district court, only to be reversed by the court of appeals, which held that the plaintiffs lacked standing and had not, in any event, made out a sufficient case for *preliminary* relief.[59] The Supreme Court affirmed the court of appeals on the standing issue without reaching the merits of the case.[60] The Supreme Court's ruling did not terminate the case. Subsequently, the Sierra Club amended its complaint, alleging sufficient injury to local club members to conform (apparently) to the Supreme Court's standards, and also adding a further claim under the NEPA.[61] As this is written, the case is still pending.

Of the several legal issues in the case, the question of standing has attracted the most attention. The legal arcana involved in the development of private parties' standing to sue government[62] need not detain us long, for the holding of the Court is quite simple. Earlier decisions applicable to cases of this kind established a twofold test of standing: the parties must show an "injury in fact" and an injury to an interest "arguably within the zone of interests to be protected" by the statutes which the agencies were alleged to violate.[63]

The Supreme Court in Mineral King held that the Sierra Club, simply in its capacity as a general defender of the environment, had shown no injury in fact. Justices Douglas and Blackmun, dissenting, would have granted standing because of the special need to permit the litigation of environmental issues. For Justice Douglas, the simple solution was merely to allow such issues to be litigated:

> in the name of the inanimate object about to be despoiled, defaced or invaded by roads and bulldozers and where injury is the subject of public outrage. . . . Then there will be assurances that all of the forms of life which it represents will stand before the court—the pileated woodpecker as well as the coyote and bear, the lemmings as well as the trout in the streams. Those inarticulate members of the ecological group cannot speak. But those people who have so frequented the place as to know its values and wonders will be able to speak for the entire ecological community.[64]

Despite a certain poetic appeal the concern that prompted it seems much exaggerated. Notwithstanding the anguish it caused to conservationist groups, the majority's opinion does not seem to be a serious barrier to their easy access to the courts on virtually any controversy they feel is worth contesting. The Court did *not* hold—as some have implied—that environmental injury, including mere aesthetic impairment, could not constitute such injury. It held merely that parties must allege some particular impact on *them*. The Sierra Club had not done so; it had not alleged, for example, that any of its members ever used Mineral King. The requirement is hardly a very stringent one, as the Sierra Club demonstrated shortly after the Court's opinion by alleging such injury. Just how easily the criterion is satisified was more recently underscored by the Supreme Court itself in a case strongly suggesting that the Mineral King decision was little more than a "sport."[65]

Several substantive legal issues are presented by the case but we can forego an examination of them. None of them go to the heart of two important policy issues which are raised by the size and character of the proposed development, which in turn raise larger questions concerning the appropriate development of national forests for recreational use.

The size of the original planned investment of $35 million does not make Mineral King uniquely large, even for a small area.[66] But the dimensions of the original planned development indicate that the valley was planned for very intensive use. Disney's plan projected nearly a million annual visitors by 1978 (60 percent in the summer). They would have been accommodated with the following facilities: a village with chapel, ice-skating rink, convenience and specialty shops, conference center, theater, general store, post office, hospital, ten restaurants (total seating capacity of over 2,000), lodging accommodations for over 3,000 persons, parking facilities (for some 3,600 cars) twenty ski lifts and other recreational facilities for skating, swimming, and "snow play."[67]

In the face of protracted litigation, Disney scaled down its original plans.[68] The highway and overhead transmission line have been abandoned in favor of a cog railway with a buried line. The new plan would cost between $18–20 million, rather than $35 million. Estimated peak use has been decreased from 14,000 per day to 8,000. The number of ski lifts has been cut from twenty to ten. But the Sierra Club and others believe that in the words of Macbeth, they have "scotched the snake, not killed it." They continue to oppose any development of Mineral King. Those in need of this kind of recreation can, critics say, go elsewhere for their pleasure.

There is not a little snobbery involved in *some* of the opposition to intensive recreation. Witness this comment by one critic explaining the difference in attitudes between "recreationists" and "protectionists": "One seeks immediate gratification for himself; he wolfs down pleasures and seeks out more. He is hedonist, recreationist. The other defers his gratifications, saving them for later generations. He is puritan, protectionist."[69]

The controversy has aspects of a modern morality play, in which the Forest Service, along with Disney, is not with the virtuous. Justice Douglas, in his dissent in the Supreme Court's decision in Mineral King, accused the Forest Service of being "captured by special interests."[70] Another critic charged the Forest Service with "bureaucratic empire building," and contrasted its behavior to the conscientious Park Service, which reportedly opposed the development of Mineral King.[71] To the Forest Service this last criticism must seem a cruel irony given the fact it is the Park Service that has the history of empire building—generally at the expense of the Forest Service! And although there is no reason to suspect the good-faith motive of Interior or of the Park Service, it bears notice that the likely outcome of a prolonged contest over Mineral King will see the valley included within the national park, and it is the Park Service "empire" that will be the greater. Perhaps inclusion in the park, as has been proposed, would be the best resolution of the controversy.[72] But that decision ought not to be forced by political machinations. And it ought not to be made simply on the strength of righteous pronunciations as to which of the two agencies, the Forest Service or the Park Service, is more the "captive" of "special interests."

However, in retrospect, the Forest Service decision on Mineral King seems to be unwise. The size of development is too grand for a small valley. And the character of some of the development is at odds with the spirit, if not the letter of the agency's policy of permitting only a rustic-type of recreation compatible with the rural character of the national forests. Granted the alpine village will be well designed to fit the surroundings, suitability should be more than a matter of form. It is a matter of proportion and character as well. A movie theater (planned for the village) designed as a log cabin is quaint perhaps but not rustic.

What sets Mineral King apart is both the valley itself and the symbol it has come to represent. If the Forest Service were unwilling to respond to the first as a matter of principle, it should have responded to the second as a matter of pragmatism. As with Hetch Hetchy sixty years ago,[73] Mineral King may have more importance as a banner for rallying opposition to future development than it has as a present controversy. Even if the Forest Service prevails in court (by no means a sure thing), the "victory" will be a profitless one indeed if it fosters increased public animosity and opposition. Some such opposition is no doubt a good thing for the public, and, in the long run for the Forest Service itself. But to the extent it generates further emotional and ideological struggle, no one will be well served. It need not be supposed that a reversal of its position would cause the Sierra Club to embrace the service as a new-found friend in order to suppose that it might help to arrest the deterioration of the Forest Service's general public image in this environmentally self-conscious age.

However, such a reversal here would have to be accompanied by suitable admonitions that the case is a unique one, and that retrenchment on this issue does not mean retrenchment on recreational developments generally. The fact remains that a growing population demands outdoor recreation in a degree and of a kind not satisfied by opening up a few backpacking trails. One visitor to Mineral King wrote of the experience:

> I hiked its trails, drank from its clear streams, watched its mountains change shape and color as the sun passed overhead. I did not encounter a single other human being, happily, the entire day. . . . I do not remember a day since then, quite as well spent. And I wonder now how my experience in the Valley will contrast with that of the thousands of visitors who will come to the Disney development. There is something to be said for leaving a place like Mineral King free from the works of men. But it is difficult gospel to preach. It almost has to be experienced. . . . [74]

For such an experience, a Mineral King must perhaps be preserved. But it is indeed a difficult doctrine to preach, or at least preach widely—for reasons quite different than those suggested by the above enthusiast. What do we do with the thousands of visitors to come? Or the millions to follow them, not to Mineral King perhaps but elsewhere? Granted the problem of resource use should not be solved simply by a nose count (as preservationists are a little too fond of telling us), neither can it be solved by counting trees or pileated woodpeckers. Plainly, a more refined calculus is necessary.

Meeting the Demand for Recreation

The dramatic character of the controversy over Mineral King has perhaps obscured the larger problem with which it was introduced. Whatever the eventual outcome, the disposition of this case will only faintly affect the greater problem of satisfying the huge and growing demand for outdoor recreational activity on the national forests. Even the precedential effect will likely have slight impact on this problem.

Suppose Disney is kept out of Mineral King, the broadest conceivable ruling a judge could render in the case, on the basic question of leasing authority, would affect only the winter sports sites on national forests, and not all of them. Even then it would affect them for only such time as Congress required to supply the authority needed (which they would very likely soon do). Such a decision might shift *some* of the pressures of winter sports use to other public or private lands, but it would have a very small impact on the overall recreation demands of summer campers and winter snowmobilers.

Suppose, on the other hand, Disney were given carte blanche, and the Forest Service, in a spirit of gay abandon, permitted Mineral King to become (as some have already labeled it) a "Disneyland in the mountains." That might help ease some of the local strains, but, again, it seems unlikely to do much to solve the problems of the supervisor of, say, the Monongahela National Forest in West Virginia. He must still prepare for a steady increase in campers, boaters, fishermen, hunters, and the like, who are unlikely to be much diverted from this use by Disney's blandishments in California.[75]

All of this is not to discredit the Mineral King controversy as trivial, either in its own right or as a dramatization of the conflict in land use and land use values. The point is that the larger problem of satisfying or controlling the demand for recreational resources is unlikely to be very far resolved by judicial decree, or even a hundred such decrees. Some particularly objectionable uses can perhaps be stopped. Some areas can be preserved entirely, and it is well they should be—to a point.

But what of the hordes of picnickers or campers pursuing a day's bucolic pleasure in the woods? Ultimately one may suppose the problem generates its own corrective mechanism. Since congestion impairs the special quality of the outdoor recreational experience, eventually it should reach the point where people turn elsewhere for their pleasure. Unfortunately, all indications are that congestion must be almost unbearably great before that phenomenon occurs. Yosemite is sad testament to that.[76] Many recreationists already use the national parks and national forests much as they do their city parks and playgrounds.[77] Too, the average recreationist is nearly as gregarious on vacation as he is at home; at least he is responsive to many of the same popular attractions for which people congregate. Even in the most open spaces, people, like turkeys, will flock together until they have all but smothered themselves. By the time the limits of congestion are reached, it is too late; the environment—at least all that made it specially valuable—has been destroyed. For those seeking some special experience in the outdoors beyond that obtainable in the city park, the main point of outdoor recreation has been lost.

Expansion of Facilities. Therefore, if the recreationists will not or cannot control their use, the land manager must do something. No one doubts this. What that something should be is another matter. The most popular solution is to expand the supply of recreational land and facilities. Such was the judgment underlying the Land and Water Conservation Fund Act of 1965. The results of this program have been significant. From 1965–72, over a million acres of federal recreational land have been acquired by the three federal agencies supported by the fund; the Forest Service share has been nearly 680 thousand acres.[78]

No doubt such additions to recreational land help, but more land is not in itself a solution to the problem. Granted, addition of new land theoretically should permit some of the increase in demand to be diverted to new areas, relieving some of the pressure on present lands; but that hardly takes care of the problem. First, there remains the tendency of people to congregate, particularly in well-known, popular areas. They will not necessarily disperse simply because there is an opportunity to do so. Second, dispersal of use is not a total solution in any event. Indeed, in some respects dispersed use, by its very nature, complicates the problem of administration, cleanup, and environmental protection. Not only is enforcement made more difficult, but there are probably diseconomies of scale in the provision of certain facilities, such as sanitation services.[79] Thus, the addition of new lands does not eliminate the need for relatively intensive site development, nor does it modify the need for increased maintenance and the development of new facilities.

Increase in Appropriations. To accomplish these things the Forest Service must depend on annual appropriations. The Land and Water Conservation Fund is neither available for maintenance of existing facilities nor for development of new ones. Appropriations have not been especially generous. Although recreation management has the second largest appropriation within the service, in relationship to what has been sought by the agency it is a poor contender indeed.[80]

Whether appropriations for timber and recreation management fairly accord with their respective contributions to the gross national product (GNP), I leave to others to determine. It would not be an easy calculation, and, in the end, it would not answer the question of how much more should be spent and how the money should be raised. In any event, it is very unlikely that the Office of Management and Budget or the Congress will be moved by exhortations alone to increase appropriations dramatically; some deeper incentive is needed. Here we come to the core of the problem. Whatever their respective contributions to the GNP, one very notable difference between timber and recreation is that the former produces substantial revenues to the federal government while the latter contributes relatively little.[81]

User Fees. In contrast to timber, outdoor recreation has generally been furnished by the federal government free or at modest charges well below the cost of providing the recreational opportunity and use. One consequence of this is that there is diminished incentive to invest in new or expanded recreational facilities. In the absence of significant cost recovery from the users, the cost of increased investment must be borne by the general taxpayers—many of whom do not use the recreational facilities or opportunities which they are asked to support. Obviously this makes such investment relatively unattractive compared with other public spending purposes, which either return substantial sums to the treasury or at least have widespread popular taxpayer support.

More important than the disincentive to invest in additional supply of recreational land or facilities is the fact that not charging, or charging prices below cost, for recreation use places no effective constraint upon the demand for recreational land and facilities.

In light of these rather obvious consequences and the increasing difficulty of keeping pace with public demand for outdoor recreation, the wisdom of continuing to provide public recreational opportunities and facilities free or at minimal costs must be questioned. Yet Congress, far from responding to the problem by authorizing a more effective fee system, has moved in the opposite direction by restricting the authority of the Forest Service (along with other federal recreation agencies) to charge only for a limited type or special facility or service. The course of legislative restrictions imposed by the 1972 and 1973 amendments to the Land and Water Conservation Fund Act was outlined earlier. As noted, these restrictions were eased somewhat in 1974 to correct an inadvertent elimination of virtually all forest campsite fees. However, the law still reflects a congressional attitude that is basically hostile to individual fee charges. In particular, Congress reflects the view that user fees are an inappropriate tool for constraining demand for, or allocating the use of, the increasingly scarce recreational resources of the federal lands.[82] Not only has this encouraged a misallocation of federal land use, it has also undoubtedly produced a more general misallocation of use among federal, state, local, and private facilities for which higher charges are made.[83]

The motivations behind the restrictions on user fees are varied and confused. The 1972 amendments appear in part to have been motivated by a desire to establish some form of uniform charge for federal lands—a desire which could only be realized by reducing all fees to a least common denominator, a minimum fee. However, as the 1973 amendments indicate, Congress was not merely interested in uniformity, but also in establishing a clear policy of confining fees to special uses while providing general recreational use and opportunity without cost.

Recreational Facilities as Public Goods. The word "free" will no doubt attract the scorn of economist critics who will know that, even in the woods, lunch is not free. However, scorn is probably too harsh a reaction, for the basic idea does reflect a notion about recreation as a "public good" that claims intellectual respectability. We need not pause long to consider the theory of public goods[84]; a few comments will suffice to indicate its general thrust and the fact that none of the arguments in support of it warrant the conclusion that the public good must inevitably be a zero-priced good. The most restrictive concept of public goods is the so-called collective consumption good, consumed "collectively" by the public at large and one which cannot be withheld from individuals unwilling to pay.[85] If one applies the concept rigorously, there are few goods which qualify. Other than national defense, it is difficult to think of goods the consumption of which is inherently indivisible and which cannot be withheld from "free riders." The fact that most cases of actual governmental expenditure do not fully meet the criteria suggests an apparent artificiality of this theory.[86] Certainly it is doubtful that outdoor recreation qualifies as such a good. It is true users cannot be excluded from many public lands where multiple access exists. The Forest Service has made this point as a reason for not charging extrance fees in many areas.[87] The short answer to this is that it has nothing to do with the public goods theory; if it is uneconomic to impose a charge for particular areas, it should not be done, but that is hardly a reason for precluding user fees on principle.

The limited scope of the collective consumption good has led some economists to develop a broader category of public goods. These are "merit goods," goods provided by the private market, but not in the amount which society, through the political process, deems appropriate.[88] Whether this concept is anything more than a description of those goods that are, in fact, provided by collective choice may be debated. Certainly it seems to be an elastic concept. However, even accepting it as a normative basis for public choice, what exactly is the public "merit" in outdoor recreation calling for public supply beyond that which individuals would be willing to buy?

First of all, it should be evident that the mere fact that outdoor recreation is widely enjoyed by the public does not, *ipso facto,* make it a public good—no more than, say, ice cream or automobiles. Second, it is not clear that recreation confers any distinctive public benefit beyond the aggregate benefit to each individual. No doubt the happy, healthy citizen is an asset to the community. But the notion that outdoor recreation, particularly of the kind we are here considering, contributes distinctively to this condition seems most dubious. From this point of view I see no reason to believe the provision of free campgrounds will contribute to the health of the body politic any more than providing free golf.[89]

There may be some general public benefits in recreation-related conservation or preservationist policies, which by their nature are not well measured by market choice. But this is another matter altogether. Such a public benefit would not favor promoting mass outdoor recreation. On the contrary, it would clearly favor precisely the opposite policy, for mass outdoor recreation is a threat to the natural environment—which is the concern of such special public choice. Providing (even promoting) free use of natural lands thus ultimately proves to be destructive of the merit of outdoor recreation. Aldo Leopold believed outdoor experiences have special social value and that "a man may not care for golf and still be human, but the man who does not like to see, hunt, photograph, or otherwise outwit birds or animals is hardly normal."[90] However, as he wisely observed, the value is quick to disappear when it becomes the object of public promotion:

> [L]et me tell of a "wild" river bluff which until 1935 harbored a falcon's eyrie. Many visitors walked a quarter mile to the river bank to picnic and to watch the falcons. Comes now some alphabetical builder of "country parks" and dynamites a road to the river, all in the name of "recreational planning." The excuse is that the public formerly had no right of access, now it has such a right. Access to what? Not access to the falcons, for they are gone.[91]

The arguments I made above, if faithfully pursued, might suggest that not only is there no basis for the public provision of *free* outdoor recreation, but there is no basis for public provision of this resource at all. That does not follow. There are other, sound reasons justifying public involvement (investment) in outdoor recreation. The most convincing is also the simplest: the public already has an investment in the basic recreation resource by virtue of its ownership of the land. So long as public ownership is retained, public involvement in recreation seems inevitable.[92] But, again, this justification for governmental investment provides no rationale for giving the fruit of the investment away free—or at nominal prices. The government does not, after all, give away its timber, nor its forage. Even its wildlife is not given away free, although under the present (questionable) scheme it is the states which impose the user fees on hunting and fishing.[93]

However, even if there were *some* undifferentiated public benefit from outdoor recreation beyond that measured by the aggregation of individual users, it would not support a policy of providing it at zero or minimal cost. At the very most it would support provision at a price somewhere short of recovery of the full cost of the resource, the "deficit" reflecting the general "social" benefit.[94] I have weaseled on defining the appropriate "cost" here, as between full cost and marginal cost. Theoretically, the distinction could be substantial, but as a practical matter it is not likely to be of much importance, because it is fairly clear we are nowhere near the point of charging the full costs of recreation use. At present the fees generated do not even cover the marginal cost of maintaining recreational facilities.

We come then to the ultimate rationale for free goods: equity, as some call it; distribution of wealth, as others prefer. The free provision of goods can often be explained not as an allocation policy but as one of income distribution. In outdoor recreation one encounters this notion in the form of statements that user fees are inappropriate because they "discriminate" against the poor. No doubt they do; they have that in common with all prices. But that is not a compelling reason to provide free public recreation facilities and opportunities. Although this is hardly the occasion to explore the general problems of wealth distribution, several comments can dispose of redistribution as a rationale for free provision of outdoor recreation.

At the outset I described the general objection to distribution of goods in kind as inappropriate paternalism. Redistribution of income in cash transfers would be "more efficient," that is, more in accord with market-directed allocation of resources, and would give recipients freer choice of goods.[95] There are, however, countervailing considerations of practical expediency and of principle. One reason for the widespread reliance on redistribution through provision of free goods is that alternative forms of income redistribution (e.g., taxation) are very inadequate. A second reason is that public policy, or at least public sentiment, does not unequivocally support either private choice or market allocations.[96] Still, acknowledging the legitimacy of a policy of providing some goods, say, public housing, does not establish a rationale for providing outdoor recreation. In the former case, the effect (or at least the design) is to shift a form of wealth to the poor; but what evidence is there this is achieved in the latter case? To all appearances the effect of providing free (or minimally priced) outdoor recreational opportunity on the federal lands is to shift wealth from a majority of the public to a minority who engage in outdoor recreation, and from relatively low-income groups to the well-to-do.[97] Even the most casual observation should show the regressive effect of free provision of outdoor recreational facilities. If the average picnicker, camper, hiker, and sportsman is representative of America's needy, we need to rethink our "war on poverty." Yet it is undeniable that, insofar as this outdoorsman pays less for outdoor recreation than its cost, he is receiving a subsidy from the general taxpayer (many of whom never use the federal lands as playgrounds). To talk about helping the needy by not charging even a moderate fee for the use of the recreation resource thus becomes a cruel hoax on the *real* poor who cannot afford the travel or other expenses of using the resource in any case.

Thus, far from an "equity" favoring zero or minimal pricing, the reverse would seem more nearly true. However, it must be emphasized that equity is not the core concern in any event. It is not conceivable that establishing high user fees for those federal recreational facilities now provided free will have any meaningful impact on low-, high-, or middle-income persons. What is conceivable is that user fees will have an impact on the use of the recreation resource itself.

The nature and degree of this effect is difficult to estimate in the abstract. In terms of regulating total recreational demand, it might be intuited that user fees for individual areas would not significantly constrain use because they are such a small part of the total cost of engaging in recreational activity. Thus, a New Yorker planning a trip to Mineral King Valley (after reading so much about it in *The New York Times*) is unlikely to be affected much by the addition of a user charge of a few dollars to a total trip cost of several hundred. However, both the example and the general assumption it supposedly illustrates are misleading.

Recreational use and its demand seldom consist of a single, simple, indivisible activity. It is more commonly a composite of many distinct and severable activities, each of which may be affected by considerations not affecting other parts of the whole.[98] In economic terms, the aggregate demand can be affected at the margin, with each individual component of the total activity being viewed as marginal in this respect. Thus, our New Yorker may not be deterred from visiting Mineral King, but if faced with a daily user charge, he may decide to spend only five days there instead of seven. Or it may not deter his visit to Mineral King, but it might well affect other parts of his trip out and back. Faced with a charge to camp in the Wasatch National Forest en route, he might forego that pleasure. Among other things, he might very well decide to stay at a private campground.

The latter possibility is a particularly important one to emphasize.[99] One of the most serious consequences of the lack of an adequate user-fee system for national forest lands—or federal lands generally—is that they misguide resource use between public and private recreational facilities. It is not, as I have already insisted, that the former is free and the other is not. The public facilities are not free, they are simply not fully priced to the user, whereas the private facilities are—and must be so—in the absence of a taxing power to recoup the costs from other pockets.

No attempt has been made, so far as I am aware, to measure the magnitude of this misallocation, but there is good reason to suppose it is substantial. It should be a matter of very great concern, not merely from some interest in achieving efficiency in the economy, but because the effect of this misallocation is to put an *unnecessary* additional burden on already overburdened federal lands. No doubt it is true and many agree that private campgrounds are an inadequate substitute for national forest campgrounds. If so, presumably campers will be willing to pay *at least* the same amount to use the latter as the former. But I think it cannot be seriously supposed everyone would so conclude (even if such agreement were possible the federal government would still have accomplished another important objective in internalizing at least a part of the use costs to those who enjoy their benefits).

User fees, properly designed, could also be an effective tool for reallocating demand among national forest areas, relieving congestion in popular areas. This would, of course, require variable fees. Unfortunately, this is something the Forest Service, Congress, and others seem to have overlooked in supporting uniform fees for public lands. Such fees make very little sense in terms of primary management objectives. The virtue of uniform fees is that they are simple to administer and easy for the public to understand. But surely these are subsidiary objectives. The main aim is to ration demand, and this can be done most effectively with differentiation of fees. Such differentiation merely would reflect the fact that fees should be related to cost (marginal cost at least), and congestion is a cost.[100]

CONCLUSIONS

The problem of providing adequate outdoor recreational opportunity and facilities on the national forests—and other federal lands—is clearly becoming more acute. The difficulty would be serious enough if the rising demand for outdoor recreation simply reflected rising population. But the demand has far outstripped population growth, and every indication is that it will continue to do so for years to come. With it will come more congestion, resulting in deterioration of the quality of recreational experience and, ultimately, of the land resource as well. In the face of such a trend present land use policy seems woefully wanting. So far from meeting the problem it has, in fact, compounded it by continuing to regard recreational use as a free good. By refusing to grant the Forest Service and other agencies suitable pricing authority Congress has not only removed any economic constraint on aggregate demand, but has eliminated a potentially effective tool for controlling the use of particular areas in which congestion is most serious.

On the latter point the prevailing attitude appears to be that while congestion is a serious problem, it can be adequately handled through administrative controls without the use of price rationing.[101] This view is not confined to Congress. The Forest Service, while it has sought some authority to make minimal charges for recreational use as a means of meeting management costs, has been reluctant to acknowledge the role of pricing as a means of rationing use. It too has adhered to the view that administrative controls should be the primary means of control.

This preference for the use of regulatory mechanisms over economic incentives is a common one in government—a reflection, I would suppose, of the prevalence of what I have earlier labeled the "bureaucratic" approach. From the vantage point of the bureaucrat this bias for administrative management is understandable, for it fits his role. Administrative fiat is, in a sense, his life style. But why others, congressmen or the public generally, should share that bias is, to me, one of life's minor mysteries. Granted, economic incentives may sometimes not work well: the market is not suitably structured to produce an efficient result. And granted, economic incentives may be sometimes inappropriate, for reasons of equity. But neither qualification seems applicable here. And we can set aside any practical considerations of administrative cost and convenience. As noted earlier, whether a fee is practicable for a particular area is irrelevant to the issue of general policy being debated. This is especially evident where the question is the choice between administrative control and economic control; for if the former is practicable, the latter certainly should be. And if the latter is not feasible, then it is plain the former would not be. The preference for administrative control mechanisms seems, in the end, to come down to a matter of taste more than reasoned judgment—an aversion to using price as a control device even where the alternative is to use direct coercion. Somehow, even as a matter of taste, this is a puzzlement.

The use of a fee to control access to a falcon eyrie is perhaps distasteful. But so too is an administrative edict that turns away those last in line. Again, putting equity aside, the only thing one can say of the latter is that it rewards the early riser and those who are fortuitously close to the site; neither person seems morally more deserving than the person who expresses the intensity of his interest by the money he is willing to pay for the privilege. Permitting the demand to be rationed by money has the undoubted merit that it is a simple, objective, and commonly used basis for choice.

Contrary to popular supposition, this use of prices does not mean the rich or well-to-do will always outbid those of moderate means, or the poor.

Whether they will do so depends upon their preferences for the good in question (their respective "utility functions" as the economist might express it). Smith whose income is, say, $45,000, may or may not be willing to pay more for the sight of our high-priced falcon than Jones whose income is, say, $15,000. Perhaps Smith would prefer to spend his money to watch the Philadelphia Eagles rather than a peregrine falcon. I see no obvious reason for being more concerned that poor Jones will be deprived of his bird-watching pleasure than for being concerned that Smith will be deprived of his football-viewing pleasure by pricing entry to the stadium. The only basis on which one might become concerned is where the high cost of the fees would be beyond his means. But, as I have said, this simply will not wash. Those who are that poor do not have the means to meet the larger expenses of the trip in any event.

No doubt the adoption of higher, more adequately structured fees for outdoor recreation would not be the complete salvation for our overworked federal lands. Even so its promise of modest improvement seems too substantial to reject simply because it does not have the ecological elegance of other "solutions" to the overuse problem—such as that of wilderness preservation.

NOTES

1. Aldo Leopold, *A Sand County Almanac With Essays on Conservation from Round River* (New York: Ballantine, 1966), p. 280.

2. U.S. Department of Agriculture/Forest Service, *1972–73 Report of the Chief of the Forest Service*, p. 21.

3. For a short useful history of the development of outdoor recreation policy, see Edwin M. Fitch and John F. Shanklin, *The Bureau of Outdoor Recreation* (New York: Praeger, 1970).

4. 13 Stat. 325 (1864). The lands were receded to the United States in 1906 to be incorporated into Yosemite National Park. 34 Stat. 831 (1906), 16 U.S.C., § 48.

5. 17 Stat. 32 (1872), 16 U.S.C., § 21.

6. Before 1916 the parks were administered separately, some by the army, some by Interior. For a detailed history, see John Ise, *Our National Park Policy: A Critical History* (Baltimore: Johns Hopkins University Press for Resources for the Future, 1961).

7. For a brief history, see U.S. Department of Agriculture/Forest Service, *Outdoor Recreation in the National Forests*, Agricultural Information Bulletin 301 (1965), pp. 12–16.

8. Quoted in Michael Frome, *Whose Woods These Are: The Story of the National Forests* (Garden City, N.Y.: Doubleday, 1962), p. 330.

9. 38 Stat. 1101 (1915), 16 U.S.C., § 497.

10. In 1924 recreation visits to the national forests were roughly 4.7 million, and were approximately doubled within the following decade. See U.S. Department of Agriculture/Forest Service, *Outdoor Recreation*, p. 91.

11. Ibid. From 4.7 million visits in 1924 use grew to a peak of 18 million in 1941, then dropped during the war years, but rose quickly to 18.2 million in 1946. Thereafter the number of visits nearly doubled by 1953. By 1960 it had reached 92.6 million. It is difficult to make comparisons of these data with current published Forest Service data that measure not visits, but visitor-days. This is perhaps as good a place as any to note that the visitor statistics do not simply measure demand; they measure both demand and supply. (See Marion Clawson and Jack L. Knetsch, *Economics of Outdoor Recreation* (Johns Hopkins Press for Resources for

the Future, 1966), pp. 105–116.) It is, for that reason, a very imperfect measure of future demand. In this context, however, it is a fairly good measure of the pressure on recreation facilities and, correspondingly, on management resources.

12. See William C. Everhart, *The National Park Service* (New York: Praeger, 1972), pp. 182–190, for a discussion emphasizing the competitive rivalry in outdoor recreation planning.

13. The only published product was a U.S. Department of Agriculture/Forest Service bulletin, *Outdoor Recreation*.

14. 78 Stat. 897 (1964), *as amended*, 16 U.S.C., §§ 460L-4 to L-11.

15. Land acquired under the Weeks Act can be used for recreation provided either of the two statutory purposes of the Weeks Act (as amended by Clarke–McNary) are satisfied; that is, the land is acquired primarily for timber production or for watershed protection. However, with such conditions, Weeks Act purchases are not an adequate vehicle for acquiring forest lands primarily for recreational purposes. Also under the General Exchange Act, 42 Stat. 465 (1922), 16 U.S.C., §§ 485-6, and the Transfer Act of 1960, 74 Stat. 205, 5 U.S.C., § 511, exchanges of land within the external boundaries of the forest can be made for recreational purposes. But these are inadequate for major acquisitions for recreational purposes in areas where they were needed.

16. 16 U.S.C., § 460L-9.

17. The condition apparently reflects two concerns: first, concern about increased federal landownership in the West (the same concern that caused Congress in 1910 to limit further reservation of forest lands by presidential order); and, second, concern that the major focus of increased recreational opportunities ought to be on eastern lands. See Daniel P. Beard, "Meeting the Costs of a Quality Environment: The Land and Water Conservation Fund Act," in Richard A. Cooley and Geoffry Wandesforde–Smith, eds., *Congress and the Environment*. (Seattle: University of Washington Press, 1970), p. 104. Whatever the legitimacy of these concerns it is curious that only Forest Service acquisitions were so limited. No such limit appears on acquisitions for national parks or wildlife refuges.

18. For a discussion of the terms of the federal grant-in-aid provisions and the results of the program through June 1969, see Fitch and Shanklin, *The Bureau of Outdoor Recreation*, ch. VII.

19. See U.S. Department of Agriculture/Forest Service, *1972–73 Report of the Chief of the Forest Service*, pp. 21 and 25. In 1973 approximately 762,000 acres of land were classified as developed recreation sites, about 73 percent of which is actually developed for recreation, the remainder consisting of so-called peripheral area. This represents nearly a 300 percent increase in developed recreation site acreage over 1972 (Ibid., pp. 16–17).

20. See generally, the Forest Service Manual, § 2351.1. I have also drawn on discussions with Forest Service officials for much of the following.

21. The Forest Service itself does not operate any commercial facilities. In the rare case where it has constructed such a facility (e.g., Timberline Lodge in Oregon), it is still operated by private concession.

22. See the Forest Service Manual, § 2330.3.

23. Ibid., §§ 2303, 2340.3(3e).

24. See *United States v. Grimaud*, 220 U.S. 506 (1911).

25. 65 Stat. 290 (1951), 31 U.S.C., § 483a.

26. Bureau of the Budget, Circular A-25 (1959). The evolution of executive recognition of user fees generally, and Circular A-25 in particular, is traced in Thomas Waggoner, *User Fees*, Study for the Public Land Law Review Commission (Springfield, Ill.: Cleaning house for Federal Scientific and Technical Information, 1970), pp. 282–290.

27. This was implemented by Executive Order No. 11200, 30 Fed. Reg. 2645 (1965), which, among other things, designated all existing fee areas and delegated authority to make future changes or additions to the recreation agencies. The secretary of the interior was given the responsibility for coordination of fees to provide uniformity among agencies.

28. 82 Stat. 354 (1968).

29. See U.S. Congress, House Subcommittee of Committee on Interior and Insular Affairs, *Hearings on H.R. 6730*, 92 Cong., 1 sess., 1971, ser. 92-11.

30. 86 Stat. 459 (1972).

31. Under the Senate version of the 1972 amendments such fees could have been charged only at sites where admission fees were charged. The House version, and the final amendments

which adopted its language, evidently contemplates use fees for special facilities or services wherever furnished. Such is the Forest Service interpretation (Forest Service Manual, § 2331.23) the interpretation of other agencies, and the sensible policy whatever the specific intent. As a consequence of the 1972 amendments and the requirement for specially identified facilities or services as a prerequisite to use fees, the Forest Service abandoned fees at many day-use campsites, reducing the total number of charge sites from some 2,850 before to 2,235 after 1972 (figures provided by the Forest Service).

32. The 1973 amendments restated the 1972 limit on user fees—restricting them to "specialized sites, facilities, equipment or services furnished at federal expense." They then provided specifically that no such fee may be charged for facilities which virtually all visitors might be expected to use, such as picnic areas, roads, trails, and toilet facilities. This adopted the substance of prior Forest Service policy (see Forest Service Manual, § 2331.25a. However, the amendments went on to limit user fees to campgrounds where *all* of the following are present: flush restrooms, showers, access and circulatory roads, sanitary disposal stations, visitor protection, designated tent or trailer spaces, and refuse containers. As a result of the amendments the number of charge sites on the national forests dropped from some 2,235 to 37—of which all but one are located in the East and the South (figures provided by the Forest Service as of 1973).

33. 88 Stat. 192 (1974). The agency's fee authority now covers something over 2,000 campgrounds. Another 3,000 national forest campgrounds do not contain the requisite facilities to come within the statute. I am told by Forest Service officials that the agency has not sought—and has no interest in obtaining—fee authority for these undeveloped grounds.

34. See generally, the Forest Service Manual, § 2700, for current policy and requirements.

35. Ibid., § 2400.

36. U.S. Department of Agriculture/Forest Service, *1972–73 Report of the Chief of the Forest Service*, pp. 17 and 21. These data are given for "winter sports sites," but these are all ski areas. See Forest Service Manual, § 2342. National forest ski areas account for more than 80 percent of the major ski areas in the West [U.S. Department of Agriculture/Forest Service (PA 525), *Skiing* (1970)]. Some idea of the growth in this particular recreation demand can be gleaned from the fact that in just three years, 1970–73, visitor-days increased by about 30 percent. See ibid., and U.S. Department of Agriculture/Forest Service, *1970–71 Report of the Chief of the Forest Service*, p. 69.

37. Roscoe Herrington, *Skiing Trends and Opportunities in the Western States*, Forest Service Research Paper INT-34 (1967), pp. 1 and 7. This includes trip, clothing, and equipment expenditures. It is not indicated precisely how much of this is attributable to national forest skiing, but since over 80 percent of the ski areas are on national forests, it seems reasonable to so attribute at least 80 percent of the expenditures.

38. For the qualifications, see Forest Service Manual, § 2712.1.

39. Minor recreation concessions, such as gas stations or stores, boat marinas, and the like are typically not sufficiently attractive to call for competitive applications.

40. Although one would suppose that a major basis for choice is the amount of the fee which applicants bid, I am told this is infrequently a dominant criterion. The character of the proposal and its planned development are typically given greater weight than the fee. Thus the process of choice is quite different than in the sale of timber—which, no doubt, reflects primarily the fact that there are more variables left for private initiative in recreation than in timber sales (where specifications are definite and uniform).

41. See 38 Stat. 1101 (1915), 16 U.S.C., § 497.

42. Forest Service Manual, §§ 2711.2, 2716.2, and 2716.3. The Forest Service treats nonpayment of fees as a "termination" rather than a revocation, for reasons that escape me, since the basic process seems to be the same.

43. Ibid. The manual provides that the discretion is normally to be exercised only when land "is needed for more important use [or] the present use has become unsatisfactory or undesirable." This is not much of a limit perhaps, but then for a one-year term it hardly matters.

44. Ibid., § 2783.11.

45. On management plans, see generally, ibid., §§ 2310, 2311, 2314; and Forest Service Handbook, § 2309.13. An excellent description is also given in Herman Ruth and Associates, *Regional and Local Land Use Planning*, Study for the Public Land Law Review Commission

(Springfield: Clearinghouse for Federal Scientific and Technical Information, 1970), pp. 99–119. Again, much of the discussion here draws also on interviews with Forest Service officials.

46. In recent years there has been some effort to develop regional plans. This is in contrast to other management areas such as timber, range, or wildlife where regional functional planning has not generally gone beyond general multiple-use guides. See Ruth, *Regional and Local Land Use Planning,* pp. III-106-7. It is not clear how this will tie in with the new land use planning system which tends to stress smaller-unit planning.

47. Forest Service Manual, § 2314.36-37. The scheme is essentially that proposed in 1962 by the Outdoor Recreation Resources Review Commission, and subsequently formulated by the Bureau of Outdoor Recreation.

48. Ibid., § 2314.3 requires composites to be incorporated within the national forest recreation plan.

49. Recreation Advisory Council, *Federal Executive Branch Policy Governing the Selection, Establishment and Administration of National Recreation Areas* (1963).

50. See, for example, 82 Stat. 928 (1968), 16 U.S.C., § 90c-1 (Ross Lake and Lake Chelan NRAs, administered by Park Service); 79 Stat. 844 (1965), 16 U.S.C., § 460p-4 (Spruce Knob–Seneca Rocks NRA, administered by the Forest Service).

51. This is the projection on which current budget plans are made. The corresponding population projections used by the Forest Service indicate an increase in population from 204.8 million in 1970 to 227.1 million in 1980. (Both sets of figures are from the Forest Service's division of recreation.) No up-to-date projections for visitor use beyond 1980 exist. The last projection to the year 2000 was made in 1961 and is considered unreliable for planning purposes.

52. Descriptions of Mineral King and its history abound. I have drawn primarily on a Forest Service pamphlet, U.S. Department of Agriculture/Forest Service, *Mineral King, A Planned Recreation Development* (1969); "Mineral King Valley: Who Shall Watch the Watchmen?" *Rutgers Law Review,* vol. 25 (1970), p. 103; and on the material in the Appendix to the Record before the Supreme Court in *Sierra Club* v. *Morton,* 405 U.S. 727 (1972).

53. 44 Stat. 821 (1926), 16 U.S.C., § 688.

54. Some 70,000 visitor-days in 1968, in the valley and environs. *The New York Times,* Jan. 28, 1969, p. 1.

55. Note, *Rutgers Law Review,* p. 120.

56. Appendix to the Record, pp. 47-48. In August the Sierra Club again requested a hearing. This request and a November telegram request to the secretary of agriculture were unavailing (ibid., pp. 41-46).

57. See Peter Browning, "Mickey Mouse in the Mountains," *Harper's Magazine* (March 1972), pp. 66 and 67; Note, *Rutgers Law Review,* pp. 112-119.

58. *Rutgers Law Review,* pp. 118-119. Even then there was further delay because of dissatisfaction with location and design standards.

59. *Sierra Club* v. *Hickel,* 433 F2d 24 (9th Cir. 1970).

60. *Sierra Club* v. *Morton,* 405 U.S. 727 (1972).

61. Because the act was not in effect when the development was approved no environmental impact statement was prepared. The Forest Service evidently does not dispute the requirement for such a statement now since it has prepared one (a draft impact statement was circulated in December 1974).

62. See generally, Glen O. Robinson and Ernest Gellhorn, *The Administrative Process,* (St. Paul: West, 1974), ch. 3.

63. See, for example, *Barlow* v. *Collins,* 397 U.S. 157 (1970).

64. 405 U.S., pp. 741-52.

65. See *United States* v. *Students Challenging Regulatory Agency Procedures (SCRAP)* 93 S. Ct. 2405 (1973) where law students in Washington, D.C., were granted standing to challenge the refusal of the ICC to suspend increased rail rates for scrap metal, on the argument that this would increase the cost of recycling goods, which would in turn cause increased consumption of natural resources in the Washington area which they enjoyed. If this flimsy allegation of injury is all that is required, it is hard to conceive that any artful lawyer could not create standing for any such group disposed to sue. Whether this is necessarily bad or good is a debatable matter on which I suspend judgment, but plainly it makes the conservationists' cry of anguish over the Mineral King holding seem premature if not simply foolish.

66. I am informed that development of Snowmass at Aspen, Colorado, has cost some $100 million and the more recent development of Snowbird at Alta, Utah, is planned ultimately to cost more than $50 million. These are free-wheeling guesses which I have not thought necessary to verify for detailed accuracy, but they estimate the rough magnitude of some recent developments.

67. See Appendix to the Record, 53 a-c; and U.S. Department of Agriculture/Forest Service, *Mineral King*, pp. 10–11.

68. National Wildlife Federation, *Conservation News* (June 15, 1972), p. 10.

69. Arnold Hano, "Protectionists and Recreationists—The Battle of Mineral King," *The New York Times Magazine* (August 17, 1969), p. 54.

70. 405 U.S., p. 748. Curiously Justice Douglas' reference is to the common assertion that the service has been captured by the timber interests. The relevance of that fact—if it be a fact—to the Mineral King case escapes me since no timber interests are anywhere to be found in the case. Evidently *timber interests* is a symbolic term embracing everyone but certified conservationists.

71. Note, *Rutgers Law Review*, pp. 103 and 140, quoting in part and approving a charge by *The New York Times*.

72. The original reasons for keeping it out of the park would seem no longer valid. The mineral value is not there, and it is easily as "natural" today as many national parks.

73. The secretary of the interior's approval, in 1908, of the construction of a dam in Hetch Hetchy Valley in Yosemite National Park sparked a five-year controversy of unparalleled intensity. Opponents, led by John Muir and Robert Underwood Johnson, lost the battle, and the dam was built. But Muir could with good cause claim a moral victory: "The conscience of the whole country has been aroused from sleep" [Quoted in Roderick Nash, *Wilderness and the American Mind* (rev. ed., New Haven: Yale University Press, 1973), p. 180]. It seems likely, in fact, that the defeat of the preservationists gave their movement greater strength than a victory would have done, insofar as it enhanced the symbolic meaning of Hetch Hetchy.

74. Jean Nienabler, "The Supreme Court and Mickey Mouse," *American Forests*, vol. 78 (1972), pp. 29 and 43.

75. In 1973 total visitor-days in the Monongahela National Forest in West Virginia exceeded 1.4 million. A little over 1,000 of these were accounted for by winter sports (U.S. Department of Agriculture/Forest Service, *1972–73 Report of the Chief of the Forest Service*, pp. 21).

76. See *Wall Street Journal*, Sept. 8, 1973, p. 1, for a portrait of Yosemite today.

77. See Clawson and Knetsch (*Economics of Outdoor Recreation*, pp. 170–178), who note this sad fact and propose various corrective measures, including the use of fees. It may be worth recalling here that Forest Service policy has been quite rigorous in resisting demands for urban- and suburban-type facilities such as golf courses, tennis courts, and the like. The policy has not gone unquestioned. See Kenneth P. Davis, et al., *Federal Public Land Laws and Policies Relating to Multiple-Use of Public Lands*, Study for the Public Land Law Review Commission (rev. ed., Springfield, Ill.: Clearinghouse for Federal Scientific and Technical Information, 1970), pp. 66–67. In my view, the Forest Service policy approach is unequivocally correct as a general policy. Not only would a contrary policy intensify use and impair the special quality of the outdoor recreation experience (for others who do not want such things in the woods), it would aggravate the supply problem dramatically by competing with, rather than complementing, local recreational facilities.

78. U.S. Congress, House Subcommittee of the Appropriations Committee, *Hearings on Department of Interior and Related Agencies Appropriations for 1974*, 93 Cong., 1 sess., 1973, p. 123.

79. This, of course, assumes that the same basic facilities—sanitation and the like—should be provided at intensively developed and dispersed sites. Moreover, whatever the scale economics in providing basic facilities, one must suppose there is *proportionately* (per person) less environmental damage from most kinds of dispersed use even though it is more widely spread. (This would probably have to be qualified by excluding from consideration the use of off-road vehicles such as snowmobiles or trailbikes, for which only one solution seems acceptable: i.e., to tax them out of existence.)

80. See U.S. Congress, Senate Public Lands Subcommittee of the Committee on Interior and Insular Affairs, *Hearings, "Clear-cutting" Practices on National Timberlands,* 92 Cong., 1 sess., 1971, pp. 859–863. Current appropriations for 1975 are given in Appendix B. In defense of Congress it should be noted that the erosion of Forest Service requests has typically been made by the OMB. In some cases Congress actually increased appropriations over the OMB's proposal. One other point should be noted. The appropriations for recreation do not fully measure the funds which rebound to the benefit of recreation. For example, some of the appropriation for wildlife could be regarded as for recreation, insofar as hunting, fishing, bird-watching, and the like are an integral part of outdoor recreation.

81. I do not suggest the economic motive is the only explanation for the disparity; the difference in organized political strength between the two activities is also an explanation. But the economic motive seems to me a powerful explanation—one which finds consistent application throughout federal land management.

82. This is most clearly evident in the remarks of Sen. Frank Church on the 1972 amendment. See U.S. Congress, Senate Public Lands Subcommittee of the Committee on Interior and Insular Affairs, *Hearings on S. 1893,* 92 Cong., 1 sess., pt. 1, 1971, p. 59.

It is interesting to note that, contrary to the spirit of Senator Church's remarks, the Forest Service continues to list, as one of the criteria in establishing fees, the "need to regulate, control or otherwise manage use." In actual practice, however, it appears that fees are not generally designed to do this. Certainly they do not appear to do it in fact. In a 1967 survey by Arthur G. Little, Inc., of visitors to all federal areas, only about 3 percent of the visitors surveyed reported that they had ever selected an area on the basis of the fee to be charged. (U.S. Congress, House Subcommittee of the Committee on Interior and Insular Affairs, *Hearings on H.R. 6730,* 92 Cong., 1 sess., ser. 92-11, 1971, pp. 60–61. Incidentally, the Little study cites this as corroborating other responses which indicated that visitors believed fee levels were reasonable. Little's interpretation of what visitors perceive is, of course, pertinent to the public attitude toward fees designed to regulate use, but hardly decisive, either of public acceptability or reasonableness of higher, and variable, fees to serve this objective.

83. The 1972 amendments do enable the agencies to take into account the fees charged by nonfederal public agencies in establishing charges, but Congress rejected a proposal to establish fees at the state, local, or private level. See S. Rept. 92–490, 92 Cong., 1 sess., 1971 , p. 3. The Forest Service takes account of all other fees, public and private (Forest Service Manual, § 2331.24c).

84. For an admirably concise, yet illuminating, review of the general theories and an extensive bibliography, see Peter Steiner, *Public Expenditure Budgeting* (Washington, D.C.: Brookings Institution, 1969). See also the collection of papers in *The Analysis and Evaluation of Public Expenditures: The PPB System,* Committee Print, Joint Economic Committee, 91 Cong., 1 sess., 1969. For a useful discussion of recreation as a public good, see Clawson and Knetsch, *Economics of Outdoor Recreation,* pp. 265–272.

85. See, for example, Paul Samuelson, "The Pure Theory of Public Expenditure," *Review of Economics and Statistics,* vol. 36 (1954), p. 387. The difficulty of exclusion need not be an absolute impossibility; it suffices if exclusion is too burdensome and costly to justify the effort. Somewhat related to this concept of public goods and the more general concept of "externalities"—costs and benefits not reflected in private market transactions—insofar as both are used to rationalize public choice as a surrogate for market choice. Steiner (p. 10) even treats public goods as an "extreme case of externalities: all of the output is regarded as individually unmarketable: all the benefits are external."

86. See Julius Margolis, "A Comment on the Pure Theory of Public Expenditure," *Review of Economics and Statistics,* vol. 37 (1955), pp. 347–348.

87. See Testimony of Chief of the Forest Service Edward P. Cliff in U.S. Congress, House Subcommittee of the Committee on Appropriations, *Hearings,* 87 Cong., 1 sess., 1961, pp. 1021–1022. See also Waggoner, *Users Fees,* pp. 310–311, who points out that entrance fees are not the only type of charge that could be levied. It has been proposed the government adopt a system similar to that used for hunting and fishing, with selective enforcement similar to that used for those activities. The Golden Eagle Passport is a *limited* application of this. One difficulty with this kind of fee is the vice of all uniform fees: it does not permit the fee to be used as a means of adjusting the use of different sites or the adjusting of use over time. Also, on equity

grounds such a fee has the disadvantage of subsidizing the frequent over the occasional user. See *Federal Agencies and Outdoor Recreation*, Outdoor Recreation Resources Review Commission Study Report 13 (1962), p. 24. In passing it may be noted that Congress already rejected the concept of such a fee in its 1972 amendment to the Land and Water Conservation Fund Act. A fear that the Golden Eagle Passport might develop into a general recreation fee—after the duck stamp model—induced Congress to reject a proposal to make the passport an individual permit rather than one issued for automobiles. See U.S. Congress, Senate Subcommittee on Parks and Recreation of the Committee on Interior and Insular Affairs, *Hearings on S. 1228 and Related Bills*, 92 Cong., 1 sess., 1971, pp. 52–3, 62–3.

88. See Richard A. Musgrave, *The Theory of Public Finance* (New York: McGraw–Hill, 1960), ch. I.

89. Clawson and Knetsch, *Economics of Outdoor Recreation,* p. 267, acknowledge the existence of such benefits but evidently view them as exaggerated. Ruth P. Mack and Sumner Myers, "Outdoor Recreation," in Robert Dorfman, ed., *Measuring Benefits of Government Investments* (Washington, D.C.: Brookings Institution, 1963), pp. 73–75, give a more affirmative statement of public benefits, one which I find unconvincing in its generality.

90. Leopold, *A Sand County Almanac*, p. 227.

91. Aldo Leopold, *Wilderness Values*, quoted in Outdoor Recreation Resources Review Commission, Study Report 3, p. 29.

92. See Clawson and Knetsch, p. 266. Of course public ownership of the land does not necessarily mean government provision of particular facilities or services: the present policy is to provide most such facilities through private concessionaires. Still the government is and should be involved even in these in order to ensure that recreation uses fit with other uses. In the case of dispersed recreation, private management of the area is uneconomic and cumbersome, leaving it inevitably to the federal government to provide and supervise recreational opportunity.

93. With the exception of the federal duck stamp applicable to hunting of waterfowl. In this connection is should be noted that the hunting and fishing fees, in part, serve as a user fee on outdoor recreation. Obviously, however, these fees are inadequate to allocate general recreational use. First, they apply only to a very limited recreational use. Second, they are not limited to federal lands (or even indeed to public lands).

94. See Jerome Milliman, "Beneficiary Charges and Efficient Public Expenditure Decisions," in *The Analysis and Evaluation of Public Expenditures*, pp. 291 and 310–311.

95. These are essentially the chief objections to redistribution "in kind." See, for example, Milton Friedman, *Capitalism and Freedom* (Chicago: University of Chicago Press, 1962), ch. XII.

96. See Steiner, pp. 15–16.

97. The Arthur D. Little study, mentioned earlier, estimated that persons from only about one-fifth of American households actually visited a federal recreation area in 1967. The study also indicated that persons in the lowest income levels have low outdoor recreation participation rates, from which it concluded that very low recreation fees would have limited effect on low-income participation and would accord all others an excessive bargain. See *Hearings on H.R. 6730*, pp. 58, 64–65, and 106.

98. For an analogous discussion and some useful examples of how the impact of increased costs affects local and nonlocal use of different types of areas see Clawson and Knetsch, pp. 77–85.

99. Ibid., p. 275.

100. See, for example, John V. Krutilla, "Is Public Intervention in Water Resources Development Conducive to Economic Efficiency?" *Natural Resources Journal*, vol. 6 (1966), pp. 60, 67–68.

101. See Sen. Frank V. Church's comments in *Hearings on S. 1893*, p. 59.

VI

WILDERNESS

Among the array of environmental concerns, few have so captured the fancy and the fantasy of the environmentally concerned as has wilderness. The values of wilderness have been variously expressed. Some have stressed the scientific and ecological values,[1] while others have stressed its recreational value.[2] But whatever particularized value is specified, ultimate refuge is usually taken in some aesthetic sense. Robert Marshall described it as all the senses "harmonized with immensity into a form of beauty which to many human beings is the most perfect experience of the earth."[3] Even those who have never been within sight of a real wilderness have at least some dim vision of its enchantment, due in part to the rich profusion of books celebrating its beauty in picture and poetry.

On the other hand, to many who have had neither direct nor vicarious experience with wilderness, the preservationist who insists wilderness be preserved at the sacrifice of other land uses often appears as an irrepressible romantic, or a wild-eyed zealot, depending on the intensity of his ardor. To the steely-eyed pragmatist the preservationist preaches an elitist creed in urging that land be taken out of uses serving large numbers of the public in favor of restricting it to selective use by a mere handful of enthusiasts (by definition the wilderness cannot accommodate more). The objection surely has substance when measured against the demands of some preservationists; and yet the extremes of one end of the spectrum need not propel us to the extremes of the other. The wonder of wilderness, and the value of its preservation, is recognized by many who could scarcely be described as romantic let alone fanatic.

It is not only in the personal acquaintance with pristine nature that wilderness has meaning and value. It has a larger social and cultural significance as well. It is the symbol of what modern civilization has lost. Wallace Stegner has eloquently expressed this:

> We need wilderness preserved—as much of it as is still left, and as many kinds—because it was the challenge against which our character as a people was formed. The reminder and the reassurance that it is still there is good for our spiritual health even if we never once in ten years set foot in it. It is good for us when we are young, because of the incomparable sanity it can bring briefly, as vacation and rest, into our insane lives. It is important to us when we are old simply because it is there—important, that is, simply as idea.[4]

In more prosaic, homely terms, wilderness dramatizes the opportunity cost of civilization, what we have given up in "natural" values to obtain the "artificial" benefits of social living. And in an age in which the social benefits are all too visibly promoted, there is special need to retain at least some visible reminder of our loss. Whatever the rationale, it is hard to deny the existence of a strong instinct for maintaining some tie, some residual hold upon a more primitive life, and it is from this instinct that the concept of wilderness ultimately derives its support.

The instinct is not a genetic characteristic to be sure; rather it is the product of very modern times.[5] Despite its ancient presence at the frontier of man's social world, the concept of wilderness is of recent origin. Only now that modern man is faced with its near elimination has the idea of wilderness and the desire for its preservation captured his imagination; as with most things, value comes from scarcity. For the colonist and pioneer, wilderness was just a condition of the land. There was no developed social consciousness about wilderness, no concept of it as a thing of nature, to be preserved, cherished, and valued. Of course, there were those who specially valued the wilderness and its beauty, but in a new world in which subsistence was a daily problem, this was a luxury for which little time could be spared. And any such appreciation had to be tempered with the harsh reality that the wilderness condition was the relentless barrier to future social settlement. Thus, for most persons, wilderness was only something to be overcome. The value of the natural environment lay only in its ability to sustain the physical needs of people pursuing the biblical injunction to subdue and conquer the earth.

After basic subsistence had been secured from the wilderness, pioneering and economic expansion extended the conquest. The early efforts were largely individual and private; these had an impact on the frontier, though a limited one. The real thrust of expansion followed the Civil War and was heavily promoted by the federal government (and, to a much lesser degree, by state and local governments) through land grants to public and private enterprise, and homesteads to individual pioneers. In the face of railroads, wagon trains—and in their wake, settlements and cities—the frontier quickly disappeared and with it some (though by no means all) of the wilderness.

THE EVOLUTION OF A
WILDERNESS POLICY

Early History
In the midst of expansion, however, some urged government protection and preservation of large tracts of land. A proposal to preserve vast areas of the Great Plains for the benefit of Indians and buffalo was made as early as 1832 by George Catlin, painter of the Indian West.[6] His idea received little serious attention. However, the sentiment for preservation persisted and reappeared, in modified form, in 1864, when Congress ceded lands in Yosemite Valley and Mariposa Grove to California, and eight years later when it created the first national park, Yellowstone. But national parks were not established with the idea of preserving wilderness as such; the main purpose was to secure these areas for public recreational use—and to prevent them from being monopolized by private interests who, but for the withdrawal into national parks, would patent or homestead the lands. Essentially, the decision was a pragmatic one, which gave little attention to preservation of wilderness values.[7] The significance of these withdrawals of lands from private use is not that they represented a searching exploration or acceptance of the value of wilderness as such, but that they evidenced the beginning of a public land use philosophy.

The philosophy which would later give the wilderness preservation movement its intellectual substance, however, had been developing. As urban life became more common, people took to the wilds for recreation or other uses. The early wilderness promoters were mostly idealists, romantics in the vein of Emerson, Thoreau, and later Muir, who saw wilderness as a source of insight and refreshment, which could come best from untrammeled nature. Ecologist George Perkins Marsh gave important support to later preservationists who argued that unthinking destruction of the wilds would disrupt the natural process on which men ultimately depend for survival.[8]

Toward the end of the nineteenth century a conservation movement containing and nurturing the germ of the wilderness preservation effort began to emerge. The passage of the Forest Reserves Act of 1891 provided the first comprehensive vehicle by which wilderness could be initially protected, and it showed that conservationists were starting to have some noticeable effect on land use policy. The act was not primarily preservationist. Preservationist leaders, such as John Muir (who convinced Interior Secretary John W. Noble to have the reserve section included in the bill with which it was passed), did support the act,[9] but so did Fernow and other multiple-use-oriented foresters. Conservationists of all persuasions tended to band together against the "resource raiders," as Stewart Udall later called the timber and mining interests.[10] But the lines of future conflict between managed use—conservation—and preservation were soon to emerge with the formation of the Sierra Club in 1895 and the development of the Forest Service after 1905.

During 1906–13 a skirmish flared between the advocates of wilderness preservation and wilderness resource utilization. San Francisco, which had just been shaken by an earthquake, urgently renewed its request that it be permitted to build a dam in the Hetch Hetchy Valley on the Yosemite reservation.[11] John Muir and Robert Underwood Johnson, a publisher and wilderness lover, campaigned against the dam, blocked it in Congress for seven years, and convinced Theodore Roosevelt to change his position and oppose the dam (contrary to Pinchot's advice). As never before, the conflict between preservation and use was starkly dramatized. The intense debate was an early rehearsal of controversies to come. Preservationists urged recognition of spiritual, aesthetic, and recreational values, while dam builders explained that wilderness, however good, must yield to the greater good represented by material progress. The builders won. It was a celebrated victory, but probably a pyrrhic one for, as John Muir put it, "the conscience of the whole country was aroused from sleep."[12] To preservationists Hetch Hetchy became the Alamo of wilderness, a symbol and a call to arms. The national forests soon became the principal battlefield.

The important imprint of history on the current scheme of wilderness preservation calls for a somewhat extended review of the evolution of the preservation policy.

The Forest Service early set itself against any general policy of preservation for its own sake. As Gifford Pinchot was no John Muir, so the Forest Service was definitely not preservationist. Pinchot, believing forest resources should be actively managed to satisfy the needs of those who would benefit most from their use, said: "The object of our forest policy is not to preserve the forests because they are beautiful . . . or because they are refuges for wild creatures of the wilderness . . . but . . . [is] the making of prosperous homes. . . . Every other consideration comes as secondary."[13] Pinchot's philosophy guided early policy toward productive managed use and against wilderness preservation, but his was not the sole influence. Local interests were—and still continue to be—a major influence, and they have tended to be less enthusiastic supporters of wilderness than nonlocal interests, at least where significant costs to the local economy are involved.[14]

Gila National Forest. However, with the emergence of outdoor recreation as an important concern of the Forest Service, there also came some recognition of wilderness preservation. The first wilderness policies were originated at local levels by officers who had authority, within their budget, to incorporate recreational considerations in forest use planning. Aldo Leopold, an assistant district forester in the district (region) encompassing New Mexico and Arizona, provided a major initial impetus for wilderness preservation. When plans were made to put roads into the roadless areas of the Gila National Forest, Leopold, aware the Gila area was the last big roadless area in the district, proposed the area be withheld from road development and maintained as a wilderness preserve.[15] The Gila fit Leopold's description of an area that should be preserved as wilderness: it was large and could support an extended pack trip; it had abundant game; preserving the area would not duplicate other preservation efforts; its timber was not economically accessible; and its mineral potential was not such that it had induced miners to enter the area.[16]

When his proposal evoked little initial response of any kind from the public or from the service, Leopold attempted to stimulate interest through a series of articles in which he described a philosophy of wilderness protection influential in shaping subsequent Forest Service wilderness policies. Leopold's immediate recommendation was that wilderness lands be placed in a kind of tentative holding category, enabling them to be withheld from development until a permanent decision could be made on the basis of the popular will. For the longer term he urged permanent preservation of some public lands, for which wilderness, rather than commercial use, was the "highest use."

Although couched in terms of standard progressive land use ideas, Leopold's proposals were a significant extension of those concepts. Critics inside and outside the Forest Service charged that the proposed wilderness program was elitist and would not result in the greatest good for the greatest number. It was also said that wilderness preservation would conflict with the political and professional desire to facilitate free and full use of the national forests. It would complicate fire control. And it was finally argued that the National Park Service, established in 1916, was the federal agency best equipped to provide for the recreational needs of the people and that the Forest Service should not compete with it for management of lands suitable for primarily recreational purposes.

Despite these objections, Leopold (with the support of the Sierra Club and the Izaak Walton League) convinced the district forester, in 1924, to designate an area of more than 700,000 acres of the Gila National Forest as a wilderness area, withholding it from development until it was needed for some other purpose. It was the first official wilderness area, but the idea quickly spread, and by 1925 five other areas in other regions had been so designated.

The Primitive Areas.   As finally formulated, the wilderness policy put few restraints on local forest officers, who retained broad discretion as to whether lands should be withdrawn for wilderness. In fact, the policy was little more than a recommendation to the field officials that they should consider wilderness values in their planning.[17] In 1928, the service promulgated formal regulations which increased centralized direction to wilderness protection by providing that wilderness areas—now called "primitive" areas—were to be established and abolished only by action of the chief. However, the new regulations did not greatly restrict foresters in their management efforts. The history of the primitive areas, sixty-three of which had been established by 1933, shows that economic activity occurred in many of them. In fact, logging activities were specifically permitted in twenty-three of the areas and affirmatively prohibited in only eight. Grazing took place in fifty-three and was barred in ten. In none of these areas were roads expressly prohibited.[18] Plainly, the concept as it was developed at this time was a tolerant and flexible one—too much so to satisfy preservationists; when Robert Marshall, one of the founders of the Wilderness Society, was brought into the Forest Service to head the Division of Recreation and Lands in 1937, it was a recognition that a change was needed. Marshall, however, was only partly responsible for the greater attention to wilderness. Rivalry with the Department of the Interior, which had earlier played a role in stimulating Forest Service interest in wilderness, was again pushing the agency in the direction of greater attention to outdoor recreation and wilderness preservation. As Secretary Ickes pushed his plan for transfer of the Forest Service to a Department of Conservation and the Park Service attempted to appropriate national forest lands for more parks, the Forest Service became defensive. Among the tactics suggested for dealing with these pressures was to give primitive areas more protection and permanence.

In 1938, Chief Silcox, presaging a formal change in Department of Agriculture regulations, sent to the regions orders prescribing that all primitive areas should be carefully studied, pared to eliminate commercial values that would be needed in the future, and reclassified from primitive area status to wilderness (those areas containing 100,000 acres or more) or wild (those areas having less than 100,000 acres) area status.

The new regulations promulgated in 1939 set the foundation for the present wilderness policies of the Forest Service. The regulations revealed a scheme which could provide a high level of protection for wilderness areas. Equally important, the plan (unlike previous Forest Service policy) implied a permanent commitment to wilderness preservation. The protections afforded wilderness areas were substantial. Road building, the activity which had given rise to the service's wilderness policies in the 1920s, was forbidden in wilderness areas except as needed to provide access for owners of private lands situated within the wilderness boundaries or as needed by miners who could not be barred from working their claims by the Forest Service alone. Commercial timber harvesting was completely barred. Summer camps, resorts, or other structures were categorically forbidden in the new classified areas except as needed for fire protection.[19]

The process of classification from primitive to wild or wilderness status proved to be slow. The war had a somewhat retarding effect, but probably more significant was the antagonism of many within and outside of the service to the permanent reservation of wilderness lands. Not only the pace of reclassification but its results were challenged by preservationists. Particularly distressing to them was the practice of removing valuable timberlands from areas to be classified as wilderness, thereby reducing the size of particular areas. Although there was a net gain of protected acreage between 1939–63 of more than 130,000 acres, the average size of the protected areas decreased, and of all the previously nonclassified areas added, only one of the total fourteen was of wilderness size.[20] In addition, qualitative changes occurred: the service exchanged verdant valley timber acreage for acreage above the timberline. There was, too, growing skepticism among preservationists that the Forest Service would, or even could, maintain permanent reservation for lands classified as wilderness. The mounting public demand for forest products and forest use increased the anxiety which a natural distrust of the bureaucracy instilled.

Preservationists began to seek surer protection for wilderness through congressional action; as early as 1947 the idea of a statutory wilderness system began to take shape. However, nearly a decade passed before Congress considered a bill to accomplish this, and some eight more years until Congress enacted the Wilderness Act.[21]

The Wilderness Act

The 1964 Wilderness Act created a system of statutory preservation for some 9.1 million acres of national forest lands already in wilderness status by prior Forest Service classification. In addition to the "instant wilderness," it provided for a ten-year review of primitive areas by the Forest Service with regard to their inclusion in the wilderness system. The Department of the Interior was directed to undertake a similar review and to make recommendations with regard to all roadless areas within the national parks and wildlife refuges. Lands included in the system were withdrawn from timber harvesting, road building, other commercial activities (mining exploration is to be prohibited beginning in 1984), and other uses incompatible with the wilderness character—such as those requiring motor transportation (except as required to gain access to private lands where the use of motors was well established).

The act was obviously a victory for preservationists, although it did not give them all they had demanded. The victory was not easily achieved, however, and certainly not without prolonged and sometimes bitter controversy.[22] For the most part, the debate skirted the basic question of whether any land should be preserved as wilderness. There were few interests who by the late 1950s would not at least publicly express some support for the idea of preservation. Thus, the debate was cast largely in terms of ostensibly subordinate issues: whether statutory preservation was necessary or desirable; what uses should be permitted in preserved areas; and what procedures should govern the classification process. Although these questions seemingly assumed the desirability of preservation, in fact, each of these issues vitally affected the basic issue of preservation itself.

Statutory Versus Administrative Preservation.   The question of statutory, as opposed to administrative, preservation was of course the very heart of the controversy, since that was the whole point of the legislation. Preservationists argued that administrative discretion was not adequate, in that it was subject to easy reversal and could not be relied upon to give expansive recognition of wilderness. The Forest Service initially opposed the concept of statutory preservation, arguing that it could give adequate protection to wilderness preservation under its general multiple-use management policies. It correctly saw the proposed wilderness legislation as depriving it of administrative discretion and flexibility in managing the forest and parklands.

Quite apart from the fact that the act would constrain its discretion in regard to wilderness areas, the Forest Service feared that if particular lands were dedicated by statute to some particular treatment, this could induce similar treatment of other uses—the effect of which would be to replace the agency's multiple-use system with a dominant-use scheme. Incidentally, this would also undercut the Forest Service's jurisdiction, for if land use were to be prescribed by statutory classifications of dominant use, a logical further step might be to reorganize administrative control accordingly. In particular this might mean that much of the agency's recreation functions—at least recreation-dominant areas—would pass from the Forest Service to the National Park Service.

The preservationists attempted to meet this objection by including in the proposed legislation a provision that multiple use would continue to be the goal of forest policy. It was not enough. Instead the Forest Service sought, and with enactment of the Multiple-Use and Sustained Yield Act of 1960, they obtained separate congressional ratification of the multiple-use principle. Armed with that security, the Forest Service withdrew its opposition to the Wilderness Act.

Needless to say, the Forest Service was not alone in its early opposition to statutory recognition of wilderness; it was joined by all of the commercial users of the forests. Timber, livestock, power, and mining interests all advocated maintaining multiple-use management and urged that any preservation be maintained only by administrative decision, expecting this would serve their needs more flexibly than would a statutory system.[23] This was particularly true of mining and water-development (chiefly hydroelectric power) interests. Under the Forest Service's administrative system of wilderness preservation their activities were largely unhampered. The Forest Service has virtually no power to limit or regulate mining or the construction of dams within the national forests. The initially proposed legislation would have banned both these activities. Small wonder then that these interests were particularly vocal opponents of wilderness legislation.

As suggested by the opposition of the mining and water-development interests, the question whether preservation should be prescribed by legislation was intimately bound up with the question of what uses should be permitted in areas set apart as wilderness. For activities such as timber harvesting, the statutory scheme would not, of course, change the *status quo*. Harvesting was banned under the Forest Service's administrative regulations, and it would continue to be banned by statute. For the mining and water-development interests, whose prior uses would be curtailed, the question of access to and use of wilderness lands was a major issue as they fought for special provisions to permit continued access to wilderness areas.

As the legislation was finally enacted the mining and water-development interests did obtain some concessions. Mining was banned, but the ban was not to be effective until 1984. Water development—dam construction—could continue on a finding by the president that it would be in the national interest. Except for these activities the legislation made little change in the kind and level of protection given wilderness under the prior administrative scheme. In contrast to the Forest Service's regulations, the act did ban future grazing except where it had been previously established; but inasmuch as grazing on wilderness lands had been decreasing anyway,[24] this was not an important change.

Criteria for Inclusion in the Wilderness System.   The last major issue in the controversy involved the determination of what lands should be included in the system. On the one hand, there was no real dispute that lands already classified as "wild" or "wilderness" (some 9.1 million acres) should be automatically included as "instant wilderness." Conversely, it had been agreed that parklands administered by the Department of the Interior should not be included until after a review determined whether they were of predominantly wilderness character, and whether preservation was in other respects appropriate. This left the Forest Service's primitive areas on which the Forest Service had not made a final review and determination as to their permanent status, but which were being preserved as wilderness pending permanent classification.

Preservationists urged these lands should be included provisionally in the system, subject to subsequent exclusion only on a showing that they should not be protected as wilderness. The Forest Service among others opposed such interim inclusion as unwarranted. Both sides correctly saw the issue as one of procedural strategy and political advantage. Interim inclusion would not in any way affect the level of protection accorded the lands, since primitive areas were managed as wilderness lands. But it could affect the burden of proof. Preservationists reasoned it would be more difficult for the Forest Service to exclude an area provisionally admitted to the system than to decline to add an area to the system. In the end, the preservationists lost, but in retrospect the loss was probably not important: with relatively minor boundary adjustments (which have actually increased the area recommended for preservation above that within existing primitive area boundaries), all of the primitive areas reviewed to date have been proposed for inclusion, and it seems very unlikely they will not be favorably acted on by Congress.[25]

WILDERNESS
CLASSIFICATION

The impact of the Wilderness Act on Forest Service policy is not easily measured. The instant inclusion of some 9.1 million acres already administratively classified as wild or wilderness lands may have given a more permanent status to those lands—so preservationists believe—but that is debatable. While the future of primitive areas and of other unclassified roadless areas was clearly uncertain, there is little indication that most of the lands classified as wilderness were any more susceptible to reclassification for nonwilderness use under the administrative classification than under Congress. While one might suppose administrative classifications are inherently more flexible, in this case that is not so evident; the fact is that much of the land the service transferred into that classification is land for which other uses, particularly timber production, are very limited.

The act did, of course, achieve some additional protections for wilderness and primitive lands, at least one of which—the future ban on mineral exploration—was beyond the power of the Forest Service.[26] However, for the most part, the differences between administrative and statutory protection do not now appear substantial.

The principal impact of the act, so far as the Forest Service is concerned, lay in the impetus it gave to acceleration and expansion of the scope of wilderness preservation by mandating a ten-year review of all existing primitive areas. Of course, the Forest Service was already engaged in a process of review and reclassification of primitive areas, mandated by its 1938 regulations, under which primitive lands enjoyed the protection of wilderness. However, until proposals for a Wilderness Act appeared, the Forest Service's own review and classification efforts had been desultory. It is true that by the time the act was passed, some three-fifths of the primitive acreage had finally passed into permanent wilderness. However, much of this was accomplished under the shadow of a proposed statutory scheme that would have mandated it, possibly on terms which would have limited Forest Service discretion. In short, the pendency of the legislation was undoubtedly a spur to administrative action. Moreover, without the mandate of the act to push forward with the review, the process of administrative review might have ground to a halt as it had before. Such a slowdown was particularly likely in view of the fact that the Forest Service's review process had already taken care of the easiest choices, that is, those most suitable for wilderness and those involving the least sacrifice of other valued uses.

Perhaps most important of all, the act expressed a political mood in favor of substantial wilderness preservation. While this mood did not itself create any new wilderness areas, it put political pressure on the Forest Service to think twice before excluding existing primitive areas from the permanent wilderness system. In plain political reality the act ensured that virtually all of the primitive areas would be proposed for inclusion and that the only real contention would be over boundaries. This in fact has been the case.

Currently the ten-year review is ending, essentially according to schedule, although Congress has not enacted, nor even considered, all of the proposed additions to the system. Although the administrative process of primitive area review mandated by the Wilderness Act is now substantially complete, this is by no means the end of the review and classification task. On the contrary, ahead lies a task more formidable than that which has gone before—for the review process has shifted from formally classified primitive areas to unclassified and heretofore unstudied roadless areas.

The Wilderness Act mandated an evaluation only of such forest lands as are presently within or contiguous to existing primitive areas. Thus, the principal thrust of the classification process, so far as the Forest Service was concerned, was to review its own prior classifications. In addition, however, the act permits, though it does not specifically mandate, review of other roadless areas outside of (and not necessarily contiguous to) existing primitive areas.

In 1967 the Forest Service undertook an inventory of roadless areas outside the primitive areas which might be suitable for inclusion in the wilderness system.[27] Regional foresters were directed to inventory all roadless areas of 5,000 acres or more and select those warranting future study for possible wilderness classification. This inventory was the product of mixed motivation, with part of the initiative coming from the preservationists. Aware of vast acreage of roadless forest lands outside of existing primitive areas, national parks, or wildlife refuges, the preservationists wanted to ensure that such lands were not frozen out of the wilderness system. The strength of their interest is easy to understand once it is noted that these lands comprise a total area of more than triple the size of the total existing wilderness system. Against some 15 million acres of national forest lands under wilderness or primitive classification, outside roadless areas comprise 56 million acres. Demands by preservationists were not the sole motive for undertaking this inventory. Although the Forest Service has not favored expansion of the wilderness areas, it did have a strong interest in knowing what it was or would be confronted with in the way of demand for wilderness. To facilitate resource planning (timber and recreation especially) it was essential to know what lands might become wilderness, the "maximum universe" of lands suitable for wilderness classification. The lack of information was made more acute by the fact that, as the primitive area review program progressed, numerous demands were being made to Congress to preserve individual areas outside existing primitive areas. Since the lands lay outside the primitive areas being studied, the Forest Service was hard pressed to respond to these demands in the absence of some systematic inventory. The continued addition of such individual areas not only impeded its management planning, it threatened to remove initiative and control over wilderness classification from the service and to make it subject to the caprice of local interests and pressures.

However, despite these incentives to produce a comprehensive inventory as soon as possible, little effort was made by most of the regions to complete the inventory. Washington made equally little effort to press them on it until 1971, one year before the deadline set for the completion of the inventory. At that time the chief issued new directives to the regions to complete the inventory in accordance with newly specified procedures and to report their recommendations for areas to be designated as *new study areas* by 1972. The reports were submitted in June 1972. Of the total 56 million acres, approximately 10.7 million were recommended for further study by the regional foresters. Their recommendations were in the main adopted and incorporated in a draft environmental impact statement in January

1973. After further review, followed by public response to the draft impact statement, the selection was revised with the result that over 1 million acres were added. The final list encompasses some 12.3 million acres.[28]

The Forest Service's initial selection (of some 11 million acres) evoked outrage from the Sierra Club and other preservationist groups, who proceeded to bring a suit challenging the adequacy of the selection process. The suit itself was withdrawn when the Forest Service agreed that before any of the roadless areas not selected for further study are subjected to uses incompatible with wilderness an environmental impact statement will be issued.[29] The consequences of this remain to be seen.[30]

Since the Wilderness Act states that both formally classified primitive areas and contiguous multiple-use lands of predominant value as wilderness may be admitted to the system, the first thing to be done before a detailed analysis of resource values is made, is to choose a general study area which includes primitive areas and potential contiguous wildernesses. Once the general area is defined for wilderness study, it is surveyed and evaluated according to three primary standards: suitability, availability, and need.

Suitability. The suitability test[31] is measured against the definition of wilderness given in the act—not a very precise formulation. The pristine character of the land and its natural protection against man-made interferences is the point on which most of the major controversy between the Forest Service and preservationists has centered. The Forest Service has been reluctant to include in the system any land on which there has been substantial intrusion by man, even though physical evidence of man's activities has been or will be erased by natural process. The traditional rationale has been that the inclusion of such lands is not only itself inconsistent with the wilderness ideal, but will provide a precedent for permitting ongoing activities inconsistent with wilderness preservation.[32] Forest Service policy in this respect differs from that of the Park Service which has been less purist in its approach to the problem of man-made intrusions. The Forest Service approach has been bitterly attacked as a thinly veiled attempt to restrict wilderness preservation.[33] It is that in part, although, as we will see, there is more to the matter than this somewhat simplistic criticism reveals. (There is also more to it than the Forest Service's defense implies, but more on that later.) Just as the Forest Service has sought to exclude lands showing even faint evidence of significant past use, so also has it sought to exclude lands not providing adequate natural barriers for protection against encroachments from intensive uses of adjacent lands or those which would impair the "wilderness experience" with the "sights and sounds of civilization."[34] Here it is evident the Forest Service is much more deeply concerned about the difficulty of preserving wilderness values, since impact of established commercial or intensive recreational uses are all but impossible to protect against by administrative fiat.

Availability and Need.   Once an area has passed the suitability test, an assessment of its social utility as wilderness is made under the criteria of availability and need.[35] To translate from one jargon to another, the "availability" is essentially the "opportunity cost" of wilderness, that is, the value of all of the resources whose use or management may be foreclosed.[36] The "need" criterion is, essentially, the benefit side of the cost–benefit equation. Insofar as need is anything more than the expression of a willingness to put all suitable and available lands in wilderness, determination of need theoretically considers the demand for wilderness in the particular area encountered. This takes into account the amount of wilderness land already set aside in a particular location, the population of the area, and other factors pertinent to prospective use (including whether other nonwilderness lands can satisfy the demand). The determination of need also considers, theoretically, the quality of the area in question and its ability to provide "wilderness experience," which is supposed to be influenced by the scenic quality of isolation and the variety of experiences available in the area.

I have pointedly noted that the components of need are theoretical, for it is not apparent that such determinations have had much impact. Indeed, even the availability criterion, which would seem to lie at the heart of the basic preservation decision, has not played much of a role in the review of primitive areas. A basic political commitment having been made to recommend most of the land in primitive areas, the primary use of economic considerations has been, in adjusting boundaries here and there, to exclude particular areas where valuable timbers are present. Or it has been involved to the extent of refusing to study other areas where timber contracts have been made.[37] Even in cases where some economic appraisal has been made, it has been more the product of thumbnail estimates than a careful cost analysis. In recent years, however, attention to more sophisticated cost–benefit analysis is evident; first, in the late studies of a few primitive areas[38] and in the preliminary survey of new study areas.[39]

The Wilderness Act provides that, prior to submitting recommendations to the president with respect to the preserving of any area as wilderness, public notice shall be given and hearings held. In addition, the general public, and federal, state, and local officials concerned with the area are specially invited to submit their views.

After this evaluation, the proposal is reviewed, modifications (usually minor) are made as warranted, and the revised proposals are utilized for preparing a draft environmental impact statement. The draft statement is then circulated, as required by the National Environmental Policy Act

(NEPA), for a second review by the public and its agencies.[40] When response to this review is received, it is incorporated by the regional foresters into a final report and forwarded to the Executive and then to Congress. To date, all but one of the Forest Service recommendations have been endorsed by the president.[41]

WILDERNESS PRESENT AND FUTURE— CRITICAL OBSERVATIONS

Some Preliminary Thoughts

The Wilderness Act of 1964 settled (at least for an indefinite time) the question whether wilderness lands ought to be permanently preserved. However, by the time the act was passed, that question had ceased to be an important element of the controversy over wilderness. Notwithstanding the fears of preservationists, the Forest Service appears to have already committed itself to some permanent preservation, and after 1960 it even accepted the concept of a statutory system. The timber and mining industries may not have warmly endorsed the preservationist ideal, but even within their ranks public opposition to any wilderness became increasingly infrequent in the course of debates over the Wilderness Act. The dispute concerned how much wilderness was to be preserved and on what conditions. As to the former, since the act directly incorporated all of the then-existing wilderness land (some 9.1 million acres), a large portion of the lands then identified as suitable for wilderness was removed from dispute. So far as Forest Service land was concerned the immediate focus of attention was on the primitive areas already identified as potential wilderness.

With the Forest Service's review of primitive areas substantially complete, the advantages of hindsight are now available, and in that specially favored position it seems somewhat curious that so much controversy was generated over what now appears to be relatively a small area. Other roadless areas have since been "discovered," whose total area is over ten times larger than that of primitive lands reviewable under the 1964 act. Moreover, it should have been apparent, at least by the time the review was half-completed, that most of the total primitive area would be ultimately recommended for inclusion.[42] Politically, the Forest Service had little choice but to recommend inclusion of most of the total acreage. After all, most of the primitive land had already been recognized, at least *prima facie*, as suitable for wilderness: the primitive classification itself established that. The fact that these lands had not before been elevated to permanent wilderness does suggest perhaps that they had not been the foremost candidates for inclusion. As a practical matter, however, acting under the 1964 mandate of Congress, the Forest Service could scarcely be so cautious as it had been before. The lands were also generally available for wilderness, most primitive lands having little other practicable use. Much of the land is fragile and unproductive. Timber is of little value, at least relative to the cost of access. Mineral value is not fully known, but in many areas it is plain that such value as is present would not currently justify the cost of access or extraction.

Despite their economic unimportance the debate over the inclusion or exclusion of particular areas has been vigorous and sometimes vitriolic. There are two explanations for this, and both shed some light on the character of the overall controversy. The first and most obvious explanation for the strident character of the debate over reclassification of primitive areas is that each particular occasion giving rise to contention between preservationists and multiple-use advocates, is quickly escalated into a grand debate over wilderness versus nonwilderness values, which in turn becomes an even more wide-ranging debate over the character of modern civilization. For some preservationists, each battle is but a part of a larger holy war and has a symbolic significance far beyond any measurable objective. So, too, for some of the opposition. Each side is looking, not only at immediate gains and losses, but also at future casualties in battles yet to be fought. However, it is not merely the larger struggle over ideology that is involved. Seen in the perspective of a total system of, for example, 15 million acres, the inclusion or exclusion of, say, 50,000 acres here or there does not seem much to quarrel over, but from a local perspective it may be exceedingly important. Noninclusion of 50,000 acres may not reduce by much the overall extent of the wilderness (particularly since, as it has turned out, all decisions have been more than offset by new additions), but that is small comfort to local preservationists who want their own wilderness area. On the other hand, preservation of such an area, no matter how richly endowed in, say, commercial timber, will have a negligible effect on national timber supply, but it could have enormous impact on local mills who rely upon it.[43]

Both of these phenomena—the holy war aspect and the localism—have had and will continue to have important consequences for wilderness preservation. The first aspect suggests the difficulty of using objective measures to define wilderness and to determine the extent of its preservation. This is already evident in the opposition of many preservationists to the use of an economic approach to evaluate the costs of wilderness. The second aspect, localism, compounds the difficulties of decision insofar as it impedes political settlement through tradeoffs on a national basis. From a national perspective it is chiefly the overall size and quality of the wilderness lands that is important: the inclusion of one small area can be offset by the exclusion of another. But insofar as conflicting local interests must be considered, such tradeoffs between, for example, the National Sierra Club and Wilderness Society and the National Forest Products Association, are not possible. Therefore, for the Forest Service, there is really little choice but to undertake an exhaustive area-by-area review. That is what has been done with the primitive areas and what remains to be done with other roadless areas.

Defining Wilderness

The first question which emerges in controversies over wilderness is what it is. The Forest Service characterizes this in terms of suitability of land for wilderness, which suggests practical considerations independent of the abstract question of defining wilderness. But virtually all of the practical considerations refer to the underlying abstraction.

The search for an acceptable answer has proved to be one of the most intractable problems in forest resources management. The core of the difficulty lies in the fact that wilderness is not merely a condition of the land, but also a condition of the mind evoked by the land. At the very least, this is likely to vary a great deal with individualized experience and taste. Even Thoreau, the guru of modern preservationists ("in wildness is the preservation of the world"), seems to have been of two minds on the matter. From pastoral Walden Pond he wrote wonderful words about *la vie naturale,* but the slope of a mountain in a real wilderness caused him considerable discomfiture: he found it "savage and dreary . . . [a] place for heathenism and superstitious rites."[44] With this as an example, it is not surprising those whose nearest forest is Central Park may see wilderness as any place without dogs and mounted police.[45] Obviously, something more was contemplated by Congress for, even by the loosest standards, Central Park is not a wilderness (a jungle perhaps, but not a wilderness).

But definitions are elusive. What has emerged from attempts to articulate the meaning of wilderness has tended to be the stuff of poetry, not the best guide for the land use planner. The Wilderness Act, in a burst of eloquence rare for Congress, declares wilderness to be an area "where the earth and its community of life are untrammeled by man, where man himself is a visitor who does not remain." That is not helpful. The act is not wholly without practical guidelines. It tells us that the land must be without "permanent improvements or human habitation;" it must appear to have been "affected primarily by the forces of nature with the imprint of man's work substantially unnoticeable." It further instructs that the land should offer outstanding opportunities for solitude or a "primitive and unconfined type of recreation." Finally, it must be at least 5,000 acres or of "sufficient size as to make practicable its preservation." These are minimal guidelines; and as a practical matter they simply pass the task of definition to the further working of the administrative (and political) process.

The absence of clearer guidelines from Congress has permitted debate over an extreme range of alternatives, with the Forest Service at one pole and the Sierra Club and Wilderness Society at the other. The Forest Service has rather doggedly insisted on a purist view of wilderness. It has been very reluctant to include lands where timber has been cut or roads or other still-visible structures have been built. *Parker* v. *United States*[46] offers one instructive example, and the prolonged controversy over "wilderness East," another.

Parker was a suit to enjoin a timber sale in a portion of an area contiguous to the Gore Range–Eagles Nest Primitive Area in Colorado's White Mountain National Forest. Plaintiffs contended that a timber sale in the area would in effect preclude any future consideration of the area for wilderness. Their basic contention was that once an area was determined to be suitable for wilderness, the service could not take any action which would impair that suitability until the president had the opportunity to determine whether to propose the area for inclusion. The Forest Service contended that the area was neither available—because it had long been planned to harvest the area—nor suitable—because of the presence of a small "bug road," built in the area in the early 1950s to provide access for fighting the bark beetle. The trial court found for the plaintiffs and enjoined the sale. The decision, upheld on appeal, was enthusiastically acclaimed by preservationists and roundly criticized by the Forest Service and the timber industry.

The opinion made two noteworthy holdings. First, it held that the Forest Service's determination of the area as not available was of no consequence. By the court's interpretation the act precluded the service from cutting in any area contiguous to a primitive or wilderness area if the contiguous area was of "predominantly wilderness character." While the service's recommendations to the president for permanent disposition could take such matters as cost and benefit into account, if it were determined that area were suitable for wilderness, then the agency had to stay its hands until the president had acted. The implications of this part of the decision are potentially broad, but we will defer considering them. It is the second part of the opinion which is of interest here. The court's finding that the area was suitable for wilderness gave short shrift to the purist argument of the government that the presence of the road precluded such a determination. The road had been blocked off, was partly overgrown, and because of the dense growth around it was not visible from more than 100 yards away.[47] Besides, the boundaries could be drawn to exclude it.

At first glance, the court's opinion on this point seems sensible. In fact, the finding on this score was not challenged by the government on appeal.[48] Why should the status of the entire area turn on the presence of one small bug road that would ultimately disappear? On second thought, however, this "sensible" answer raises some difficult questions. If an invisible bug road does not disqualify, what about a road once used for logging, still visible because of its continued use by hunters in jeeps.[49] After all, these roads too will eventually disappear naturally, and they can be made to disappear more rapidly by Forest Service action.[50]

Parker represents one relatively trivial illustration of the purist position of the Forest Service. Although it was overruled in that particular instance, the service has continued to insist on a rather high standard of suitability, as illustrated in the "wilderness East" controversy. Wilderness is unevenly distributed, with virtually all of it in the eleven western states and Alaska. Apart from the unique Minnesota Boundary Waters, the amount of wilderness in the East is negligible, for two reasons. One is the relatively small amount of federal landholdings in the East. The second is the fact most federal lands in the East were acquired after they had been heavily used; indeed, it was just such overuse that led to their acquisition by the Forest Service. After the passage of the Wilderness Act and the initial inclusion of a few small wilderness areas in the East, the Forest Service declared, "There is no wilderness in the East," a position which reflected its purity standard of suitability. At the same time the demand for wilderness in the East is high. The greater population density, the concrete and steel pressures of modern society, and the inaccessibility of western wilderness areas are only some of the factors that contribute to this demand. In recent years, this has been translated into two proposals: one to create a special "wild area" system of near-wilderness lands; the other to add some twenty-eight areas (a total of 471,000 acres) to the existing wilderness system.

Under the former, Congress would create a system of "wild areas," defined as primitive areas in which man may have "left his mark," but his imprint was sufficiently slight to enable the area to be restored to a natural state. The protection to be awarded these areas is similar but not identical to that given wilderness areas: timber harvesting and grazing would be prohibited; all new mining activity would be prohibited; and the use of motor vehicles and equipment restricted; but public facilities of a "rustic, primitive nature" would be permitted.[51] The rationale for a separate wild-areas system is that of maintaining the purity of wilderness areas. Most of the eastern areas proposed for wild-area status (essentially the same ones proposed for inclusion in the wilderness system) are less than 5,000 acres or show visible signs of man's influence.[52]

Most preservationists have opposed the wild-areas proposal on the ground it is a subterfuge to limit true wilderness by giving legislative sanction to the Forest Service's restrictive notions of purity.[53] Preservationists argue that the proposed wild areas qualify for full wilderness protection and have accordingly supported legislation to designate some twenty-eight areas. One proposal[54] would also amend the Wilderness Act to permit inclusion of areas where evidence of man's presence has been substantially erased and the area restored to wilderness. This proposal would specifically permit certain nonconforming uses or improvements to be present when the area was designated (the assumption being that they will be removed).

The Forest Service until recently kept a discreet silence concerning the alternative proposals. In fact, however, it was widely known that the service favored the wild-areas proposal; indeed, the proposal was really a reflection of its well-known position on purity. In the face of vocal criticism from preservationists, the Forest Service recently supported the addition to the existing system of those eastern lands restored to wilderness, carefully limiting this support to eastern lands only (i.e., lands east of the one-hundredth meridian).[55] Thus, its endorsement of the "wilderness East" proposal only partially compromises its purity policy.

Apart from this recent compromise the Forest Service has continued to embrace the purity ideal and to insist that purity, like virginity, cannot be restored. The traditional defense of this has been that the same standards which govern protection of wilderness (after it is classified as such) should govern the initial selection. Otherwise it will be unable to maintain the high level of protection against demands to permit nonconforming use. Former Chief Forester Edward Cliff explained:

> Personally I hope very much that we will not see a lowering of quality standards to make acceptable some man-made intrusions or defects of other kinds simply for the sake of adding acreage. If this is done, we will surely see an undermining of our defense against similar intrusions on land already in the system. . . . Quality standards may be eroded and significantly lowered in the future unless we keep our sights high. . . . The quality we insist on in classification will shape the character and quality of the environment that can be maintained in future management of the resources.[56]

Preservationists have attacked this rationale as inconsistent with the more flexible standard of the act (i.e., the imprint of man's work need only be "substantially unnoticeable"). It is, they argue, only an excuse for opposing expansion of the wilderness system.[57] While the latter view seems extreme, the service's rationale does appear more restrictive than the act commands; it is also a bit disingenuous, or at least incomplete, in not elaborating a deeper reason for its conservative approach. The practical importance of high standards is twofold.

First, there is the problem of maintaining standards of preservation once an area is identified as wilderness. Clearly, this problem is related somewhat to the character of initial classification. If land bearing visible signs of man's intrusions is included in the wilderness, it will be more difficult to preclude future nonconforming uses. But it is doubtful that the problem is a major one. The difficulties the service has faced in this respect are only slightly related to whether the land was once "trammeled" by man. The big problem of administration today relates to pressures from large numbers of users and those for incompatible uses (such as motorized equipment); the magnitude of both generally has little to do with how pristine the land was when it was admitted.[58]

The more significant problem relates not to management of wilderness but rather to the extent of wilderness preservation. It is not, as the preservationists claim, simply a matter of opposing wilderness expansion; but a matter of being able to draw a desirable limit to preservation. For many preservationists, the fact that an area may have been subjected to past use is a matter of relatively little concern if the natural condition and appearance has been or can soon be restored. There is some practical appeal to this: once the condition of the land is restored, who will know whether in some "distant" time (as we now gauge time, a matter of a score years or so) part of the land was used for roads, logged, or explored by miners? To paraphrase the hair-coloring ad, only the Forest Service will know for sure. And who will care: to the extent people are responding to the area as it is now, past use is unlikely to be of much consequence to most.

The difficulty is that such a flexible approach leaves too little limit on preservation. If any land can become wilderness with either natural *or* artificial restoration to its once-primitive condition, the potential expanse of wilderness becomes not only great, but greatly elastic. What Chief Cliff ought to have said was not that we should keep the standards restrictive in order to keep them high, but rather that we should keep them high in order to keep them restrictive.

Though Cliff seems to have been chary of putting it in those terms, his successor has been somewhat more candid. In urging that any lowering of wilderness standards to accommodate restored areas be confined to the East, Chief John McGuire argued:

> There are several reasons for maintaining such a distinction. If almost any of the restored eastern national forest lands . . . were deemed to meet present Wilderness Act criteria, it would be extremely difficult to define a degree of disturbance that would disqualify many millions of acres of Federal lands for wilderness consideration. These listed areas have almost all been substantially altered by man's work. Should such areas be considered as "primeval," vast areas within the various Federal land systems could also qualify. The uniqueness of the present wilderness system would disappear.
>
> The national forest system has been established for a multiplicity of land uses and services. These publicly owned lands provide timber, wildlife habitat, water, forage, and developed recreation sites and experiences. Just as it is important to assure preservation of a portion of our Nation's land heritage for wilderness purposes, it is necessary to have a relatively stable base for providing these other resources and uses on a permanent, sustained yield basis. . . .
>
> A "restored" lands definition of wilderness for all national forest lands

could markedly reduce the management options for a great portion of the national forests in the West. Wilderness designation means that a number of other resource values and opportunities are foregone. For example, watershed improvements, wildlife habitat improvement projects, timber harvesting, range improvement, other vegetative alteration projects and developed recreation are not permitted within wilderness. Even the development of limited "back-country" recreation facilities, without road construction, would be foreclosed.[59]

This, of course, poses the ultimate question, Why should they be restrictive? What began as a question of environmental suitability becomes a question of what the Service calls availability and need. Not how much land looks like wilderness, but how much wilderness can we afford to preserve becomes the focus of the issue.

Economic Criteria

It is not surprising that, in expressing Forest Service policy on the extending wilderness, Chief Cliff chose to avoid putting the issue in terms of economic allocation and cast it rather in terms of maintaining quality. As mentioned before, the Forest Service has not made much use of economic analysis in its primitive area review process until recently. Even now one senses it is groping somewhat in deciding just how and how much an economic analysis (beyond crude thumbnail calculations) will aid in decision making. The degree of enthusiasm for the kind of cost–benefit analysis used for preliminary analysis of the 56 million acres of roadless areas (out of which 12.3 million acres were finally selected for further review) varies, depending on whom one talks to in the agency. If there seems to be some ambivalence about the exact role of economic analysis within the agency, outside the agency no such uncertainty clouds the thinking of the major opponents of wilderness. The timber industry is quite certain economic analysis is necessary; most preservationists seem equally convinced such analysis is simply a tool of commodity-user interests.

The attitude of those who want to avoid considering the economics of wilderness seems to me a strange one, but it is one which needs to be reckoned with. To begin with, it is evident that this is an economic problem in that it involves an allocation of scarce resources.[60] If it were not an economic problem, it would not be a problem at all. To be sure, the issue is not merely an economic one: it is also a political, social, and even a cultural one. But that is true of virtually all problems important enough to discuss; an economic problem does not cease to be one merely because of the presence of other such elements. All of this is trivially true and would hardly warrant mention were it not for the tendency of some preservationists to regard the issue of wilderness as one somehow wholly removed from economic considerations and beyond economic analysis.

Characterizing the issue as an economic one does not itself indicate the appropriate solution; it does, however, suggest a particular way of analyzing the issues. Here, it would seem, is the real explanation for resistance to defining the problem in economic terms: it is not the economic characterization as such but the manner of the calculus generally attending it. In short, the problem may be an economic one but, so goes the argument, economic analysis is inappropriate, or at least so inadequate that it is not worth the bother.[61] This attitude is hard to categorize as anything but a confusion of what economic analysis attempts to do, as well as what it claims to accomplish. Perhaps it also reflects a confusion of economic analysis in general with a particular economic situation. In its broadest sense, however, economic analysis is simply the evaluation of alternative choices under conditions of scarcity. Its distinctive contribution is its insistence on a careful and complete valuation of the alternatives and on choosing the alternative with greater value.

It is this valuation process that is most suspect by preservationists. The notion appears to be widespread that wilderness represents intangible values impossible to measure; thus, no equation between wilderness and competing uses is conceivable. This view is by no means confined to preservationists; similar sentiment was recorded in interviews with Forest Service officials. One official asked, "How can you put a price tag on solitude and spiritual refreshment?" The question reflects a rather basic misunderstanding of how a pricing system works, and so mistakes the nature of the problem. There is nothing inherent in the value of wilderness, however intangible, that prevents it from being priced. Wilderness is no different from any other scarce resource that produces intangible satisfaction. Rubber balls are valued for the intangible thrills they produce when bouncing; a Rembrandt painting, for the intangible pleasure derived from viewing it; a church, for the spiritual uplift it affords. But we do not give away rubber balls, Rembrandt paintings, nor the building materials with which churches are made. The problem is not that the value is immeasurable it is simply that here, in contrast to rubber balls, Rembrandt paintings, and stained glass windows, the resource has not been left to market forces but has been allocated by administrative and political decision.

The economic theory is that wilderness like many other land resources is a public good for which private prices are an inappropriate measure of social value.[62] We briefly noted earlier the pertinence of the theory of public goods to outdoor recreation; it need not be reviewed.[63] I am willing to accept (with qualifications on the user-fee aspect) the reasonableness of public choice.[64] But public choice does not mean irrational choice, and in any formulation of rational choice criteria it is difficult to see how economic considerations—economic costs and benefits—can be avoided. Even a decision not specifically articulated in economic terms, clearly has an economic consequence. For example, a decision to opt for wilderness preservation without considering the value of productive uses sacrificed is tantamount to a decision that the value of wilderness exceeds any probable value of those resources. That is an economic choice, however it is rationalized. The real question is whether, and to what extent, the economic consequence will be clearly and rationally identified in the choice.

It is one thing to identify the relevance and importance of economic factors, it is another to describe the methodology and the detail of analysis to be incorporated into the decision-making process. Of course, if the choice were left to the market, the interplay of the market process would take care of the allocation process. But since it has been decided the market would be inadequate to measure the full social values, the task becomes one of applying *some kind* of benefit–cost analysis.[65]

Calculating the benefits of wilderness preservation is obviously the difficult part of the task. As emphasized earlier, this does not mean the wilderness value is intrinsically beyond the measure of price, it means only that in the absence of a market mechanism for pricing this resource, there is no clear measure of its value. One can describe in general terms some of the value, as was attempted at the outset of this chapter, but that brings us no closer to a solution of this problem.

One might construct an imputed demand schedule, based on the expenditures persons incur in connection with visits to a particular area. This technique is suggested for calculating the demand for outdoor recreation generally,[66] and it could be applied to wilderness as well. However, there are a number of difficulties with this technique, even as applied to ordinary recreation. Among them is the fact that the needed information about such costs is difficult to obtain. And when obtained it is not a complete measure of the value the visitor puts upon the visit. In the case of wilderness the difficulty is even greater in this respect. If it is true, the primary value of wilderness goes beyond the enjoyment of visitors; imputing a demand for wilderness based on visitor data will, of course, undervalue the wilderness benefit.

For example, one of the values presumably immeasurable by the visitor data is what has been described as the "option demand" for the resource.[67] Many persons who have no intention of visiting a wilderness would value (and would pay for) the option of permitting them or their children to do so in the future. Even the option-demand theory, however, does not quite reach to the heart of the broader social value which wilderness is commonly thought to have and which provides the basic rationale for public, rather than private, market choice. We might label this the *social-option value*—the value which society at large places on having a refuge against civilization—where, in Romain Gary's words, man "can feel safe from his own cleverness." [68] In part this is an aggregate on the individual option demand, but it also goes beyond it in the sense that the value is one which requires a broad social perspective, a value which specially commends itself to public choice rather than market determinations.

If the benefits of wilderness are extremely difficult to measure, the costs are not. And this is really the more important part of the benefit–cost analysis. Even if we derive no meaningful measure of the value of wilderness benefits, it is essential to rational decision making to have some notion of the costs. An initial calculation of the costs may resolve the issue without becoming mired in the difficulties of valuing benefits. If, for example, the cost of preserving a particular part is small, no significant land use conflict exists, and choice for preservation can be made without further advice. At the other end of the spectrum, if the cost were determined to be extraordinarily high, it might be that no conceivable wilderness benefits flowing from preserving, say, a marginal increment of land could override the demonstrable costs.

As mentioned earlier, just such estimates seem to characterize most of the economic analysis done in earlier stages of the classification process. Conceptually the analysis is simple: cost is measured by the value of the alternatives foregone (opportunity cost). In the case of wilderness, the cost would be the value of timber which cannot be cut, the minerals which cannot be withdrawn, and other uses (e.g., developed recreation) precluded by the wilderness status. Unlike wilderness benefits, we can obtain price figures for at least some of these uses, since they are sold in the market.

It is sometimes argued that these resources are not really sacrificed: since they are preserved for the future, they should be considered more an investment than a current cost. Quite apart from the dubious assumption that preservation status is one which can be easily reversed when resource demand rises, the notion that nothing is lost in foregoing *present* consumption is incomprehensible. This does not imply the future value of the resource should not be considered, but given reasonably efficient capital investment planning the future economic value of the resource will be taken care of in the process of maximizing the present value of a future income stream from the resource. Such calculation might or might not support nonuse of resources over a particular time period, and this might not accord with preservation (over a period of time). But quite plainly the investment decision would not necessarily accord with preservation. Even using a low rate of discount, which would favor investment, any conformity between the investment decision and preservation would be purely accidental.

Indeed, there is one important respect in which preservation would not only be unwarranted in terms of allocation of resources over time but would be antithetical to efficient capital formation. Even ignoring the foregoing benefits of consumption and use, preservation does impair the value of the resource "capital" itself. Thus timber, which we can treat as the primary capital resource considered in this context, may generally appreciate in value with rise in market prices. Against this increase, however, must be applied the quickly diminishing productivity of the forest left in the primitive state. Though conservationists are constantly and correctly reminding us that a forest left in a natural state can and does renew itself, so far as I am aware, no one would imagine the *economic* productivity of an unmanaged forest is equal to that of a well-managed forest.[69] Whether the wilderness benefit exceeds the sacrifice in economic productivity (in capital value) has still to be resolved; the point here is merely that capital value *is* sacrificed.

Many preservationists insist that refined calculations are really pointless because the total amount of land—and resources—that could become wilderness is a trivial portion of the nation's land (and resources). Thinking simply in terms of acres this is clearly true. Suppose, for example, one were to take all the presently identified but unclassified roadless areas, 56 million acres, and add them to existing wilderness and primitive areas—about 15 million acres; add a half million acres for eastern wilderness proposals, and then add all Department of the Interior lands which have to date been proposed for wilderness—about 6 million acres.[70] All of this would come to only about 10 percent of all federal lands and something more than 3 percent of the nation's lands.[71]

But this display of figures, like a parlor trick, hides more than it reveals. What we are interested in is not gross acreage but productive land; and, as anyone who has driven across the Nevada desert quickly notes (until he reaches Las Vegas), there is a lot of land that is neither productive nor wilderness. Just how much there is, I do not know. Nor do I see any reason to find out unless one wants to engage in the game of numbers, percentages, and ratios. What really matters is the productive value of the proposed and prospective wilderness, and how much of that will be lost by preservation.

Only very partial and crude estimates are available now, and they may be all that will ever be available. So far as the areas presently within the wilderness system (including primitive areas not yet reclassified as wilderness) are concerned, there does not appear to be any reliable calculation of what the total value of such lands would be in productive use. Although general surveys of minerals and timber have been made of these areas at some time in the past, many of them are old and would not reflect current market values nor other current conditions affecting value. Thus, even if early studies had been done with exacting cost–benefit techniques, we would not have a very *precise* indication of the opportunity cost of this wilderness.

However, there seems to be a consensus today—among timber and other commodity users as well as the Forest Service and preservationists—that *most* of the areas within the existing wilderness system have little productive value. So far as timber is concerned, many of the areas are not even sufficiently productive to be classified as "commercial forest,"[72] and of those which do include commercial forest much of it is marginally productive. That is why many such lands have remained roadless and "unexploited": the timber was not worth the high cost of access. To preserve such lands involves, then, little loss in timber value. And when one further considers the very poor return on investment from active management of marginal timberlands, and then adds to that the unrecovered environmental costs of access and removal from lands of low productivity, it is apparent that the opportunity cost of preserving such lands as wilderness is close to zero.[73] Indeed, quite apart from the question of wilderness preservation, it has been argued that the low rate of return on investment makes it uneconomic to manage such marginally productive lands for sustained-yield timber production.[74]

Turning from existing primitive and wilderness areas to other roadless areas, a first glance at the inventory of such areas suggests that the same generalizations hold for much of this land as for the existing system. Of a total inventory of some 56 million acres, only about 18.6 million are commercial forest and some of that is, again, in a region of low productivity which may be uneconomic to harvest.[75] On a closer look, the first appearance may be deceptive. Forest Service estimates put the total annual allowable cut for all of the 56 million acres at some 2.3 billion bd.-ft.[76] The difficulty in assessing the significance of this figure is that the estimate does not reveal how much of the volume is operable, that is, how much of it would repay the costs of road access and harvest.

More important (though also less reliable) are the estimates of *total* opportunity cost for the roadless areas, including not only timber values but the value of other major resource uses which preservationist status would foreclose, together with cost outlays for establishing and maintaining the wilderness. The cost of all 56 million acres is estimated at over $2.5 billion.[77]

The above figures suggest merely the rough parameters of what is involved in the unclassified roadless areas; they indicate that the potential costs of preservation, while not overwhelming, are not negligible either. Beyond that it is not possible to be more exact, for the specific calculations made by the Forest Service are not only preliminary, they are ambiguous as to some of the underlying assumptions: for example, whether all of the timber for which value was calculated is operable, or, in any case, economically sound to manage, in light of other investment opportunities. However, it is doubtful whether it would be worthwhile to attempt a more precise and detailed calculus for the entire roadless acreage, or even for the 12.3 million acres selected for further study (new study areas).

As previously mentioned, it would greatly simplify matters if we could deal in nationwide terms, for in the total scheme of things, compromise tradeoffs between preservation and, say, timber values, would be much easier to make. Unfortunately, a nationwide approach seems out of the question for reasons mentioned: the controversy over wilderness is inevitably a local one. The fact that a particular tract of roadless land may contribute trivially to total timber supply for the nation, a region, or even a forest becomes almost unimportant if the timber which it does or could contribute is deemed vital to the local economy. Similarly for the wilderness side, it is nearly impossible to persuade local preservation groups to give up their own wilderness in consideration of another hundreds of miles distant. It seems inevitable then that there is no alternative but to engage in a case-by-tiresome-case appraisal of the costs (and, if possible, the benefits) until every acre of potential wilderness has been examined. It will be a long process.

Where do we arrive after this tour through the economics of wilderness—which some will no doubt think better described as the wilderness of economics? Wherever we have arrived, it is certainly not far from where we began. Having only outlined some of the basic concepts and issues, nothing much has been said of the application or of the precise applicability of the concepts to the particular decision-making process of the Forest Service. While I would feel comfortable in saying these are matters which should be pursued to a degree greater than has generally been the case in the past, I would not feel comfortable in prescribing particular procedures, even if I were competent to do so. For its part, the service is giving more serious attention to economic analysis of the costs of wilderness. But just how important this analysis will be in formulating decisions remains to be seen. It is not just that the issue of wilderness preservation has been political. This, after all, is quite appropriate considering the initial premise that the decision is to be a matter of public choice. The problem is that the issue has also been insulated in a layer of emotional lard which has obscured the elements on which rational and reasonably informed choice can be made. If dispassionate analysis were to do no more than clear the air of cant and pointless rhetoric, it would do a singular service.

Preserving Wilderness

To date, paramount public attention has been fixed on the question of establishing wilderness, while problems of managing it have clearly been of secondary public interest outside of a few exceptional instances or matters of special local interest.[78] To some it will no doubt appear strange even to talk of managing a wilderness, for by common understanding as well as apparent congressional design,[79] wilderness is an area left to nature's own devices. Unfortunately, it is not so simple. Surrounded by an urban, industrialized civilization, even a wilderness cannot be preserved simply by declaration alone. At the very least, administration is required to establish or interpret and enforce restrictions on access and use.[80]

The basic statutory restrictions have been discussed earlier; essentially they forbid commercial uses such as timber harvesting,[81] livestock grazing (except where established prior to the act), and other commercial uses. As previously noted, a special exception was provided for mining and mineral exploration which could continue until 1984.[82]

For the most part, these general statutory restrictions on wilderness use do not impose any significant burden on the Forest Service of either interpretation—the courts have taken that out of its hands—or of administrative implementation—the restrictions are self-enforcing. With some of the other restrictions the administrative responsibility has been more difficult.

Use of Motorized Equipment. The use of motorized equipment has caused special difficulty. Although the act generally bans its use within wilderness, a number of exceptions are provided[83]: (1) where the use of motorboats or aircraft was established before the act, this may continue subject to agency restrictions; (2) use of equipment for mining or mineral exploration is permitted; (3) where roads or motor transport are necessary to obtain access to private land within the area, it is impliedly authorized; and (4) use of motor vehicles or other equipment is provided where necessary either to handle emergencies or for administrative purposes.

We can set aside the mineral exploration problem, for the use of particular equipment is an integral part of the larger incongruity of mining and mineral exploration. Once that basic incongruity is accepted, the use of motorized equipment poses no special problem. Conversely, if by judicial fiat mining and mineral exploration is prohibited, obviously the problem of motors is solved.

The problem of access to private inholdings is a significant one. Within the exterior boundaries of the nearly 15 million acres of national forest wilderness and primitive areas are extensive private inholdings. The only access to many of these lands is across wilderness. While the Forest Service can regulate this access, it cannot restrict it to a point where it would in effect destroy it.[84] The Forest Service has attempted to diminish this problem of regulating access together with the more general problem presented by nonconforming private uses within the wilderness area, through gradual acquisition of the private lands, by purchase or exchange.[85] However, it is not likely that with the funds at its disposal the Forest Service will be able to rid itself of this problem within the immediate future. It is more likely the problem will be compounded by the addition of the new study areas.[86]

More troublesome is the problem of determining means of access for emergencies and administrative purposes. In conformance with its approach to wilderness classification the Forest Service has taken a purist approach in regard to its own activities and those of other agencies (e.g., agencies conducting scientific investigation). Motorized equipment or vehicles are authorized only under very limited circumstances and only with the approval of the forest supervisor or a higher official.[87] As in the case of wilderness classification, the Forest Service's restrictive policies have brought it criticism from various groups, for example, outfitters and backpackers who want to use power saws to cut fuel wood or blaze trails, mining companies or agencies such as the Geological Survey that want to use helicopters to make mineral or other scientific surveys, and so on.[88]

For example, when two students in an Outward Bound program were killed in the wilderness, a local Forest Service official refused to permit the use of a helicopter to recover the bodies on the ground that since the students were already dead, no emergency existed which would justify the use of a helicopter. The refusal was later reversed by the chief who denied that the initial decision reflected Forest Service policy.[89] However, that did not prevent its criticism, on the evident assumption that it did reflect the basic attitude of the agency toward wilderness.

That assumption seems to me accurate but the criticism itself dubious. It is not at all obvious that helicopters should be used in a case involving no actual rescue. Indeed, even in many cases of rescue, the use of helicopters or other motor vehicles might be reasonably debated. Suppose, for example, a group of experienced, adult backpackers become lost in a wilderness on a scheduled ten-day trip. After they have been gone, say, three days past their scheduled return, their families ask that helicopters be dispatched to search for them. On these assumed facts it seems, to me, a questionable policy to send a helicopter or other mechanized vehicle into the area. If that seems harsh, it is so only because that is what the wilderness condition implies. Granted a sympathetic instinct and an explicit congressional recognition that emergencies justify some qualification of the wilderness condition, lines must be drawn somewhere; and if wilderness is to mean anything, the line must be a fairly harsh one. Otherwise, why stop at helicopter rescues; why not construct permanent rescue roads, aid stations, or telephone lines? At some point on this slippery slope of logical "next steps," it becomes difficult to see any real point to wilderness preservation. I am not suggesting mechanical devices ought never to be permitted for emergency or administrative purposes. What I am suggesting is that any restriction giving meaningful recognition to wilderness as an area of "primeval character" will be regarded by many (particularly those unsympathetic to the wilderness ideal) as unnecessary and harsh.

Fire Control and Disease Prevention. The problem with mechanized equipment and vehicle use for purposes of meeting the needs of administrative management raises a more general issue of what those needs are. A major consideration has been to define the proper scope of various protective activities such as fire control and disease prevention. Taking a very purist view the question of what measures to apply to protect wilderness against the depredation of fire, insects, and disease would seem to admit but a single answer—none. Whatever else a wilderness is supposed to be, according to the Wilderness Act, it is an area "affected primarily by the forces of nature." That would imply that natural fires[90] ought to be permitted to burn, and insects and disease to work their destruction—in short, free play should be given to natural ecological forces. Such a laissez faire policy is dictated not simply out of respect for the wilderness ideal, it is essential to maintain the vitality of the natural environment. Control of insects, disease, and fire interferes with the process by which the forest reinvigorates itself. With timber cutting banned from wilderness, these natural processes become the only means of removing old timber and promoting forest regeneration.

Unfortunately, a completely laissez faire solution is ruled out by the fact that these natural forces do not recognize wilderness, or even public, boundaries. The fire that sweeps through a wilderness may sweep right across adjoining public or private lands as well. The problem has been to find a balance of protection, which reasonably meets both the needs of the wilderness and the interests of other lands. The Forest Service's early response was one of vigorous prevention and control—of fire in particular. However, its policy has shifted toward giving greater latitude to natural forces. Usually insect and disease control is not undertaken unless the danger threatens to spread to other lands, or unless the epidemic presents a greater threat to wilderness values than does the method of control.[91] The stated policy on fire is a bit vague (partly because it appears to be still evolving), but in general the policy appears to be similar to that for insect or disease control, one which aims for a less aggressive control of fire in wilderness areas where it poses no danger to lands outside the area or to life and private property within.[92]

In recent years many conservationists have urged the use of controlled burning as a tool of forest management, particularly in wilderness areas.[93] Although the service has used controlled burning in aid of wildlife or range management, or as a means of cleanup and site preparation in timber harvest areas, it has been rather reluctant to embrace controlled burning as a general form of ecological control. One problem is that of controlling the spread of fire. Another is that controlled burning, while emulating natural forces, is an artificial interference with natural forces—only slightly different from cutting trees. However, both objections can partly be countered by the fact that burning is occasioned by the Forest Service's own prior suppression of natural fire, the effect of which has been to build up excessive "fuel" in the forest to the point where the outbreak of any fire creates the risk of a conflagration.[94] In apparent recognition of this the Forest Service has now endorsed controlled burning in wilderness areas, subject to approval by the chief of the Forest Service.[95] Just how vigorously such a program should be pushed at this time is debatable. Carefully implemented, there are benefits to such a policy—not only in wilderness areas but in other areas also. But at present there are substantial gaps in scientific knowledge of the ecological and economic consequences of controlled burning and of the techniques for burning effectively and safely, all of which counsel a cautious approach to controlled burning.[96]

Carrying Capacity of Wilderness Areas. The most serious threat to wilderness is far more subtle than the problem of commercial exploitation or natural depredations such as fire, pests, or disease; it is excessive use by individuals. The problem runs essentially parallel to that of recreational use of the forests in general and, like the more general problem, indications are it will become increasingly more troublesome. In 1970, nearly 6 million visitor-days were reported for areas in the wilderness system.[97] Even if this use increased only in proportion to general recreational use, the danger to wilderness is evident. In fact, however, wilderness use is expected to increase relative to general recreational use,[98] compounding an already serious future threat to wilderness preservation.

The problem of overcrowding is particularly acute for wilderness because of its very limited, and relatively fixed, carrying capacity. In part, this limited capacity is a consequence of the specially fragile character of most wilderness. As noted earlier, the very absence of exploitation typically attests to their relatively low productivity. Soils are often shallow and vegetation insecure and easily damaged, mainly by soil compaction or destruction of vegetation. Once damaged, the land and vegetation recovers very slowly—in some cases not within a human generation. The carrying capacity of a wilderness, however, is set, not by the tolerance of the physical environment alone, but by the psychological impact of use on the wilderness experience of the users themselves.[99] At least in some areas the latter aspect may be the controlling one in determining capacity insofar as it calls for a lower level of use than considerations of environmental protection. Thus, an area capable of tolerating, say, 1,000 visitor-days a month without serious environmental impact may tolerate only a fraction of that number when account is taken of "psychological congestion" effects. A wilderness in which one encounters, say, two or three campers each hour over the period of a twelve-hour day may still retain its physical vitality, but it would, at least to me, hardly seem like a wilderness.

This psychological aspect adds a most difficult dimension to the problem of overuse; unlike the physical constraint of maintaining the wilderness, experience can hardly be defined let alone measured. We are back to the question raised earlier in the context of the initial decision of whether or not to preserve land; that is, What is wilderness? Yet in a way the problem here is more vexing, for it forces the agency—and the public—to articulate more precisely the concept of wilderness (and wilderness experience).

Initial decisions to remove land from economically productive use can usually be made without any clear concept of what wilderness means. Given a political decision made to preserve some lands, a determination of suitability (as distinct from availability) can be made on the basis of scenery and a very gross judgment about the capacity for solitude, and so on, but there is no occasion for defining closely what is meant by solitude or other attributes of wilderness. A decision to establish a limit on use requires just such a definition. It is a most difficult one to make. Not only is there no ready-made standard, but there is no fully satisfactory process for setting one.

One can always poll visitors to see how they define the wilderness experience. That has been done for several areas. In general the results show most wilderness visitors seek a high degree of purity; they value solitude and react adversely to encounters with other visitors or to evidence of other use (particularly in the form of litter).[100] One difficulty with such surveys is that they test a very selected sample insofar as they are limited to actual, rather than potential, beneficiaries and users.

Thus, the sample population is biased in the direction of whatever expectations have been created for the particular area. A very pure wilderness—with low density of use, no significant evidence of use, few or no facilities—is likely to attract primarily a very select population of visitors who value that purity highly. It should follow that any poll of such a group will produce a significant majority in favor of purity. On the other hand, an area that has, and shows, a high density of use will draw visitors from a broader, more "tolerant" population. And so on. The logic can be followed through the entire spectrum of recreational experience, from a backpack adventure in the High Sierras to an afternoon at Coney Island. If the latter seems far-fetched, consider the proposal of one writer who, far from seeking solitude, proposed the construction of aerial tramways into wilderness so that all could enjoy it.[101] One wonders how the tramway rider would respond to the pollster's question, What is a wilderness?

There is much to be said for selecting as a bench mark the standard of the most discriminating wilderness visitors insofar as it provides the foundation for a high standard of purity. Indeed, for that reason recent surveys have not been content with polling visitors, but have differentiated between the true purists and those less insistent on purity. The underlying rationale is that wilderness should serve the purists, and the others may be accommodated by other recreational lands.[102] As a general proposition this is an appealing rationale. We can scarcely justify going to the opposite extreme and consulting everyone, for the very concept of wilderness preservation cuts against the grain of popular taste. If we simply counted noses, it is unlikely we would have wilderness at all.

And yet the visitor-sampling technique does not really solve the specific problem of determining the level of purity to be maintained. To define the level of purity by consulting an admittedly predetermined group of purists is evasive: by what standards is the group to be defined? If we have standards by which that group can be defined, what is the point of asking *them*: why not simply make the group-defining standards the standards of wilderness itself? Then, of course, the problem is, how do we establish the suitability—or legitimacy—of *those* standards? In short, reliance upon visitor perception would seem to be meaningful only in obtaining some measure of the nature and extent of acceptability of agency standards among those who are perceived as the primary users (not necessarily beneficiaries since, as I have pointed out, the benefits of wilderness must be supposed to extend beyond users).

It has been suggested that instead of merely asking visitors to define their ideal of wilderness, they might be asked to order their preferences according to how much they would be willing to pay for varying conditions (whether they would be required to pay is a separate issue if it is supposed their responses are candid).[103] This approach offers some advantages over the simple poll; in particular it permits the benefits associated with a particular level of wilderness preservation/use to be measured in terms which can thereby be compared with the costs of securing those benefits (e.g., the cost of restricting or channeling use to avoid encounters, the cost of additional land acquisitions, etc.). However, it does not fully answer the point raised above. Insofar as it is still directed at an already selected group, it still presupposes a certain basic standard of use.

Once a determination is made as to carrying capacity, there remains the problem of deciding how use will be controlled. We can quickly pass over the alternative of closing the wilderness to all visitors. Although the Forest Service has recognized that some areas might have to be closed in order to prevent environmental damage,[104] it is scarcely an appropriate solution to the problem of overcrowding. Even if such a measure were politically acceptable—a most dubious assumption—such a solution could be justified only in cases where no less drastic measure would be effective or practicable. It is difficult to imagine a situation where no control short of a total ban would be ineffective. Perhaps there could be some cases where the environment itself is so threatened that no further human use should be permitted. However, as noted earlier, it is the psychological character of the wilderness experience, not the physical environment, that will generally set the maximum limit on use. Where this is the case, to close the area in order to "preserve the wilderness" would make no sense at all,[105] unless there were no practicable, acceptable way of controlling the number or the concentration of visitors.

On the basis of expected use it is reasonable to predict that even an efficient system for controlling concentration will not in itself (without controlling the number of visitors) be adequate.[106] The crucial task therefore is to find an effective, acceptable basis for rationing visitor use. For reasons already explored in the discussion on managing outdoor recreation, rationing by means·of a pricing system has been forbidden by legislative fiat. Under the Land and Water Conservation Fund Act amendments, no fees may be charged except for developed recreational areas where special facilities or services are provided.[107] Even if this legislative restriction is eased for general recreation areas, there is no foreseeable likelihood it will be modified to the point of permitting charges for the use of wilderness areas. Nor is it likely that the Forest Service would impose a fee, even if permitted to do so. In view of the earlier discussion of recreation fees, we will not consider further whether this resistance to the use of a pricing system as a rationing device is sensible policy; the case for or against user charges is not much different for wilderness visitors than it is for recreation visitors.[108]

The alternative to price rationing is, of course, administrative rationing. Forest Service regulations permit regional foresters to implement administrative rationing, of both the number of visitors allowed and their length of stay, where deemed necessary either to maintain the quality of wilderness use (the wilderness experience) or of the environment itself—if lesser means of management influence (such as efforts to disperse visitors) are inadequate.[109] While the regulations do not specify the basis on which visitors shall be permitted to enter or be excluded, the assumption is a "queuing" system will be used, with permits being issued on a first-come–first-served basis. Recently such a system has been implemented in two national forest wilderness areas in California,[110] and is under active consideration in several others. A similar system is currently used in five wilderness areas administered by the Park Service. This permit system provides for reservations in advance; eventually it is contemplated that a national system for making reservations will be established for all national forest wilderness areas (for which permits are required by regional directive)—and perhaps even for the entire wilderness system.[111]

It is yet too early to know what will be the public acceptability of such rationing, although early comments are favorable. As a practical matter there is no alternative likely to be more acceptable. Aside from a pricing or queuing system the only basis for allocation is that of administrative selection based on "merit." This is a rather vague basis of selection which can conceivably encompass any number of desiderata, but as it has been suggested in this context by the noted conservationist, Garrett Hardin, the element of merit is one of physical ability to withstand the rigor of true wilderness.[112] On first hearing, the suggestion has a tone of reasonable plausibility. Certainly it does conform to the basic assumption that wilderness ought not to be modified to accommodate the effete with civilized comforts and aids. However, any system that did no more than exclude those who could not make the trip without an automobile is essentially pointless. By reasonably rigorous enforcement of wilderness quality standards, these persons are already excluded. The problem is what to do with the excessive number of visitors who can still "make it" after we have banned vehicles, motors, and other such aids.

Because it does not focus on the real problem, Hardin's proposal gives no answer, although we may suppose the logic of his solution suggests some further standards of physical prowess. That, however, would open up huge difficulties, both practical and normative. The practical are fairly obvious. Who should define the standards—the agencies or the legislature? What criteria should be used—age, skill, physical condition, mental alertness? What mechanisms should be available to supervise the exercise of administrative discretion either in setting the standards or in applying them to particular cases? Would every decision be subject to judicial review? The practical problems of establishing and administering standards of merit illuminate the very questionable, normative foundation of Hardin's merit proposal, What is the "merit" of physical vigor? As mentioned above, we assume maintaining vigorous standards of environmental purity will serve to exclude many persons not physically able to endure the wilderness on its own terms. This exclusion is not, however, based on any notion that the strong are, ethically, more deserving persons.

However, to go beyond this incidental exclusion to select only the most fit clearly assumes the most fit are the "most deserving." Hardin explains that the physically fit are best able to appreciate the true character of wilderness. Those who make it on their own, unaided by mechanical devices, are able to enjoy not merely the experience of being in a wilderness but the additional "experience of getting there," that is, self-achievement. That may be, but once one assumes all persons must minimally be able to make it on their own, without any artificial aids (radios, roads, vehicles), is there any justification for further selection on the basis of physical vigor? Is there any reason to suppose that, for example, a 20-year-old person, for whom the rigors of wilderness are only moderately challenging, appreciates the wilderness more than the 60-year-old person who can barely endure it?

If any generalizations are possible, I would be more inclined to say that just the reverse is likely to be true. But more to the point, there is simply no real basis in psychology for drawing any general inferences about the keenness of a person's experience or appreciation from his physical condition. And even if there were, it would not provide a moral basis for "merit awards" (in the form of permits to use the wilderness) to those with keener sensitivities. Whether such a notion of merit positively offends one's ethical sensibilities, it certainly is difficult to explain or justify by reference to any widely accepted sense of distributive justice. It is curious, to say the least, that Hardin concludes that the allocation of visitor permits through the marketplace would be rejected as "unfair," but that allocation to those with the keenest physical abilities and mental faculties would not be. Whatever inequities there may be in the distribution of wealth which cause persons to be suspicious about the marketplace, inequity is no less pervasive in the distribution of physical vigor or mental sensitivity. If one measures ethical merit independent of original endowment, there is no a priori reason to prefer health over wealth in the distribution of "merit goods." [113]

I put it this way in order to state the equivalence of the two cases in general normative terms. However, as I urged earlier, it is incorrect to suppose that a market system reflects nothing more than relative endowments of wealth. It also reflects relative preference in the choice of goods. For this reason, the common supposition that the rich would always outbid the poor in buying wilderness permits is foolish. Whether they would do so would depend on their individual preferences (their "utility functions," as the economist would put it). Moreover, notice that to the extent a pricing system would favor those who are relatively well-to-do, such is the case without a permit system; for the nongovernment-controlled costs of making a typical visit already serve to exclude the poor from the wilderness. Thus, a fee system would serve largely to ration demand among a relatively affluent group. Seen in that light, it is not easy to become excited about the ethical problem of charging the poor to enjoy wilderness.

It would draw us too far afield to pursue these matters further into the realms of ethical justice and economic welfare. It is enough to have pointed up the very basic problems intruding upon even such a seemingly obvious problem of resource management. It is safe to predict these issues will be largely avoided in practice by the expedient of an arbitrary, but apparently neutral, queuing system.

CONCLUSIONS

The wilderness preservation controversy has ranged over virtually all the basic issues confronted in federal land management. For the land manager, all the questions concerning land use allocation policy are posed. Should any large land area be given over to a single use or nonuse? By what criteria should such lands be chosen? How can the tradeoffs between economic use and preservation be measured? The allocation considerations lead to other questions of administrative management. How shall land use be regulated to conserve the resource? Should use of the resource be rationed by a pricing system or by administrative controls?

And underlying these substantive policy questions are those concerning the structure and processes of decision. What is the role of public participation in making decisions? What relative weights should be given respectively to national and local public interests? Should decisions be aimed at achieving an optimal balance of resource use within particular regions, or over the nation as a whole?

Finally, there is the further question for decision makers outside the Forest Service, notably those in the legislature and in the courts, How much discretion should the agency have in answering all of the above questions?

Quite obviously none of these questions have produced anything resembling a consensus among interested parties. Perhaps they never will. Certainly, there are some very substantial impediments to be overcome, one of these being the orientation of national forest policy generally with its emphasis on regional and local interests, and local needs. Giving preeminent consideration to regional and local land use interests would appear to complicate land use policy. For one thing, more individual decisions must be made. This not only adds to the burdens of land use administration, but it increases the potential for conflict. For another, focusing on local and regional interests precludes the possibility of tradeoffs across geographic regions. Specialization of land use is limited in favor of achieving balance within each geographic area.

Such a policy of decentralized land use is not without its political and social virtues, the same virtues which underlie the federal structure of the nation. Whether these virtues require the degree of balkanization which has characterized land use policy—wilderness policy in particular—is debatable.

The other major impediment to consensus on wilderness preservation is what was earlier termed the *holy war* aspect of the controversy. The conflict over wilderness is not simply a conflict of practical interests, but of basic social values as well. Such conflicts are hard to resolve by consensus. The "naturalist" who deeply believes the world is too preoccupied with material goods is unlikely to be persuaded that wilderness should be sacrificed to produce more of them, just as the "utilitarian" is unlikely to be enchanted with the idea that utilitarian benefits should be sacrificed to preserve the spiritual values of wilderness.

What this suggests is that it is probably futile to seek consensus on the broad issues of wilderness preservation. Attention to the general, abstract issues can only exacerbate the conflict among partisans on both sides of the preservation controversy, and make compromise more difficult. Instead, the general issues must be broken down into their smallest components and each of these examined as individual problems, with, it is hoped, a modest degree of rationality and a minimum amount of moralizing.

NOTES

1. See generally, David Bower, ed., *The Meaning of Wilderness to Science* (San Francisco: Sierra Club, 1960); and the Outdoor Recreation Resources Review Commission (ORRRC), *Wilderness and Recreation,* Study Report 3 (1962), pp. 31–33.

2. ORRRC, *Wilderness and Recreation,* pp. 28–31.

3. "In the Wilderness," *The Living Wilderness,* vol. 19, no. 49 (Summer 1954), p. ii (editorial). For a sampling of other, comparable expressions, see Roderick Nash, *Wilderness and the American Mind* (rev. ed., New Haven, Conn.: Yale University Press, 1973).

4. Quoted in ORRRC, *Wilderness and Recreation,* p. 34.

5. Nash (*Wilderness*) gives an excellent history of the wilderness concept, from which I have drawn substantially in the following discussion.

6. Ibid., pp. 100–101.

7. See John Ise, *Our National Park Policy* (Baltimore: Johns Hopkins University Press for Resources for the Future, 1961); and William C. Everhart, *The National Park Service* (New York: Praeger, 1972)

8. See George Marsh, *Man and Nature* (1867; facs. ed., Cambridge, Mass.: Harvard University Press, 1965), p. 327.

9. Nash, *Wilderness,* p. 133.

10. Stewart L. Udall, *The Quiet Crisis* (New York: Holt, Rinehart & Winston, 1963), pp. 64–80.

11. On the Hetch Hetchy episode, see Ise, *Our National Park Policy,* pp. 85–96; Nash, *Wilderness,* ch. 10; and Everhart, *The National Park Service,* pp. 15–17.

12. Quoted in Everhart, *The National Park Service,* p. 16.

13. Quoted in Samuel Hayes, *Conservation and the Gospel of Efficiency: The Progressive Conservation Movement* (Cambridge, Mass.: Harvard University Press, 1959), p. 42. See also, Gifford Pinchot, *Breaking New Ground* (New York: Harcourt Brace, 1947), pp. 31–32, 183–185, and 266.

14. This is well illustrated by the controversy over wilderness proposals in West Virginia, discussed in Kenneth P. Davis et al., *Federal Public Land Laws and Policies Relating to Multiple-Use of Public Lands,* Study for the Public Land Law Review Commission (rev. ed., Springfield, Ill.: Clearinghouse for Federal Scientific and Technical Publications, 1970), pp. 32–37.

15. For a full account of this early history, on which I have drawn heavily, see James P. Gilligan, "The Development of Policy and Administration, of Forest Service Primitive and Wilderness Areas," Ph.D. Thesis, University of Michigan, 1954.

16. ORRRC, *Wilderness and Recreation,* pp. 115 and 286.

17. See Gilligan, "The Development of Policy," p. 101, quoting from a 1926 Forest Service Bulletin.

18. Ibid., p. 134.

19. Ibid., p. 193.

20. J. M. Hughes, "Wilderness Land Allocation in a Multiple Use Forest Management Framework in the Pacific Northwest," Ph.D. Thesis, Michigan State University, 1964, pp. 259–260.

21. 78 Stat. 890 (1964), 16 U.S.C., §§ 1131–1136.

22. On the general legislative history of the act, see J. Michael McCloskey, "The Wilderness Act of 1964: Its Background and Meaning," *Oregon Law Review,* vol. 45 (1966), p. 288; and Delbert V. Mercure, Jr., and William M. Ross, "The Wilderness Act: A Product of Legislative Compromise," in Richard A. Cooley and Geoffry Wandesforde-Smith, eds., *Congress and the Environment* (Seattle: University of Washington Press, 1970).

23. See McCloskey, *The Wilderness Act,* pp. 298–299.

24. See ORRRC, *Wilderness and Recreation,* p. 89.

25. Although individual proposals by the Forest Service have been frequently attacked by preservationists, it is noteworthy that, in those wilderness proposals made up to 1973, the

service's recommended additions to the wilderness system have exceeded by over 400,000 acres the acreage in primitive areas which were the basis for those proposals. See *Ninth Annual Report on the Status of the National Wilderness Preservation System*, H. R. Doc. 194, 93 Cong., 1 sess., pt. 1, 1973, appendix III.

26. In *Izaak Walton League of America* v. *St. Clair*, 353 F. Supp. 698 (D. Minn. 1973) a federal district court, finding mining to be incompatible with wilderness, held the former to be prohibited notwithstanding the fact that the Wilderness Act specifically defers such a ban to 1984. This decision was reversed on appeal on the basis of the language of the statute permitting mining until 1984 and remanded to the agency for further findings on the effect of mining on the wilderness. The appellate court stated: "[T]he factual questions regarding the effect of mining activity upon the wilderness, and whether a permit should issue with restrictions that would be adequate to protect the wilderness quality of the [area] are those types of questions peculiarly within the competence of the Forest Service, and statutorily delegated to it by the Wilderness Act." 497 F. 2d 849, 852–53 (8th Cir. 1974).

Attempts have also been made to change the mining provisions of the act through legislation. A bill was introduced in the Ninty-third Congress which would have amended the act to prevent mining and mineral exploration on wilderness areas immediately. The Forest Service opposed the bill, preferring an administration bill which would have revised the mining laws to allow the federal government to control mining and mineral activity on all public lands through a leasing system. See U.S. Congress, Senate Public Lands Subcommittee of the Committee on Interior and Insular Affairs, *Hearings on S. 1010,* 93 Cong., 1 sess., 1973.

27. The basis on which the Forest Service undertook the inventory was the Multiple-Use and Sustained Yield Act of 1960 which, of course, recognizes wilderness as a use of the national forests. Presumably, the reason for basing the inventory on the 1960 act rather than on the Wilderness Act was that it was thought they would have greater flexibility under the former. A detailed account of the roadless area review program is contained in the pleadings and statements filed in *Sierra Club* v. *Butz*, Civil No. 1223-72 (D.D.C. 1972). For most of the following chronicle, I have relied on the Statement of Material Facts As To Which There Is No Genuine Issue, filed in that case. An outline of the process is also contained in U.S. Department of Agriculture/Forest Service, *Final Environmental Statement on Roadless and Undeveloped Areas* (1973), pp. 14–77.

28. See U.S. Department of Agriculture/Forest Service, *Final Environmental Statement,* pp. 14–76. This includes some areas that had been previously recommended for such study, independent of the 1971 directive.

29. See *Sierra Club* v. *Butz,* Civil No. 1223-72 (D.D.C. 1972). The case was later transferred to San Francisco and was there withdrawn (*Wall Street Journal,* Dec. 4, 1972, p. 8).

30. On the basic procedures and standards for review and classification discussed here, see The Forest Service Manual, § 2320; and Forest Service Handbook, § 2309.13. The discussion here also draws on study reports of individual wilderness areas and conversations with Forest Service officials, as well as other identified sources.

31. See Forest Service Manual, §§ 2314.36 (c) (5); and 2321.11.

32. See, for example, Edward P. Cliff, "The Wilderness Act and The National Forests," in Maxine E. McCloskey and James P. Gilligan, eds., *Wilderness and the Quality of Life* (San Francisco: Sierra Club, 1969).

33. See, for example, *The Wilderness Report* (November 1972), p. 5.

34. See, for example, Testimony of Chief of the Forest Service, Edward P. Cliff, U.S. Congress, Senate Subcommittee of the Interior and Insular Affairs Committee, *Hearings on San Gabriel, etc., Wilderness Areas,* 90 Cong., 2 sess., 1968, p. 8. This consideration was one of the reasons for the agency's insistence, prior to the act, that wilderness areas be large. Size is still an important consideration, both under the act (5,000 acres or "sufficient size to make practicable its preservation and use in an unimpaired condition") and Forest Service policy; despite pressures to add small parcels of land here and there, of the areas recommended by the service through 1973, only three under 35,000 acres were included (*Ninth Annual Report on the Status of the Wilderness System,* appendix III).

35. Forest Service Manual, § 2321.12-.13.

36.   Ibid., § 2321.12 lists the following examples of "unavailable" lands:

1.   Areas where the need for increased water protection and on-site storage is so vital that the installation for maintenance of works and facilities incompatible with wilderness is an obvious and inevitable public necessity.
2.   Areas where wilderness classification would seriously restrict . . . the application of wildlife management measures of considerable urgency and importance.
3.   Highly mineralized areas which . . . clearly show economic mining potential of such an extent that restrictions necessary to maintain the wilderness character of the land would not be in the public interest.
4.   National forest areas supporting heavy stands of high quality timber, all of which is essential to the economic welfare of existing dependent communities.
5.   Areas containing natural phenomena of such unique or outstanding nature that general public access should be provided.

37.   As in *Parker* v. *United States,* 448 F. 2d 793 (10th Cir. 1971), *cert. denied,* 405 U.S. 989 (1972).
38.   The Idaho Primitive Areas, one of the largest and most controversial areas, is an example; here a full cost–benefit analysis was undertaken.
39.   See U.S. Department of Agriculture/Forest Service, *Final Environmental Statement,* pp. 25–46. The analysis reflected in this impact statement is noteworthy, not only for its detailed quantification of opportunity cost, but also its attempt (not totally successful) to give some measure of benefit (need). The latter was measured by calculating the quality of each area (as rated by the regional forests, evaluating scenic value, isolation, and variety of experience), and multiplying that by the size of the area to arrive at an "effectiveness" index. Cost was measured by two indexes: one, the value of timber foregone and, two, the value of *all* resources—minerals, recreation, timber—together with the costs of establishment and administration. Comparing these provided the primary basis for screening roadless areas into those with highest and lowest potential for inclusion, and finally for selecting out 235 areas for final identification and temporary protection (pending final study) as new study areas. Subsequent data corrections and response to public impact then produced net increase of 39 areas, for a total of 274 (ibid., pp. 46–64).
40.   The requirements of the Wilderness Act are more specific in regard to public participation than those of the National Environmental Policy Act (NEPA). As discussed in Chapter II, NEPA specifically requires that, for major actions having a significant impact on the environment, the comments of other federal agencies be solicited. Notice to the public is mandated in accordance with the procedures of Section 3 of the Administrative Procedure Act (Section 3 is the so-called Freedom of Information Act). While NEPA does not itself mandate public hearings, or even the affirmative solicitation of public views, these have been mandated by subsequent Executive Order. As a result there is substantial overlap between the requirements of the Wilderness Act and NEPA.
41.   The High Uintas recommendation is the lone exception of which I am aware; endorsement was withheld pending further examination of conflict with the Central Utah Water Project (*Fifth Annual Report on the Status of the Wilderness System,* H. R. Doc. 58, 91 Cong., 1 sess., pt. 1, 1969, p. 5.)
42.   By the end of 1973 the Forest Service had recommended for permanent preservation a total area approximately 13 percent greater than the area contained in the present boundaries of those primitive areas reviewed (*Ninth Annual Report on the Status of the National Wilderness Preservation System,* appendix III).
43.   See, for example, Davis et al., *Federal Public Land Laws,* pp. 32–37, who discuss the local impact of preservation in the Monongahela National Forest in West Virginia.
44.   Nash, *Wilderness,* p. 91.
45.   Testimony of E. D. Cleveland in U.S. Congress, House Public Lands Subcommittee of the Committee on Interior and Insular Affairs, *Hearings on Wilderness Preservation System,* 87 Cong., 1 sess., 1961, ser. 12, p. 311. Noteworthy in this regard is an informal

report of a survey by researchers in the Department of Sociology at the University of Minnesota of campers returning from wilderness trips. The following is a list of conveniences they desired to have in the wilderness:

Conveniences	Percentage of interviewees desiring conveniences
More campsites	82
First aid stations	52
Garbage disposal areas	79
Toilets	78
Picnic tables	60
Fireplaces	54
Wells for drinking water	72
Places to buy groceries	49
Public telephones	21
Planned recreation	16
Showers and washrooms	15
Electricity	12

46. 309 F. Supp. 593 (D. Colo. 1970), aff'd, 448 F. 2d 793 (10th Cir. 1971), cert. denied, 405 U.S. 989 (1972).

47. The plaintiff's proposal for the wilderness area was to draw the boundaries in such a way as to exclude the road. This was not such a unique idea. The boundaries of the Boundary Waters Canoe Area (BWCA) in Northern Minnesota have been very greatly gerrymandered to exclude nonconforming roads as well as some private landholdings. However, the Forest Service has always insisted that the BWCA is a unique area not fully conforming to the standards prescribed for other areas and one which is not managed the same as the others.

48. The government's main challenge was to the first holding of the court, the one that was clearly seen by the agency as the most important [448 F. 2d 793, 796 (10th Cir. 1971)].

49. See U.S. Congress, Senate Public Lands Subcommittee of the Committee on Interior and Insular Affairs, Hearings on San Gabriel, etc., p. 17.

50. In fact, the Forest Service does attempt to eliminate such evidence of man's intrusions. Sometimes they have done so to the discomfiture of those who use the area. A well-known example of the latter occurred when the Forest Service was directed by Congress (on the insistence of local preservationists) to include Marion Lake in the Mt. Jefferson Wilderness Area. The agency had opposed the inclusion because of the heavy use of the lake and surrounding area and the existence of various man-made improvements. After its inclusion, the Forest Service removed certain facilities such as picnic tables, fireplaces, water pumps, and a boathouse along the lakeshore. This provoked the criticism that the agency was simply trying to get back at Congress and its local supporters. See U.S. Congress, Senate Public Lands Subcommittee of the Committee on Interior and Insular Affairs, Hearings on S. 316 and Related Bills (Eastern Wilderness Areas), 93 Cong., 1 sess., 1973, p. 27.

51. See generally, U.S. Congress, Senate Subcommittee of the Committee on Agriculture and Forestry, Hearings on S. 3699 and Related Bills, 92 Cong., 2 sess., 1972.

52. Testimony of Izaak Walton League, ibid., pp. 19–20. At least one conservation group has supported the wild areas proposal on the assumption that in time, these areas would develop into wilderness. Others have doubted that such will ever be the case under Forest Service management (ibid., p. 71). Another argument advanced in favor of a wild areas concept is that it would permit greater recreational use than wilderness (ibid., p. 35). However, that seems to run counter to the intent of many of the bills which would expressly restrict public use to a level consistent with retaining the primitive characteristics of the area.

53. See, for example, testimony of the Sierra Club, Wilderness Society, and Friends of the

Earth in U.S. Congress, House Subcommittee of the Committee on Agriculture, *Hearings on H. R. 14392 and Related Bills,* 92 Cong., 2 sess., 1972, pp. 46, 57, 122, and 136.

54. See U.S. Congress, Senate Public Lands Subcommittee of the Committee on Interior and Insular Affairs, *Hearings on S. 316 and Related Bills.*

55. Ibid., p. 21–22.

56. Cliff, "The Wilderness Act," p. 9. See also Richard J. Costley, "An Enduring Resource," *American Forests,* vol. 78, no. 6 (June 1972), p. 8. (Costley was head of the Recreation Division under Cliff and one of the modern architects of the Forest Service's wilderness policy).

57. See, for example, *The Wilderness Report* (November 1972), p. 5, which states, "No agency policy is more clearly misconceived, nor more deliberate an effort to frustrate the Wilderness Act."

58. This requires some qualification. Where the area is *still* extensively used the problem here can be significant. The problem typically is not that offending man-made improvements cannot be removed, it is that the improvements may be necessary to prevent hordes of recreation users from damaging the area. For example, an outdoor privy can be removed, but where a large number of visitors use the area, removal of all privies can only lead to toilet paper being strewn randomly around the forests, not to mention possible pollution of the local water supply. Fire grates or rudimentary campgrounds present a similar problem. To the person who seeks pure wilderness a fire grate or a cleared campground may be an unwelcome reminder that he is still within the frontier of man's dominion. But these are not conveniences for the visitor; they are intended to limit the risk of nonnatural fires. At some point the density of use becomes so great that it is impossible to protect the area without significantly altering the wilderness character. That, of course, always leaves the option of simply closing the area to use, or at least restricting it.

59. U.S. Congress, Senate Subcommittee of the Committee on Interior and Insular Affairs, *Hearings on S. 316,* pp. 23–24.

60. The best single discussion of the economics of wilderness preservation is that of the ORRRC, *Wilderness and Recreation,* ch. 6, which also contains a useful bibliography of the pertinent theoretical literature. Other analyses include: J. M. Hughes, "Wilderness and Economics," *Forestry,* vol. 66 (1968), p. 855; Lawrence G. Hines, "Wilderness: Economic Choice, Values and the Androscoggin," in *Wilderness and the Quality of Life,* pp. 74–80. Hines is generally critical of economic analysis, at least to the extent of formal cost–benefit analysis.

61. See, for example, Hines, "Wilderness," who argues against cost–benefit analysis because it too closely simulates private market choices which he finds inadequate.

62. A useful analysis of the concept of public goods applied to wilderness is given in the ORRRC *Study Report 3,* pp. 205–207.

63. See generally Peter Steiner, *Public Expenditure Budgeting* (Washington, D.C.: Brookings Institution, 1969).

64. As a noneconomist, I do not feel compelled to justify this in terms of traditional economic theories, such as the Sammelson–Bowen collective consumption good. For now at least, I am content with Steiner's looser definition of collective goods as what "some segment of the public collectively wants and is prepared to pay for a bundle of goods and services other than what the unhampered market will produce" (Ibid., p. 7). As he notes, collective goods need not be always publicly provided; however, in the present case I doubt that it could be otherwise, hence collective good equals public good.

65. A very helpful treatment (particularly for the lay reader) is found in E. Mishan, *Cost-Benefit Analysis* (London: Oxford University Press, 1971).

66. See Marion Clawson and Jack L. Knetsch, *The Economics of Outdoor Recreation* (Baltimore: Johns Hopkins University Press for Resources for the Future, 1966), pp. 64–77.

67. See Burton Weisbrod, "Collective-Consumption Services of Individual-Consumption Goods," *Quarterly Journal of Economics,* vol. 18 (1964), p. 471.

68. Quoted in ORRRC, *Wilderness and Recreation,* p. 31. See also the general discussion of valuation on pp. 213–219. It is in valuation of the benefits of wilderness that I am most disposed to Hines' critical view of cost–benefit analysis cited earlier (Note 61). It should be noted, however, that difficult as it may be to calculate usefully the benefits of wilderness under the circumstance of public choice, one can construct reasonable means for comparing different areas

in terms of this relative benefit. The Forest Service has done this in its preliminary analysis of unclassified roadless areas, evaluating the "effectiveness" of different areas according to certain criteria: size, scenic quality, isolation (and likely dispersion of visitors) and variety of experience available. See U.S. Department of Agriculture/Forest Service, *Final Environmental Statement on Roadless and Undeveloped Areas* (1973), pp. 25–27. The criteria are components of the "need" criterion which the Forest Service has, at least in theory, applied in all of its wilderness-review processes (see Forest Service Manual, § 2321.13). However, the roadless area review program appears to be the first time these components have been weighted and quantified to measure the relative need for particular areas. Notice, however, that these factors still do not measure "benefit" as such; for that reason they appear to me to have quite limited utility in cost–benefit analysis.

69.   For illustrative data, see, for example, U.S. Department of Agriculture/Forest Service, *The Outlook for Timber in the United States,* Forest Research Report 20 (1973), ch. III, estimating that selective management practices—only those justified by the condition that they would yield at least 5 percent return for the investment—could increase yield 3 percent by 1980 and by 25 percent in the year 2020 above that which would be produced by present management practices (which already produce more than unmanaged yield).

70.   As of July 1973, of some 28.5 million acres in the National Park System scheduled for study, 200,000 acres have been classified as wilderness and 5 million have so far been recommended for inclusion. Of 29.6 million acres in the National Wildlife System, 100,000 acres have already been designated as wilderness and another 900,000 proposed. Finally, the BLM has classified approximately 154,000 acres as primitive (these are not formally part of the wilderness system). U.S. Department of Agriculture/Forest Service, *Final Environmental Statement,* pp. 10, 11, and 13. Probably more than 6 million acres will ultimately be proposed for wilderness, but I think it unlikely the figure will go very much higher.

71.   The gross area of the United States, including Alaska and Hawaii, is 2.3 billion acres, of which about 762 million is owned or managed by the federal government. U.S. Department of the Interior/Bureau of Land Management, *Public Land Statistics* (1973), p. 1.

72.   As noted in Chapter IV, the Forest Service standard for commercial timberland requires an annual yield of 25 ft.[3] per acre.

73.   See Marion Clawson and Burnell Held, *The Federal Lands: Their Use and Management* (Baltimore: Johns Hopkins University Press for Resources for the Future, 1957), p. 77.

74.   As discussed earlier, in Chapter III, this was the conclusion of the so-called Bolle report on the Bitterroot National Forest. [*Report of the Select Committee of the University of Montana on the Bitterroot National Forest* (1970), reprinted as *A University View of the Forest Service,* S. Doc. 91-115, 91 Cong., 2 sess., 1970; *cf.* Marion Clawson, "Conflicts, Strategies, and Possibilities for Consensus in Forest Land Use and Management" in Clawson, ed., *Forest Policy for the Future* (Baltimore: Johns Hopkins University Press for Resources for the Future, 1974), pp. 105, 168–181.] It should be noted that the northern region and northern portions of the intermountain region, to which Bolle's conclusions were primarily directed, account for a giant share of the current wilderness system. For example, approximately half the existing national forest wilderness and primitive land is in four states: Idaho, Montana, Utah, and Wyoming. See *Eighth Annual Report on the Status of the National Wilderness Preservation System,* appendix V.

75.   See U.S. Department of Agriculture/Forest Service, *Draft Environmental Statement on Roadless Areas* (January 1973), appendix A at 2-a. It is particularly noteworthy that the intermountain region accounts for some 11.5 million acres in roadless areas, one-fifth of the total; however, the total annual allowable harvest from such lands is a mere 172 million bd.-ft. less than the cut of some single forests in the Pacific Northwest. The total annual allowable cut calculated for the entire 18.6 million acres of commercial forest is 2.3 million, half of which is in the Pacific Northwest (Oregon and Washington) and Alaska.

76.   Ibid., p. 37, and appendix A at 38-a. On the 12.3 million acres finally selected as new study areas, the estimated annual allowable harvest is 299 million bd.-ft., about 2 percent of the current total for the national forests. See also U.S. Department of Agriculture/Forest Service, *Final Environmental Statement on Roadless and Undeveloped Areas* (1973), pp. 70, and 90.

77.   U.S. Department of Agriculture/Forest Service, *Draft Environmental Statement,* ap-

pendix A, 37-a. The figure for the finally selected new study areas only is approximately $238 million (U.S. Department of Agriculture/Forest Service, *Final Environmental Statement*, p. 77).

78. Probably the most noteworthy example is the BWCA where controversy has raged for years over allowing timber cutting, mineral exploration, and the use of motorboats and snowmobiles in the wilderness. See, for example, *Izaak Walton League of America v. St. Clair*, 497 F. 2d 849 (8th Cir. 1974) *petition for cert. filed*, 43 U.S.L.W. 3108 (1974), (mineral exploration); and *Minnesota Public Interest Research Group v. Butz*, 498 F. 2d 1314 (8th Cir. 1974) *aff'd*, (timber cutting). Recently the BWCA controversy has escalated in response to the Forest Service's proposed multiple-use plan which, by steering a middle course between preservationists on the one hand and users on the other, has resulted in displeasing both sides equally. See U.S. Department of Agriculture/Forest Service, *Boundary Waters Canoe Area Management Plan* and *Environmental Statement* (1974). *Minnesota Public Interest Research Group v. Butz*, No. 4-72, Civil-598 (D. Minn. Sept. 18, 1974) (challenge to adequacy of environmental statement). The BWCA, however, is an exceptional case; many of the activities and uses (e.g., timber cutting and use of motors) have been permitted in the area under special legislation unique to the BWCA.

79. By Forest Service directive too. See Forest Service Manual, § 2320.

80. On the agency's management functions within wilderness, see generally Cliff, "The Wilderness Act and the National Forests," pp. 10–11.

81. One exception is Minnesota's BWCA. When the area was first set aside for special administrative protection, timber harvesting in parts of the area (the so-called portal zone) continued to be permitted. In 1930 Congress—prompted primarily by proposals to construct hydroelectric power projects in the area—enacted the Shipstead–Nolan Act which gave special statutory protection to the area in order to conserve its natural beauty [46 Stat. 1020 (1930), 16 U.S.C., §§ 577-577b]. As with the prior administrative scheme, the statute did not establish the BWCA formally as a wilderness area, and it specifically recognized continued logging in the area (logging, however, was prohibited within 400 ft. of the lakeshore). The Wilderness Act specifically provides that the terms of the Shipstead–Nolan Act continue to apply [16 U.S.C., § 1133 (a) (2)] and that, notwithstanding the act, the management of the BWCA shall continue in accordance with prior regulations of the secretary of agriculture "in accordance with the general purpose of maintaining, without unnecessary restrictions on other uses, including that of timber, the primitive character of the area" [16 U.S.C., § 1133 (d) (5)]. The Forest Service continued to permit timber cutting in the portal zone (outer boundaries) of the area, prompting challenges from local conservationists. Recently cutting was enjoined until a determination could be made concerning the adequacy of the agency's environmental statement and the legality of cutting under provisions of the Wilderness Act. *Minnesota Public Interest Research Group v. Butz*, No. 4-72, Civil-598 (D. Minn., Sept. 18, 1974). For prior history of the case, see *Minnesota Public Interest Research Group v. Butz*, 358 F. Supp. 584 (D. Minn. 1973), *aff'd*, 498 F. 2d 1314 (8th Cir. 1974).

82. The exception for a time was eliminated by a federal district court decision in *Izaak Walton League of America v. St. Clair*, 353 F. Supp. 698 (D. Minn. 1973), which declared that mining and mineral exploration necessarily conflicted with the wilderness objectives and that the latter overrides the former. The decision was reversed by the court of appeals, 497 F. 2d 849 (8th Cir. 1974), *petition for cert. filed*, 43 U. S. L. W. 3108 (1974), which found Congress' language to the contrary controlling (ibid., p. 853). It remanded the case to the agency for a determination by it whether a permit should be issued and, if so, what conditions were necessary to protect the wilderness. The court of appeals decision seems sound. While one might agree, as a matter of personal taste, that mining and mineral exploration are incompatible with wilderness, it is surely a remarkable piece of arrogance for a court to nullify Congress' very clear authorization to permit it nevertheless. If, in fact, the consequence is to destroy the wilderness character, is it not within the power of Congress to do so? If Congress wishes to declare an area as a "wilderness, vacation and training ground for the 7th Cavalry Division," are we to suppose that Congress could not do so because "wilderness," "vacation," and "training ground for the 7th Cavalry," are, to all reasoning minds, inconsistent?

83. See 16 U.S.C., § 1133; and Forest Service Manual, § 2326.1.

84. Quite apart from the provisions of the act which preserve private right of access, any

substantial curtailment of access would impair the value of the private land, and such an impairment would presumably constitute a "taking" of land for which the Fifth Amendment requires compensation.

85.   Purchases are made under Section 6 of the Land and Water Conservation Act of 1965, 78 Stat. 903 (1964), *as amended,* 16 U.S.C., § 460L-9. Exchanges are made under authority of the General Exchange Act, 42 Stat. 465 (1922), 16 U.S.C., §§ 485-6; and the Transfer Act of 1960, 74 Stat. 205 (1960), 5 U.S.C., § 511.

86.   This will depend in large measure on how much latitude is given the agency in drawing the boundaries of wilderness so as to exclude areas with substantial private inholdings.

87.   See Forest Service Manual, § 2326.11.

88.   See Cliff, "The Wilderness Act and the National Forests," p. 11.

89.   Statement of Sen. Mark Hatfield in U.S. Congress, Senate Public Lands Subcommittee of the Committee on Interior and Insular Affairs, *Hearings on S. 316,* p. 29.

90.   I am informed by Forest Service officials that in western forests lightning-caused fires greatly predominate over those caused by man; this would be particularly true of wilderness areas where human use is relatively slight. This is in contrast to the incidence of wildfires nationwide, which for the period 1966-70 were predominantly manmade. Glascock, "Forces Shaping the Public Opinion Toward Fire and the Environment," in *Symposium on Fire and the Environment,* U.S. Department of Agriculture/Forest Service, no. 276 (1972), p. 65.

91.   Forest Service Manual, § 2324.1-.12. The second part of this policy seems contrary to the wilderness ideal, but it can perhaps be justified on the grounds that to the extent fire is artificially controlled, it eliminates the natural check on the spread of insects and disease.

92.   See Forest Service Manual, § 2324.2-.24.

93.   See, for example, Estella B. Leopold, "Ecological Requirements of the Wilderness Act," in *Wilderness and the Quality of Life,* pp. 188-197; and Miron L. Heinselman, "Preserving Nature in Forested Wilderness Areas and National Parks," *National Parks and Conservation Magazine,* vol. 44 (September 1970), p. 8.

94.   See Leopold, "Ecological Requirements."

95.   Forest Service Manual, § 2324.24.

96.   For an interesting discussion of some of the uncertainties in controlled burning, see John A. Zivnuska, "Economic Tradeoffs in Fire Management," in *Proceedings of a Symposium on Fire and the Environment,* U.S. Department of Agriculture/Forest Service, no. 276 (1972).

97.   *Report of the President's Advisory Panel on Timber and the Environment* (1973), p. 494.

98.   For example, Robert C. Lucas, "Wilderness Perception and Use: The Example of the Boundary Waters Canoe Area," *Natural Resources Journal,* vol. 3 (1964), pp. 394 and 398, estimates a tenfold increase in wilderness visitor days as against a threefold increase in general outdoor recreation visitor days.

99.   Here I use the term in a broad sense, to include persons who enjoy or appreciate wilderness vicariously or indirectly, as well as those who actually enter wilderness areas.

100.   See George H. Stankey, "A Strategy for the Definition and Management of Wilderness Quality," in John V. Krutilla, ed., *Natural Environments: Studies in Theoretical and Applied Analysis* (Baltimore: Johns Hopkins University Press, 1972), p. 88.

101.   See Jubler, "Let's Open Up Our Wilderness Areas," *Reader's Digest* (May 1972).

102.   See Stankey, "A Strategy," pp. 96-97.

103.   See Anthony C. Fisher and John V. Krutilla, "Determination of Optimal Capacity of Resource-Based Recreation Facilities," in John V. Krutilla, ed., *Natural Environments,* p. 115. Although the authors consider willingness to pay separate from actual payment, they also do propose a user charge to ration use. Such user charges are now prohibited by statute.

104.   Forest Service Manual, § 2320.

105.   In effect the "wilderness *experience*" would be preserved by destroying it. One thinks instantly of Hue, South Vietnam, and of the military's celebrated statement that it was necessary to destroy the city in order to save it.

106.   On methods for dispersing visitors, see Forest Service Manual, § 2323.12.

107.   See 16 U.S.C., § 460L-5.

108.   As a matter of taste perhaps some who would not object to a fee to enter a camp-

ground in Sequoia National Forest might object to a fee to enter the High Sierras—the notion being that there are some things that just ought to be "free" (more accurately, that ought to appear to be free). Too, there might be a difference in the level of fees needed to achieve an effective control. It is plausible to suppose that the demand for wilderness is somewhat less price elastic than for recreation, a supposition based on two assumptions: the typical wilderness user has a higher income and fewer close substitutes for wilderness.

109. Forest Service Manual, § 2323.12a.

110. These are the San Gorgiono and San Jacinto areas in southern California. The system went into effect in both areas in 1973; the use of a permit began in 1971; however, permits were not restrictive but used simply for keeping track of visitors and obtaining visitor information.

111. Various possible methods for reservation have been suggested. One is to use a well-known private communications system, such as Western Union; another is to use the post office. A more sensible system would simply establish a central federal reservation center which would have communications links with all national forests and which would handle reservations essentially in the same manner as, say, nationwide motel or hotel reservation systems. The cost of such a system would not, of course, be negligible, but a fee could be charged to cover this cost. And, in fact, I am told that the Forest Service contemplates such a fee, which would appear to be outside the restriction of the Land and Water Conservation Fund Act insofar as it is based not on use of the resource but on the provision of the reservation service.

112. See testimony of Garrett Hardin in U.S. Congress, House Subcommittee of the Committee on Government Operations, *Hearings on Effects of Population Growth on Natural Resources and the Environment,* 91 Cong., 1 sess., 1969, pp. 90 and 95–96.

113. Indeed, the contrary was once argued with some plausibility by Henry Simons:

Let us imagine a competitive economy, without inheritance, where all persons have substantially equal talents for straight thinking, imagination, salesmanship, and chicanery, but are enormously unequal in physical strength. Here, of course, the millionaires will be the persons with strong backs; and the apology of productivity ethics will be that they are entitled to share in the social income according to their respective differential contributions (productivity). A dose of Calvinist theology would make this doctrine more palatable to the masses; but persons of a critical temper might be led to restate the implications and to revise the conclusions simply be reversing them. If a person has been greatly favored by the Creator in the dispensation of rare physical blessings, it is hard to regard that initial good fortune as a basis for preferential claims against his fellows with respect to scarce goods whose distribution is amenable to some deliberate human control. Indeed, one is almost obliged to admit the reasonableness of the opposite system of ethical book-keeping, whereby rare physical blessings would be debited to the recipient's account with the universe.

Henry Simons, *Personal Income Taxation* (1938), excerpt reprinted in R. W. Houghton, ed., *Readings in Public Finance* (Middlesex: Penguin Books, 1970), p. 25.

VII

THE
RANGE
RESOURCE

Grazing was among the earliest uses of the forests. Long before there was significant timber harvesting, western forests were extensively used for grazing of livestock.[1] So long as the forests were part of the public domain, their access and use was virtually unrestricted. As a consequence, many of the lands were heavily overgrazed by the time the Organic Act of 1897 was passed. When management responsibility was transferred to the Forest Service, regulation of grazing, through a system of permits and grazing fees, was established as one of the first and foremost management tasks. Since no statute specifically provided for grazing permits or fees—indeed, grazing was not even mentioned in the Organic Act of 1897 or the Transfer Act of 1905—the permit and fee system was soon challenged. In the celebrated *Grimaud* case,[2] the Supreme Court affirmed the power of the secretary of agriculture to regulate and charge for grazing on the national forests—a power derived from the general framework of the act of 1897. It was not, however, until the 1950 Granger–Thye Act[3] that grazing was specifically recognized by statute as a use of national forests and range management as a responsibility of the Forest Service.

Today livestock grazing is permitted on some 105.5 million acres of Forest Service land.[4] In 1972, over 3.7 million head of livestock (cattle, horses, sheep, and goats) grazed more than 8 million animal unit-months.[5] Despite these impressive figures the national forests nationwide are not as dominant in forage as they are in timber. Only about 3 percent of the total forage production is contributed by all the federal lands, and the national forests and grasslands are but a part of that.[6] There is every indication, moreover, that the role of the national forests will decrease. If, as seems inevitable, livestock operations continue to shift from the West to the South and East, grazing will, of course, shift from public to private lands. Recent Forest Service studies have shown such a shift to be economically desirable for increased forage production,[7] not to mention the conservation benefits of relieving an overgrazed western range.

Still, the national forest range does play a significant role, particularly in the western states, in providing summer range for livestock—a vital element in western livestock operations.[8] Certainly, if one measures by the protest from western livestock interests when the Forest Service raises fees or reduces permitted use, or by the controversy which the subject of public range management has engendered over the years, one must conclude something important is at stake.

RANGE MANAGEMENT— THE BASIC SCHEME

The Permit System

All livestock use in the national forests and grasslands is subject to the requirement of a permit.[9] A variety of permits are in use, paid permits being the most important. Approximately 16,500 paid permits were outstanding in 1972. Of these, most are ten-year permits held by western ranchers.[10] In addition, there are a variety of nonfee permits issued for temporary purposes, such as grazing of milk cows and noncommercial work animals, crossing permits for trail animals, or so-called private land permits to persons who control grazing lands intermingled with national forest land and who waive exclusive use of these lands in return for a permit on forest lands.[11] Though the nonfee permits are large in number—nearly 82,000 in 1972[12]—they have little economic significance. Of the fee permits, the ten-year permits are in use primarily in the western regions. Grazing in the eastern and southern regions is pursuant to annual permits. This reflects the lesser importance of grazing on federal lands in the East and the South. In the West, where a large portion of the range is federally owned, and where livestock owners are heavily dependent upon it, the Forest Service since 1926 has recognized the need for the security of long-term commitments to the rancher and has provided for it.

Issuance of permits is primarily the responsibility of the forest supervisor, subject, of course, to the quite specific and limiting requirements of departmental regulations and service directives.

The basic requirements for term permits remain largely unchanged from those established in the early years of administration.[13] First, the applicant for a permit must be a citizen, a requirement common to most public licensing laws in this country. More important are the requirements that the permittee own the livestock grazed on the area, and also that he own base ranch property. In addition, a permittee must establish that the base land he owns or controls is "commensurate" with the forest range in its capacity to support the permitted livestock during the period such livestock are not permitted on the forest range. [This commensurability need not be satisfied entirely by the base ranch property; it may be satisfied also through private leaseholds or through permits held from other public agencies such as the Bureau of Land Management (BLM).]

The ownership and commensurability requirements were originally linked with another requirement, one that the rancher be dependent on the forest range for grazing in order to round out his operation, that is, maintain a full-season grazing capacity. This dependency criterion has been eliminated, as a requirement. It remains as a theoretical criterion for establishing priorities in the allocation of permits, but even here it has no practical importance beyond the requirement of ownership of base land and livestock.

The ownership and commensurability requirements have caused difficulty over the years. As will be noted, the latter in particular has been the basis for challenging elements of the current fee system. The ownership, commensurability, and dependency requirements were all designed to reserve the forest range for the homesteaders who used the range as part of their regular ranch operations and to eliminate the "nomad" or "tramp" herds and flocks which had previously used the range. This reflected, in part, a social and economic policy of aiding ranching interests, but it was also a conservation policy. The lands were heavily overgrazed; much of this was attributed, no doubt correctly, to owners of large transient herds who had little interest in maintaining, and no interest in improving, the public range. On the other hand, the nearby ranch operator who used the range as more or less an extension of his own land would have such an interest, provided that others were not given a "free ride" on his contributions to the range. In the circumstances in which they were first instituted, these requirements probably were necessary to serve the best interests of range conservation. Today, that is not so clear, but this is a matter which we can defer until an outline of the permit systems has been completed.

Permits are acquired in a variety of ways. Original grants were issued in accordance with a set of priorities: existing users over new applicants, those adjacent to the range over those more distant, those most dependent upon the range over those less dependent, and small operators preferred over large. These "preferences" are still recognized. However, the occasion for so-called grant permits (i.e., permits issued for the first time) in the western range are relatively rare. Because most of the rangeland has been initially allocated, licensing deals chiefly with modifications of existing permits or with reissuance of permits to transferees of permitted livestock or base property. In some cases, however, new grazing allotments will be created as a result of a large vegetative-type conversion (such as from brushland to grass), in which case new grant permits may be made. More commonly, changes in grazing range are made through adjustments (increases or decreases) in allotment boundaries or in grazing capacity, both of which would normally result only in modification of existing permits.[14]

Term permits are renewable and have traditionally been renewed as a matter of course at the end of each term. It is primarily in this respect that the "preference" of prior users over new applicants is recognized today. In practical fact, this preference of renewal over new applicants establishes a tenure which is permanent until voluntary relinquishment (which would normally occur upon the sale of the permittee's land or livestock).

This tenure—or as it is sometimes more commonly and confusingly called, preference—does not preclude adjustments or even termination of permits under certain circumstances other than voluntary reliquishment. Term permits may be adjusted or terminated under a variety of conditions; however, except in unusual circumstances, such as violation of service regulations or withdrawal of allotment from grazing use, permits would not be terminated altogether. More commonly, permits are adjusted with respect to the number of livestock permitted. Primarily, this was done for purposes of range conservation. One of the earliest tasks of forest management was to survey the range to determine its carrying capacity (measured in terms of animal unit-month) to ensure sustained-yield conservation and to adjust grazing use accordingly. The task of surveying the range and adjudicating individual permits to conform with range capacity began in 1910. Sixty years later it is still unfinished, and range improvement continues to be a major concern of management. Reduction in the number of permanent livestock is not considered to be the sole, nor even the primary, range-improvement practice. Reductions in stocking continue to be made in areas where the range has been deteriorated beyond recovery through practices short of reduction, but the emphasis has shifted to other means. Greater emphasis is now placed upon better patterns of grazing: for example, through the use of "rest-rotation" and similar grazing formulae which permit a range to recover and be treated during grazing use. Emphasis has also been placed on range development by the permittee.

Independent of the limitations fixed on the size of the herds permitted to each livestock owner in accordance with the capacity of the particular allotment, the service has always set an overall upper limit on the total number of stock (by type) which any permittee may be authorized to graze on national forests. The limits, set for individual localities (generally forests) by the regional forester,[15] are intended to prevent permittees from monopolizing or obtaining an unfair share of the range in the particular locale.

Permits are not transferable, at least in theory. A person who transfers either his land or his livestock or both cannot transfer with it his permit. However, if the transferor–permittee reliquishes his permit, and thereby his preferential status over new users, the Forest Service will reissue the permit to the transferee of the land or livestock, provided that the transferee satisfies all of the requirements and conditions for holding a permit. Theoretically, this reissuance is discretionary with the service, reflecting the fact that the permit is considered by the service to be a privilege, not a property right. However, the immemorial administrative practice has been to reissue the permit as a matter of course to any qualified purchaser of permitted livestock or range property. If the new permittee does not quite acquire the same preferred status as that held by his predecessor, this is largely irrelevant, since he does obtain a "preference" of his own entitling him to indefinite renewal. The Forest Service may choose to insist that the permit nevertheless remains a privilege and not a property right,[16] but the practical reality is that admininstrative practice has accorded the permit at least some of the major earmarks of a property right—defeasible, conditioned, and regulated, but nevertheless substantial.

Of course, the fact that the permittee's formal status is described as a mere privilege does not affect his individual rights to fair process. The permit is subject to regulation: it is subject to termination, and reissuance to a transferee of land or livestock may be denied. But all of these actions are subject to the due process limitations of an appeal and hearing, as prescribed by the Forest Service appeal procedures, and in conformance with justiciable due process standards for administrative action. Whether the permit itself represents a privilege or a property right is irrelevant to this procedure. This is now a well-recognized legal principle, not disputed between livestock interests and the Forest Service. However, the question of the permittee's status does continue to be the subject of dispute in defining the *substantive* limits of Forest Service discretion in regulating permits. It is at the heart of recurring disputes over withdrawals of rangelands from grazing use, reduction in stocking of permitted livestock, and other regulatory actions, including a continuing controversy over grazing fees.

The Fee System

The first fees for grazing,[17] instituted in 1906,[18] were based on the general and loose criterion of "reasonableness." In 1920 a major study was undertaken to determine a reasonable fee schedule in accordance with the fair value of the permit, measured by rental rates or other determined value for comparable private rangelands. In accordance with the results of this study a fee schedule was approved, beginning in 1927, under which most fees were increased substantially over a four-year period through 1931. The 1931 fee then became the base fee which was thereafter adjusted annually in accordance with an index based on the average market prices for beef and lamb. The fees charged under this scheme were far from uniform, since the base fee varied among regions, among forests, and even among allotments, depending upon the varying local private range lease rates and other factors on which the base fee was paid.

The Forest Service system of fees also differed notably from the fee system implemented in 1936 by the BLM for grazing lands which it administered under the Taylor Grazing Act of 1934. Under the BLM system no attempt was made to charge for the full value of the land. Instead, a modest, uniform fee was set, intended to cover merely the cost of administering the grazing program.

Although these two fee systems remained in effect for some three decades, for most of that period they were recognized as inadequate by both agencies. One source of concern to the agencies was the lack of uniformity between the two systems. However, given that the lands administered by the two agencies are of disparate quality, the absence of a single-fee system was not regarded as the major problem. The more serious problem was that neither system of fees adequately reflected the true market value of grazing on public lands. The Forest Service fee system of 1929 had been designed to reflect a market value in accordance with the best measure of comparable private land values, although, after a time, it came to lag behind them. The BLM system, on the other hand, had never attempted to recover the market value of its grazing lands. Indeed, under the Grazing Service, the BLM's predecessor, these fees did not even come close to recovering the full cost of administering the agency, contrary to the stated intent of the Department of the Interior at the time the Taylor Grazing Act was enacted.

Accordingly, the BLM and Forest Service, in 1961, began a joint program of grazing fee studies to develop new methods and models for determining range values and to evaluate the respective fee structures in light of those values.[19] The basic model upon which the studies proceeded was essentially similar to that adopted in 1929. The initial premise was that the government should charge a fee for the use of its lands, a premise no one really disputes today. The second premise was that the fee should reflect the economic value of the grazing to the permittee, a premise generally (although guardedly) accepted even by large stock interests. The third premise—and one that gives rise to dispute—was that the economic value is correctly and fairly measured by market values. The difficulty here, of course, is that there is no market for public land grazing permits. There could be if permits were sold in public auction, but the Forest Service and the BLM have rejected this alternative on the ground it would produce instability of ranch operations dependent upon public grazing. In the absence of an auction market the problem is to estimate the values obtained in a market and to derive what the economists would call a "shadow price" for this nonmarket good.

Two alternative economic models for developing such a price were considered in the BLM and Forest Service studies. Analytically, both rest on the same simple premise that, in a perfect private market for grazing privileges in which both public and private lands freely compete, the price of lands yielding comparable benefits will be equal. Disregarding transaction costs (which, of course, would contradict the perfect market model), the price for the use of each land would be equivalent to the marginal cost of the use of that land—resulting in an efficient allocation of grazing resources. To the extent public land fees have been kept below those of private lands, however, the artificially reduced price has signaled demand away from the private lands to public lands. To the extent the demand has exceeded the supply of public lands, it has had to be restrained by permit rationing. The result of the shortage has given the permit a capital value corresponding to the differential between private and public land use fees. It was the design of the new fee system to recover the value for the public as owner of the land and by so doing also to remedy the misallocative effects that have been caused by the past system.

The method chosen for measuring the value of use was to determine the total cost of operation to the user on privately leased grazing land and to subtract from this private cost the total nonfee cost of operation to the user of public rangelands. This difference is the amount the rancher should be willing to pay for the public range. The difference was $1.23 per animal unit-month, which was taken as the measure of the full economic value of the public rangelands for which the livestock owner should pay. Although the new fee structure required substantial increases in most existing grazing fees, the new fees were to be implemented only over a ten-year period. At the end of the period, grazing fees are brought to a uniform base level of $1.23 per year, and adjusted annually in accordance with a so-called forage value index based on the preceding year's private lease rates.

The new fee system has not yet brought uniformity to grazing fees. The new fees apply to all national forest and BLM lands in the eleven contiguous western states, plus South Dakota and Nebraska. But they do not apply to the national grasslands, nor to any forests in the eastern and southern regions. These lands were excluded because of the different circumstances which set them apart from the western range and made it inappropriate to implement the same fee system for both. Most important, the use of many of these lands has been on an annual, temporary basis, and the fees have always managed to stay in line with private lease rates. A discrepancy between fees and market value has not developed in the East and the South as it has in the West. However, fee studies for these lands have been undertaken, and it is possible these lands will be brought into the new fee system.

Range Management and Planning

Administration of grazing permits is part of the broader task of range management.[20] The basic geographic unit for planning, management, and administration is the range allotment of which there were some 11,900—9,400 for cattle and horses and 2,500 for sheep—in the national forest system in 1970.[21] Most allotments are based on historic patterns of grazing that existed at the time the Forest Service took over the forest reserves. Following one of the primary aims of the permit system in the early years of Forest Service administration of the range, the allotments were designed to compliment the range operations of existing range users in such a way that the rancher could use the forest range to round out his operations and maintain a full-season grazing capability. Thus, where possible, the allotment would be contiguous to the permittee's private lands, within the same drainage area or within areas having common topographic and vegetative characteristics. As would be expected from the nature of their design, the allotments have no fixed or uniform size. A western range allotment could be 1,000 acres or more, but this varies a great deal with the natural characteristics of the land and the circumstances of use. Most allotments are smaller than, and are fully contained within, a ranger district (which will generally administer several such allotments). Sometimes allotments cross district boundaries, in which case they are managed under a single, jointly prepared management plan and administered by one of the rangers, unless grazing is not compatible in one of the districts. When the latter occurs, allotments are redesigned.

Planning for the allotment begins with a *range environmental analysis* which provides the basic resource information for the allotment-management plan. Primary responsibility for inventory analysis in planning is given to the district rangers who receive technical assistance as needed from conservationists, wildlife biologists, soil and water specialists, and others on the forest supervisor's staff. Permittees using the allotment also participate in the process. The range environmental analysis builds on a basic inventory of the range. Today such inventories are made largely through aerial photographic maps which record topographic, vegetative, and other characteristics of the land. Traditionally, an inventory of the allotment was prescribed periodically. However, where an intensive inventory has been made within the past ten or twenty years, a full reinventory is seldom now necessary.

The inventory examines the basic characteristics of the land—the types of vegetation, availability of water, soil conditions, topographic characteristics—relevant to determining the general suitability of the area for grazing. These general characteristics of the land do not materially change very often, and provided that an adequate inventory has been made, changes can and will be readily made in the inventory record as they occur. The condition of the range and the trend in range health can, however, change markedly within a short period of time, both from use and to a lesser extent from natural events. The condition and trend require periodical field survey and analysis. This is done through the use of permanent trend plots, a series of sample plots established in the allotment from which the condition and apparent trend in the health of the plant, the stability of the soil, and the extent of use by livestock and wildlife are measured. The frequency of the survey and analysis varies, depending upon what is already known about the range and its condition, the extent of use, and other factors, not the least of which is the budget and the priorities set by the forest supervisor; however, a survey and analysis within at least five years is generally required.

From these data an analysis is made of management problems and alternative objectives, and a program is formulated. Choosing among alternatives involves at the outset an initial decision as to what, if any, corrective action must be taken with respect to the range resource itself. When range resource needs are provided for, there remains the choice of management alternatives in light of other constraints. For many rangelands, this will mean simply formulating a grazing program which yields, on a sustained basis, a maximum value in terms of the number of animals carried, animal weight gains, or other livestock-oriented output measure. However, multiple-use considerations may impose constraints. As in timber management and other resource planning, a multiple-use analysis, or, as it is now generally known, an *environmental analysis report* must be prepared; this is designed to analyze the effect of the management action upon other resource uses in the area. The analysis is formally independent of the range-allotment analysis, but it becomes part of the management plan and provides a basis for implementing the multiple-use plan.[22]

In range management, as in other areas of resource planning, the decision-making process has been improved as a consequence of interdisciplinary effort. But the value of that input depends on the capability to analyze and make effective use of it in arriving at a final plan which can provide an efficient allocation use of resources. For this, more sophisticated tools of analysis are required. As mentioned earlier, the Forest Service researchers and planners have in recent years devoted extensive energy to the creation of computer program models designed to provide such an analytic tool. Like their fellow planners in other resource areas, range planners have devoted substantial energy to the development of computer models for analysis of a part of their Forest Range Environmental Study (FRES).[23]

The FRES model is similar to Timber RAM; it is a linear program designed to evaluate output production alternatives for given resources, subject to specified constraints. Unlike Timber RAM, FRES is, of course, oriented toward optimal use of the range resource rather than timber production, but this is a relatively minor design difference; the basic mathematical framework is similar for both. The most important difference between the two models is that while Timber RAM is designed to be implemented in the field in planning particular timber-management practices at the forest level, FRES is a broad nationwide plan, designed to aid in very broad policy strategies. Thus, it is a comprehensive study of all the nation's range environments, including those outside the forest. Its broad purposes include a clarification of the functions and values of rangelands, an analysis of the present situation and projection of future needs, a determination of alternatives for future Forest Service policies and for devising a system for effecting and continuing analysis of the range.

General public involvement in range-management planning has traditionally been, and continues to be, quite limited. Those most immediately affected, the permittees, are invited to participate in the planning process at every stage, from the inventories to the implementation of the plan. Other groups—wildlife organizations and state conservation officers most notably—are also normally consulted on those aspects of planning which affect their particular interests. In the course of routine management planning on established allotments, general public participation is usually not formally solicited unless the public has demonstrated an interest in the area because of wildlife, watershed, recreation, or other uses. In the case where planning involves a major project development—for example, where a new allotment is created as a consequence of type conversion or range rehabilitation for which a formal environmental impact statement is required under the National Environmental Policy Act (NEPA)—then public participation is formally solicited in accordance with general NEPA procedures.

Based on the long-term management objectives, specific management actions are scheduled for implementation on an annual basis and included in the permittee's annual plan. This annual plan, developed with the permittee, is both a directive to the permittee and an agreement between him and the Forest Service regarding their respective obligations and responsibilities. It includes, for example, a description of the assignment of responsibilities for development and maintenance work on the range, any required adjustments in stocking or season of use, the permittee's grazing formula (pattern of grazing and sequence of rotation, if a rotation system is used), and other detailed directions and assignment of responsibilities for herding, salting (for cattle), and other ongoing management activities such as allotment examinations.

Within the framework of these detailed directions set forth in the annual plan, the district ranger and his staff have the continuing responsibility for supervising permittee use through periodic allotment examinations. In addition to providing a survey of the condition and health of the range and the impact of use upon it, the allotment examination also determines that the range is being used only by authorized livestock, and that such use is in accordance with the permittee's annual plan of use.

PROBLEMS AND
CONTROVERSIES

The Permit System

When established in 1905, the permit system was bitterly attacked by livestock interests who, having used the public domain as they wished, suddenly found themselves required to obtain a permit which not only limited their use of the range but charged for it as well. Ultimately, of course, the opposition abated, and the permit requirement, accompanied by a modest fee, became acceptable. However, when the remainder of the public domain was put under a permit system by the Taylor Grazing Act of 1934, some of the early opposition to the permit system, and to some of the restrictions imposed by it, surfaced again. It would be an exaggeration to say that the permit requirement itself is a matter of important controversy today. Proposals have been made, most notably by the Public Land Law Review Commission (PLLRC), for disposing of some of the federal lands used primarily for grazing by sale to permittees.[24] This would, of course, eliminate the permit system and public management generally to that extent. However, there is little pressure from livestock interests in this direction, probably for the simple reason most realize that they would not obtain use on the lands as cheaply by outright purchase as they do now under the permit. In any event, this proposal would affect only a portion of the lands, mostly BLM lands having no other important purpose. For the remainder of the land, the continuation of some form of permit requirement is not controversial.

However, while there appears to be no significant challenge to the permit requirements as such, there is nevertheless substantial criticism, and proposals have been made for a major reform in the permit system administered by both the Forest Service and the BLM. Most of these are summarized in the PLLRC's report, which clearly reflects the general view of the livestock industry in this respect. They have also been included in proposed amendments to the Taylor Grazing Act, covering grazing districts administered by the BLM.[25] For reasons not clear, similar legislative proposals have not been made for the forest lands. The commission proposals are addressed to both grazing districts and national forests. Perhaps the reason for focusing only on BLM lands is that they are deemed to be the more significant in terms of grazing use. But this too seems unwarranted, for although those lands are somewhat more extensive than the forest range, the difference is not that substantial; and it is offset by the fact that the national forest lands provide a critically important, high-quality summer range for the livestock in the western states. A more plausible speculation for the focus on Taylor Act's grazing lands is that it is intended as a first step toward an ultimate attempt to change both systems. Certainly, it is clear the basic controversy generated over the reform proposals of the commission and livestock interests cuts as deeply against the Forest Service as against the BLM.

Rights and Privileges. The criticisms and the proposed changes are several, although all share a single general objective, that of transforming the status of the permit from one of privilege to one of right. As noted earlier, the question of the permittee's status has long been a major controversy between the stockman and the government in various contexts: over limitations on permitted use, over withdrawal of lands from grazing use, or over grazing fee adjustments.[26] At the heart of these issues has always been the claim of the industry that the permits either do confer or should be recognized and altered to confer a property right to the ranchers. With equal insistence the Forest Service and BLM have continued to reiterate that the permit is, and should continue to be, a mere privilege.

Before turning to particular aspects of this controversy, it is important to emphasize what was noted briefly earlier. The question of right versus privilege is not the same issue here as is the known and much commented upon right–privilege issue in constitutional law.[27] Although superficially both may appear similar insofar as they deal with the status of recipients of government benefits, the right–privilege issue in constitutional law has been concerned with the question of procedural due process as a prerequisite to denial, revocation, or alteration of government benefits. Under an old line of legal authority surviving until fairly recently, the grant of these benefits—licenses, public employment, welfare benefits, and many other similar benefits—was considered to be a mere privilege whose dispensation was within the broad discretion of the government, unconfined by any requisites of due process, notice, public hearing, etc. That line of authority has now been effectively overruled.[28] It is now clear that the requirements of procedural due process extend to recipients of government benefits, whether such benefits are called privileges or rights. To the extent of the law's protection, these beneficiaries do in fact have rights. But the term *rights* in that context is not really different than what the government still calls privilege in the present context.

There is not much controversy on this point. The livestock industry is not arguing for *procedural* due process, and the government is not arguing for the discretion to act summarily. What the industry, supported by the PLLRC, seeks is a kind of substantive right in the rangeland which would have many of the attendant characteristics of a private property right, as a closer look at the particulars will show.[29]

The PLLRC's first recommendation for a major change in the permit system would allow permits to be freely transferable, apparently eliminating the current base property and commensurability requirements. The second recommendation urges that the allocation of new permits for increased levels of use, made possible through increased forage production on existing allotments, be made by an open, competitive market rather than by allocating the new permits among existing permittees. (Existing permittees would, however, be free to compete for the new-use permits.)

Closely related to these recommendations are several proposals designed to increase the tenure and to accord greater security to existing permittees. One measure would fix a statutory term for permits. Though the commission report does not specify the period of time, a more recent proposal called for doubling the present ten-year renewable term to twenty years.[30] A second measure would specify in the permit the terms under which it would be adjusted, in lieu of the present practice of allowing an adjustment in use levels for "conservation and protection of the resource." Similarly, the exact terms under which a permit could be cancelled would be identified specifically in the permit. A more important measure would eliminate use limits on permits generally, substituting instead a requirement that the permittee maintain specified range conditions, under the threat of permit cancellation or other penalty should he fail to do so. A fourth measure, which would go further toward conferring a property right on the permittee than any of the others, would require that permittees be compensated when permits are canceled to satisfy other land uses, whenever grazing had been designated as the dominant use of the land. Under the permit system as modified by these proposals, permits would continue to be subject to annual fees, as now, although the commission proposes a number of major changes in the fee structure, in line with the position taken in the past by the livestock interests. These will be discussed below; it need only be noted here that the changes in the fee system tie in closely with the overriding thrust of the changes designed to confer upon the permittee a greater protective right in use of the range.

Base Property and Commensurability.   The proposals to eliminate the commensurability and base property requirements for permit issuance and to allow the direct transfer of permits among livestock owners are intimately related. The elimination of the commensurability in base property requirements is important primarily in the context of transfers of the permits, and free transferability would be greatly enhanced without these current requirements. However, the proposals are separable, and it is convenient to deal with them on their independent merits.

The first proposal seems to be among the best in the set of the PLLRC's recommendations on grazing. The commensurability and base property requirements had their origin in an early Forest Service policy aimed at favoring the homesteader who operated a regular ranch operation. This was partly a conservation aim, since it was assumed that local owners had greater incentive to conserve the range and use it wisely than did those who owned no property in the area. At the same time it also reflected an economic and political policy of encouraging an industry organization comprised essentially of small, but stable, ranchers. Whether the requirements were ever necessary to serve the first end, and whether the second end was appropriate, it is hard to defend the requirements today.

First, the requirements of landownership and commensurability seem too tenuously related to proper conservation to deserve consideration on that score. To the extent that incentives are needed beyond currently imposed standards, it would seem enough that the permittee has a long-term use of the lands, often for generations as a practical matter. Enhanced yield on the allotments is a strong incentive in these circumstances. Also, if the permittee were allowed to transfer the land, he would be in a position to receive capital values which conservation in wise use would add to the grazing permits.

Second, no defensible economic policy still exists, if it ever did exist, to subsidize small ranchers. The trend in agriculture generally has been quite the contrary for the simple reason that the smaller farmer is a less efficient producer. Nor is there any defensible political or social policy justifying requirements designed to favor small ranchers at the expense of larger operations. If the idea is to protect the small ranch owner, it is enough to say that he is protected unless he wants to sell his current permit. It is difficult to see what social benefit is received either by society at large or by the individual rancher himself in restricting his freedom of operations. That the elimination of these requirements would greatly facilitate the transferability, and this transferability would encourage greater economic efficiency, seems unquestionable. Through a market system, permits would tend to be used where they have the highest economic value.

This, in turn, raises the question of transferability and the second major recommendation of the commission. Both the Forest Service and the BLM have opposed transferability of the permits on the grounds that it would tend to create a property interest in the permit. Their objection, however, seems too doctrinaire. There is nothing wrong with private property, nor with the creation of private property interests in this area, so long as they are consistent with the overall objective of social policy. Broad public interests such as conservation of the range or multiple use of resources may justify a policy of restraining private property interests so that they do not impede these aims. But this is not a problem unique to the range resource. Regulation of private resource use by law, in order to protect the public, has been inherent in private ownership from time immemorial. It has been an increasingly important limitation on landownership in recent years, with the growing concern over environmental protection and the attendant proliferation of restrictions on land use. Such regulation is clearly not incompatible with free transferability.

A more substantial problem, with the recognition of a transferable interest in the permit, is that it allows the private individual to reap capital values properly belonging to the public. In general, however, the objection to transferability on these grounds seems weak. The government can and should charge the permittees for the full value of the lands. With the new fee formula established in 1969, a system has been established which seems soundly designed to do so. The recognition of a transferable interest, it is true, might be a precedent for giving the permittee a greater private interest in the lands than public management policy should allow. That is only because of the tendency to think about property rights in absolute terms instead of as a functional concept defining a whole array of rights and interests, which can and do vary from situation to situation. The Forest Service's own continued reference to "property rights" in such absolute terms has merely clouded sound policy prescription, and it has provided the basis for confusing and misleading others as to the character and the consequences of particular management policy.

Finally, there is an aura of empty formalism in the objection to transferability. Transferability has become a practical reality, even if it is not an acknowledged right. An explicit recognition of transferability with a statement of the exact terms and conditions to which range use would continue to be subject would be a candid and clear acknowledgment of the reality that persists behind the administrative theory.

Competitive Auction for New Permits. For the reasons touched on above, the proposal to auction rights to additional grazing use above current permitted levels seems to be sound. Reliance on a market for allocation of resources cannot always be justified. Where important values cannot be represented in the market, other allocative mechanisms, or at least other allocative influences, may be warranted.[31] The proper case for public ownership in this area rests on just such a principle, and on the whole I think validly. But here we need not be concerned with nonmarket values: the choice is between two users of the range, both using it for the same purpose (grazing) with like intensity (assuming both would be equally subject to range-management regulation). Is there any reason why the allocation should not be, and could not be, made by auction?

The one sound reason for not relying on a market would be that existing permittees had built up an equity in further increased yield from the allotment. As noted earlier, to the extent this is the result of their own effort, it properly belongs to them, not to the public. It is, however, theoretically possible to separate out the investment of the permittee and that of the government, allowing the former to obtain the increased use to the extent of his investment, while the latter would be auctioned to the highest bidder (which might, of course, be the existing permittee). Whether this is administratively practicable is not known, but certainly it bears further study.

Use Limits. The first proposal to eliminate use levels deserves consideration. In cases where major range rehabilitation was required, the Forest Service probably should continue to exercise a direct management role in order to effect adequate improvement measures. Also, in cases where grazing conflicts with other uses, direct managerial responsibility will still be necessary to ensure a proper accommodation of such uses in conformity with multiple-use principles. However, in cases where no significant conflicts exist and where the only role of administrative management is supervision of grazing use to ensure maintenance of the range condition the elimination of use levels in favor of a simple quality control standard would seem to have merit.

The argument against it rests essentially on the suspicion that users cannot be depended on to maintain the range. That suspicion has plausible historic precedent, if one considers how the range was used in earlier years, but it is very questionable that historic precedent alone should prevent an experimental trial to test it in light of current circumstances. In any event, the Forest Service would not be abandoning control through administratively defined quality standards enforced by permit cancellation or fine (coupled with the reintroduction of use levels if necessary). Admittedly, such a system would not eliminate all the burdens of administrative responsibility. The task of designing and enforcing quality standards would be a substantial one. However, under this scheme the government would become a regulator more than a manager; such a role could give greater flexibility and induce greater private initiative and innovation in range management than exists under the current system. At least the promise of this seems sufficiently persuasive to justify its experimental implementation.

Compensation for Loss of Use The proposal to compensate permittees for loss of grazing use is more troublesome than the proposal for lifting use levels. The effect of the proposal is obvious: grazing permits would acquire additional value at the expense of any other existing or potential users, since application of the land to other uses would be clearly determined by the necessity to compensate ranchers. Not only would this dramatically change the current system of grazing, it would also create a very important, even compelling, precedent for application of a similar principle in other areas. If ranchers deserve compensation, what of private timber companies who are precluded from purchasing public lands for timber rights when the land is withdrawn for, say, recreation or wilderness use? And by the same token, what of similar withdrawals affecting mining or mineral exploration? A moment's reflection indicates that this principle is potentially applicable to any of a number of uses of public lands. There are even some implications outside the area of land management. In applying the same principle, should not the government also compensate radio broadcast licensees, whose licenses are modified as a consequence of a reassignment of their frequencies? Other occasions for compensation require only slightly freer imagination.

These examples, of course, only show the reach of the principle involved; they do not in themselves dispose of the issue. One may well ask, after all, why not compensate in all these cases? As a matter of economic theory one could argue that the compensability is indeed a test of the efficiency and allocation—a test of whether the resulting reallocation of resources is, in the economists' lingo, *Pareto optimal.* (According to the theory of Pareto optimality, a position of optimal social welfare is reached when change can be made without making someone worse off. And according to subsequent refinements on this theory, the test determining whether a change is in the direction of optimal welfare is whether the winners could compensate the losers.[32]) But, even accepting this theory of economic welfare, and it is not at all fully accepted,[33] application of the theory here would not support compensation, for the theory of compensability, as a test of welfare, is separate from the question of whether payment is actually made. The purpose of the test is to provide a calculus for determining whether as a whole society's benefits exceed its losses and, thus, whether the allocation of resources is efficient. The question of actual compensation is said to go to an independent issue of wealth distribution or equity, on which economic theory purports to have little to say. But in terms of equity, what is the justification for compensation here? If the rancher or other user has purchased a vested interest from the government, equity would presumably demand compensation. Obviously, however, there is no such vested interest. Until recently most permittees fell far short of covering the fair market value for current use of the range, let alone the fair market value for long-term security interests in the range, which would justify the compensation proposal made.

One might make a theoretical case for selling to users a full, exclusive property interest in the public lands. That would, of course, be a termination of public ownership (with possible residual regulatory control comparable to that which exists under current zoning laws) in favor of private ownership and a substitution of the economics of private market transactions for public management. Elsewhere, that is what the PLLRC recommends for some of this land. And, in those cases where the private market would satisfactorily reflect all the relevant social values, there is a great deal to be said for doing just that—as an economic policy and as a social policy. There are obvious difficulties and limitations on private market economics here and elsewhere, but as a possible approach to at least some areas this proposal deserves careful consideration. But this is all quite tangential to the immediate issue here, because the compensation proposal does not rest on any clear and carefully considered policy of relying on market economics.

In this context, neither the ranchers nor the commission is proposing that all rangeland be auctioned off to any private user who bids the highest price. Even if that solution proved to be economically efficient and socially acceptable, it would not give the livestock interests what they clearly now want. What the stockmen are seeking is not a sale of the land to them but more in the nature of a homestead right or a mining patent. Given our long experience with both the homestead and the mining laws, it would seem dubious wisdom to follow their precedent here. In any event, it ought not be done by indirection. If such a sweeping change is to be made, from public to private ownership, then all of the economic and social issues involved in such a proposal ought to be squarely raised. Nothing here contradicts what was said earlier about measures which would increase reliance upon private markets, for example, by eliminating certain restrictions on holding permits and allowing free transferability. Those could be carried out, and would increase efficient land use, without creating full private ownership of the kind entitling the permittee to compensation whenever government regulation restricted his use of the range. In short, the matter is one of degree; the question of property rights, as mentioned earlier, is not an absolute thing. To give the permittee certain rights, certain freedoms—for a price—it is not necessary to give him complete and unfettered property rights. Whether to take that further step is a genuine, and debatable, issue, but it is not one to be reached by indirection, as would be the case if the commission's recommendations on compensation were adopted.

The Grazing Fee Issue

Like the entire permit system with which they are intimately associated, grazing fees have been the subject of recurrent controversy both for the Forest Service and for the BLM.[34] Though any opposition to the power to charge for the use of forest range was set to rest in the *Grimaud* case in 1911, the livestock interests have persisted with their criticism of the fees as adjusted from time to time. When a major change in the Forest Service fee system was made in 1927, the great majority of permittees vigorously opposed any increases. Although they conceded the fairness of the methods by which the fees were determined, they nevertheless opposed "as a business proposition" increases reflecting those methods. Similar, even more intense opposition has been directed at the fee system established for Taylor Grazing Act districts, first implemented in 1936. When the service and the BLM established the present uniform fee structure in 1968, opposition developed as expected and has continued to be pressed by the livestock interests, in the courts and Congress. To date, the stockmen have not been successful in either forum. A U.S. Court of Appeals upheld the revised fee system in 1970.[35] And, although hearings were held in 1969 by the Committee on Interior and Insular Affairs,[36] no action was taken despite the inclinations of influential committee members who have always been quite responsive to the pleas of livestock interests. However, the opposition by livestock interests has continued to be pressed before Congress, so the issue remains alive although somewhat attenuated.

Insofar as the opposition can be explained on principled grounds (which by no means accounts for all of it), the case against the new fee structure rests mainly on an objection to the government's calculation of grazing costs for public lands, in comparing them with private lands, and on the impact which increased fees will have on barely profitable ranching operations. Although these are somewhat distinct grounds for challenge, they are closely related.

Generally the first objection is simply stated, although in refinement it becomes a bit complex. Both the livestock interests and the government agree with the basic assumption of the model that the total cost of grazing on public lands should be made equal to that of private lands. Both sides also agree that the permit for the use of public lands has acquired a value, one which would not have developed if user fees in the past had been set higher. However, the livestock interests contend this value has been capitalized into the ranch costs, and, thus, in comparing public and private land-grazing costs, the capitalized value of the permit should be included as a cost of the use of public lands.[37] This would reflect the fact that in the course of past purchases and sales of base property or permitted livestock, the value of the permit has been included in the sale price of these assets and hence should be regarded as part of the investment costs to be recouped by the rancher. If this "cost" were included, the discrepancy in cost between privately leased and public lands would be erased; indeed, for the national forest lands, including the capitalized value of the grazing permit would have made the cost of grazing higher on the public than on the private lands. Thus, there would be no basis for an increase in grazing fees in order to equalize the two costs.

The government's position was, and continues to be, that the economic value of the permit has developed because of a disparity between private and public grazing charges, and it cannot be recognized as a cost for purposes of setting the fee, even if the market price at which base property and livestock associated with the permit has included a sum which affects the value of the permit. To recognize this "premium" value put on private base property or livestock, because of the entitlement of the owner to graze on public lands, would be tantamount to recognizing that the permittee had a vested right, one transferable with the base property or livestock. Both the Forest Service and the BLM have long insisted that grazing is a nontransferable privilege; therefore, there is no basis for recognizing any private market values assigned to it. To treat the value which ranchers have put on the permit as a cost would be equivalent to official recognition that said permit was a right—one which could not be impaired by the government without compensation.

In realistic terms, the government's reliance on a distinction between right and privilege may be a poor rationale. Even though the BLM and the service have continued to insist that their permits conferred only a privilege, both agencies were aware of the fact that permits were acquiring a capital value which, when transferred, became a cost to the transferee.

The livestock owner thus has some support for his argument in the fact that the government stood by and did nothing to recover this capital value. However, the argument has been grossly overstated. The fact is, much of the permit's value created by the gap between the fee for and the market value of the permits is a fairly recent phenomenon. The Forest Service and the BLM did respond as early as 1961, when their fee study began. Unfortunately, governments often act slowly, and in this case it took eight years. However, one would think the livestock interests can hardly complain of that, since their opposition was one factor in the delay in implementing the study results.

There is, too, a scent of the red herring about the stockmen's objections to the refusal to recognize capitalized permit value insofar as it suggests that all of the ranchowners have been trapped into paying premium prices for ranch investment, only to be told that this price would not be recognized as a valid cost for purposes of the fee. Most of the permittees undoubtedly made that investment before the permits acquired a substantial part of their current value. Thus, their capital costs do not in fact include a substantial premium for the permit value. To the extent that they do, however, much of this cost has been amortized by paying lower fees over the period between the time of acquisition of the ranch property and the time when the full-market-value fee is to be paid.

CONCLUSIONS

The volatile controversies that once surrounded public range management in the West have now passed into history. In the midst of current battles over timber management, recreation, and wilderness preservation the problems in range management that do persist attract relatively little public attention. The problems are nevertheless important, in their own right and as illustrations of more general issues in public land management.

One such issue is that of private rights in the use of the range which is raised by a series of PLLRC proposals. The Forest Service has resisted all efforts to recognize private property rights in the public range as being incompatible with public ownership and its own administrative responsibility for managing the range. Though one must admire the spirit of public responsibility which underlies the Forest Service position, I believe that the service has been too inflexible in insisting that recognition of greater private "rights" is incompatible with public ownership and management. What is urged here is not the creation of absolute property rights free of government conditions and control. Indeed, it is not necessary to speak in terms of conferring property rights at all; it would be more accurate to characterize the issue here as one of defining the appropriate character and scope of administrative regulation of rangeland use. The Forest Service has tended to view the issue by asking, What are the private entitlements of users in public resources? Expressed in that fashion the question invites a simple negative answer. The answer is less simple when the question is, What are the reasonable interests of the public in regulating public land use? More particularly: What public interest is served by restricting use to local landowners? What public interest is served by forbidding transferability of range use permits?

The first restriction follows a more general Forest Service policy of favoring local interests in managing forest resources, a policy that is particularly evident in timber management. But why should local interests be thus favored? Is such continued favoritism of local interests compatible with *national* ownership? The second restriction cannot, for better or for worse, be explained in terms of a policy of localism; there is no reason to suppose that preventing local owners from transferring their permits aids local interests. The rationale for such a restriction is more legalistic than economic: transferability is disfavored because it would give permittees a greater private "right" in the use of the public. My response to that is, so what? Granted the legitimate concern over maintaining public control over public resources, it is very hard to see any loss of necessary public control involved here. The Forest Service seems to be concerned with the precedent which a loosening of regulatory restrictions might set; there is certain commonsensical wisdom in that concern, but the appropriate response to it is to define carefully, clearly, and firmly the metes and bounds of the "right" being conferred.

It is not clear why this could not be done consistent with continued administrative responsibility for proper resource conservation and use. Here there is no implication that the user would be given the right to use the range resource in any manner whatsoever. It was suggested earlier that the service in certain situations, should consider the possibility of giving greater latitude to private initiative in range use. However, nothing in this suggestion implied an abdication of public responsibility for establishing and enforcing appropriate standards of conservation and use.

Also, greater freedom in private use of the public range would not in any way imply free use. Forest Service policy here has been correct in insisting on recovery of the full market value of the range resource—this despite the seductive arguments that such fees will hurt the poor rancher and drive up meat prices to the ultimate detriment of the public. Forest Service policy seems all the more commendable by being somewhat at odds with the general tenor of agricultural policy with its crop subsidies, price supports, special loans, services, and countless other aids and comforts.

Admittedly in this larger context of lavish agricultural aids, the importance of insisting on recovering full value for public land use is considerably diminished. What, after all, is the point of the government's troubling over collecting a few million dollars in fees when it is giving away billions in direct and indirect subsidies? Within the perspective of broad government policy, the question is perhaps unanswerable. But within the framework of land-management policy, the answer is relatively simple. Whatever the excuses for general policies of income redistribution to agriculture, there is no justification for allowing them to pass in disguise. If the subsidies are to be made, it is better to make them as open and direct as possible. Not only does this allow them to be openly seen and evaluated by the decision maker and the public, it is also more conducive to a more rational resource allocation, including a more rational choice of resource use by the farmer himself. This is all familiar learning to economists. Admittedly, it is not an inexorable principle of economic social theory that all subsidies must be in direct financial aid. In some cases there is defensible reason for such aids. For example, if we want people to have better housing, giving the money may not be acceptable since they will not buy housing! They might buy a new sports car. That it may be paternalistic of the grantor to dictate that the recipient must buy a house and not a car does not mean that the condition is indefensible.[38] But assuming that the purpose of the subsidy is fulfilled, it is surely preferable that subsidies be made directly, with the least interference and with efficiency in resource allocation.

In the case of range use, there is no justification for granting free use of the land—that is, use at a price less than full value—simply for the purpose of aiding the rancher. This can only have the effect of inducing misallocation of the land as between grazing and other uses. Or it can have the effect (as indeed it has had) of inducing a misallocation of resources between private and public lands, which in turn creates an excess burden on the latter. It is because of this misallocation, resulting from a skewed fee system, that wildlife conservation groups have supported the revised fee system. Encouraging grazing to an uneconomic degree by retaining an economically inefficient fee system has significant implications for other uses of the land, most particularly uses of the land for wildlife conservation.

Nor is it necessary in terms of some overall purpose of subsidization to refrain from charging the full economic value of the range. The amount of the subsidy which would be conferred by such free or less than full-value use, measured against other subsidies, is not large. Charging full value for range use will not undermine any overall aims of agricultural subsidization.

Despite the strong economic case for a fee system which recovers the approximate market value of public land use, it is by no means certain that this goal will be achieved. As is often the case in affairs of state, political considerations do not necessarily pursue sound economic policy; and in the politics of farm policy, they rarely do so. There is the ever-present prospect of political alteration. Such has been the history of range management, and such is its probable future.

NOTES

1. For an early history, see *The Western Range,* S. Doc. 199, 74 Cong., 2 sess., 1936; and Paul H. Roberts, *Hoof Prints on Forest Ranges: The Early Years of National Forest Range Administration* (San Antonio, Texas: Nayler, 1963).

2. *United States* v. *Grimaud,* 220 U.S. 506 (1911).

3. 64 Stat. 88 (1950), 16 U.S.C., § 580 (1).

4. The figure is somewhat misleading in that only about one-half that acreage, 58 million acres, is classified as "suitable for grazing," and of this, only 54 million acres are listed as "open for grazing." Nearly 90 percent of this land is in the six western regions. U.S. Department of Agriculture/Forest Service *1970 Annual Grazing Statistical Report.*

5. U.S. Department of Agriculture/Forest Service, *Report of the Chief, 1972–73,* p. 37. An animal unit-month is the standard grazing measurement; it is equivalent to one cow or horse or five sheep or goats grazing for one month.

6. Public Land Law Review Commission, *One Third of the Nation's Land* (1970), p. 105.

7. See U.S. Department of Agriculture/Forest Service, *The Nation's Range Resource,* Research Report 19 (1972), pp. 94–95.

8. See Marion Clawson and Burnell R. Held, *The Federal Lands: Their Use and Management* (Baltimore: Johns Hopkins University Press, 1957), p. 60. On this I can offer some personal nonscholarly corroboration as the reluctant heir to a large interest in a cattle ranch in southern Idaho which grazes on both Taylor grazing districts and national forest lands. Without the latter, the livestock operations of this modest enterprise would surely be in jeopardy. The ranch, moreover, has a somewhat larger private acreage than other ranches in the area.

9. In addition to the Forest Service Manual, § 2230 *et seq.,* I have drawn generally on University of Idaho and Pacific Consultants Inc., *The Forage Resource,* A Study for the Public Land Law Review Commission (Springfield, Ill.: Clearinghouse for Federal Scientific and Technical Information, 1970); and U.S. Department of Agriculture/Forest Service, *Grazing Fees on National Forest Range* (1969). Discussions with Forest Service officials also contributed very greatly to my understanding. Data on grazing use are from the U.S. Department of Agriculture/Forest Service, *Report of the Chief, 1972–73,* p. 37.

10. Other types of paid permits include temporary (annual) permits; crossing permits (many are also issued free); commercial transportation permits (for commercial packing, dude ranching, and others). See 36 C.F.R., § 231.3.

11. See 36 C.F.R., § 231.3. There are other categories as well, but these are the important ones.

12. This includes private land permits as well as those classified as "exempt." See U.S. Department of Agriculture/Forest Service, *Report of the Chief, 1972–73*, p. 37.

13. See 36 C.F.R., § 231.3; Forest Service Manual, § 2231 *et seq.*

14. Where a new permit is issued or a modification of an existing permit is made to increase grazing, it is normally for a temporary period (one to five years) to determine the suitability and capacity of the range. At the end of this period, a regular ten-year permit is issued.

15. For example, in the Intermountain Region (the dominant grazing region of the National Forest System) the current limits run from 300–800 head of cattle or horses and from 4,000–12,000 head of sheep or goats. Forest Service Manual, § 2231.7; R-4 Supp.

16. See, for example, Testimony of Chief of the Forest Service, Edward Cliff, in U.S. Congress, Subcommittee of the House Committee on Interior and Insular Affairs, *Hearings on Grazing Fees,* 91 Cong., 1 sess., 1969, pp. Ser. 91-1 and 124–125.

17. For general sources, see ibid., and U.S. Congress, Senate Subcommittee of the Committee on Interior and Insular Affairs, *Hearings on Grazing Fees on Public Lands,* 91 Cong., 1 sess., 1969, *The Forage Resource*; and U.S. Department of Agriculture/Forest Service, *Grazing Fees.*

18. On the early history of fees, see Walter Dutton, "History of Forest Service Grazing Fees," *Journal of Range Management,* vol. 6 (1953), p. 393.

19. For a history, a description, and the Forest Service's defense of the fee structure, see U.S. Department of Agriculture/Forest Service, *Grazing Fees*; see also Testimony of the Chief of the Forest Service Edward P. Cliff in U.S. Congress, House Subcommittee of the Committee on Interior and Insular Affairs, *Hearings on Grazing Fees,* pp. 121–126.

20. See Forest Service Manual, § 2200 *et seq.,* and *The Forage Resource.* I have also drawn heavily on a variety of Forest Service publications, most notably: *Range Allotment Analysis,* PA-623 (1964); *Region 4 Training Guide for Grazing Management* (1971); and on discussions with service officials.

21. U.S. Department of Agriculture/Forest Service, *1970 Annual Grazing Statistical Report,* p. iv.

22. While the environmental analysis survey is expected to recognize every use of the rangelands, cases in which other uses seriously conflict with grazing are infrequent, and most are readily resolved without substantial sacrifice to either use. Special attention is generally required in areas where big game use the same range. Although livestock and game do not generally browse the same species of vegetation, any grazing by cattle in particular may result in the destruction of game forage by trampling or soil impact. Every allotment plan is therefore required to estimate and provide for the needs of big game, giving first priority to those needs over those of livestock.

23. See U.S. Department of Agriculture/Forest Service, *The Nation's Range Resource.*

24. PLLRC, *One Third of the Nation's Land,* p. 115 (Recommendation 42).

25. See *S. 2028;* and U.S. Congress, Senate Subcommittee of the Committee on Interior and Insular Affairs, *Hearings on Administration of Grazing Districts,* 92 Cong., 2 sess., 1972.

26. Ibid.

27. See Kenneth C. Davis, Administrative Law Treatise, §§ 7.11-7.12 (St. Paul: West, 1958 and 1970 Supp.).

28. See, for example, *Cafeteria Workers* v. *McElroy,* 367 U.S. 889 (1961); and ibid.

29. On all of the following proposals, see PLLRC, *One-Third of the Nation's Land,* ch. 6.

30. See *S. 2028,* 92 Cong., 2 sess., 1972.

31. For excellent, concise statements, see Peter Steiner, *Public Expenditure Budgeting* (Washington, D.C.: Brookings, 1969); and William Baumol, *Welfare Economics and the Theory of the State* (2d ed., Cambridge, Mass.: Harvard University Press, 1965).

32. The so-called Kaldor–Hicks criterion. See Nicholas Kaldor, "Welfare Propositions of Economics and Interpersonal Comparisons of Utility," *Economics Journal,* vol. 49 (1939); and John R. Hicks, "The Foundations of Welfare Economics," ibid., p. 696.

33. I. M. D. Little, *A Critique of Welfare Economics* (2d ed., London: Oxford U. Press, 1957), pp. 84–116.

34. For a history of the controversy with the BLM, see Phillip Foss, *Politics and Grass: The Administration of Grazing on the Public Domain* (Westport, Conn.: Greenwood Press, 1960), pp. 86–88.

35. *Pankey Land and Cattle Co. v. Hardin,* 427 F. 2d 43 (10th Cir. 1970).

36. See U.S. Congress, House Subcommittee of the Committee on Interior and Insular Affairs, *Hearings on Grazing Fees;* and parallel Senate hearings.

37. The core position is set out by two agricultural economists from Utah State University, in U.S. Congress, Senate Subcommittee of the Committee on Interior and Insular Affairs, *Hearings on Grazing Fees,* pp. 10–14.

38. For an excellent short rationale for transfers in kind, see Lester Thurow, "Cash Versus In-Kind Transfers," *American Economic Review,* vol. 64 (1974), p. 190.

VIII

WILDLIFE

Lands within the national forest system are home for a variety of wildlife not equaled by any other single system of federal lands.[1] This includes the commonly recognized forest fauna: deer, bear, elk, turkey, fowl, freshwater fish, and birds of nearly every variety. It also includes a large number of unique, rare or endangered species. For many such species, the national forests are the sole habitat and last refuge against extinction. The California condor, the Kirtlands warbler, the Florida manatee, the American alligator, and the eastern timber wolf are a few of those precariously situated on the forests. The merely rare species range from the spotted bat to grizzly bear.[2]

This suggests the importance of the forests to wildlife, but says relatively little about the role of wildlife conservation and management in general, and of the Forest Service's activities in particular. Until recently there has been regrettably little wildlife conservation.[3] Even in the case of major game species, where an economic resource could be readily identified, conservation policy was late in coming. Game laws designed to regulate hunting of certain game species appear as early as the seventeenth century in several of the Colonies, and these were succeeded by state game laws in many states.

224

However, most of these were limited in scope, loosely enforced, and generally ineffective. It was not until the end of the Civil War that any significant effort was made for the protection of wildlife. By that time many species had been totally eliminated from the eastern states, through uncontrolled hunting or careless destruction of habitat, and some had been eliminated altogether. Among them was one that has become the modern symbol of man's destructiveness: the last passenger pigeon died in 1914 in the Cincinnati Zoo; two decades earlier their numbers had been estimated in the billions.[4]

LEGISLATION TO PROTECT WILDLIFE

The first and only significant effort to protect wildlife, at least until the past couple of decades, was directed at game species. Between 1850–85, legislation to protect game against uncontrolled hunting (including particularly commercial hunting) and unlimited destruction was enacted in all of the states and territories. In 1900, Congress made its first effort with the passage of the Lacey Act.[5] This act was intended primarily to support the state laws against commercial hunting of wildlife, by prohibiting the shipment across state boundaries of game and nongame species (or parts of them, such as bird plumes and furs in which there was extensive traffic), contrary to the laws of the state where taken. The act also regulated the introduction into the country of exotic species of birds and mammals in order to protect native species against foreign wildlife. The Lacey Act was only partly successful; it proved incapable of stopping illegal hunting and shipment of waterfowl into commercial markets across the country. One of its main weaknesses was the inadequate protection it gave migratory game birds. Migrating across U.S. and Canadian boundaries and many states, these game birds were outside the jurisdiction of any state.

As a result, Congress, in 1913, passed the Weeks–McLean Law to protect the migratory birds.[6] Because of doubts as to Congress' power to pass such a law under its commerce clause power, however, the United States negotiated a treaty with Canada incorporating the substance of the law. This treaty was ratified in 1918 by the Migratory Bird Treaty Act[7]; its constitutionality was upheld in *Missouri v. Holland*,[8] a landmark decision on the treaty power of the United States. Although primarily aimed at the protection of game fowl, through regulation of hunting and elimination of sale of birds, the act also extended federal protection to all migratory birds.

Both the Migratory Bird Treaty and the Lacey Act were important measures in the protection of wildlife, but insofar as they were aimed at the protection of wildlife through regulation of hunting, both were somewhat exceptional intrusions into what was recognized as primarily the responsibility of the states, as owners of the wildlife. The basis for a broader federal responsibility in wildlife conservation came with the recognition of the importance of the federal lands as wildlife habitat. The role the federal lands could play was seen as early as 1894 when Congress passed the Yellowstone Park Protective Act, which made unlawful the killing of wildlife in Yellowstone Park.[9] This set a precedent that was later followed in other parks, one which is enforced today in nearly all national parks. It also set a precedent for establishing other national wildlife refuges. Probably the most important step in the development of refuges was taken with enactment of the Migratory Bird Conservation Act by Congress in 1929,[10] providing for the establishment of a national system of waterfowl refuges administered by the Bureau of Biological Survey within the Department of Agriculture.[11]

But the national wildlife refuges and the national parks accounted for only a part of the protected wildlife habitat provided by the federal lands. Far more extensive and potentially far more important were the vast acres of forests and western rangelands. The importance of the forests as a wildlife habitat was recognized as early as the first withdrawals of forest lands from the public domain. Many of the early forest reserves were established with the explicit intent to provide protection to an important wildlife habitat. Unlike the refuges, the forest reserves were not closed to hunting or fishing; though such a restriction was considered in the early era of the reserves, it was rejected by Gifford Pinchot, who persuaded President Theodore Roosevelt to limit such complete sanctuaries to the special refuges. However, the forest reserves did provide a substantial measure of protection for the wildlife habitat which could not be provided by the public domain lands. Unfortunately, it was not until 1934 and the enactment of the Taylor Grazing Act that the public domain was closed, and active conservation policies could be pursued. Even then wildlife remained a limited concern, its interest being subordinate to the interest of livestock.

The early years of the wildlife conservation movement were devoted largely to policies of protection of wildlife and preservation of wildlife habitat. Relatively little attention was given, either by the states or the federal government, to active management of the game stock or of the habitat.

To assist the states in wildlife conservation, Congress, in 1937, enacted the Federal Aid in Wildlife Restoration Act[12]—commonly known as the Pittman–Robertson Act—which provides aid to the states on a 75 to 25 percent matching basis, to be used by the states for wildlife management and research, including land acquisition and development. (The federal funds are provided by an excise tax on the manufacture of sporting arms and ammunition and, by a recent amendment, on pistols. The state's share is provided through state hunting license fees, which under the act must be allocated to wildlife purposes.) In 1950 this precedent was used to provide federal aid to sport fisheries management with the so-called Dingell–Johnson

Act,[13] the federal funds being provided from an excise tax on fishing tackle. While these acts provided financial support to states for wildlife conservation work (including state-supported wildlife programs on federal lands), neither involved any direct federal intervention in wildlife management. Federal land agencies such as the Forest Service did concern themselves with habitat management, but even this effort was minor and incidental until recently.

The past decade has seen a broadening of federal conservation authority over wildlife. The seminal measure was the Endangered Species Act of 1966,[14] which was intended "to provide a program for the conservation, protection, restoration and propagation of selected species of native fish and wildlife . . . that are threatened with extinction." In furtherance of this purpose, the secretaries of the interior, agriculture, and defense were mandated to protect species threatened with extinction, and "insofar as practicable and consistent with the primary purposes" of the agencies, to preserve the habitats of such species on lands under this jurisdiction. The secretary of the interior was given the leadership role in endangered-species protection. He was given the responsibility for determining which species are "threatened" with extinction as well as authority to "encourage" and "assist" other federal agencies in carrying out the purposes of the act. Authority was also given to the land agencies to acquire land for conservation of endangered species. In 1969, the Endangered Species Conservation Act[15] amended the 1966 law to prohibit (with certain exceptions) the importation of species threatened with "worldwide extinction."

The 1966 and 1969 acts were less important for the actions they directly mandated than for the general policy of wildlife protection they espoused and the precedents they established for expanding the role of the federal government in this area.[16] In fact, the acts in themselves provided rather weak protection for endangered species. They did not purport to protect any species until actually endangered; species merely threatened were not covered, and there was no statutory prohibition against trapping or killing endangered species. Although the 1966 act may have implied a discretionary authority to federal land agencies to prohibit taking of protected species on lands within their respecive jurisdictions,[17] it did not purport to assert any federal authority over such species on nonfederal lands. These and other limitations on the scope of the original act induced conservationists to press for more expansive federal legislation. At the same time, the threat of increased federal authority in an area traditionally regarded by the states as their exclusive concern produced countervailing pressures to curtail federal jurisdiction in favor of restoring the states' paramount jurisdiction.[18]

After some vigorous contention, the former prevailed. In 1973, the 1966 and 1969 acts were superseded by a new Endangered Species Act which greatly expanded federal authority over endangered species.[19] Among many changes in the scope of endangered-species protection,[20] probably the most important is a provision forbidding the "taking" (defined broadly to include not only killing and trapping but any harassment or harm, or attempt to engage in such conduct) of protected species, on federal, state, or private lands except in accordance with a federally approved state program of protection.

This assertion of federal authority over wildlife on nonfederal lands represents a dramatic and controversial departure from the traditional federal role in wildlife conservation. Federal preemption of the state role is not complete, however. The act provides for cooperative agreements between the federal government and any state which establishes and maintains an "adequate and active program for the conservation of endangered species and threatened species," subject to approval by the secretary of the interior. Under such agreements the states, with financial assistance provided by the federal government, retain their management responsibility. However, while the act thus provides for (and the legislative purpose plainly relies upon) the retention of substantial state responsibility, it is a responsibility subject to continuous federal supervision.[21]

The Endangered Species Acts of 1966, 1969, and 1973 have brought us to a new era in wildlife conservation, but their effect on the broader realm of wildlife management beyond endangered-species protection remains unclear. Before considering some implications, we need to examine further the Forest Service's management role.

THE MANAGEMENT SCHEME

On federal lands, at least on multiple-use lands such as the national forests or the public domain lands of the Bureau of Land Management (BLM), wildlife conservation and management has generally been the shared responsibility of state and federal governments. As landowner the federal government has jurisdiction and responsibility for habitat management, while the states have traditionally been conceded primary authority over the taking and stocking of wildlife itself. However, this scheme is subject to a number of exceptions. One of these, just noted, is protection of endangered species. Another exception involves lands specially reserved for recreation or preservation. For example, on most national parks and other lands administered by the National Park Service, hunting is prohibited by statute.[22] Similarly, on national wildlife refuges hunting is specially restricted (though not necessarily prohibited) by federal law.[23] The scope of federal authority over wildlife has been the subject of sometimes acrimonious controversy between state and federal authorities. For the most part, the Forest Service has been extremely chary of asserting authority over hunting and fishing on the forests.

Long-established service policy has conceded general authority over wildlife to the states, confining federal jurisdiction to management of the wildlife habitat, a policy expressly incorporated into the Multiple-Use and Sustained Yield Act of 1960. This policy has recognized some exceptions; for example, direct authority of hunting and fishing has been asserted in some instances to protect the habitat from depredation.[24] (Of course, such authority is now mandated by the 1973 Endangered Species Act to the extent states do not develop an approved plan of management for endangered species, but currently it is not possible to tell whether many, or any, such occasions will arise.) Apart from such special cases the jurisdiction over national forest wildlife remains divided. *Divided* may, however, be a somewhat misleading term. As a practical matter, it might be more accurate to say that responsibility is *shared* in view of the extensive cooperative effort between state wildlife agencies and the Forest Service in habitat-management planning and wildlife conservation. Before looking at this further, an outline of the basic functions of the Forest Service management functions is required.

Management Functions
The importance of an active management to conserve wildlife on forest lands has been recognized in the Forest Service since the time of Aldo Leopold. Despite this early recognition of its importance, however, wildlife management has certainly not traditionally figured as one of the major concerns of the Forest Service. It was not recognized as such by statute until the Multiple-Use and Sustained Yield Act of 1960. Even with that formal recognition, wildlife management has continued to be more of a by-product of other resource management functions than a major function of independent statute. In recent years, the increased attention given wildlife conservation generally has brought with it a more substantial role for wildlife–habitat management within the Forest Service. However, while it is coming into its own as an important concern of forest management, wildlife management continues to struggle for independent recognition; in most national forests it must still be considered a distinctly secondary, even incidental, function. The paramount task of Forest Service wildlife managers is to provide advice and guidance on and coordinate plans for interaction of resource uses and management actions on wildlife.[25]

Apart from this advisory service function of wildlife specialists, there are many affirmative habitat-improvement programs. These vary substantially from area to area depending on the nature of the wildlife, the environment, the size of the administrative staff for the particular unit, the interest of local Forest Service officials and the interests of other wildlife groups with whom they work. In heavily forested areas, this might involve special cutting or prescribed burning to promote browse for wildlife.[26] In desert areas, preparation of water holes for game is a common activity. Often, of course, these activities also serve purposes other than those beneficial to wildlife. Thinning of trees, for example, is likely to be part of a general program of timber stand improvement, as is disposal of debris or slash; preparation of water holes will often be part of general range-management activities intended for the coordinate benefit of livestock and game. Beyond these relatively routine efforts, however, the increased emphasis on wildlife as an important natural resource has led to more substantial management efforts, including special habitat programs designed to restore, preserve, or enhance the wildlife habitat. This has given greater significance to long-term management planning.

Administrative and Biological
Management Plans

The planning process in wildlife management is somewhat more varied than that of timber or range management. In this respect it resembles more the kind of diversified planning utilized in outdoor recreation. As with outdoor recreation, a variety of plans and several levels of management planning may be involved in planning a single area.[27] There are two general types of management plans: administrative and biological unit plans. The former is a general habitat-management plan covering all the wildlife activities within the particular administrative unit (i.e., forest or ranger district). The biological unit plan provides special planning direction for a particular species in a specified area.

Primary planning authority rests with the forest supervisor, and it is at this level that nearly two-thirds of the professional wildlife specialists in the service are assigned. However, the district ranger is directly and substantially involved in the planning process insofar as individual plans are prepared for each ranger district. As would be expected, individual plans vary considerably in degree of detail and sophistication among forests and even among districts. Much of the variation is attributable, of course, to differences in the wildlife situations and their management needs. While there is variation among wildlife plans, most district and forest plans have certain common features. Typically, an administrative unit plan contains data on the various wildlife species and on their pertinent habitat conditions; a history of wildlife management in the area; a list of the various state and federal agencies and private organizations, with whom management planning and activities are coordinated; a discussion of general objectives and policies, including multiple-use coordination requirements affecting wildlife; and finally, directions for habitat management. The management directive is more or less specific, depending on the unit for which the plan is prepared. District plans, of course, are more detailed and include an *action plan* which schedules particular work projects for the current year and for a future three- to five-year period.

PROBLEMS AND CONTROVERSIES

The Question of Jurisdiction

An old Chinese encyclopedia classified all animals as: "(a) belonging to the Emperor, (b) embalmed, (c) tame, (d) suckling pigs, (e) sirens, (f) fabulous, (g) stray dogs, (h) included in the present classification, (i) frenzied, (j) innumerable, (k) drawn with a very fine camelhair brush, (l) *et. cetera,* (m) having just broken the water pitcher, (n) that from a long way off look like flies."[28]

The classification faintly suggests the American legal order with respect to animals, at least if one removes the Chinese whimsy, which is not to be found in the American structure. Nowhere is this more apparent than in the area of wildlife management. The chief difficulty has been in identifying the first of the above types—those belonging to the emperor. Or, perhaps more accurately, the difficulty is to identify who is the emperor.

In recent years the increase in federal management efforts to protect wildlife has regenerated old controversies between federal and state authorities over the question of jurisdiction.[29] As noted earlier, wildlife on the federal lands has traditionally been a shared responsibility between state and federal agencies, with the latter managing the wildlife habitat and the former the conservation of the wildlife itself, particularly the regulation of fishing and hunting. While there have always been exceptions, most notably in the case of national parks and wildlife refuges, the pattern of divided jurisdiction or shared responsibility has prevailed for most federal lands; for the national forests, it has been in effect since the time of the forest reserves. Generally, the arrangement seems to have worked well enough. In the use of the national forests, the relations between state and Forest Service wildlife officials appear to have been reasonably successful. However, the push for more active federal protection of wildlife creates potential for conflict in the future. The issue has been sharply posed by the enactment of federal wildlife protection laws, such as the endangered species legislation, which in some cases is in opposition to state game laws.

The Endangered Species Act of 1966 was not intended to preempt state laws, even for endangered species on federal lands. However, insofar as it directed the federal landowning agencies to protect species, it did provide a basis for assumption of jurisdiction by federal land agencies, such as the Forest Service, to adopt restrictions on hunting and fishing which would supplant inconsistent state laws. For many of the endangered species, this conflict between federal and state authorities was more a matter of principle and a threatening precedent (to the states) for other preemptive federal jurisdiction than of immediate concern. There was no real conflict over protection of endangered songbirds, for example. There was, on the other hand, an increasingly bitter conflict over game or predator species that were within state game or predator control laws.

There can be no reasonable doubt that an extension of federal control over wildlife on federal lands would be within the constitutional power of the Congress, under the property clause of the Constitution. Although the states have refused to concede such power, arguing that the states "own" all wildlife within their respective borders, it is now difficult to take that claim very seriously.[30]

Whether the federal government and the Forest Service in particular *should* expand its authority over wildlife management beyond its traditional concern with habitat, is not as easily answered as the question whether they could. For one thing, it is probably pointless to debate in the abstract whether the Forest Service, for example, should take over all aspects of wildlife management on the national forests. They are not about to do so, and, so far as appears to date, there is no reason why they should desire to do so. The issue is whether in particular situations, and contrary to state law, they would find it in their interest to assert control over hunting, fishing, or stocking of wildlife. The last condition should be stressed since there is no real point to the dispute if state law and federal policy concur. One doubts that there would be many occasions for such an assertion of federal authority so far as the Forest Service is concerned. The likely occasions would be cases involving forest refuges,[31] wilderness, or other special wildlife-management areas where the special character of the area dictates restrictions or a comprehensive federal management scheme. Even here one must suppose the exceptional case when state authorities would not join in the management plan or cooperate by adopting appropriate state regulations to conform to the needs of the federal plan.

However, freed of the notion that the federal government simply has no business in wildlife beyond the management of the habitat, one can assume such occasions would arise. Certainly that is the assumption made by the states. Legal aspects aside, the states present a number of arguments against any extension of the federal role. The following summary, by one state game commissioner, appears to be more or less representative of these arguments[32]:

1. Unless state ownership and exclusive control over wildlife is confirmed, private landowners may assert the same right to manage and control resident wildlife as does the federal government.

2. Denial of the states' exclusive jurisdiction would in effect give the federal government authority it does not want and does not have the requisite expertise or manpower to administer.

3. If the wildlife ownership theory is not laid to rest it will result in a checkerboard pattern of wildlife-management jurisdiction impossible to administer.

4. State game and fish departments are the most convenient agencies for protecting and controlling wildlife and for achieving uniformity of management.

5. Federal agencies are simply not equipped to enforce hunting and fishing regulations on the federal lands, and additional enforcement officers and magistrates would be too costly.

6. Separate federal programs would require an unnecessary additional tax burden and might divert funds which ought to be available to the states.

The first argument can be quickly dispatched. It does not follow that what the federal government can do as landlord and sovereign, the private landlord can do. In any case it is not clear what the concern here is: are state officials so jealous of their authority that they do not want to encourage private landowners to practice wildlife conservation?

The second argument appears to be true; however, the question is not really whether the Forest Service or the other agencies want to "take over." In a general sense they plainly do not. Rather, the question is whether they find it in their interest to exercise a marginal increase in federal power to promote certain interests or programs. Here, even the Forest Service, a consistent supporter of state jurisdiction, occasionally asserts its superior authority.

The main weakness of the third and fourth arguments is the fact that wildlife management is already a checkerboard, with different state and federal agencies exercising overlapping functions; it is doubtful that a more affirmative role by the federal government would make it more so.

The fifth argument seems plausible except that it assumes the federal government could or would increase its management efforts without appropriate funding measures, an assumption undermined by the last argument. The last argument simply disregards the question of whether the funds diverted "ought to be available to the states." That question can only be answered by judging whether state and federal expenditures are most efficiently spent. Implicit here seems to be an additional assumption—that federal agencies like the Forest Service have access to large, untapped sources of appropriate funds with which to finance their operations. In truth, the wildlife appropriations for the Forest Service are not as sparse as they are sometimes thought to be, but by the measure of the tasks it is asked to perform, one can hardly say the service is embarrassed with riches.

The Economic Factor

In 1972, in a special message to Congress on environmental protection, President Nixon stated:

> Wild places and wild things constitute a treasure to be cherished and protected for all time. The pleasure and refreshment which they give man confirm their value to society. More importantly perhaps, the wonder, beauty, and elemental force in which the least of them share suggest a higher right to exist—not granted them by man and not his to take away. In environmental policy as anywhere else we cannot deal in absolutes. Yet we can at least give considerations like these more relative weight in the seventies, and become a more civilized people in a healthier land because of it.[33]

It is eloquently stated. Unhappily, the wisdom for implementing this policy has the characteristics of rare and endangered species—it is hard to locate and harder to reproduce. So is the money. And unfortunately, when presidents or conservationists speak of giving wildlife "more relative weight" the tug at the heart strings is often canceled by an equal tug on the purse strings. Therein lies the true heart of the matter.[34]

Forest Service appropriations for wildlife management in 1975 totaled some $9 million.[35] That is by no means an insignificant sum, but neither is it an embarrassment of riches. In fact, given the growth of the agency's wildlife-management responsibilities in recent years (under the mandate of legislation such as the NEPA, the Endangered Species Act, and others) it seems insufficient. Important Forest Service plans for wildlife-improvement programs must be shelved in the absence of more adequate funding,[36] while other possible future plans cannot be undertaken in the absence of some stronger likelihood of increased funding. For all the attention given to preservation of endangered species by protecting them against hunting, it is noteworthy how slight and passing seems to be the attention given to problems of wildlife-habitat management. Yet, in terms of the goals espoused by the Endangered Species Act, habitat improvement is likely in the end to be decisive in the preservation of endangered or threatened species.[37] However, the plight of endangered or threatened species or even rare species should not be allowed to obscure the larger concern for wildlife generally and for appropriate consideration to the habitat needs of wildlife and of the role for affirmative management programs. And this means, among other things, the necessary funds.

An important part of the funding problem is that wildlife has not generally been identified as an economic good. As a consequence, in economic competition with other "productive" goods such as timber, wildlife needs have suffered. The reluctance to put wildlife into an economic frame of reference appears to stem from two views. One is the view that economic analysis is inappropriate insofar as the values at stake transcend the "materialistic" values with which economics is (supposedly) concerned. The second view is that economic analysis is not useful in the field of wildlife conservation because the values are not measurable in terms amenable to economic analysis.

The first view is but another aspect of a general notion discussed previously in the context of wilderness. It requires little further attention here beyond a paraphrase of the basic point made earlier. We can accept the common sentiment that wildlife has value beyond the materialistic benefits to man (whatever that means). Being in the realm of value judgments, it is not really disputable anyway; nor is it very useful. Contrary to frequent supposition, this sentiment, however lofty, does not carry us beyond the economic realm.

The issue in the present context is not the question of how much we should value wildlife in some personal ethical sense. It is rather, how much of other goods—and other satisfactions[38]—we should sacrifice to protect and preserve wildlife. This is plainly an economic question which cannot be avoided by attempting to cast it in other terms. It is more than a matter of semantics; it is a matter of functioning effectively in an economic world. Those who are reluctant to deal with the economic aspect of, say, wildlife are ill-equipped to do business on the terms in which business is transacted. It seems contradictory, for example, to ask for funds to aid and support wildlife values in one breath while with the next we deny that wildlife values can be measured in economic terms.

That is not to understate the substantial difficulties of economic measurement, particularly measurement of benefits. As in wilderness preservation, while the costs of wildlife conservation and management are visible and measurable, the benefits are plainly less so. The dollars needed to fund a particular habitat program, the opportunity cost of restricting grazing in an area where game and livestock compete, the cost of foregone revenues in restricting timber cutting to protect a fishery—all can be measured in value terms (more or less) uniform among taxpayers. Attempts to find a comparable measure for valuing 4,000 warblers in Michigan or a few hundred timber wolves in Minnesota are bound to produce frustration. (In the latter case it is also bound to cause some friction among a few taxpayers who, far from willing to pay to preserve the beasts, would pay to have them exterminated.) We are not totally without bench marks for economic value as means of measuring the worth of wildlife management. At least in some areas, wildlife is an identifiable economic good. It is true we do not have a direct market for it because we no longer permit commercial hunting of most of these wildlife species. However, even though state law, backed by federal law, has prohibited the commercial sale of most of these wildlife species, there nevertheless is a very measurable market benefit associated with private sports hunting and fishing.

In attempting a benefit–cost analysis of the Forest Service wildlife-management activities, one can approach a measure of the economic "value" of its efforts simply by imputing some portion of the monies spent privately on fishing, hunting, bird-watching, and related activities. This is only one component of the wildlife-management program, but nevertheless it is one measure which would help to support appropriations for this purpose. And there are various other means of imputing values to what the Forest Service does by establishing what the economist calls "shadow prices" for the activities involved. Economic studies have developed the analytic method for shadow pricing, and a number of studies have been made for particular wildlife programs.[39] The kind of figures one could derive for national forests as a whole in this regard must be extremely speculative in the absence of more complete data, not to mention a more reliable calculus (one capable of imputing expenditures to the correct "accounts"). Some general data are available from which some crude estimates can be derived for all federal lands and could by further extrapolation be derived for the national forests.[40] Even after discounting for imprecision in the basic data and in the derivation from them, the purely economic contribution of forest wildlife is impressive—far more impressive, I might add, than congressional appropriations for wildlife management.

Such imputed values, carefully constructed, can be useful counters in bidding against other economic uses for fiscal support. Unfortunately perhaps, the imputation of value, in itself, is seldom fully persuasive to budget makers. As I have argued, it is probably better than nothing, but it is far less effective than demonstrated revenue production. Here is a major disadvantage of wildlife insofar as it must compete with major federal revenue-producing activities such as timber. Of course, wildlife directly yields revenue in the form of hunting and license fees, but this goes to the states. Even the federal tax on hunting and fishing equipment goes to the states under the Pittman–Robertson and Dingell–Johnson acts. Perhaps a very wise legislature, interested in the general public welfare, would not discriminate between value added and revenue received, but there is reason to think that Congress does.

One way of correcting this, of course, would be to levy some kind of federal user fee for hunting and fishing on federal lands. That is what the PLLRC recommended,[41] and it has considerable appeal. Congress itself has remained unpersuaded. In fact, the 1972 amendments to the Land and Water Conservation Fund Act expressly prohibited such fees.[42] In part this appears to reflect continued attachment to the old chestnut, encountered earlier, that wildlife enjoyment on federal lands should be essentially a "free" good. (Unfortunately, when it is time to appropriate funds to provide this free good, it becomes very dear.)

More than this, however, congressional reluctance to adopt a fee system rests on the basic premise that such charges are properly the province of states which "own" the wildlife. That has been the traditional Forest Service view, and, of course, the vigorously expressed view of state wildlife officials.[43] Insofar as this species of "federalism" turns on ownership of the wildlife, it seems most dubious. The imposition of user fees does not turn on any of the legal conundrums of ownership of the wildlife, discussed earlier. Who owns the wild game itself is irrelevant to the right to collect a fee for entrance to the land to hunt or fish. The right to control access—and to charge for it—is an incident of landownership everywhere recognized. Private landowners have this right, and the federal government, as landowner, should have no less right, regardless of who owns the game.

Somewhat more plausibly it is argued that a hunting and fishing fee would discriminate unreasonably between consumptive and nonconsumptive "use" of wildlife; for example, the bird watcher is not charged.[44] It is not clear, however, why this is any more an objection to federal fees than to state fees. It could be argued that the state hunting and fishing fees are not entrance fees (as the federal fee would be) but fees for the consumption of fish or game; but that argument seems a little flimsy. If a sportsman returns empty-handed, can he claim a refund of his license fee? Obviously, the fee is for permission to engage in the activity, and as such it is scarcely distinguishable from what a federal fee would be.

Of course, there are some practical difficulties. One is the administrative cost of collection. A second difficulty is that any general federal charge would be imposed on top of existing state fees. State wildlife officials contend that such a federal fee would substantially impair the state's ability to collect fees, with the result that revenues would be diverted from state to federal programs.

As to the former difficulty, it is not apparent that the administrative costs would be prohibitive, at least judging from the experience with the federal waterfowl fee system.

The second difficulty is more substantial, but it rests on a questionable assumption that users are already being charged all the traffic will reasonably bear. Even assuming that there might be some diversion, it does not follow that the loss would exceed the gain.

Against these uncertain costs there are certainly some tangible gains to be realized from even a modest federal fee. Consider, for example, the revenue obtained if a charge of one dollar were made for every deer *killed* (not for every hunter licensed) on the national forests. In fiscal 1973, this alone would have yielded over $375,000 dollars for the Forest Service.[45] This income could be obtained from a modest fee on *deer killed.* But suppose, caught up in the spirit of commercial enterprise, the Forest Service were instead to charge every hunter and fisherman for the visit, say, a half-dollar per visitor-day. The revenue yield in 1973 would have been over $14 million, a sum nearly double the total agency appropriations for wildlife management within that year.[46]

The revenues generated by special user fees would, of course, benefit nonusers who merely take satisfaction in knowing that somewhere out there in the wild the grizzly bear lives, but this is not a reason to forego charging direct users for their more identifiable benefit. If there is a "consumer surplus" representing an additional increment the American sportsman is willing to pay for the unquestionably tangible benefit of putting meat on his table or a trophy on his wall, it makes good sense to tap it.

CONCLUSIONS

The public interest in wildlife conservation as a major, independent aim of public land management, and of conservation policy generally, has become increasingly evident in recent years. The plenitude of special legislative enactments—of which endangered species legislation is but one illustration—is testament to that. But a gap between the goal and its effective realization exists, and it cannot be filled merely by statutory directives to preserve and protect wildlife. Before such mandates are to be translated into working policies, programs of wildlife management must be established in which wildlife needs are affirmatively promoted. And if the policies and programs are to be more than paper, they must be adequately funded.

Herein lies the impediment to an enlarged role for wildlife management in the national forests. There is, so far as one can readily discern, no shortage of Forest Service plans and programs. What is wanting is their strong financial support. It is evident that funding for wildlife management has increased in recent years; however, it is not apparent that it has kept pace with the goals which have been set by the Forest Service or, for that matter, by Congress. In competition with the demands of other resource interests, wildlife has yet a long way to go before it has economic support commensurate with its proclaimed position as a major public land resource.

It is often said that the difficulty in obtaining adequate financial support for wildlife is the difficulty of setting monetary values on wildlife, at least that which has no commerical value (including sport hunting and fishing). That is no doubt true, but only in part. The fact is that with imaginative economic analysis monetary values can be estimated for most wildlife programs. The larger difficulty has been in obtaining recognition for such imputed values from budget makers, particularly when such values are set against measured revenues from other, competing resource uses.

As has been suggested, this problem might be overcome by a system of modest federal user fees. That there are some practical difficulties with such a scheme is apparent, as I have mentioned. Not the least of the problems would be the strong opposition of state wildlife officials to any such federal encroachment on what has long been regarded as state prerogative. It was such opposition that led Congress, in 1972, to forbid the Forest Service and others from assessing federal user fees. That would seem to settle the matter for now, but Congress has been known to change its mind. It is now beyond belief—or hope—that they will do so here, at least to the extent of permitting modest experimentation with a fee system.

NOTES

1. Quantitative data on the contribution of forest wildlife to recreational and commercial use, though hardly a full measure, either of wildlife value or of the importance of the national forests as a wildlife habitat, provide at least one bench mark by which the importance of the national forests can be judged. For example, it is estimated that national forest lands account for nearly a third of the total *harvest* (the term has somewhat disagreeable connotations but is a common one) of big game. See U.S. Department of Agriculture/Forest Service, *Wildlife for Tomorrow* (PA-989), (1972), p. 12. Similar data are not available for fish or waterfowl, but they are likely to be comparable considering the importance of national forest waters. It is estimated, for example, that more than 40 percent of the salmon taken by commercial and sport fisherman off the Pacific Coast states are spawned in waters within the national forest (ibid., p. 21). In 1973 about 30 million visitor-days were spent in the national forests hunting and fishing. See U.S. Department of Agriculture/Forest Service, *1972-73 Report of the Chief of the Forest Service,* pp. 20–21. This does not, of course, account for the nonconsumptive enjoyment of millions of additional visitors.

Measures of the economic contribution which this makes are not available. Some measures have been made for the federal lands as a whole, but these are necessarily crude. See G. A. Swanson, *Fish and Wildlife Resources on the Public Lands,* study for the Public Land Law Review Commission (Springfield, Ill.: Clearinghouse for Federal Scientific and Technical Information, 1969), ch. X.

2. Of the more than ten wildlife species currently classified as rare or endangered, over half have been identified on or near the national forests. See U.S. Department of Agriculture/Forest Service, *Wildlife for Tomorrow,* p. 222.

3. For a short history of wildlife conservation, see James B. Trefethen, "Wildlife Regulation and Restoration," in Henry Clepper, ed., *Origins of American Conservation* (New York: Ronald Press, 1966), pp. 20–35.

4. U.S. Department of Agriculture/Forest Service, *Wildlife for Tomorrow,* p. 6.

5. 31 Stat. 187 (1900), 16 U.S.C., §§ 667 (e) and 701.

6. 37 Stat. 847 (1913).

7. 40 Stat. 755 (1918), 16 U.S.C., § 703.

8. 252 U.S. 416 (1920).

9. 28 Stat. 73 (1894), 16 U.S.C., § 26.

10. 45 Stat. 1222 (1929), 16 U.S.C., § 715 *et seq.*

11. The bureau, first established in 1889, was later merged with part of the Bureau of Fisheries in the Commerce Department to become, first, the Fish and Wildlife Service, and second, the Bureau of Sports Fisheries and Wildlife, within the Department of the Interior.

12. 50 Stat. 917 (1937), *as amended,* 16 U.S.C., § 669.

13. 64 Stat. 430 (1950), *as amended,* 16 U.S.C., § 777.

14. 80 Stat. 926 (1966), *as amended,* 16 U.S.C., § 668aa-668ee.

15. 83 Stat. 282 (1969). An earlier, minor amendment in 1968 imposed limitations on the disposal of lands acquired as part of the National Wildlife Refuge System.

16. In 1971, Congress, in a spirit of nostalgia for the Old West, enacted the Wild Horses and Burros Act, 85 Stat. 649 (1971), 16 U.S.C., §§ 1331 *et seq.,* to protect wild free-roaming

horses and burros as "living symbols of the historic and pioneer spirit of the West." The act is not a direct descendent of the endangered species legislation. In fact, in purpose and scope it resembles rather the Bald Eagle Protection Act of 1940 [54 Stat. 250 (1940), *as amended,* 16 U.S.C., § 668], which protects the eagle (the act was subsequently amended to the golden eagle) as a national "symbol of the American ideal of freedom." However, the Wild Horses and Burros Act probably owes a greater political debt to the Endangered Species Act than to the Bald Eagle Act.

17. This is expressly provided in the case of lands within the National Wildlife Refuge System [16 U.S.C., § 668dd (c) and (d)]. For other lands, such a power was implied in the basic policy provisions of the Endangered Species Act (see 16 U.S.C., §§ 668aa and bb), coupled with other applicable laws conferring general management authority—such as the Forest Service's Organic Act of 1897.

18. See, for example, U.S. Congress, Senate Committee on Commerce, *Hearings on S. 1232 and 1401,* 91 Cong., 1 sess., 1969, ser. 91–24.

19. 87 Stat. 884 (1973).

20. Among the more important changes made by the 1973 act is the extension of protection to "threatened" wildlife species which may become endangered, as well as for those already endangered. Under the 1966 act, only those species in actual peril were protected as endangered. It also extends protection to species threatened *in any significant portion* of their range. This provision is particularly important for species such as the eastern timber wolf, which is endangered in the continental United States (where the only significant population is found in Minnesota), but is not endangered worldwide (viable populations exist in Canada and Alaska). The 1966 law purported to protect only species endangered with worldwide extinction (though the timber wolf was protected despite the fact it was not so endangered). The 1973 law also makes numerous other changes such as extending federal authority for land acquisition to be used as endangered species sanctuaries and for cooperative assistance to states which develop an approved plan of protection. The 1973 law also provides for a study of threatened or endangered plant species, looking toward future preservation and protection of such species.

21. Section 6 of the act not only requires the secretary of the interior's approval of any state program; it also requires the secretary to reconfirm such approval annually. In addition, the secretary retains a rulemaking power in conjunction with his authority to allocate assistance funds. Presumably this gives him additional substantive management authority.

22. The Yellowstone Park Protective Act, 28 Stat. 73 (1894), 16 U.S.C., § 26, is the paradigm. For a discussion, see Swanson, *Fish and Wildlife,* ch. 2.

23. See, for example, Sections 6 and 7 of the Upper Mississippi River Wildlife and Fish Refuge Act, 43 Stat. 651 (1924), 16 U.S.C., § 726, and Section 10 of the Migratory Bird Conservation Act, 45 Stat. 1224 (1929), 16 U.S.C., § 715i.

24. In *Hunt* v. *United States,* 278 U.S. 96 (1928), the Supreme Court affirmed the power of the federal government to protect its lands against depredation. The aptly named *Hunt* case involved killing of deer on the Kaibab National Forest as a means of reducing the deer population which, because of a state prohibition against hunting (the Kaibab was in a state game preserve) and an elimination of natural predators, had grown to excessive size—far greater than the forest could support. The result of the overpopulation was that thousands of deer starved, but they also overbrowsed the forest. Despite this the state challenged the Forest Service's contravention of state law, an objection which the Court brushed aside: "[t]he power of the United States to thus protect its lands and property does not admit of doubt—the game laws or any other statute of the state to the contrary notwithstanding" (278 U.S., p. 100).

25. Swanson, *Fish and Wildlife,* ch. 11, contains an excellent summary of some of the major interrelationships, drawing on a number of individual studies. See also the National Academy of Sciences, *Land Use and Wildlife Resources* (Washington, D.C.: National Academy of Sciences, 1970), pp. 96–113.

26. Prescribed burning is practiced quite extensively for a variety of purposes, including, but not limited, to wildlife management. See, for example, U.S. Department of Agriculture/Forest Service, *Symposium on Fire in the Environment,* FS-276 (1972); Devet, "Use of Fire in Multiple-Use Management," in B. Bateman, ed., *Forest Wildlife Management* (Washington, D.C.: American Forestry Association, 1967), pp. 97–101.

27. For an outline of the plans and the planning process, see the Forest Service Manual,

§ 2620-264.4. The discussion in text is also drawn from a variety of individual management plans.

28. Quoted in Michel Foucault, *The Order of Things: An Archeology of the Human Sciences* (New York: Pantheon, 1970), p. xv.

29. For a useful discussion, see Swanson, *Fish and Wildlife,* ch. 1.

30. In *Hunt* v. *United States,* 278 U.S. 96 (1928), the Supreme Court declared it to be "beyond dispute" that the federal government had paramount power to enact laws and regulations contrary to state law in order to protect its lands. It would also seem beyond dispute that this power is not narrowly restricted to protecting the land, but includes a plenary power to control and manage the natural resources found on the land—state law to the contrary. This appears not to be seriously contested in the case of other natural resources. So far as I am aware no one has seriously suggested that the states could control—over federal opposition—the harvesting of timber on federal lands or the use of the lands for grazing or recreation. Even in the parallel situation involving water rights, where state law has traditionally applied until very recently, it appears not to be contested that the federal government has constitutional power to use and dispose of waters arising on federal land.

In support of state control it is frequently said that the states "own" the wildlife within their borders. To support this contention reference is made to judicial statements made in the course of affirming the power of the state to control private taking or disposal of game. See, for example, *Greer* v. *Connecticut,* 161 U.S. 519 (1896). But the concept of "ownership" here is merely confusing. Ownership is merely a popular shorthand used to describe a varying assortment of prerogatives (in the case of private individuals it is more common to talk of "rights") with respect to the thing owned. As it appears in the early legal literature and case law, the concept of public or common ownership of wildlife really describes two distinct things: first, a common law rule excluding *private* ownership in wild animals (animals *ferae naturae,* as the venerable texts call them) until committed to possession, and second, a paramount state interest to regulate the taking of wild animals for the benefit of the public. In neither aspect does this concept of public ownership embody or in any way imply the modern notion of federalism—of state's rights vis-à-vis the federal government (indeed the basic legal concepts here are as ancient as Roman law). It simply expresses relationships between individual rights and sovereign power. Thus, a *private* landowner under the above principles cannot claim a property right to wild animals on his land except when reduced to possession, or in accordance with state law. But it is difficult to see how any of this affects the federal government. The assumption of the states' rights proponents appears to be that the federal government, in its capacity as owner of federal lands, is like private landlords whose incidents of title and right stem from and are subject to state sovereignty. This ignores the fact that the federal government is not merely a landlord; it is a *sovereign.* Congress is empowered under the Property Clause to enact laws "respecting the Territory or other Property belonging to the United States." This is more than a simple expression of the private rights of landlords; it is an expression of constitutional sovereignty, one superior to the states under the Supremacy Clause of the Constitution.

Finally, it should be noted that in particular situations other constitutional bases of jurisdiction may be present. As indicated earlier, the Treaty Power provides the basis for the Endangered Species Act of 1973, as it did earlier for the Migratory Bird Treaty Act. See *Missouri* v. *Holland,* 252 U.S. 416 (1920). The Commerce Clause may be pertinent in some cases. *Cf. Toomer* v. *Witsell,* 334 U.S. 385 (1948), which forbade the exercise of *state* power over commercial fishing because state legislation burdened interstate commerce. Finally, the General Welfare Clause and the Spending Clause could be construed to support federal power. *Cf. United States* v. *Gerlach Livestock Co.,* 339 U.S. 725 (1950), which involved the power of the United States to take private water rights.

31. Under 48 Stat. 400 (1934), 16 U.S.C., § 694, the president, on the recommendations of the secretaries of agriculture and commerce, and subject to approval of the appropriate state legislatures, may establish refuges for fish and game within "specified and limited areas" of the national forests. Taking of wildlife within such areas is prohibited except for regulated taking of predators, 16 U.S.C., § 694a-b.

As a general policy, the Forest Service opposes wildlife reserves within the national forests on the basis that they limit management flexibility and undermine the aim of multiple use.

32. Testimony of the Director of the Colorado Division of Game, Fish and Parks in U.S.

Congress, Senate Subcommittee of the Committee on Commerce, *Hearings on S. 1232 and S. 1401*, 91 Cong., 1 sess., ser. 91-24, 1969, p. 40.

33. *Weekly Compilation of Presidential Documents* (Feb. 14, 1972), pp. 218, 223.

34. For a useful survey of some economic aspects of wildlife, see Swanson, *Fish and Wildlife*, ch. 10.

35. See Appendix B.

36. One noteworthy illustration is an ambitious joint program of the Forest Service and the State of Missouri for habitat management on the Mark Twain and Clark National forests.

37. The case of the eastern timber wolf in Minnesota is illustrative. For all of the controversy over killing of the wolf, the larger threat to its continued existence in the state is posed by the decline of the whitetail deer, its main prey. The deer is declining—in the wolf's primary range—because of the advancing maturity of the forest and the reduced browse. See testimony of Milton Stenlund in U.S. Congress, House Subcommittee of the Committee on Merchant Marine and Fisheries, *Hearings on Endangered Species*, 93 Cong., 1 sess., 1973, ser. 93–9, p. 326.

38. I stress "other satisfactions" in response to the sometime observation that decisions here ought not be governed by such materialistic considerations as money. As was pointed out earlier in discussing wilderness values, one should distinguish the ultimate satisfaction from the medium of exchange by which it is secured. The point is perhaps trite but nevertheless worth making in order to counter the assumption of some wildlife enthusiasts that money is an inadequate measure of wildlife value because of the nonmaterial satisfactions involved. By that turn of logic we could say the same about money as a measure of the value of almost anything— from yoga lessons to eyeglasses (used for enjoying nature—including wildlife). The point, of course, is that not just money is given up for wildlife, but all of the other satisfactions that money buys are sacrificed.

39. See, for example, Gardner Mallard Brown and Judd Hammack, "A Preliminary Investigation of the Economics of Migratory Waterfowl," in John V. Krutilla (ed.), *Natural Environments: Studies in Theoretical and Applied Analysis* (Baltimore: Johns Hopkins University Press for Resources for the Future, 1972), p. 171; and studies cited in Swanson, *Fish and Wildlife*, ch. X. Illustrative of Forest Service applications in cost–benefit analyses of management programs is U.S. Department of Agriculture/Forest Service, Eastern Region, *Fisheries Plan for the Ottawa National Forest* (no date).

40. See Swanson, *Fish and Wildlife*, pp. 219–238, which estimated recreational user (consumptive and nonconsumptive) valuation of wildlife to be over $8 billion annually (based on old data—1965 and earlier). No precise figure was estimated for the share which federal lands might claim, but the data imply that in the western states at least, a one-third share would be conservative. The national forest's share of this would be presumably *at least* equal to its proportion of land holding. All of this, incidentally, is recreational-use value only and does not measure the substantial commercial value of the West Coast fishery. It has been estimated that streams on federal lands contributed in 1965 some $7–9 million in commercial value (ibid., p. 237).

41. *One-Third of the Nation's Land* (1970), pp. 169–173.

42. 86 Stat. 459 (1972), 16 U.S.C., § 160 L-6a.

43. See, for example, the arguments of the states in *New Mexico v. Udall*, 410 F. 2d 1197, 1202 (10th Cir.), *cert. denied*, 396 U.S. 961 (1969).

44. See U.S. Congress, House Subcommittee on National Parks and Recreation of the House Committee on Interior and Insular Affairs, *Hearings on HR 6730 and Other Bills*, 92 Cong., 1 sess., 1971, ser. 92–11, p. 56.

45. Based on estimated harvests, see *1972–73 Report of the Chief of the Forest Service*, p. 39. "Yielded for the Forest Service" implies that the revenues are earmarked when, in fact, most service revenues are not. My assumption, however, is that appropriations for wildlife management would rise in *some* proportion to the revenues earned.

46. Based on nearly 30 million visitor-days for hunting and fishing in 1973 (ibid., pp. 20–21). The total appropriations for wildlife habitat management for 1973 were $7.7 million [U.S. Department of Agriculture, *Information Digest*, no. 1630 (1973)].

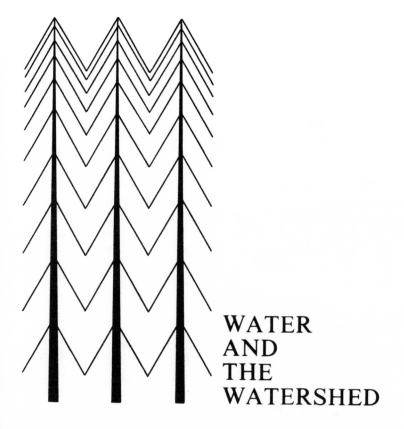

IX

WATER
AND
THE
WATERSHED

The national forests are one of the nation's most important sources of water. It is estimated, for example, that in the eleven contiguous western states, over one-half of the annual runoff is from national forest lands.[1] There is, of course, more to a watershed than water. Water is simply one of the many resources for which the forest watershed is base. The soil and water of the forest are the basic resources on which all others are ultimately sustained. The character and condition of these basic resources are determinative influences on every other forest resource—timber, forage, recreation. Obviously, watershed conservation must be all-pervasive in the management of the forest resources.

Watershed protection was in fact the first aim of forest management.[2] In the first comprehensive report on forestry, prepared for Congress in 1878, more than one-fourth was devoted to forest influences on climate and streamflow. Early efforts to obtain legislation to reserve forest lands from the public domain were based in part upon the need to protect water supply. "Securing favorable conditions of water flows" was one of the two purposes for administering the forest reserves stated in the Organic Act of 1897. The other was to furnish a continuous supply of timber.

Just as protection of the watershed was a basic purpose of the 1897 act, so later was it the primary aim of the Weeks Act of 1911, which created the power to acquire lands on the watersheds of navigable rivers in order to provide for "the regulation and flow of navigable streams." Indeed, until the Clarke–McNary Act of 1924, protection of the watershed was the sole purpose for which the federal government could acquire forest lands. Despite dispute over the precise effects of forests on climate and streamflow, the Weeks Act reflected a concern—which had been growing since the early days of the Forest Reserves Act—for the effect which various unregulated management practices on the forest lands were having on the amount, quality, and timing of the water flow off forest watersheds. It also reflected the then-unsubstantiated belief that the forests could be manipulated so as to increase the natural yield of water from forest watersheds, and authorized research into the effects of various manipulative management techniques on water yield.

THE WATERSHED-MANAGEMENT SCHEME

Today watershed-management activities encompass a variety of management actions.[3] In very broad terms these are classified by the Forest Service in two main categories: "environmental management support" and "watershed restoration and improvement." This twofold classification is somewhat crude as a description of the various particular functions, but it does provide a convenient guide and a basic orientation to watershed management in general.

Environmental Management Support

At present environmental management support is the primary management activity of the Forest Service, and the first priority for the Soil and Watershed-Management Division. It is essentially a supporting service for other management functions, primarily timber, range, wildlife, and recreation. The division surveys and analyzes the soils, waters, and geological characteristics of those forest areas being actively managed for other particular purposes and provides management prescriptions for their protection and improvement. The work entails extensive inventorying and mapping of soil and water data, monitoring of water quality, flood control surveys, impact and multiple-use surveys, and other studies of varying intensity and scope. Some of this work is conducted for purposes of comprehensive, long-range, land use planning. The degree of such long-term planning varies among the different regions, depending upon the regional program's emphasis and priorities. Some have made major steps toward the development of a comprehensive inventory and mapping system designed to provide a geomorphologic and basic resource map for complete watersheds.

However, under the circumstances prevailing over the national forests as a whole, the present level of funding is considered inadequate to support such work as a high priority, and it is generally subordinate to the more immediate needs of surveying and analyzing particular forest-management activities such as timber sales, road construction, and recreational development, where the potential for immediate environmental impact requires the attention of water and soil scientists. Even here Forest Service officials indicate that they are able to meet only a fraction of the current demands for survey and analysis work. This does not mean that no watershed analysis is made for certain projects, but rather that it often will not be accomplished professionally with the aid of trained hydrologists, soil scientists, or geologists, or that it will be incompletely performed. The consequences of this deficiency are all too obvious, particularly in the area of timber harvesting where inadequate attention has been given to watershed impacts of particular sales and construction, a problem already noted in connection with the clear-cutting controversy.

Watershed Restoration and
Improvement

The current emphasis on preventive service work is of recent origin. Historically, watershed management was more heavily oriented toward what the service describes as watershed restoration and improvement. If it no longer receives the emphasis it once did, restoration and improvement nevertheless continues to be an important part of watershed management. Although the service lumps such programs into a single category, there are actually two quite distinct kinds of functions included here. One is concerned with environmental protection, that is, improvement of watershed conditions in order to protect the soil and water. The other is concerned with manipulation of the watershed and its cover to improve water yield, and to increase the amount or the timing of the water flow from the watershed. Though both functions are properly compatible, they differ in their approach. Watershed protection tends to emphasize measures which would generally increase water retention and impede overland flow; improvement of water yield tends to emphasize measures which generally increase overland flow through reduced water retention.

Watershed management has traditionally been designed either to preserve or to restore the watershed conditions and to stabilize the soils and vegetation, maintaining a high quality of water yield. As noted earlier, however, forest scientists in the beginning years of forestry believed that water was affected not only as to quality but also as to amount and timing by the forest, and that, through manipulation of the forest, the amount and timing of the water yield could be altered. Research and experimentation into the effects of the forest on streamflow have confirmed that water yield can be significantly manipulated. Since the establishment of the first experimental watersheds by the Weather Bureau and the Forest Service in 1909 at Wagon Wheel Gap in Colorado, the Forest Service has established experimental watersheds in every region of the country to investigate the effects of various management practices on water yield. Experiments on these watersheds, conducted by or in conjunction with the Forest Service experimental stations, have demonstrated that water yield can be influenced by a variety of management techniques.[4] Essentially, these can be classified into three basic categories: snow management on high-elevation watersheds to alter the timing and, to a degree, the amount of yield; manipulation of timber and other vegetation of the timber harvest zone; and type conversion of deep-rooted stands of brush or timber or other vegetation to shallower-rooted stands of grass.[5]

Although the results of experimental work today have demonstrated to the satisfaction of most hydrologists the capability for water yield improvement, they are not readily translated into predictions or management prescriptions for ordinary forests. Most of the work has taken place under the highly specialized conditions of experimental watersheds.

In order to bridge the gap between the conditions of the experimental forests and the operational, multiple-use forests, the Forest Service has established a number of "barometer" watersheds on operational forests for the purpose of carefully studying the characteristics of the watershed and the effects of the forest and forest practices on water yield. These barometer watersheds have been established within national forests throughout the country. The size of the watershed and the conditions vary from region to region; the design is to provide a representative sample of a watershed containing typical programs of multiple-use management, timber harvesting, livestock grazing, recreation, wildlife, etc. The basic function of the barometer watersheds is to provide a means of measuring the general direction and magnitude of change over time in the quality, quantity, and timing of water yield in soil conditions, sediment production, and a means of relating these changes as measured naturally to various land-management practices. They are not, strictly speaking, experimental watersheds but rather instrumented watersheds; however, they do also have an experimental purpose in providing a basis for testing on an operational forest, under multiple-use guidelines, various soil and water prescriptions based upon research findings from experimental watersheds. After the watershed has been established, forest supervisors are required to prepare a special barometer watershed-management plan.[6]

Although the establishment of barometer watersheds is a step toward making possible the translation of experimental results into operational water yield-improvement programs, there has been very little such work on a nonexperimental basis. In recent years four major water-management programs have been developed, three in the Southwest (Arizona and California) and one in Colorado.[7] The Colorado project to date is a minor one; it is aimed at increasing water yield through snow manipulation in high alpine lands. The three Southwest projects are all type-conversion projects, involving the conversion of brush to grass which retains less water. Each of these is a rather special effort and not at all representative of current program emphasis throughout the Forest Service generally. In fact, interest in implementation of water yield-improvement programs appears, if anything, to be on the decline. Although there are a number of barometer and municipal watersheds where possible projects are being studied, there seems to be very little enthusiasm on the whole for extensive water yield-improvement programs. This reflects a distinct change from a decade ago when Forest Service officials and scientists regarded water yield manipulation as one of the most important promising management functions for the future. Although there continues to be interest in this aspect of management among some Forest Service scientists, overall interest is clearly very low. Not only is there no particular disposition to engage in extensive programs, there is very little evidence that water yield improvement is a significant element in the planning of timber sales.

Thus, such watershed input that goes into timber management deals typically with protective considerations and not with considerations of water yield improvements, even though it is possible to manipulate water yield as an incident of a timber-management program.

Management Planning

In discussing Forest Service management functions no mention has yet been made of the long-term planning processes as such.[8] As with most other management functions, the planning process, both for general protective management work and for special project work, is the primary responsibility of the forest supervisor, in accordance with regional directives. In actual practice, however, long-range planning gets relatively little emphasis in the Forest Service generally. Many forests do not have a current watershed-management plan covering general management functions. Theoretically, all forests are supposed to have a management plan for each watershed within the forest, as well as an overall plan for specific restoration projects, containing a backlog of individual plans for each such project equivalent to two year's work. However, with the existing budget constraints, and with the high emphasis on current, short-term service work, little attention has been given to long-term planning as such except in a few cases where special circumstances exist; for example, in barometer or municipal watersheds, or special restoration and improvement projects.

With the advent of the new multiple-use planning scheme, watershed-management plans will probably disappear altogether.[9] For some resources, it is expected the functional plans will continue to be an important part of the planning process and will be simply incorporated in some way into the unit plans; however, in the case of watershed management, where functional plans have never been of major importance, it is presently contemplated they will generally disappear altogether. The exceptions will be special projects, restoration projects, or water yield-improvement programs calling for special, individualized plans. At the time this was written one could not say what will be the exact effect of the new planning system on watershed-management planning, assuming it ever becomes fully operational. The expectation is that under the new integrated form of multiple-use planning, watershed management will have a larger role in, and a larger impact on, Forest Service planning and management generally. However, this is likely to depend not so much on the form of the planning scheme as on the basic funding and staffing of the watershed-management function to ensure that the services needed are actually available.

Toward the ultimate objective of comprehensive watershed- and soil-management planning, steps have been taken in some areas toward the development of computerized map-inventories of all watershed characteristics and conditions—geologic, hydrologic, soil, and vegetative—for individual watersheds.[10] When completed, such computerized inventories would permit easy retrieval of watershed data to be combined in many different forms to facilitate planning. For example, information on timber stands could be combined with information on geologic or soil characteristics to yield information as to how much and where timber can be harvested without endangering soil stability. This kind of inventory would then provide the basis for management prescriptions for individual functional areas; it would also provide basic data to which computer programming could be applied. In this regard, it is noteworthy that watershed scientists have taken the lead in developing a comprehensive resource program for computers, the so-called Resource Capability System (RCS).

FORESTS AND WATER—
PROBLEMS AND
CONTROVERSIES

Adam Smith chose water as an example of a useful commodity having no value. In contrast to diamonds which were valuable but not useful, "Nothing is more useful than water: but it will purchase scarce any thing; scarce any thing can be had in exchange for it."[11] In eighteenth-century Kirkcaldy, Scotland, the illustration was no doubt apt. In twentieth-century Tucson it would be scorned. So, too, in countless other cities and rural places within the arid West. As nature did not endow the West with diamonds, neither did it bless it with water.

On the other hand, only man could make it *scarce*. Other elements, from cactus plant to Gila monster adjust; man does so fitfully at best. Perhaps if more people had listened to John Wesley Powell's cautious reports of arid lands west of the one-hundredth meridian instead of the promoters' siren songs about the "Golden West,"[12] the problem would have proved more tractable. There would not be more water, but there might be fewer people, and (possibly) better conservation. But this, of course, is facile speculation; the crush of population, and the corresponding press for more water, increases even now. In Arizona, water is becoming more like diamonds every day.

There is no need to explore the general problem of water supply here. While water is scarce, studies of what to do about it are not.[13] In any event, the general subject is beyond the scope of the present study. However, insofar as management of the public lands, forest lands particularly, do have an important impact on water supply, we should at least take notice of that aspect of the problem. Primarily, the focus of discussion is on the western lands; while federal landownership and management has some impact on eastern watersheds, it is principally in western states that the role of the federal landowner is centrally important and most controversial.

Improvement of Water Yield

In contrast to the persistent concern over preservation of water quality, interest in water yield improvement has, as mentioned earlier, received very little attention except in the technical literature on water research. One recent exception to this is a study for the Public Land Law Review Commission (PLLRC), which noted that a substantially greater program emphasis on water yield improvement within the Forest Service could be one means of remedying serious water shortages in many western states.[14]

That there would be important benefits from increased water yield, by even a modest amount—and all indications are that the amount of possible increased yield would be quite substantial[15]—is perhaps too obvious to mention. In the West where water is not merely scarce but virtually precious, even a modest increase in yield, particularly during the late summer months, would relieve at least some of the conflict among competing water users. Agricultural, industrial, power, and municipal users would all unquestionably benefit. Admittedly, the benefits are somewhat speculative at this point, as are the costs. Some benefit–cost analyses have been made which show significant potential benefits from an active program of water yield improvement.[16] But more detailed analyses must be done before extensive programs could be developed, and interest in such programs today is generally slight; consequently, interest in benefit–cost analyses which would assess their value is relatively neglected.

The reasons for this are diverse and complex. One immediate reason for the current lack of attention is the continued uncertainty of just how significantly water yield can be altered over a sustained period of time. Most of the work to date has focused on the experimental watersheds, under management conditions that could not be duplicated on most operational forests consistent with managing them for other uses. For example, type conversion designed to replace one type of ground cover with one that utilizes less water is possibly the most important and the only semipermanent technique for increasing yield. In theory, such conversion might be made of any species, but as a practical matter it is confined to conversion of brushlands to grass. One proposal suggested that in Colorado extensive stands of noncommercial timber, such as aspen, could be converted to grasslands.[17] That seems an unlikely possibility in view of environmental and aesthetic considerations. And, so far as is known, no one has seriously proposed converting even marginal commercial timber stands to grasslands. Obviously then, this is a very limiting factor. There are a number of water-poor areas where type conversion of brush to grass can be made and, as mentioned earlier, there are several such conversion programs currently operating in the Southwest. However, so far as the national forest system as a whole is concerned, type conversion offers a very limited opportunity for water yield improvement.

Even apart from these limitations, there is skepticism as to the results reported on experimental forests. Although there is no question that cover manipulation has altered the immediate yield from these forests, some still doubt that the increased yield results in a significant increased streamflow at any very substantial distance from the area and on a sustained basis over time. Skepticism concerning the practical state-of-the-art explains only a small part of the overall lack of interest in water yield improvement. Most forest scientists believe the results achieved on experimental forests, and on a few operational forests, such as those in the Southwest, are significant, and agree that substantial water yield gains can be provided to ultimate water users.[18] In any event, the results achieved would certainly justify greater attention than that currently given to further investigation on operational forests. Particularly is this the case in light of the important potential benefits to be obtained from a major effort in this area.

Environmental Costs. But the benefits also have costs. The first of these, and from the viewpoint of the public, probably the most significant one, is the environmental cost to other uses and enjoyment of the forest. Many environmentalists would question the Forest Service's ability to adjust the water cycle without damage to the environment, at least in most forest areas. There are risks, to be sure. Except for limited measures to modify snow drifting (e.g., by the construction of snow fences), water yield-improvement measures require extensive cover manipulation.

In forested areas, this means clear-cutting, and it probably also means treatment of the clear-cut area with herbicides in order to maintain water yield—otherwise ground cover will reappear so soon after the cut that no significant effect on yield would be obtained. Obviously, this creates a problem of erosion; it increases the possibility of flooding, and under some conditions it could result in loss of soil nutrients. And, of course, there may be aesthetic impairment. All of these, even the aesthetic effect, probably could be avoided by careful planning and close supervision. The greater the constraint, the more limited the results and the higher the economic cost. But even assuming that worthwhile results could be achieved without significant harm to the environment, this is almost beside the point.

The real question is not what the Forest Service can do, but what *will* the Forest Service do, or more important in terms of public response, what does the public *believe* the Forest Service will do. The later point deserves particular stress, for, as the debate over clear-cutting generally makes plain, the nonrational components and controversies over the environment commonly overwhelm the rational ones. In any event, the anticipation of such opposition from environmentalist groups to water yield-improvement measures has dampened all enthusiasm for yield improvement. Only where local segments of the public, such as local water users, actively support water yield improvement does the service appear willing to commit itself in an important way.

Economic Costs. The real or imagined environmental costs account for only part of the lack of interest in water yield-improvement measures. A second and even more substantial factor is the economic cost of such programs. The first and most obvious constraint on what the Forest Service itself can do is its limited appropriations for watershed management generally, and the relative priorities within the Forest Service for use of those funds. At current levels of appropriation for soils and watershed management, it is hardly any surprise that the level of interest in this particular activity is relatively low. Water yield improvement ranks among the lowest, if not *the* lowest, of priorities—far below the "service" functions which are top priority and well below the restoration and rehabilitation work as well.

Within the tasks assigned to the Soils and Watershed-Management Division, it is hard to quarrel with these priorities. At the same time one might well ask why, in the context of resource management generally, the production of water should not be considered as important as the production of timber or forage. Whether the question is asked of the Forest Service or of

Congress, the plausible answer is the same: unlike timber or range, the production of water yields no revenue either to the Treasury or to the Forest Service (one possible, highly relevant exception would be reclamation water rights). Granted there are many activities undertaken by the Service and supported by Congress that are not revenue-producing. Sometimes this is because the benefits are not measurable in economic terms; sometimes it is because they are sufficiently public so that the cost is appropriately met through taxes; and too often, it would seem, it is because some influential group of beneficiaries has managed to persuade the general public to pay it a subsidy. In the case of water, the first two explanations do not apply, while the last has been largely limited to the benefits of reclamation projects.

The absence of a salable resource offers a plausible explanation for the present lack of interest in efforts to increase water production. It is noteworthy in the case of the largest water yield-improvement program on the Tonto National Forest in Arizona that local water users support a significant part of the program's cost.[19] And, of course, there is nothing unique in the water resource that prevents it from being sold like any other resource. Under western water law, a market for water does exist in which private water rights are actively exchanged. One obstacle to the sale of water rights by the federal government lies in its limited ownership. The reserved rights doctrine gives the government paramount title to such water as is reasonably necessary to management of reserved land. However, this claim on water, though large, it is not limitless.[20] An appropriation of water simply for the purpose of resale for other uses not related to the public land would probably not be within the purview of the doctrine. Apart from the reserved-rights doctrine, title to the water would depend on appropriation in accordance with state law. Lacking a clear, paramount title to forest waters, the government has nothing to sell.[21] However, the issue here has nothing to do with natural water yield, but with the production of a higher yield through a special program of watershed management. To charge the users for the benefits of such a program requires no ownership interest.

All this would seem too elementary to warrant discussion were it not for the fact that, in response to suggestions by Forest Service personnel that they support water yield-improvement programs, some water users asserted that the federal government could not charge for additional water yield produced on the forests, because it does not own the water. That is about the same as saying that a fee for commercial cloud seeding, based on the value of the rain produced, depends upon the ownership of the clouds. How common such simple-mindedness is among water users is unknown, but it is apparently not exceptional. Possibly the ownership issue is simply subterfuge, hiding a speculation that the Forest Service will ultimately undertake this work in any event, whether or not a user fee is charged. If that is the assumption, it is not exactly simple-minded, but it is naïve. The Forest Service will not undertake such work in significant degree at the present time because of limited appropriations, which have to be allocated among other higher-priority programs. The priorities are not likely to be changed without special incentive. Given the present concern over environmental protection that will clearly continue to get first priority for funding, there is no reason to expect a switch in other priorities for the use of these funds. Nor does it seem likely that Congress will raise appropriations for the Forest Service to do the work—at least not without demanding that some kind of user charge be imposed to cover the cost of the work.[22] That is not to say that Congress has stopped giving out, in kind or in coin, large subsidies to private groups; however, in the absence of an influential political group to lobby for them, it is doubtful they will be offered. And none of the water users have thus far shown much interest in seeking additional water yield.

CONCLUSIONS

Again, in an attempt to briefly summarize the management problem, the question of economics emerges as a focal point for analysis. No simple alchemy exists by which money can be converted to water. But it is hard to avoid the conclusion that the problem of water supply suffers from the absence of economic incentives which would not only ration existing use but would induce measures to augment the supply through established, but costly, technical means. Perhaps when the shortage becomes more acute some changes in the economic structure will appear and will provide rational incentives for more effective production as well as more efficient use of this invaluable resource.

NOTES

1. See Charles F. Wheatley, Jr., et al., *Study of the Development, Management, and Use of Water Resources on the Public Lands,* study for the Public Land Law Review Commission, S-31 (Springfield, Ill.: Clearinghouse for Federal Scientific and Technical Information, 1969). Water for domestic and municipal supplies is obtained directly from about 1,100 watersheds within the national forest system. These watersheds range in size from hundreds of acres to hundreds of thousands of acres. In addition, water flowing from thousands of other watersheds on national forest system lands, mixed with water from other areas, is used by municipalities far removed from the national forests. Statistics are not available on the exact number of communities dependent on water from national forest watersheds. Some of the larger distribution systems supplying water to major metropolitan areas draw their water from more than one watershed, while many of the watersheds provide water to several municipalities. Available data show that at least 700 watersheds supply municipal and domestic water to small, rural communities. (The above information was provided to me by Forest Service staff.)

2. For a short history of water conservation, see W. Soper, "Water Conservation," in Henry Clepper, ed., *Origins of American Conservation* (New York: Ronald Press, 1971), pp. 101–131.

•

3. Forest Service Manual, § 2520 *et seq.*
4. The extensive research literature is reviewed in Wheatley, *Study of Water Resources,* pp. 523–544. The experimental work continues, although not without criticism. Luna Leopold offers the following grounds for criticism:

1. Research is pursuing questions already answered.
2. Research is divergent from the main concerns of the forest managers who make operational decisions and who are not concerned with water-yield increases but with timber production and the watershed impact of reservation, grazing, wildlife interests.
3. Research is conducted under experimental conditions that diverge substantially from those present on nonexperimental lands. For example, "good" logging practices on experimental watersheds do not conform to commercial logging.
4. New harvesting practices—such as clear-cutting on lands on which it has not traditionally been practiced—have created new problems, but experimental research has not been reoriented toward them.
5. Research work is inadequate in a number of other areas, for example, effects of cutting and road building on the chemical quality of water, or the use of fire as a management technique. (See Luna Leopold, *Hydrologic Research on Instrumented Watersheds,* printed in U.S. Congress, Senate Public Lands Subcommittee of the Committee on Interior and Insular Affairs, *Hearings on "Clear-Cutting" Practices on National Timberlands,* 92 Cong., 1 sess., 1971, pp. 491–519.)

5. See U.S. Department of Agriculture/Forest Service, *Harvesting the National Forest Water Crop* (1967), p. 6.
6. See Forest Service Manual, § 2535.
7. These are discussed in U.S. Department of Agriculture/Forest Service, *Harvesting the National Water Crop,* pp. 12–13.
8. See Forest Service Manual, § 2511–12.
9. I am informed by agency officials that, for this reason, functional management plans are not being revised or updated at this time except for special watersheds, such as barometer or municipal watersheds.
10. This is the so-called WRIS (Watershed Resources Inventory System) program.
11. Adam Smith, *Wealth of Nations* (1776; Harvard Classics ed., New York: Collier & Son, 1909), p. 35.
12. Powell's struggle to educate a nation to the reality of the arid West, and to debunk the fantasies of promoters such as William Gilpin and the pseudoscientific theories of early surveyors and writers. ("rain follows the plow"), is superbly told in Wallace Stegner, *Beyond the One Hundredth Meridian* (Boston: Houghton–Mifflin, 1954). See also, Daniel J. Boorstin, *The Americans: The National Experience* (New York: Random House, 1965), pp. 223–241.
13. Most recently the subject has been explored in numerous studies of the National Water Commission. The special role of public lands is explored in a two-volume study for the Public Land Law Review Commission (Wheatley, *Study of Water Resources*). Individual studies are nearly without number. Among major studies of water supply, Jack Hirshleifer, James C. De Haven, and Jerome W. Milliman, *Water Supply: Economics, Technology and Policy* (rev. ed., Chicago: University of Chicago Press, 1969); and John V. Krutilla and Otto Eckstein, *Multiple Purpose River Development: Studies in Applied Economic Analysis* (Baltimore: Johns Hopkins University Press for Resources for the Future, 1958) are noteworthy general analyses.
14. Wheatley, *Study of Water Resources,* pp. 541–544.
15. See U.S. Department of Agriculture/Forest Service, *Harvesting the National Water Crop,* p. 6, which estimates that, in the West, 9 million acre-ft. (1 acre-ft. equals approximately 326,000 gallons) of increased annual water yield could be obtained, the value of which (for agricultural, industrial, and domestic uses) is almost $500,000 annually. The annual cost is estimated at $13 million. The above is derived from a number of individual studies, some of which are reviewed in Wheatley, ibid., pp. 529–544. See also a more recent study, U.S. Department of Agriculture/Forest Service, Pacific Northwest Region *Water Yield Improvement Potentials on National Forest lands Tributary to Ochoco Reservoir* (1969).

16. Ibid.

17. U.S. Department of Agriculture/Forest Service, *Harvesting the National Water Crop*, p. 9.

18. One official in the agency expressed such skepticism to me; however, in this he was almost alone. Every other hydrologist contacted, not to mention virtually every study, made it clear that increased water yields could be obtained and delivered to users on a sustained basis. Of course, such estimates are based on the assumption of a continued treatment.

19. U.S. Department of Agriculture/Forest Service, *Harvesting the National Water Crop*, p. 12.

20. For an extensive discussion of the reserved rights doctrine and its implications for land management policy, see Wheatley, *Study of Water Resources*, pp. 6–382.

21. See Marion Clawson and Burnell R. Held, *The Federal Lands: Their Use and Management* (Baltimore: Johns Hopkins University Press for Resources for the Future, 1957), pp. 228–229, who point out the drawback of this legal status inasmuch as it destroys any incentive for efficient watershed management. A similar conclusion is reached by Thomas Waggoner, *User Fees, and Charges for Public Lands and Resources,* a study for the Public Land Law Review Commission (Springfield, Ill.: Clearinghouse for Federal Scientific and Technical Publications, 1970), pp. 307–309.

22. Although a few officials doubted the Forest Service's authority to charge a fee to water users, not only the authority but the *duty* to charge fees for any *special* benefits conferred on private users is clearly stated in Title V of the Independent Offices Appropriation Act of 1952, 65 Stat. 268, which provides that whenever the federal government provides anything of value to any person or group, such activities shall be self-sustaining to the fullest extent possible. It was further specified that fee regulations within agencies of the executive branch should be as uniform as practicable, and that fees should be "fair and equitable," considering (1) direct and indirect cost of the government, (2) value to the recipient, (3) public policy or interest served, and (4) other pertinent facts. This is further implemented by Budget Bureau Circular A-25 (1959). A subsequent bureau report [*National Resource User Charges* (1964)], issued to guide agencies, specifically applied the above principles to national resources. Interestingly, water was not among the resources mentioned, but that undoubtedly reflected the fact that under present legal arrangements there is no basis for a federal user charge on water supply *generally.* However, where the federal government undertakes a special program to augment water supply, it seems clear the agency can and should charge for it under the above authority, at least to the extent that specific beneficiaries can be identified. Although one Forest Service official, with whom this was discussed, doubted that the latter condition of specific beneficiaries could be met, I do not see the problem. Obviously, beneficiaries must be identified or no charge could be levied, but that should be no greater problem here than in the case of federal reclamation water. The point in any case is rather moot, for the Forest Service is unlikely to engage in significant yield-improvement work unless local water users take the initiative in seeking it and agreeing to support it financially, as is currently done in the Southwest. Obviously, voluntary support does not require user fee authority.

X

THE
FOREST
SERVICE
IN
RETROSPECT

Surveying individually the diverse aspects of public land management, as we have done, leaves a dissatisfying sense of disjunctiveness. One instinctively searches for some principle that will bring all of these problems into a common framework by which they can be judged. It is easy to generalize about the nature of the problems in all these different areas. Basically the problem is scarcity, which breeds conflict, which in turn creates problems. That is hardly a profound statement; indeed, the same could be said about most of the social issues we face. Yet despite the banality of this observation, it has frequently been forgotten or ignored—sometimes even denied. This is especially evident in the area of public resources, where a rich endowment of land and natural resources has fostered the illusion that the supply could never run short.

It will perhaps be said that we now know better as the new "ecological conscience" dramatically shows. Unfortunately, this new conscience has not awakened all, nor has it activated all who have been so awakened. Knowing we cannot have everything is but the *beginning* of wisdom, and a very modest beginning at that. What follows is a better understanding of the mechanisms for allocating scarce resources among competing demands. This is the foremost institutional problem which challenges the Forest Service today in managing the national forests. For that matter, it is a problem the agency has probably always faced; however, increased scarcity of resources and the deepening conflict among resource uses has given new importance and dimension to the problem in the past two decades. In the context of individual resource-management tasks I have already critically commented on how the Forest Service and others (such as Congress) have responded to particular problems of resource allocation and use. Here, I shall return to the Forest Service as an institution in order to offer some further generalizations about its professionals, its biases, and its organization.

THE FOREST SERVICE
BUREAUCRACY

Bureaucrat is a term few government personnel use when describing themselves. Their reluctance is scarcely surprising considering the pejorative tone which the word has acquired. The Forest Service official is no different in this respect, unless it be that, to a greater degree than most government bureaucrats, he regards himself as professional, that is, one relatively independent of outside political influence and control. On the whole it is a fairly accurate image.

Influence of Special Interests

Although the professional expertise of the agency is not generally disputed, some critics (modern conservationists mostly) would qualify the claim of independence. It is said, for example, that the Forest Service, far from being independent, has been "captured" by the dominant industry interests, mainly (but not exclusively) the timber industry.[1] The claim of industry capture is scarcely unique to the Forest Service; it is broadly asserted by critics of nearly every governmental agency. It has been most frequently leveled against the independent regulatory commissions, but virtually no agency that has any significant dealings with particular industry interests has escaped the charge of industry capture.[2]

There is considerable substance to the basic criticism: it seems to be endemic to our bureaucracy that administrators more easily identify with private industry interests than with the public interest. However, this criticism tends to ignore the larger generalization of which industry capture is only a part: all bureaucracies develop close ties to particular "clientele" groups. The client may or may not be "industry"; it may also be a particular segment of the public, say, a conservationist group. That such groups often parade under a general label of public interest representation does not alter the basic fact that they are but components of the public whose interests are not necessarily broader, nor more representative of society's interests as a whole, merely by virtue of this banner of "public good" under which they act. Friedrich Nietzsche said, "Truth seldom resides in the temple men have built in her honor, or where priests have been ordained to her service." So, too, with the so-called public interest.

This is not to say, of course, that all special interests are the same, or that it is a matter of indifference whether an agency responds to one group of clientele interests or another. It is merely to assert that the term *special interest* is a tag put around many different necks, not the least of whom are those quick to inveigh against such interests and the influence they exert. Thus, the hue and cry often raised over industry capture tends to avoid the real issue: whether the particular interests being served are sufficiently coincidental with broader public interests to justify the agency in responding to them. This becomes a question of the particular merits of each individual controversy.

For example, in deciding whether a given area should be designated as a wilderness there is probably no way in which the Forest Service could respond to this issue without giving in to a special interest on one side or the other. If it refuses to designate the area as a wilderness, it would almost certainly be accused of giving in to the timber industry or other commodity interests. However, if it establishes the wilderness area, thus precluding any of the commodity users, it would seem equally valid to say it was giving in to the special interest of wilderness preservationists. The claim of special interest capture can be made for either outcome.[3]

The latter example will no doubt strike some as unreal. Whatever special interests the Forest Service may align with, it is not the Sierra Club. Not even the timber industry, for all its recurrent complaints that the Forest Service is inadequately attentive to public timber needs, would suppose that the Forest Service is *generally* preservationist in its leanings. (This, however, does not mean that it is not often accused of giving in or selling out to preservationist groups on particular matters.) Probably not even the timber industry could reasonably deny that, on the contrary, the Forest Service has traditionally given paramount attention to commodity-type resources, chief of which has been timber.

The Forest Service's strong interest in the timber resource is an old one. Contrary to the evident assumptions of some critics that present timber supply policies indicate the agency's fall from a state of prior conservationist grace, these policies are essentially in the tradition of Gifford Pinchot and other early conservationist leaders. The fact that more timber is cut on the national forests today than, say, two decades ago does not indicate the contrary. More timber products are now demanded. What the increase in timber cutting does show is that the utilitarian conservationism of an earlier era was far more compatible with a preservationist spirit. Both were easily accommodated in the capacious and slightly utilized national forests. But any notion that Pinchot would be shamed by the agency's present timber policies must be rejected out of hand. If anything, Pinchot would react adversely, not to the service's timber orientation but to its increasing attention to preservation and other "nonproductive" uses.[4]

Although the Forest Service has considerably intensified its efforts in the area of timber supply over the past decade, it has also intensified all of its management activities with regard to other uses as well, especially recreation. At this higher level of intensified management, it does appear that the service is moving in the direction of a more balanced attention to resources other than the traditional commodity resources of timber and forage. Still it has proved to be an exceedingly difficult thing to do, for several reasons.

Budget Considerations

First of all, there is the problem of the budget. Even the most vocal critics of the Forest Service acknowledge that the emphasis on commodity use in management policy cannot be attributed to the agency alone. After all, it is Congress and the Executive, who by their budgets and their general policy directives to the agency provide the basic constraints within which it must operate. It is yet to be shown that Forest Service policy does not fairly reflect the basic priorities in resource allocation of Congress and the Executive.[5] If the Forest Service has been "captured" by the commodity interests, so too have Congress and the Executive. They have been seduced into thinking they need more houses or more paper products when what they need is more wilderness. But let us not pursue this latter possibility—not because it is an unimportant consideration, but simply because it is too large a problem for us to grapple with here. It is enough for us to see simply that the Forest Service, for all its relative political independence, is not, to borrow John Donne's metaphor, an "Iland intire of it selfe" but a "peece of the *Continent*, a part of the maine." Certainly this is evident in the budget which is the ultimate, unavoidable constraint on forest resource policy. Other directives are quite commonly cast in such general and indefinite terms as to leave the agency large discretion. Appropriations are less malleable. While the agency has some discretion to reallocate funds within general accounts, it does not have the power to reorder the basic priorities represented by the appropriations.

Personnel Policy

If Forest Service policy reflects congressional and executive priorities, it also reflects the traditional outlook of the forestry profession, which has been heavily oriented toward timber (and to a lesser degree toward other commodity resources). A 1963 study by the Society of American Foresters reported that, while foresters accepted the theory of multiple-use management, in practice they "continued to think and speak of forests as consisting only of trees, and of forestry as essentially the management of forest lands for the production and utilization of timber."[6] Forestry education has reflected and helped to shape this viewpoint.[7] This bias in the profession, and in the educational scheme that underlies it, can in turn be attributed to several economic and noneconomic factors. The Society of American Foresters' study explained:

> This tendency to identify forestry with timber production has several causes. A forest, by any modern definition, is an area in which trees are the dominant element, and trees provide the raw material for the support of some of the major industries. By and large, most of the direct financial returns from forests have come, now come, and will continue to come chiefly from wood and other tree products. . . . Economic forces consequently tend to focus attention on timber, particularly in the case of the private owner, to whom it is his bread and butter. Another reason for the emphasis on timber is the common but mistaken belief that effective management of the forest for the primary purpose of timber production automatically results in effective management of water, wildlife, and recreation. Although this belief is gradually being abandoned with increasing knowledge of the effect of managerial practices on various resources, its influence is still strong.[8]

In the decade since these observations were made the forester's role and his education have broadened, but the basic observations of the 1963 study still seem pertinent and generally valid.

Of course, the forestry profession is not the sole supplier of Forest Service professionals. In fact, as noted earlier, the percentage of foresters in the agency has steadily declined. Still, it is evident that forestry continues to be the dominant profession.[9] In this respect it should be noted that the important measure of its status is not simply the percentage of positions held in the agency (50 percent in 1973) or in the National Forest System (52.5 percent), but rather in the percentage of top-level, policy-making positions. Here it appears that the forestry profession still dominates the agency and its policies to a degree far greater than their numbers in the agency as a whole would indicate.

If the traditional attitudes of the forestry profession have helped to shape Forest Service policy the reverse is also true. A forester's education is not complete when he enters the agency; in many respects it has just begun. The ways in which the agency shapes attitudes has been discussed previously. This "acculturation" process is reinforced by a recruitment and promotion policy which rather strictly limits lateral entry into the agency. In some degree the practice is inherent in the structure of the civil service system which favors internal promotion. However, Forest Service policy goes beyond any dictates of the civil service. Indeed, the policy of internal promotion antedates the civil service. The policy was established by Pinchot for filling ". . . vacancies by promoting [Forest Service] people instead of looking for new blood outside. We were fully and rightly convinced that our own strain was the best available, and the results confirmed our conviction." [10]

Pinchot's convictions notwithstanding, this policy is not without its problems. Insofar as it limits the agency's exposure to different viewpoints, it obviously strengthens the kind of traditional biases noted above, and has given the agency an image in the eyes of some that it is too inbred. The criticism warrants further examination.

Earlier it was observed that the Forest Service is neither monolithic in organization nor single-minded in its views. For all the emphasis on shared values, experience, and conformity to generally traditional policy norms, there does persist among the various professional groups a spectrum of views on forest management. The wildlife biologist and the specialist in timber management may share many common traditions and experiences, but, as would be expected, they do not necessarily share the same view on the role of importance of their respective specialties. Even among line officers whose broad responsibility theoretically embraces all functions, it would be a mistake to suppose there is perfect uniformity throughout the system, or even throughout a particular region. With its emphasis on tradition and conformity, the Forest Service from a distance may resemble a marching army. On a closer observation, however, quite a few of the mass appear to hear a different drummer. They may all march in the same direction, but not all at the same cadence.

Neverthless, this individual diversity only qualifies, it does not refute, the common observation that the service tends to be an insular bureaucracy. There may be unevenness in the ranks, but a common direction and identity sets this particular troop apart from others. Moreover, and more important, this identity is strengthened as one progresses through the ranks to senior leadership positions. Differences of view persist, but tend to be diminished by the promotion process which selects out "generalists" with broad, though traditional, experience. There are positions at the top echelons for professionals with a specialist role and viewpoint. But few who have a specialty diverging radically from the mainstream tradition of the generalist forester make it to the important policy-making positions. So this process tends in the direction of conformity, whether it is called inbreeding, self-containment, or acculturation. Whether we label it bad or good is less obvious and deserves further consideration.

There are several rationales to support the policy of *self-containment.* One derives from the need for managerial experience. The Forest Service, whose major management responsibilities are preeminently tasks requiring experience as well as professional competence has always had a strong need for such experience. By "experience" I mean not simply technical experience, the kind one obtains after years of working in a particular professional activity. That type of experience, after all, can be obtained from supply markets outside the service. As noted earlier, there are virtually no areas of occupational specialty where the Forest Service is unique; all of the relevant professional specialties—at all levels of experience—can be found in other land-management agencies, industry, or numerous other public and private institutions. Rather the kind of experience that provides the special justification for a policy of self-containment is more varied and more related to nontechnical aspects of professional management. Broadly speaking, it is management experience in dealing with people, both within and outside the Forest Service; and it is experience in dealing with a variety of different management tasks. The Forest Service has always put particular stress on this. Its top-echelon personnel are expected to be generalists, well versed in the wide variety of distinctive tasks performed by the agency. This is the case with most large public and private organizations. More so than most organizations, however, the Forest Service promotes this actively through a practice of frequent and varied personnel transfers as a means of exposing its professionals to all major segments of the organization. (As noted earlier, a person can decline transfers, but he does so at peril to his advancement.) In this way, then, the Forest Service professional is exposed to the wide variety of work and management problems the agency faces as a distinctive institution. Obviously, this kind of experience is not easily purchased on the open market.

Even here, however, the Forest Service is not unique in providing managerial experience and sophistication. Again, these talents can be found without difficulty in many agencies and institutions outside the service. What is unique about the Forest Service experience is not managerial skill but managerial perspective, the acculturation to the special traditions and attitudes of the service. What the agency gets by relying on its own is not so much special competence as it is organizational loyalty. To bring in too many outsiders is to take a risk that the opinions and attitudes which the outsider brings to his job will be at odds with the agency's outlook and settled policies. Relying on internal promotion—restricting lateral entry into mainline agency positions—is thus an important tool of control. It gives a cast to agency policy that is more or less dependably uniform and conservative.

However, to express the problem in terms of maintaining control of agency action may state the matter too narrowly. What is also involved is an intangible something called image or identity. In the private sector organizational imagery and identity are well-recognized needs. Corporations avidly promote, not only the distinctive identity of their products, but also the general corporate image as well. In part the latter is an aspect of the former, but only in part. The need for a corporate image has deeper roots in the consciousness of corporate management, as the countless varieties of corporate status symbols clearly attest. A similar phenomenon is found within bureaucracies. But few organizations, public or private, have so assiduously promoted a distinctive identity as has the Forest Service. From the early efforts of Pinchot to develop a core of professional foresters to replace the amateurs charged with forest conservation, the service has actively cultivated an image of an institution of professionals with a grand mission and a distinctive competence to perform it. As a trademark, Smokey the Bear has been promoted and protected (against imitations which would cheapen the image) with a success that would warm the collective hearts of Batten, Barton, Durstine and Osborn.[11]

There is a practical side to this concern for a distinctive identity. In its major resource responsibilities the service competes with other federal agencies, most notably with the National Park Service and the Bureau of Land Management (BLM) within the Department of the Interior, but to a lesser extent also with other agencies such as the Bureau of Outdoor Recreation (BOR) and the Bureau of Sport Fisheries and Wildlife (BSFW). Maintaining a distinctive identity is not merely a means of keeping its basic policies separate from the actions of other agencies, with whom it frequently (not invariably) disagrees; it is also a means of competition and, ultimately, even of survival as a separate agency. Against the recurrent efforts to merge the Forest Service with, or transfer various of its functions to, agencies in the Department of the Interior, the service has sought to maintain its independence and integrity as a multiple-function agency by establishing a *distinctive* competence in all aspects of resource management. Similarly, in a constant competition for jurisdiction over particular areas (frequently arising in connection with proposals to convert forest lands to national parks or other areas controlled by the Park Service), the Forest Service has generally sought to protect its jurisdiction of the multiple-use principle and its distinctive competence to manage that policy.

Given the desire to promote this special identity, the policy of professional *inbreeding*—or to employ a less pejorative term, *self-containment*—is quite logical. Within the agency self-containment builds loyalty and esprit, a kind of clubby togetherness that is indispensable to a clear, distinct corporate personality. Outside the agency, the same process reinforces the image of the service as a unique organization of dedicated professionals whose careers and lives are devoted to the Forest Service.

This image of dedicated professionalism has served the service well in another important respect. It has helped it to escape, at least in part, from the degree of political manipulation that has plagued some of its sister agencies within the Department of the Interior. To a degree unique among federal land-management agencies, the Forest Service has been relatively insulated against direct political changes in the top-level appointments, and this in turn has secured the independence of lower echelons from indirect political change. By contrast, the BLM has been much more subject to this effect; even the Park Service, more independent and stable than its sisters in the Department of the Interior, has never enjoyed quite the same degree of political independence as the Forest Service. One explanation for this is that the multiple clientele of the Forest Service has enabled it to counter one political influence with another opposite one and to achieve a kind of neutral balance. But in itself this probably would not have sufficed unless the agency had been able to project an image of solid and distinct professionalism. A system in which positions are filled by professional standards of experience and tenure, without any *visible* intrusion of politics into the internal selection and promotion of personnel, may serve to remove some of the incentive for Congress or the president to attempt political manipulation in response to some particularly influential political group.

If all of the above considerations are pertinent rationales for the Forest Service's self-containment, they are certainly not dispositive of its merits. On the other side of the scale, a number of substantial difficulties appear, and, on balance, they indicate the need for a thorough rethinking of agency policy.

Consider the experience element. No doubt it is useful that senior officers and staff should have some understanding of the traditions of the Forest Service as well as a managerial experience commensurate with the level of responsibility involved. But it does not seem necessary, or, in the long run, useful to adopt a policy in which virtually every important position, at every level within the National Forest System, is filled from within the agency. Such an exclusive emphasis on self-containment converts the virtues of experience into the vice of narrowness. True, Forest Service experience does provide a fairly wide window on the world. However, the view is still one limited by its particular perspective: those with views from other houses may see something quite different. The fact that the agency specially seeks predominantly in-house experience is evidence that it recognizes that this experience is distinctive. That the agency should deliberately insulate itself from the disturbing influence of outsiders with different viewpoints is very troublesome. The service should realize this. For all the tradition it obviously cherishes, it has in recent years publicly professed its willingness to reevaluate its policies, priorities, and perspectives. It has, as we have seen, taken some steps toward this aim in redesigning its policy and decision-making processes. However, a far more important step toward opening up the process of planning and decision making would be to introduce greater openness by broadening lateral entry into the various levels of the organization.

Quite apart from the fact that it could broaden the perspectives of the service, a greater openness of entry into the organization should commend itself to the agency on grounds of pure self-interest. Earlier I noted the virtue of limited entry in developing a distinctive image of a professionally expert organization, insulated against direct political manipulation and control. But it is not unambiguously virtuous to be professional. There is today a skepticism of professional expertise left to its own devices. The whole movement toward public involvement and decision making is testament to this. Some of this may be more a matter of fashion than fundamental politics; nevertheless it reflects a skepticism about professionalism (and bureaucracy) quite healthy to the body politic.

In any event this skepticism toward insulated professionalism does exist and the service ignores it at its peril. Indeed, the independence the Forest Service has built in part through its image of professionalism, may be threatened by a too rigorous insistence on that same image. The major threat to the agency's independence comes less from industry-sponsored political control, than conservationist-sponsored political control. The ability of the service to resist direct political control depends not simply on its image of professionalism but also upon the character of that professionalism. The image of inbred specialization, worn by Forest Service in many quarters, is poor defense against outside intrusion by public interest groups insisting that this specialization is ill-equipped to view the forest resource in a perspective broad enough to serve all the public needs. In short, professionalism serves to remove part of the incentive for political interference only when the professionals are *perceived* as open-minded and experienced persons. Whatever its actual effects, a policy of self-containment undermines that image and the public confidence in the agency.

What is said here does not imply that the Forest Service should dramatically shift away from a policy of internal promotions as a norm. Nor does it imply that all positions at every level should be opened to all qualified persons regardless of past service experience. Any such effort would surely cause mass disaffection among agency personnel who found their careers substantially impeded; in final effect, it would destroy the cohesiveness and integrity of the organization. What is suggested is that the times require a broader view of forest management than the traditionally restrictive attitude toward lateral entry seems capable of allowing. To accomplish this it is not necessary to leave all the organizational doors wide open; it is enough to leave a few more ajar.

PLANNING AND
DECISION MAKING

Among the common criticisms leveled against government agencies is their neglect of long-term planning. It is a charge that has been especially prominent in the case of the independent regulatory commissions. However, such a charge cannot reasonably be leveled at the Forest Service. Whatever else one may say of Forest Service planning, one cannot fairly say it does not engage in sufficient, long-range planning. A significant percentage of the agency's professional staff is devoted to little else but preparation of management plans. At all levels, and for virtually every activity, plans are bountiful; in fact, the trouble is that there are probably too many separate plans, inadequately coordinated and integrated.

A major difficulty is in integrating various components of the functional planning system. As noted earlier, the number of these plans varies among regions and forests. However, for most forests, the primary administrative planning unit will have at least one functional plan for each resource function and each protective or supportive function. In some cases these are forestwide; in others these plans are prepared for each individual district or other geographic subunit (e.g., an allotment for range management or watershed management). In some cases, plans may be prepared within the regional, district, or other subunit levels. Even disregarding the multiplication of plans and planning directives resulting from the two or more levels of planning (say, district and forest or forest and region), the task of fitting these together into a coherent planning scheme is obviously an enormous one. And it is one which has been rather neglected until very recently. Until the late 1950s, virtually no planned integration of different functions existed, particularly among the five major resource functions.

Multiple-Use Planning

The introduction of multiple-use planning was a significant step toward coordination of the different resource functions, but it never developed a fully integrated planning system and falls far short of helping to redress the imbalance among resources. For all of the emphasis given to multiple-use planning in the Forest Service Manual and other official directives, multiple-use plans never achieved the preeminent stature among management plans. In theory, multiple-use guides and plans provided a general framework of integrated planning within which individual functional plans were developed. Individual functional plans were thus theoretically subordinate and were developed from or at least were subject to the multiple-use planning documents.

The reality was something else. In practice, multiple-use guides and plans became little more than guidelines for coordinating the more or less autonomous functional plans. As guidelines for multiple-use coordination they were not perhaps without some utility. The underlying concept of the system of zoning classifications, such as scenic zones, travel-influence zones, water-influence zones, and the like, as well as special management prescriptions for each zone, provided a framework for coordination among functions and a more balanced consideration of the different resource uses. However, their practical importance for some time has been a matter for some skepticism. In most cases the guidelines were little more than common-sensical directives.

The basic weakness of multiple-use planning was that it was inadequately integrated into the mainstream of management planning and operations. Instead of attempting to coordinate a number of different, largely autonomous functions, there was a need to integrate multiple-use planning into a single-stage system. Such a new system was needed, not merely to give greater recognition to appropriate multiple-use constraints on individual functions, but also to develop a comprehensive land use plan in which each forest resource activity would be integrated. Individual functional plans would be developed where appropriate, but these would be derived from the comprehensive land use plan. Thus, the new plan would be the primary land use plan, not merely a coordinating document for connecting autonomous functional plans.

Essentially, this is the thrust of the new "land use" (the currently preferred term for the multiple-use planning process) planning system which has been implemented by the service in recent years. As this is written, the new planning system has not been fully developed, and there remain some uncertainties about its practical implementation and effects. The main uncertainty is how well the new planning process will achieve its intended purpose of integrating resource planning. In particular it remains to be seen whether the new land use planning will materially alter the relative priorities among resource uses, whether it will, as was intended, achieve a greater balance among the five major resource uses. At the early stage of implementation—when I interviewed Forest Service officials in the field—some skepticism was voiced by many with whom this was discussed.

It is too early to predict effects; many years must pass before they will become publicly visible. What can be said is that the design of the new land use planning approach to multiple-use forestry does look in the right direction of more fully integrated resource planning.

Economic Considerations

Ultimately, of course, changes in planning and decision-making processes can be effective only to the extent that they are economically or politically supported. It is not enough to talk of a more balanced functional planning process. Any reallocation of forest resource use must be supported by an appropriate allocation of funds by Congress. This, in turn, can be expected only as a consequence of a shift in political pressures or a change in economic incentives, or both. Reform in the management-planning and decision-making processes is thus not a sufficient condition of better resource management. Still it is an important and necessary one. An efficient management-planning system is essential, not only to respond effectively to political and economic demands, but also to provide an intelligent framework in which the respective political and economic demands can be intelligently created and guided to serve some public objective.

All of which prompts a generalization about planning incentives in a bureaucracy: a central problem of bureaus is the difficulty of evaluating productive efficiency in the absence of a market in which their services can be measured. Economist Anthony Downs has perceptively pointed out:

> Unlike most other large organizations, bureaus are economically one-faced rather than two-faced. They face input markets when they buy the scarce resources they need to produce their outputs. But they face no economic markets whatever on the output side. Therefore they have no direct way of evaluating their outputs in relation to the costs of the inputs used to make them.[12]

This economic perspective is useful for analyzing one respect in which incentives and constraints in government *may* differ from those of private firms. And it has particular interest in the case of the Forest Service for the very reason that some of its functions are more directly influenced by market rewards than others. By implication of Downs' thesis we would expect to see different effects in those areas where the service has a market for its output and those where it does not. And it is reasonable to hypothesize that we would expect to find greater emphasis in areas where the market provides some measure of productivity than in areas such as watershed management where no such market measurement generally exists. It may be noted that, for the market to exert such influence, it is not necessary that the agency itself directly receive (or suffer) the rewards of a market transaction. It is enough that in some degree the president, the Congress, or others who exercise substantial political influence have some regard for the market, and that appropriations (and other rewards, such as promotions, etc.) respond accordingly. There are strong indications that the market in this respect clearly influences the Forest Service: appropriations reflect it, and the service responds to the appropriations.

Of course, the market incentives do not work in a vacuum; they are either reinforced or countered by political forces. Often these reinforce the market incentives; in the case of timber, for example, the market incentives for intensive management are strongly reinforced by timber-interest groups acting through Congress and through the Executive. Increasingly, however, the nonmarket forces of environmental interests have been effective in countering both the market incentives and the political influence of commercial interests. The Forest Service is caught in the position of having to respond to these crosscurrents. It is a frustrating predicament, for it cannot respond fully to both.

The crucial problem is to find some common measuring rod, some vehicle for determining the appropriate tradeoffs between the competing functions.

It is a difficult problem. The environmental and aesthetic functions have no readily determined market price. A market might be established for many of these simply by asking the proponents of nonexploitative uses to pay others to leave the forests alone. But that is unlikely since the entire thrust of their movement lies in a rejection of market evaluation. How then can the Forest Service respond?

One commentator, a director of forestry at West Virginia University, gives the following account of the problem:

> The use of forests should be subject to rules and analysis that promote efficiency and social welfare. Ideally, then, we should have accurate data on the costs and benefits of alternative policies and practices, and should be able to make sound judgments based on a comparison of the cost-benefit ratios. In the world of private enterprise this function is performed by the free market: the production of a good that promises a profit bids strongly for the needed resources. But in the question of timber versus recreation, the free market is of little use as an allocation mechanism because one of these "products," recreation, does not generally enter into a market. The forest administrator has some pretty good data to show the social utility of timber. He receives bids on timber sales and can observe the prices of timber products in the open market. But against this quantitative information must be weighed the demands for other rival uses, such as recreation, which often pass through no market and carry no market derived dollar value.
>
> The only recourse for the forest administrator in this dilemma is to remain acutely sensitive to the impulses he receives from the political sphere, from citizens, and from organized groups. It is not difficult to conjure up an image of the forest administrator adjusting his various uses to the point where the screams emanating from the various interest groups have about the same decibel count. In the end, his final decision is a matter of informed judgment.[13]

The image of measuring decibel counts is a caricature, but like all caricatures it bears a resemblance to reality.

The absence of the market in which the competing uses can be measured and valued need not, however, preclude the use of economic tools to aid in decision making. Cost–benefit analyses can provide a workable tool for analyzing at least some of the competing alternatives and giving direction for an efficient choice among them.[14] To aid in analyzing the alternatives and tradeoffs in more complex problems, the Forest Service now has numerous computer programs. In some circles, particularly among the younger professionals, college-trained in the use of such techniques as linear programming, there is considerable enthusiasm about the use of such analytic tools as aids in planning resource allocation. The enthusiasm is not universal, particularly among some conservationists. Quite apart from the more general anxiety which many feel toward the computer age, there is a special distress over the image of Smokey the Bear with a pocket computer instead of a shovel. It has not, of course, reached that stage, and it probably never will, but the apprehension does persist. Insofar as this apprehension and antagonism is anything more than an aesthetic distaste for trying to put nature into a linear program, it appears to be the association of computer programming with more intensive economic management.

As was said of economic analysis, computer programming is not necessarily or inevitably biased. The results depend on what the program inputs are and how they are defined. Neither computers nor economic analysts can offer an easy solution to the matter of public choice, but both are clearly an improvement over a decibel meter. Computer capability, which has been in short supply, is now being provided down to the forest level.[15]

The Role of Economists

However, trained analysts, especially those trained in economics, are still in short supply. As of January 1973, the Forest Service employed a total of twenty-two economists; of these, only four worked in the National Forest System.[16] This is woefully inadequate for an agency charged with responsibility for annually allocating resources whose direct economic value must be estimated at more than $1 billion.[17] The absence of economists with important decision-making and advisory roles in the National Forest System is particularly striking when set against the burgeoning interest outside the agency in natural resource economics. While the Forest Service does maintain an acquaintance with the economics of natural resource management through its research arm (where most of its economists are situated) the influence of the agency's research economists on the formation of agency policy appears to be slight.

Perhaps the fact that the present chief of the Forest Service, John McGuire, has economic training will alter this past neglect. But I am skeptical. The absence of economists in the mainstream of agency decision making in the National Forest System is not an oversight. The institutional neglect reflects an underlying professional bias against modern economic analysis and economists on the part of the traditional foresters who still dominate the agency. The bias is to an extent inherent in professional forestry itself. Notwithstanding that economics is a component of silviculture—the centerpiece of traditional forestry—it has tended to be dominated, if not overwhelmed, by the biological aspects. Traditionally, even the forest economist has tended to be more a forester who specialized in economics than an economist who specialized in forestry. Therein lies a significant difference, in training and in analytic approach. And for the generalist forester who does not specialize in economics, the difference is even greater.

I do not wish to overstate the professional differences between forester and economist. No doubt the differences which appear between some foresters (most notably those in the Forest Service) and some economists (most notably those outside the service) reflect generational gaps as much as professional differences. In this aspect the Forest Service's personnel policies are explicable in part as a bias toward traditional, conservative forestry and forest economics, as against some of the more "radical" views of some current economic analysts. This is strikingly evident in the area of timber management where the agency has followed very conservative (and, I believe, economically dubious) policies toward sale administration, allowable-cut determinations, and other matters of timber supply in general.

It is not necessary to suppose that professional economists would uniformly quarrel with Forest Service economic policies in order to believe, as I do, that the addition of a significant number (at the very least four or five for each regional staff and a similar number in the Washington office) to important staff positions in the National Forest System would produce changes in agency policies looking toward greater economic efficiency in resource allocation. The reluctance of the agency to expose itself to more economists is, I believe, a measure of its reluctance to consider major alteration in current economic policies.

The Role of Lawyers

Economists are not alone in being virtually excluded from positions of influence. Lawyers too appear to have little, if any, role in the making of agency policy. The Forest Service does not have a legal staff of its own; its attorneys are formally assigned to the General Counsel's Office within the Department of Agriculture. However, this is of little more than formal significance, for those who are assigned to the agency are regarded as its lawyers. Even so, the role of lawyers is a limited one. It is evident that the lawyer is not closely involved in agency policy or decision making except perhaps when a clear legal issue is obviously raised by the decision to be made or action to be taken. Even here it appears that many actions are taken without the guidance of competent legal advice or assistance. Perhaps I should stress the word "competent" here, for the external evidence is consistent with either of two judgments: first, the agency is not guided by legal counsel, or, second, the agency receives incompetent legal advice.

This is perhaps most evident in situations subject to the requirements of the NEPA, which have provided the basis for a large and growing legal role in land-management planning. One would suppose that lawyers would naturally be drawn into the decision-making process to ensure adequate compliance with the NEPA. At the very least, one would think that the NEPA statements themselves would be carefully prepared by lawyers reasonably conversant with the trend of judicial decisions on previous NEPA statements. But even a casual survey of impact statements indicates that they received little, if any, competent legal guidance.

I make no argument for lawyers as land use planners, a role in which neither training nor experience qualifies them to serve. But it is an unavoidable fact that land use decisions are no longer the province of administrative expertise. For better or for worse, land use decisions have moved into the lawyer's arena. The courts in particular have assumed jurisdiction to supervise not merely the formalities of decision-making procedures (such as preparation of impact statements and public participation) but the substantive rationality of the decisions and policies. The Forest Service, I believe, has yet to accept or fully to appreciate this fact. As a consequence, it has not sufficiently recognized the unavoidable need for closer involvement of legal counsel in the planning and decision-making process in order to prepare itself adequately to meet the demands of judicial review.

Public Participation

One of the changes now occurring in policy-planning and decision-making processes within the Forest Service is increased emphasis on public participation. This is partly the consequence of the internal reforms in planning and decision making, but mainly it is the result of external demands for increased public involvement in governmental decision making. Current thinking about participatory democracy attaches enormous significance to public participation in governmental processes. This is particularly so in the area of environmental concerns where expanded public involvement has been increasingly looked to as the "great white hope" (more appropriately perhaps the "great green hope") for saving the environment. The law has pushed strongly in this direction in recent years. Through judicial decision, legislative action, and administrative prescription, public participation has become an accepted norm of the planning and decision-making processes of administrative government.

The Forest Service has responded to this movement with mixed emotions. The *concept* of general public participation, at least in broad planning decisions, appears to be well and widely accepted within the service and, particularly in the areas of comprehensive land use planning and in major project or program planning, public input is now actively solicited. This has not always been the case, and in some areas, especially those involving particular resource-management actions such as individual timber sales, there is still some resistance to extensive public involvement. Like most agencies, the service has long regarded itself as the expert and the guardian of the public interest within its realm. Moreover, to a degree far greater than most agencies, the service has had an important and continuing informal contact with a fairly broad spectrum of public interest groups. These contacts had been thought sufficient to keep it informed of the public needs and interests, but the current mores of participatory democracy have dictated a more formal involvement of public groups, and the service has had to adapt. The results to date are hard to measure. It is apparent that some frustration has been felt both by agency officials and by public groups. The latter are frequently heard to complain, not only that the agency has been resistant to giving the public the information it needs for effective participation, but also that it has not listened when the public has participated. On the other hand, some Forest Service officials have complained that the participants have not fully represented the broad spectrum of public interests, but only the more limited interests of special groups; the result has been a highly polarized confrontation between opposing groups rather than a reasoned consideration of alternatives.

Based on a number of particular cases—chiefly those involving timber cutting or wilderness decisions—both sides can find some support for their complaints. But any definitive statement on public participation in Forest Service planning and decision making must await a thorough investigation of the subject. Moreover, any meaningful evaluation of public participation requires a clearer enunciation of purpose than any that has to date appeared. This is a general problem that extends beyond forest management to administrative government generally. In all of the clamor for greater public involvement in administrative planning and decision making, there seems to have been little attention given to the question, To what aim and for what purpose? It is commonly said in support of public participation that it provides an important input into the administrative process. Seldom, however, is any attempt made to penetrate behind this jargon to define what kind of input is provided.

It is important, I think, to distinguish two major functions of this input. One is the purely informational function, that of providing the factual data and experienced opinion the agency cannot readily obtain from its own resources. A second is what might be called the social or political function, that of permitting the public some measure of influence over decisions affecting their interests.[18]

Obviously, these functions are interrelated and not necessarily antagonistic. Nevertheless, they are rather distinct, and it by no means follows that a form of public involvement which fulfills one aim will adequately serve the other. In some cases one objective may interfere with the other.

The Information Function.   Consider the information function. In terms of providing the agency with concrete facts and informed opinion about, say, a timber-management plan, a consultation with private timber interests (e.g., local mill owners and/or local timber industry associations) and with conservationists (e.g., the Sierra Club and like-minded groups) is important. But from a purely information-seeking viewpoint, the scope of participation beyond a bare handful of interest groups is likely to be unproductive. In fact, at some point as the number of participants grows, the information function is not only not furthered, it may be undermined: useful information becomes obscured by the sheer volume of commentary of little informative value. On the other hand, limiting participation to those whose contribution of information outweighs its cost would scarcely serve the social or political objective of participatory democracy, which dictates a broader public involvement than can possibly be justified by any narrow consideration of information input.

The Sociopolitical Function. Of those two major objectives, probably the most difficult to serve adequately is the sociopolitical. We can set to one side the limited case of participation by individuals with personal and legally protected interests adversely affected by agency action. Such persons are entitled to individual hearings under the agency's appeals process. While that process is itself subject to some criticism,[19] these are not of major significance to the question of general public participation. The agency appeals process is not designed to serve as a mechanism of general public participation in agency decision making. At most, it provides a procedure either for vindicating personal rights or for airing public complaints upon action already taken. The need and the concern is for a means of registering *general* public opinion *before* decisions are made. The problem is not so much one of finding procedural mechanisms by which the public can air its views. The Forest Service employs a number of methods for soliciting public opinion that are all adequately designed to reach the public: public hearings, "listening sessions," correspondence, and solicitation of written views.[20] The difficult problems are not mechanical but normative, How extensively should the canvass of the public be? In formulating a management plan for a wilderness area in northern Minnesota, should the agency hold hearings in Chicago or in Cleveland?[21] How should the public responses be evaluated (apart from the information content); how much weight should be given to the "votes" cast?

As mentioned earlier, some Forest Service officials have indicated their disenchantment when the views received have represented the more extreme interest groups and interest viewpoints. Such disenchantment seems to me a bit naïve. Anyone who views the course of public participation in the administrative process elsewhere finds essentially the same thing, whether it relates to FDA standards for food additives, FCC regulation of telephone rates, or Forest Service management of clear-cutting on the national forests. For such matters as these, the silent majority does exist; whether it is conservative or liberal I do not know (it is too silent to tell), but that it does in fact exist I have no doubt.

One easy resolution of this problem is simply to ignore those who do not "vote" or otherwise express their views. The public view would be determined simply by evaluating those who chose to speak up. A case can be made for giving special weight to the intensity with which persons hold certain views, and the trouble that people take to express themselves is one indication of that intensity. This would seem to return us to our decibel meter; however, in this instance there is no assumption that the meter readings would be dispositive of the final decision, but merely dispositive of the "public view."

It probably goes without saying that we are broaching some rather basic issues of political principle, issues which we cannot discuss in detail here. Suffice it to say that the problem of measuring and fairly weighing public votes deserves far more consideration by the Forest Service and by other administrative agencies, which are now being confronted with the phenomenon of public participation for the first time. The problem is not an easy one to resolve; it is complicated by the fact that virtually every participant purports to speak for more than himself. In fact, most presume to speak "for the public" or at least for the "public interest." As I have already said, such claims should be skeptically received. Whether they do represent the public interest is, I suggest, a question to be determined only after the entire controversy has been fully reviewed from all viewpoints.

All of this would seem too obvious to mention if it were not for the fact that, in the context of discussing public participation, many seem to assume what we were really talking about is participation by environmentalist, or at least popularly oriented, groups. The assumption appears to be not that the industry interests are not entitled to be heard, but that they represent only their own individual interests, and not any broader public interest. Without meaning to suggest in any way that industry interests are adequately representative of the public, I would insist it is silly to suppose that such interests represent no interests other than their own particular enterprise purpose. On the assumptions that no one lived in houses, no one used paper, no one had any use for timber products generally, then it would be true that the timber industry, for example, could not speak for a very broad segment of the public, or the public interest. But then, of course, there would not be any timber industry. In short, the mere existence of a viable industry here, as well as elsewhere, demonstrates that an important public need is being served. That the timber industry serves this need for private gain and not out of some larger sense of public obligation is surely irrelevant to whether the need and the interest are sufficiently public to be recognized as such. I do not confine this observation to industry groups. The same recognition of the broader constituency, of the broader interest represented (to the extent one can be discerned) should be given for all participants. The only caution is not to become confused by the labels or the advertising every group employs to enhance its product.

CONFLICTS IN LAND USE POLICY

The inconsistencies, conflicts, and competition among the federal land agencies have been the subject of much critical attention over the years. Most of it has been directed toward proposals for consolidation of the Forest Service with the major land agencies of the Department of the Interior. Such proposals have become a hallmark of nearly every new administration's land use policy. The forest reserves were no sooner transferred from the Department of the Interior than proposals were made to transfer them back or to consolidate them in some other way with other land use functions. Of course, at the time of the original transfer there were few other functions to be consolidated. But as they grew within the Department of the Interior so, too, did the efforts to consolidate the Forest Service's responsibilities with them. Proposals to transfer either the national forests or the service itself to Interior have been made with monotonous regularity since as early as 1913.[22] The most forceful, and most nearly successful, advocate of consolidation was Harold Ickes, FDR's redoubtable secretary of the interior, whose consuming ambition was to merge the Forest Service with the Department of the Interior (to be renamed the Department of Conservation). But Congress proved no more agreeable to his idea than it had been six years earlier when it rejected a consolidation plan of the Hoover Administration to merge all of the land functions into the Department of Agriculture.[23] Still, Ickes' failure did not deter others from endorsing the consolidation idea. In 1949 the Hoover Commission unanimously recommended the consolidation of land functions, but (like the earlier Hoover Administration proposal) within Agriculture, rather than Interior.[24]

If the Hoover Commission's recommendations for unification of the land-management functions had any practical impact, it is not apparent. About the most one can say is that they kept the idea of reorganization alive, and others have since come forward to promote the cause. The most recent is the proposed Department of Energy Natural Resources, proposed by the Nixon Administration in 1972,[25] which would have unified all land management under an Administration for Land and Recreation Resources, which would coordinate timber and wildlife production, grazing, recreation, etc. The chief of the Forest Service would set policy for all national forests from Washington, and this would be implemented in the ten geographic regions by an administrator approximately the equivalent of the present regional forester. Organization below the regional level would presumably remain roughly the same as it is now. The proposed unification is now moribund if not altogether dead—for political reasons that need not concern us. But the interesting question of the merits of unification remains alive. It awaits only the discovery by a new administration to resuscitate it.

While history seems insufficient reason in itself for retaining a particular organization, it does nevertheless establish at least a weak presumption of normalcy not to be lightly cast aside. Such a presumption would require any reorganization of such far-reaching import as that contemplated here to show not merely that the existing scheme is inadequate, but that the new one will probably be better. On this last score I confess some mild skepticism, not strong enough perhaps to reject a new organization, but substantial enough to restrain enthusiasm for it.

The main case for unification of the land agencies rests on the perception that the management responsibilities of the different land agencies are closely interrelated and in many cases substantially overlapping. Even our earlier brief discussion of the land agencies demonstrates the accuracy of this observation. There is not a single Forest Service function not also substantially performed by at least one, and in some instances as many as four, Interior agencies.[26] However, the question is not whether many agencies share functions, but rather what is to be gained by their consolidation. Intuitively, one would suppose two basic things; first, simplification and more efficient administration, and, second, greater integration of land-management policy.

On the first, it is hard to doubt that simplification and efficiency of administration would be good, but there is reason to suspect it would not be readily obtained by mere consolidation. If it were all so easy, one wonders why the land agencies within the Department of the Interior continue to display much of the same kind of duplication of administrative effort among themselves as between each of them and the Forest Service. The point, of course, is that each of these bureaus, although ostensibly unified under a single department, perform pretty largely as independent agencies. Each has its own set of statutory responsibilities; each has, in fact, its own traditions and its own political constituency. The proposed reorganization would not itself appear to affect any of this significantly: the Forest Service would be carried intact into the new department, along with each of the other bureaus.

Essentially, the same point must be made with regard to the second promised benefit, greater integration of policy. That there are many disparities in land use policy can pass without contradiction,[27] it is the cause and the cure that is subject to dispute.

As to cause, it should be noted that more is involved here than organizational separation. Often the inconsistencies that are the major target of such reform have nothing to do with organizational structure.[28] This does not, of course, say that all disparities and inconsistencies are compelled by different legislative provisions. It is an accepted fact that each of the land agencies does have, and each rather self-consciously cultivates, its own land use philosophy and policies, some being consistent, others not. However, here too, the differences reflect in part distinctive, if not contradictory, legislative mandates to the different agencies. These differences, even if only faintly discernible in particular statutory directives, are made more pronounced by the particular agency's primary constituency, which works to shape its perspective along a particular path. The point is transparent but important. One expects the Bureau of Sport Fisheries and Wildlife to be more wildlife oriented than the Forest Service and the Forest Service to be more timber oriented than the Park Service, and so on. In some degree the agencies are thus reflecting merely the tensions between the resource functions and basic policy objectives which are unlikely to disappear with organizational change.

Of course, there is a good deal of bureaucratic rivalry between the agencies even in pursuit of common aims. Quite apart from differences in underlying policy or philosophy, the division of responsibility among agencies is more likely to stimulate competition than coordination. It is part of the territorial imperative of bureaucracy. An agency sees a particular function, say, outdoor recreation, as commanding a more or less fixed amount of public and legislative support. The agency's share of the pie depends on its role and the scope of its responsibility in performing that function; each agency can be expected to do its best in promoting its distinctive role and expanding the scope of its responsibility—at the expense of other agencies if necessary.

The rivalry between Interior agencies and the Forest Service is part of the folk tradition of Washington. As history it is well documented by many episodes, from Pinchot's early battles through successive contests (most notably between the Forest Service and the Park Service) over jurisdiction or policy. Few doubt that it still exists. The celebrated "Treaty of the Potomac" in 1963,[29] in which Secretary of the Interior Stewart Udall and Secretary of Agriculture Orville Freeman pledged mutual cooperation, assistance, and an end to warfare, served more to focus public attention on the rivalry than to end it. Only two years later the two departments found themselves at loggerheads over the development of Mineral King Valley. More recently, they have openly clashed on many issues of policy, particulary in the recreation area, where the Forest Service and the National Park Service continue to compete for jurisdiction and to pursue somewhat different philosophies.[30] (The growth of national parks and national recreation areas at the expense of the Forest Service continues.)

While some critics view such rivalry as simply the quest for larger appropriations and power, I think something more is involved. Agencies may be acquisitive, but they are seldom simple highwaymen. They serve their own interests, but not without identifying them with a broader public interest. The Forest Service and the Park Service are notable illustrations: each has ample self-regard and a distinctive sense of high purpose, well cultivated by tradition. Small wonder each views the other's actions suspiciously when they encroach on what each regards as its special competence.

As a general matter one would not wish it otherwise. It would be a poor agency indeed that thought so little of its worth, or the importance of what it did, as to be indifferent to its sphere of influence. Some such rivalry is not only understandable, it is desirable. The antithesis of competition is monopoly; as we fear monopoly in the private sector, so should we be apprehensive of it in government. One reason is that it could deprive us of the opportunity to compare agency performances and policies.[31] More than depriving us of yardsticks for evaluating performance, however, monopolization can retard incentive and innovation in public land management. Economist Sir John Hicks once supposed that the "best of all monopoly profits is a quiet life."[32] If true, it would seem as great an indictment of the monopolistic bureaucrat as of the monopolistic entrepreneur.[33]

On the other hand, rivalry can prove wasteful. Among other things, competition may not spur product improvement as much as product differentiation, and, at least in public resource management, this must be regarded as a most dubious benefit. Also, if there are economies in consolidation (which was earlier doubted, but which must remain open as a possibility), these are sacrificed by maintaining competitive institutions.

But whether the rivalry is defended as competition or challenged as bureaucratic waste, there is very little reason to think that any proposals so far made will eliminate it. I return to the Department of the Interior paradigm: if departmental unification would eliminate rivalry, why has it not done so in Interior where the rivalry between bureaus is at least as strong and in some cases stronger than that between any of these bureaus and the Forest Service?

Despite the negative cast of the above comments, the case for unification of agencies continues to have a nagging appeal, even though I have attempted to smother it with skepticism. That should come as no surprise, I suppose, considering how durable these reorganization proposals have been over the years. One source of its continued appeal is doubtless its simplicity and its generality. In the face of confoundingly complex problems, it appears as a solution which all can grasp. In the face of vexing diversity, it is a universal antidote. Unfortunately, its appeal is its danger. Reorganization might make some problems of land use policy more tractable, but these are likely to be few in number and slight in importance. It would be a poor gain if, to make a few problems easier, attention were diverted from the great mass of others which would be unaffected.

CONCLUSIONS

The high tide of conservationist concern that has swept over the country in recent years has bathed the Forest Service in controversies over its resource-management policies. It is hardly the first time the agency has been in this position. Virtually since its origin it has been knee-deep or chin-deep in controversies of one kind or another. On the other hand, it can be said that probably at no time prior to the 1960s had the service been in such a defensive posture against so many popularly based adversaries, those who have challenged the agency's traditional claim to leadership in resource conservation.

In its early years the agency was challenged by timber, livestock, power, and other interests, but few criticized it as anticonservationist or successfully challenged its claim of leadership as the foremost conservation organization in the country. Even Harold Ickes, who made rival claims of leadership for his Department of the Interior, could not credibly attack the record of the Forest Service on conservationist grounds. Not until the late 1950s and the decade of the 1960s was there any significant discontent with the agency's management policies which seriously undermined its preeminence as a conservationist organization. Today that discontent seems to have reached an all-time high as criticism of Forest Service policies and the agency itself have become increasingly more organized and more vocal.

Though there are some who view this modern disaffection as due to some decline in the agency's vigor, that seems a superficial interpretation. As has been mentioned, it is obvious to anyone familiar with the history of the agency that the change has been in the economic and social circumstances (the change in the character and intensity of conflict among resource demands), not in the Forest Service itself. Indeed, the more plausible ground for criticizing the Forest Service is precisely that it has not changed, or not changed enough to recognize modern environmental circumstances, needs, and demands: first, the agency has failed to gauge adequately the intensity of modern concern over resource preservation and environmental protection; second, it has not adequately recognized the breadth of public and political support which this concern has come to command; and third, it has been reluctant to share its management responsibilities with outside agencies or groups or to open up its decision-making processes to public scrutiny and intervention.

While much of the criticism of the Forest Service and of its policies seems to me questionable, and certainly exaggerated, there is substance in the claim that the agency has in many respects been slow to recognize the modern mood of an environmentally conscious public. At the very least it has lost much of the initiative of leadership in the eyes of a large, and seemingly growing, part of the public. Of late, there are many indications of a sincere and diligent effort to recapture its position in the forefront of American conservation. Whether it will be fully effective, it is too early to say. There are some institutional barriers to be met. One is the tradition of self-reliance. Though the agency has made important strides in opening up some of its planning processes to public participation, the image persists of an agency resistent to sharing major responsibilities either with outside professional agencies or public groups. More important, outside entry into the higher policy-making levels of the bureaucracy is still uncommon. Thus the views of outsiders who are consulted are still filtered through the perspectives of inside professionals. It will no doubt be noted that this is true of any large bureaucracy. Perhaps, but the strong traditions of the Forest Service, together with its heavy reliance on internal career advancement, present a somewhat special case. In any event it is a significant impediment to developing relationships with the outside public, whether it is unique to the service or not. Of course, the Forest Service's reliance on its own tradition and its own cadre of professionals trained in that tradition is not without its virtues. These have been examined earlier, and need not be reviewed. Here it is necessary only to make the point that the consequence of a *too* assiduous pursuit of those virtues has tended to insulate the agency from the outside public. Certainly, that is the perception of a seemingly broad segment of the public, and, in terms of developing a secure and confident relationship and understanding with the public, this perception is quite as important as the reality.

A second bias toward conservatism in the structure of the agency is decentralization of authority. Since Pinchot's day it has been an ideal of Forest Service organization that land-management responsibility was to be delegated, so far as practicable, to the "man on the ground," subject only to general policy guides from Washington. To a considerable degree the ideal is achieved in practice; not only is significant responsibility and discretion delegated to regional foresters, much is still further delegated to individual forest supervisors. Again, the rationale of this has been examined, and it was noted that generally such a policy is eminently sensible. It places responsibility on those who have direct experience with the resources and the effects of resource use; and, other things being equal, it permits a greater exposure of agency bureaucrats to the affected local public (viewed at least as consultants, if not as active participants in decision making). At the same time decentralization of authority can be a drag on flexibility in adjusting policies, particularly in response to national public demands. Delegation of management discretion to local levels enhances the importance of local public interests vis-à-vis national interests. A priori one might suppose that localism would not impart a bias for or against change; there are, after all, public demands for and against change at the local level, as well as at the national level. As it happens, however, traditional resource uses are likely to be more strongly defended at the local than the national level. The economic and social impact of a change, say, toward curtailment of timber cutting in favor of preservation, is almost certain to be magnified at the local level when compared to the national level. It is true, of course, that in many areas vigorous local conservation and preservation groups have not been without influence in pushing for changes in allocation policy. But judging from experience to date, it appears they have less influence at the local levels than at higher levels. Quite apart from any inherent disposition toward conservatism that may be imparted by local management discretion, decentralization necessarily shows the process of changing traditional policies simply by requiring more independent decisions. The diffusion of significant policy authority among nine regional foresters and some 146 supervisors below them is necessarily an impediment to swift adoption of changes in national policy. Regional and local authorities influence not only the implementation of policy, they are important components in the development of policies themselves. Thus, any interest group seeking practical change over the entire national forest system faces not one but several centers of authority.

It is unlikely that the Forest Service will ever recapture the preeminence it once enjoyed in Pinchot's time as the leading force in American conservation. Such preeminence is as much a matter of public image as achievement. On that score the agency is almost hopelessly handicapped in competition with agencies such as the Environmental Protection Agency (EPA) or private conservation organizations such as the Sierra Club, which can have single-minded concerns and no responsibility for the consequences of any positions they advocate. Still, the agency seems to have become unnecessarily neglectful of the opportunity to improve its public image with little, if any, sacrifice to "principle." Mineral King is an example; having made what it reasonably considered to be a principled though debatable decision on the development of Mineral King, it refused to give much, if any, weight to how its decision would be generally perceived by a wide segment of the public. It is not that the agency is unconcerned about its image. On the contrary, as I pointed out earlier, it has consciously cultivated a distinctive image of professionalism highly dedicated to forestry and conservation. But that image is not enough to hold the imagination of the public today. Professionalism has become suspect, at least where it appears to be too much insulated from outside influence. Forestry and conservation include today a broader range of concerns than when the agency's traditions were being developed by Pinchot. The Forest Service is not unaware of this: it was the service, after all, that first developed and implemented the idea of wilderness preservation; the Forest Service was an early leader in outdoor recreation, and it has been prominent in wildlife conservation and management. The achievements seem to outstrip the current image which the service continues to present to the public. I do not suggest that what the agency needs is more public relations work in the form of engaging bears, owls, or other forest denizens dressed in ranger uniforms. What is wanted is a somewhat greater sensitivity to public sensibilities, even those that may be based on misdirected anxieties.

NOTES

1. See, for example, Justice Douglas' dissenting opinion in *Sierra Club* v. *Morton,* 405 U.S. 727 (1972).

2. See Louis Jaffe, "Book Review," *Yale Law Journal,* vol. 65 (1955), pp. 1068 and 1071. As Professor Jaffe elsewhere points out, the phenomenon is "much less a disease of certain administrations than a condition endemic in any agency or set of agencies which seek to perform such a task [of regulating an industry]." See Louis Jaffe, "The Effective Limits of the Administrative Process: A Re-evaluation," *Harvard Law Review,* vol. 67 (1954), pp. 1105 and 1113–1119.

3. Indeed, if one were to base this upon a mere nose count to see which was the "special" interest and which was the "public" interest, it is apparent that the wilderness proponents would merit the epithet of special interest even more than would the various other groups.

4. See Nelson M. McGeary, *Gifford Pinchot: Forester–Politician* (Princeton: Princeton University Press, 1960), p. 87.

5. See Appendix C for a quantitative measure of the relative budget priorities. The priorities are indicated not so much by the amounts allocated to the respective functions as by the differences with respect to the percentage of the agency's request actually granted by the OMB and by Congress. Compare, for example, the increases for timber and wildlife, respectively. Note, too, that this does not take into account the prior scaling down of requests as a consequence of prior inability to obtain funds. Repeated failure to obtain a requested level of funding for a particular activity is likely to lead, eventually at least, to diminished expectations and, in turn, reduced requests in the future. It is probable that some of the requests in underfunded accounts reflect this. Note, for example, the rather dramatic reduction in requested appropriations for outdoor recreation, falling from a requested increase of approximately $32 million in 1967 to $3 million in 1971. Given the huge increases in outdoor recreation use the reduction of requests must reflect either the agency's conclusion that higher requests were futile or a direction from the department (or from the OMB) not to forward higher requests.

6. Samuel T. Dana and Evert Johnson, *Forestry Education in America: Today and Tomorrow* (Washington, D.C.: Society of American Foresters, 1963), p. 7.

7. See ibid., pp. 116–118, and 139 (curricula) and p. 142 (faculty staffing).

8. Ibid., pp. 5–6.

9. See William McWhinney, *The National Forest: Its Organization and Its Professionals* (Los Angeles: UCLA Graduate School of Business Administration, 1970), pp. 128–130. McWhinney notes that the agency has "begun a transition into a multidisciplined agency." In the sense that multidisciplined means an increased number of specialists with different skills, the Forest Service has for a long time been multidisciplined, as was indicated earlier. In the sense it means an increased percentage of professionals outside of the forestry career field, this too is true, as previously indicated. However, multidisciplined should not be read to imply that the forester is no longer dominant in those positions responsible for setting major policy. In fact, McWhinney appears to agree with my impressions that the generalist forester is still "dominant" in this latter sense.

10. Gifford Pinchot, *Breaking New Ground* (New York: Harcourt Brace, 1947), p. 283.

11. A study conducted in 1968 revealed that, for children of elementary school age, Smokey was the favorite among five selected cartoon characters which included: Pinocchio, Tony the Tiger, Bullwinkle, and the Jolly Green Giant. Among teen-agers and adults Smokey was more readily identified, and more favorably received, than, among others, the Bell System's symbol—a perhaps dubious but still noteworthy achievement. U.S. Department of Agriculture/Forest Service, *Public Image of and Attitudes Toward Smokey the Bear and Forest Fires* (1968), pp. 7–14.

12. Anthony Downs, *Inside Bureaucracy* (Boston: Little, Brown, 1967), pp. 29–30.

13. Quoted in Kenneth P. Davis, et al., *Federal Public Land Laws and Policies Relating to Multiple Use of Public Lands*, Study for the Public Land Law Review Commission (Springfield, Ill.: Clearinghouse for Federal Scientific and Technical Publications, 1970), p. 50.

14. See generally, E. Mishan, *Cost-Benefit Analysis* (New York: Praeger, 1971); and Roland McKean, *Efficiency in Government Through Systems Analysis* (New York: Wiley, 1958).

15. National forests now have or will soon have computer terminal facilities linked, in turn, to regional and national computers.

16. Data supplied by the Forest Service. Most of the other eighteen are in Experimental Forestry. It should be noted that there are others who have economic training even though they are not professional economists. For example, the service has some forty-seven management analysts, who presumably have some economic training.

17. The amount, of course, is a crude generalization since most of the resources used are not priced. However, there can be doubt that, by even the most conservative of horseback estimates the value is over a billion. Receipts for priced resources alone were nearly a half billion dollars in 1973. See U.S. Department of Agriculture/Forest Service, *1972-73 Annual Report*, p. 53.

18. A possible third function, more or less converse to the above two, would be that of enabling the *agency* to explain and justify its programs to the public (through the participants in its processes). This is not a common justification of public participation; indeed, so far as I am aware it is one never specifically and clearly articulated. However, it is my impression that many within the Forest Service conceive this to be an important product of public involvement. There is no reason why it should not be so regarded, on the reasonable assumption that learning understanding should be a two-way process.

19. Mainly for its unnecessary complexity and vagueness. See 36 C.F.R., § 211.20-.37. Thus, the distinction between a Class-one appeal (from decisions raising issues relating to a breach of the terms of a written instrument) and a Class-two appeal (from decisions having effect on the *enjoyment of use* under a written instrument) is a truly obscure one. Also, the meaning of a Class-three appeal ("appeals from other appealable decisions involving the administration and management of national forests which do not fall into Class One or Class Two") is something less than clear in not specifying what is an "appealable decision."

20. See generally, U.S. Department of Agriculture/Forest Service, *A Guide to Public Involvement in Decision Making* (1974).

21. In the course of developing a multiple-use plan for the Boundary Waters Canoe Area (BWCA) in Minnesota, public interest groups requested that public hearings be held in Chicago on the grounds that the BWCA receives a significant number of visitors from the Chicago area. Underlying this request was, of course, the reasonable assumption that those in Chicago—or those from out of state generally—would be more in favor of preservation-oriented restrictions because the cost of such restrictions would be, for them, negligible. For those within the state, and for those in the immediate locale particularly, the costs are plainly more substantial. For example, the loss in revenue (and thus the "cost" of the restriction) is in inverse proportion to the distance from the area. So, too, is the foregone enjoyment of motor vehicles, if these are restricted (the use of motors is predominantly a local or at least an in-state use).

The Forest Service in this case denied the request to hold hearings in Chicago. From the standpoint of obtaining useful factual information that refusal seems eminently sensible: there were cheaper ways of getting such information as Chicagoans were likely to produce. From the standpoint of recording the "vote" of wilderness visitors, the refusal is more troublesome, as a much stronger case can be made for allowing this group of distant visitors to record a "vote" at least as a sample of a special group of "interested persons." Of course, allowing the vote does not decide the question next raised, How much weight should be given the vote?

22. See Henry Clepper, *Professional Forestry in the United States* (Baltimore: Johns Hopkins University Press for Resources for the Future, 1971), p. 60; and Marion Clawson and Burnell Held, *The Federal Lands: Their Use and Management* (Baltimore: Johns Hopkins University Press for Resources for the Future, 1957), p. 367.

23. Ibid.

24. *Report of the Commission on Organization of the Executive Branch* (1949), p. 25. This followed the recommendation of the commission's task force on agriculture. A minority

of the commission opted for the recommendation of the Task Force on National Resources to create a new department of natural resources.

25. See President Nixon's State of the Union Message, January 20, 1972. The details are outlined in *Papers Relating to the President's Departmental Reorganization Program,* Part IV (February 1972). The proposal, part of a sweepingly ambitious proposed reorganization of the entire executive branch, is largely the product of recommendations of the President's Advisory Council on Executive Organization—the so-called Ash Council, named for its chairman, Roy Ash. Subsequently, a proposal for the natural resource department was altered to add to the proposed department certain governmental functions of managing and regulating energy. This later addition was an effort to add sex appeal to the proposal by capitalizing on the current excitement over the "energy crisis."

26. For example, outdoor recreation, shared by the Bureau of Outdoor Recreation, the National Park Service, the Bureau of Sports Fisheries and Wildlife, the Bureau of Reclamation—all in Interior—and several others not in Interior (e.g., the Corps of Engineers and TVA).

27. However, in the interest of clarity it is useful to distinguish between mere differences and direct conflict. Since most lands are managed by a single agency, inconsistent policies between agencies can exist without creating conflict between the agencies or seriously disrupting the functions of either. For example, the Forest Service and the BLM have different policies toward the use of sealed versus oral auction bidding in timber sales. Here is an inconsistency without a "conflict"; the two policies can be jointly pursued without jeopardizing either agency's timber-management programs. Occasionally, the different attitudes of the agencies can cause conflict which threatens the effective performance of the agency. For example, in the Mineral King controversy the Park Service's opposition to a winter ski resort, on Forest Service lands, has given rise to direct conflict insofar as it is in a position to block access to the area.

In drawing this distinction I do not mean to imply that inconsistency is of no consequence except when it ripens into conflict. The only point is to suggest that mere inconsistency is a far less serious problem where it does not impede the performance of agency functions.

28. Illustrative is the disparate treatment of revenues from timber sales on Forest Service and BLM lands, cited by the Hoover Commission as an example of the need for reorganization. As pointed out in Clawson and Held, *The Federal Lands,* p. 371, the example is an exceptionally poor one since organization has nothing to do with the disparity, but is part of the substantive law governing management of their respective lands. It is noteworthy that differences in the in-lieu-of-taxes return exists even within the national forest system. For example, a different formula (payment of three-fourths of 1 percent of the fair appraised value of the land)—yielding a higher than 25 percent return—is applied to the Superior National Forest in Minnesota under the Thye–Blatnik Act, 62 Stat. 568 (1948), 16 U.S.C., § 577g, on the rationale that, because so much of the federal land had been locked into wilderness, commercial revenues are unusually small in relation to the land base.

29. See Michael Frome, *The Forest Service* (New York: Praeger, 1971), p. 194. The *causus pacis* was a joint study for the future development and management of the North Cascades area in the State of Washington, in which both the Forest Service and the Park Service owned lands.

30. The degree of rivalry has been exaggerated by critics, by journalists, and innocent but gullible readers of political gossip. Consider, for example, the statement by Senator Moss, in 1967, that rivalry between Forest Service and Park Service field personnel over a then-proposed North Cascades National Park almost resulted in "bitter bloodshed." See U.S. Congress, Senate Subcommittee of the Committee on Government Operations, *Hearings, Redesignate the Department of Interior as the Department of Natural Resources,* 90 Cong., 1 sess., 1967, p. 123. However, as Moss himself concedes, the North Cascades was an extreme situation. It can scarcely be cited as a representative example. For a contrasting view to that of Moss, see, William Everhart, *The National Park Service* (New York: Praeger, 1972), p. 182.

31. Clawson and Held, *The Federal Lands,* pp. 372–373.

32. John R. Hicks, "Annual Survey in Economic Theory: The Theory of Monopoly," *Econometrica* vol. 3 (1935), pp. 1 and 3. Hicks' dictum about lethargy or monopolistic enter-

prises has not gone undebated. For a recent exchange of views, see Schwartzman, "Competition and Efficiency: Comment," *Journal of Political Economy*, vol. 81 (1973), p. 756; and Harvey Leibenstein, "Competition and X-Efficiency: Reply," ibid., p. 765.

33. See Somers, "The President, The Congress and The Federal Government Service," in *The Federal Government Service* (2d ed., New York: Columbia University Press, 1965), pp. 70 and 87. See also William Niskanen, *Bureaucracy and Representative Bureaucracy* (Chicago: Aldine–Atherton, 1971), ch. 15, for a rather elaborate analysis of the respective efficiency of competition and monopoly from the perspective of legislative appropriations and cost minimizing incentives.

Appendix A

NATIONAL
FOREST
SYSTEM
AREAS

Note: The tables in Appendix A are from the U.S. Department of Agriculture/Forest Service.

Table A–1.   Areas by Forest Service Regions, as of June 30, 1973

Region and unit	No. of units	Gross area within unit boundaries (acres)	National forest system lands (acres)	Other lands within unit boundaries		
				In the process of acquisition (acres)	Other (acres)	Total (acres)
United States and Puerto Rico	—	226,171,028	187,255,013	127,604	38,788,411	38,916,015
National forests	155	219,911,065	183,014,294	114,353	36,782,418	36,896,771
Purchase units	30	2,176,505	241,501	13,251	1,921,753	1,935,004
National grasslands	19	3,881,157	3,808,202	—	72,955	72,955
Land utilization projects	17	58,570	58,570	—	—	—
Research and experimental areas	26	131,767	120,501	—	11,266	11,266
Other areas	22	11,964	11,945	—	19	19
Division of the Above Between Forest Service Regions 1–6 and 10, Regions 8–9, and Puerto Rico						
Regions 1–6 and 10	—	179,579,494	163,488,539	35,845	16,055,110	16,090,955
National forests	104	175,448,516	159,578,989	35,845	15,833,682	15,869,527
Purchase units	4	150,930	3,617	—	147,313	147,313
National grasslands	17	3,843,077	3,770,122	—	72,955	72,955
Land utilization projects	5	20,640	20,640	—	—	—
Research and experimental areas	8	112,959	111,799	—	1,160	1,160
Other areas	10	3,372	3,372	—	—	—
Regions 8 and 9 and Puerto Rico	—	46,591,534	23,766,474	91,759	22,733,301	22,825,060
National forests	51	44,462,549	23,435,305	78,508	20,948,736	21,027,244
Purchase units	26	2,025,575	237,884	13,251	1,774,440	1,787,691
National grasslands	2	38,080	38,080	—	—	—
Land utilization projects	12	37,930	37,930	—	—	—
Research and experimental areas	18	18,808	8,702	—	10,106	10,106
Other areas	12	8,592	8,573	—	19	19

Table A-2. Areas by States, as of June 30, 1973

State	Unit	Gross area within unit boundaries (acres)	National forest system lands (acres)	Other lands within unit boundaries			Unit headquarters	Region
				In the process of acquisition (acres)	Other (acres)	Total (acres)		
Alabama								
William B.								
Bankhead	NF	348,917	179,224	—	169,693	169,693	Montgomery	8
Conecuh	NF	171,177	83,955	80	87,142	87,222	Montgomery	8
Talladega	NF	723,022	361,690	2,446	358,886	361,332	Montgomery	8
Tuskegee	NF	15,628	10,778	—	4,850	4,850	Montgomery	8
Total	NF	**1,258,744**	**635,647**	**2,526**	**620,571**	**623,097**		
Talladega	PU	12,159	768	—	11,391	11,391	Montgomery	8
State total		**1,270,903**	**636,415**	**2,526**	**631,962**	**634,488**		
Alaska								
Chugach	NF	4,733,904	4,717,179	—	16,725	16,725	Anchorage	10
Tongass	NF	16,043,477	16,000,057	—	43,420	43,420	Juneau and Ketchikan	10
State total		**20,777,381**	**20,717,236**	—	**60,145**	**60,145**		
Arizona								
Apache	NF	1,228,085	1,188,769	—	39,316	39,316	Springerville	3
Coconino	NF	2,010,773	1,834,797	—	175,976	175,976	Flagstaff	3
Coronado	NF	1,784,443	1,713,143	—	71,300	71,300	Tucson	3
Kaibab	NF	1,755,566	1,711,662	—	43,904	43,904	Williams	3
Prescott	NF	1,405,215	1,250,527	632	154,056	154,688	Prescott	3
Sitgreaves	NF	884,901	814,436	640	69,825	70,465	Holbrook	3
Tonto	NF	2,961,908	2,870,279	—	91,629	91,629	Phoenix	3
Total	NF	**12,030,891**	**11,383,613**	**1,272**	**646,006**	**647,278**		
Santa Rita	ER	52,163	51,003	—	1,160	1,160	Tucson	3
State total		**12,083,054**	**11,434,616**	**1,272**	**647,166**	**648,438**		

Abbreviations: EA, experimental area; EF, experimental forest; ER, experimental research area; LU, land utilization project; NF, national forest; NG, national grassland; and PU, purchase unit.

(*Continued*)

289

Table A-2. (Continued)

State	Unit	Gross area within unit boundaries (acres)	National forest system lands (acres)	In the process of acquisition (acres)	Other (acres)	Total (acres)	Unit headquarters	Region
					Other lands within unit boundaries			
Arkansas								
Ouachita	NF	1,961,275	1,329,739	752	630,784	631,536	Hot Springs National Park	8
Ozark	NF	1,488,917	1,107,048	2,483	379,386	381,869	Russellville	8
St. Francis	NF	29,607	20,843	103	8,661	8,764	Russellville	8
Total	**NF**	**3,479,799**	**2,457,630**	**3,338**	**1,018,831**	**1,022,169**		
Ozark	PU	12,862	517	—	12,345	12,345	Russellville	8
Crossett Exp. Forest	EF	1,675	1,675	—	—	—	Crossett	8
Other areas		160	160	—	—	—	Hot Springs National Park and Russell-ville	8
State total		**3,494,496**	**2,459,982**	**3,338**	**1,031,176**	**1,034,514**		
California								
Angeles	NF	691,054	649,786	273	40,995	41,268	Pasadena	5
Calaveras Bigtree	NF	380	380	—	—	—	Sonora	5
Cleveland	NF	566,913	393,993	324	172,596	172,920	San Diego	5
Eldorado	NF	884,824	664,849	533	219,442	219,975	Placerville	5
Inyo	NF	1,828,486	1,776,924	—	51,562	51,562	Bishop	5
Klamath	NF	1,892,458	1,671,073	26	221,359	221,385	Yreka	5
Lassen	NF	1,372,590	1,056,039	1,293	315,258	316,551	Susanville	5
Los Padres	NF	1,964,390	1,750,229	300	213,861	214,161	Santa Barbara	5
Mendocino	NF	1,079,463	873,302	3,147	203,014	206,161	Willows	5
Modoc	NF	1,979,418	1,633,149	—	346,269	346,269	Alturas	5
Plumas	NF	1,412,015	1,152,114	121	259,780	259,901	Quincy	5
Rogue River	NF	61,031	53,840	—	7,191	7,191	Medford, Oreg.	6
San Bernardino	NF	812,633	625,464	2,530	184,639	187,169	San Bernardino	5

Sequoia	NF	1,180,794	1,119,487	—	61,307	61,307	Porterville	5
Shasta	NF	1,645,009	1,026,329	2,114	616,566	618,680	Redding	5
Sierra	NF	1,395,553	1,285,431	—	110,122	110,122	Fresno	5
Siskiyou	NF	39,918	33,604	—	6,314	6,314	Grants Pass, Oreg.	6
Six Rivers	NF	1,112,865	968,745	—	144,120	144,120	Eureka	5
Stanislaus	NF	1,089,967	895,894	40	194,033	194,073	Sonora	5
Tahoe	NF	1,198,967	747,472	—	451,500	451,500	Nevada City	5
Toiyabe	NF	696,049	633,397	—	62,652	62,652	Reno, Nev.	4
Trinity	NF	1,176,992	1,036,603	172	140,217	140,389	Redding	5
Total	NF	**24,081,774**	**20,048,104**	**10,873**	**4,022,797**	**4,033,670**		
Northern Redwood	NF	147,179	2,005	—	145,174	145,174	Eureka	5
Butte Valley CF-22	PU	18,315	18,315	—	—	—	Yreka	5
San Joaquin								
Pasture CF-21	LU	800	800	—	—	—	Porterville	5
San Joaquin	ER	4,580	4,580	—	—	—	O'Neals	5
Institute of Forest								
Genetics	EA	187	187	—	—	—	Placerville	5
Fire Research Lab	EA	9	9	—	—	—	Riverside	5
Other areas	EA	51	51	—	—	—	San Francisco	5
State total	NF	**24,252,895**	**20,074,051**	**10,873**	**4,167,971**	**4,178,844**		
Colorado								
Arapaho	NF	1,090,037	993,448	—	96,589	96,589	Golden	2
Grand Mesa	NF	351,628	346,143	—	5,485	5,485	Delta	2
Gunnison	NF	1,768,139	1,663,269	—	104,870	104,870	Gunnison	2
Manti-LaSal	NF	27,145	27,105	—	40	40	Price, Utah	4
Pike	NF	1,283,373	1,104,851	—	178,522	178,522	Colorado Springs	2
Rio Grande	NF	1,961,789	1,850,213	—	111,576	111,576	Monte Vista	2
Roosevelt	NF	1,082,425	781,642	—	300,783	300,783	Fort Collins	2
Routt	NF	1,247,628	1,125,145	42	122,441	122,483	Steamboat Springs	2
San Isabel	NF	1,240,820	1,107,291	—	133,529	133,529	Pueblo	2
San Juan	NF	2,101,381	1,866,920	—	234,461	234,461	Durango	2
Uncompahgre	NF	1,044,027	943,525	280	100,222	100,502	Delta	2
White River	NF	2,051,369	1,939,348	—	112,021	112,021	Glenwood Springs	2
Total	NF	**15,249,761**	**13,748,900**	**322**	**1,500,539**	**1,500,861**		

Abbreviations: EA, experimental area; EF, experimental forest; ER, experimental research area; LU, land utilization project; NF, national forest; NG, national grassland; and PU, purchase unit.

(*Continued*)

291

Table A-2. *(Continued)*

State	Unit	Gross area within unit boundaries (acres)	National forest system lands (acres)	Other lands within unit boundaries			Unit headquarters	Region
				In the process of acquisition (acres)	Other (acres)	Total (acres)		
Comanche	NG	419,093	419,093	—	—	—	Pueblo	2
Pawnee	NG	193,060	193,060	—	—	—	Fort Collins	2
Fountain Creek CO-2	LU	560	560	—	—	—	Colorado Springs	2
State total		**15,862,474**	**14,361,613**	**322**	**1,500,539**	**1,500,861**		
Connecticut								
Forest Insect and Disease Lab	EA	10	10	—	—	—	Hamden	9
State total		**10**	**10**	**—**	**—**	**—**		
Florida								
Apalachicola	NF	632,588	557,446	323	74,819	75,142	Tallahassee	8
Ocala	NF	430,349	366,899	299	63,151	63,450	Tallahassee	8
Osceola	NF	161,814	157,231	—	4,583	4,583	Tallahassee	8
Total	**NF**	**1,224,751**	**1,081,576**	**622**	**142,553**	**143,175**		
Ocala	PU	29	29	—	—	—	Tallahassee	8
Forest Resources Lab	EA	10	10	—	—	—	Lehigh Acres	8
State total		**1,224,790**	**1,081,615**	**622**	**142,553**	**143,175**		
Georgia								
Chattahoochee	NF	1,569,827	737,522	7,064	825,241	832,305	Gainesville	8
Oconee	NF	261,645	103,808	511	157,326	157,837	Gainesville	8
Total	**NF**	**1,831,472**	**841,330**	**7,575**	**982,567**	**990,142**		

Chattahoochee	PU	71,088	1,786	—	69,302	69,302	Gainesville	8
Oconee	PU	531	466	—	65	65	Gainesville	8
Lakeland Flatwoods GA-21	LU	9,340	9,340	—	—	—	Gainesville	8
Forest Sciences Lab	EA	4	4	—	—	—	Athens	8
State total		**1,912,435**	**852,926**	**7,575**	**1,051,934**	**1,059,509**		
Idaho								
Bitterroot[a]	NF	461,034	460,812	—	222	222	Hamilton, Mont.	1
Boise	NF	2,958,356	2,642,453	—	315,903	315,903	Boise	4
Cache[a]	NF	264,442	263,942	—	500	500	Logan, Utah	4
Caribou[a]	NF	1,067,404	972,626	—	94,778	94,778	Pocatello	4
Challis	NF	2,471,536	2,451,246	2	20,288	20,290	Challis	4
Clearwater	NF	1,753,738	1,675,471	2,560	75,707	78,267	Orofino	1
Coeur d'Alene	NF	801,314	723,516	—	77,798	77,798	Coeur d'Alene	1
Kaniksu[a]	NF	1,059,912	892,250	156	167,506	167,662	Sandpoint	1
Kootenai[a]	NF	46,395	46,395	—			Libby, Mont.	1
Nezperce	NF	2,241,105	2,198,492	—	42,613	42,613	Grangeville	1
Payette	NF	2,419,809	2,307,355	—	112,454	112,454	McCall	4
St. Joe	NF	1,075,666	862,918	5,304	207,444	212,748	St. Maries	1
Salmon	NF	1,793,551	1,769,824	—	23,727	23,727	Salmon	4
Sawtooth[a]	NF	1,782,266	1,721,155	—	61,111	61,111	Twin Falls	4
Targhee[a]	NF	1,355,220	1,311,635	—	43,585	43,585	St. Anthony	4
Total	NF	**21,551,748**	**20,300,090**	**8,022**	**1,243,636**	**1,251,658**		
Curlew	NG	75,245	47,659	—	27,586	27,586	Pocatello	4
State total		**21,626,993**	**20,347,749**	**8,022**	**1,271,222**	**1,279,244**		
Illinois								
Shawnee	NF	714,644	243,564	981	470,099	471,080	Harrisburg	9
Shawnee	PU	125,081	7,230	—	117,851	117,851	Harrisburg	9
Other areas		10	10	—	—	—	Harrisburg	9
State total		**839,735**	**250,804**	**981**	**587,950**	**588,931**		

a Unit is in two or more states: total area on pages 307 and 308.

Abbreviations: EA, experimental area; EF, experimental forest; ER, experimental research area; LU, land utilization project; NF, national forest; NG, national grassland; and PU, purchase unit.

(Continued)

Table A-2. (Continued)

State	Unit	Gross area within unit boundaries (acres)	National forest system lands (acres)	Other lands within unit boundaries			Unit headquarters	Region
				In the process of acquisition (acres)	Other (acres)	Total (acres)		
Indiana								
Hoosier	NF	645,042	172,177	4,204	468,661	472,865	Bedford	9
Hoosier	PU	82	82	—	—	—	Bedford	9
White River-Martin County IN-21	LU	324	324	—	—	—	Bedford	9
Other areas		626	626	—	—	—	Bedford	9
State total		**646,074**	**173,209**	**4,204**	**468,661**	**472,865**		
Iowa								
Southern Iowa IA-2	LU	360	360	—	—	—	Milwaukee, Wisc.	9
State total		**360**	**360**	**—**	**—**	**—**		
Kansas								
Cimarron	NG	107,700	107,700	—	—	—	Pueblo, Colo.	2
Independence Shelterbelt Research Site	EA	206	206	—	—	—	Fort Collins	2
State total		**107,906**	**107,906**	**—**	**—**	**—**		
Kentucky								
Daniel Boone	NF	1,357,089	514,605	9,026	833,458	842,484	Winchester	8
Jefferson[a]	NF	54,614	961	—	53,653	53,653	Roanoke, Virginia	8
Total	NF	**1,411,703**	**515,566**	**9,026**	**887,111**	**896,137**		

Redbird	PU	687,061	110,302	13,251	563,508	576,759	Winchester	8
Other areas		89	89	—	—	—	Winchester	8
State total		**2,098,853**	**625,957**	**22,277**	**1,450,619**	**1,472,896**		
Louisiana								
Kisatchie	NF	1,017,288	595,175	960	421,153	422,113	Alexandria	8
Kisatchie	PU	40	40	—	—	—	Alexandria	8
State total		**1,017,328**	**595,215**	**960**	**421,153**	**422,113**		
Maine								
White Mountain[a]	NF	53,561	40,563	—	12,998	12,998	Laconia, N.H.	9
White Mountain[a]	PU	27,755	5,381	—	22,374	22,374	Laconia, N.H.	9
Southern Maine ME-21	LU	465	465	—	—	—	Laconia, N.H.	9
Northeastern Forest Exp. Station	EF	11,977	3,694	—	8,283	8,283	Upper Darby, Pa.	9
State total		**93,758**	**50,103**	**—**	**43,655**	**43,655**		
Michigan								
Hiawatha	NF	1,281,668	862,648	5,711	413,309	419,020	Escanaba	9
Huron	NF	694,097	416,795	330	276,972	277,302	Cadillac	9
Manistee	NF	1,331,585	495,024	1,578	834,983	836,561	Cadillac	9
Ottawa	NF	1,559,891	915,417	80	644,394	644,474	Ironwood	9
Total	NF	**4,867,241**	**2,689,884**	**7,699**	**2,169,658**	**2,177,357**		
Alpena S.F.	PU	1,240	1,240	—	—	—	Cadillac	9
Fife Lake S.F.	PU	240	240	—	—	—	Cadillac	9
AuSable Adm. Site MI-2	LU	2	2	—	—	—	Cadillac	9
N. Muskegon Sand Dunes MI-21	LU	437	437	—	—	—	Cadillac	9

[a] Unit is in two or more states: total area on page 308.

Abbreviations: EA, experimental area; EF, experimental forest; ER, experimental research area; LU, land utilization project; NF, national forest; NG, national grassland; and PU, purchase unit.

(*Continued*)

295

Table A-2. (Continued)

State	Unit	Gross area within unit boundaries (acres)	National forest system lands (acres)	Other lands within unit boundaries			Unit headquarters	Region
				In the process of acquisition (acres)	Other (acres)	Total (acres)		
S. Muskegon Sand Dunes MI-22	LU	600	600	—	—	—	Cadillac	9
W. Ottawa Sand Dunes MI-23	LU	39	39	—	—	—	Cadillac	9
Northern Hardwoods Lab	EA	7	7	—	—	—	Marquette	9
State total		**4,870,859**	**2,693,502**	**7,699**	**2,169,658**	**2,177,357**		
Minnesota								
Chippewa	NF	1,599,599	649,954	2,166	947,479	949,645	Cass Lake	9
Superior	NF	3,305,780	2,055,527	157	1,250,096	1,250,253	Duluth	9
Total Superior	NF	**4,905,379**	**2,705,481**	**2,323**	**2,197,575**	**2,199,898**	Duluth	9
	PU	705,952	91,568	—	614,384	614,384		
State total		**5,611,331**	**2,797,049**	**2,323**	**2,811,959**	**2,814,282**		
Mississippi								
Bienville	NF	382,821	176,978	318	205,525	205,843	Jackson	8
Delta	NF	118,200	59,159	—	59,041	59,041	Jackson	8
DeSoto	NF	796,369	499,663	197	296,509	296,706	Jackson	8
Holly Springs	NF	519,952	145,025	—	374,927	374,927	Jackson	8
Homochitto	NF	373,497	189,079	120	184,298	184,418	Jackson	8
Tombigbee	NF	119,155	65,284	—	53,871	53,871	Jackson	8
Total DeSoto	NF	**2,309,994**	**1,135,188**	**635**	**1,174,171**	**1,174,806**	Jackson	8
	PU	280	280	—	—	—		
Forestry Sciences Lab	EA	10	10	—	—	—	Gulfport	8

Unit	Type	Location						
Forest Hydro. Lab	EA	Oxford	8	15	15	—	—	—
Forestry Sciences Lab	EA	State College	8	7	7	—	—	—
Southern Hardwoods Lab	EA	Stoneville	8	3	3	—	—	—
Other areas	EA	Jackson	8	1,245	1,226	635	19	19
State total				**2,311,554**	**1,136,729**	**635**	**1,174,190**	**1,174,825**
Missouri								
Clark	NF	Rolla	9	1,744,725	802,486	585	941,654	942,239
Mark Twain	NF	Springfield	9	1,198,753	628,235	1,952	568,566	570,518
Total	NF			**2,943,478**	**1,430,721**	**2,537**	**1,510,220**	**1,512,757**
Cedar Creek	PU	Rolla	9	77,064	—	—	77,064	77,064
Mark Twain	PU	Springfield	9	48,129	765	—	47,364	47,364
Cedar Creek MO-21	LU	Rolla	9	12,944	12,944	—	—	—
State total				**3,081,615**	**1,444,430**	**2,537**	**1,634,648**	**1,637,185**
Montana								
Beaverhead	NF	Dillon	1	2,196,102	2,113,397	—	82,705	82,705
Bitterroot[a]	NF	Hamilton	1	1,189,469	1,115,083	—	74,386	74,386
Custer[a]	NF	Billings	1	1,200,400	1,113,711	—	86,689	86,689
Deerlodge	NF	Butte	1	1,353,685	1,176,321	99	177,265	177,364
Flathead	NF	Kalispell	1	2,626,860	2,364,614	—	262,246	262,246
Gallatin	NF	Bozeman	1	2,135,641	1,714,921	40	420,680	420,720
Helena	NF	Helena	1	1,159,339	969,053	—	190,286	190,286
Kaniksu[a]	NF	Sandpoint, Idaho	1	491,856	446,966	—	44,890	44,890
Kootenai[a]	NF	Libby	1	2,093,629	1,767,335	13	326,281	326,294
Lewis and Clark	NF	Great Falls	1	2,001,695	1,835,264	—	166,431	166,431
Lolo	NF	Missoula	1	2,614,867	2,089,673	—	525,194	525,194
Total	NF			**19,063,543**	**16,706,338**	**152**	**2,357,053**	**2,357,205**
Other areas	NF	Missoula	1	158	158	—	—	—
State total				**19,063,701**	**16,706,496**	**152**	**2,357,053**	**2,357,205**

[a] Unit is in two or more states: total area on page 307.

Abbreviations: EA, experimental area; EF, experimental forest; ER, experimental research area; LU, land utilization project; NF, national forest; NG, national grassland; and PU, purchase unit.

(Continued)

Table A-2. (Continued)

State	Unit	Gross area within unit boundaries (acres)	National forest system lands (acres)	Other lands within unit boundaries			Unit headquarters	Region
				In the process of acquisition (acres)	Other (acres)	Total (acres)		
Nebraska								
Samuel R. McKelvie	NF	116,819	115,703	—	1,116	1,116	Chadron	2
Nebraska	NF	229,592	140,771	—	88,821	88,821	Chadron	2
Total	NF	**346,411**	**256,474**	—	**89,937**	**89,937**	Chadron	
Oglala	NG	94,344	94,344	—	—	—	Chadron	2
Hastings Shelterbelt Research Site	EA	144	144	—	—	—	Fort Collins	2
State total		**440,899**	**350,962**	—	**89,937**	**89,937**		
Nevada								
Eldorado[a]	NF	53	53	—	—	—	Placerville, Calif.	5
Humboldt	NF	2,680,333	2,528,076	—	152,257	152,257	Elko	4
Inyo[a]	NF	62,348	60,576	—	1,772	1,772	Bishop, Calif.	5
Toiyabe[a]	NF	2,690,331	2,521,922	536	167,873	168,409	Reno	4
State total		**5,433,065**	**5,110,627**	**536**	**321,902**	**322,438**		
New Hampshire								
White Mountain[a]	NF	798,305	679,099	86	119,120	119,206	Laconia	9
White Mountain[a]	PU	6,839	4,155	—	2,684	2,684	Laconia	9
State total		**805,144**	**683,254**	**86**	**121,804**	**121,890**		
New Mexico								
Apache[a]	NF	650,031	616,328	—	33,703	33,703	Springerville, Ariz.	3
Carson	NF	1,491,500	1,391,263	304	99,933	100,237	Taos	3

Cibola	NF	2,110,357	1,621,731	—	488,626	488,626	Albuquerque	3
Coronado[a]	NF	71,541	68,936	—	2,605	2,605	Tucson, Ariz.	3
Gila	NF	2,797,617	2,704,710	13	92,894	92,907	Silver City	3
Lincoln	NF	1,271,069	1,103,270	—	167,799	167,799	Alamogordo	3
Santa Fe	NF	1,718,805	1,580,704	12	138,089	138,101	Santa Fe	3
Total	**NF**	**10,110,920**	**9,086,942**	**329**	**1,023,649**	**1,023,978**		
Kiowa	NG	136,505	136,505	—	—	—	Amarillo, Tex.	3
Cuba-Rio Puerco NM-22	LU	240	240	—	—	—	Santa Fe	3
Other areas		3,163	3,163	—	—	—	Albuquerque and Santa Fe	3
State total		**10,250,828**	**9,226,850**	**329**	**1,023,649**	**1,023,978**		
New York Hector NY-21	LU	13,259	13,259	—	—	—	Rutland, Vt.	9
State total		**13,259**	**13,259**					
North Carolina Cherokee[a]	NF	327	327	—	—	—	Cleveland, Tenn.	8
Croatan	NF	308,226	156,589	—	151,637	151,637	Asheville	8
Nantahala	NF	1,349,000	451,377	1,678	895,945	897,623	Asheville	8
Pisgah	NF	1,076,511	482,312	436	593,763	594,199	Asheville	8
Uwharrie	NF	220,202	45,747	88	174,367	174,455	Asheville	8
Total	**NF**	**2,954,266**	**1,136,352**	**2,202**	**1,815,712**	**1,817,914**		
Nantahala	PU	17,027	737	—	16,290	16,290	Asheville	8
Yadkin	PU	194,496	—	—	194,496	194,496	Asheville	8
Forestry Sciences Lab	EA	27	27	—	—	—	Research Triangle Park	8
Other areas		8	8	—	—	—	Asheville	8
State total		**3,165,824**	**1,137,124**	**2,202**	**2,026,498**	**2,028,700**		

[a] Unit is in two or more states; total area is on pages 307 and 308.
Abbreviations: EA, experimental area; EF, experimental forest; ER, experimental research area; LU, land utilization project; NF, national forest; NG, national grassland; and PU, purchase unit.

Table A–2. *(Continued)*

State	Unit	Gross area within unit boundaries (acres)	National forest system lands (acres)	Other lands within unit boundaries			Unit headquarters	Region
				In the process of acquisition (acres)	Other (acres)	Total (acres)		
North Dakota								
Cedar River	NG	6,717	6,717	—	—	—	Billings, Mont.	1
Little Missouri	NG	1,027,732	1,027,732	—	—	—	Billings, Mont.	1
Sheyenne	NG	70,340	70,340	—	—	—	Billings, Mont.	1
Denbigh	EF	40	40	—	—	—	Bottineau	1
Denbigh	PU	600	596	—	4	4	Bottineau	1
Souris	PU	160	160	—	—	—	Billings, Mont.	1
State total		**1,105,589**	**1,105,585**	**—**	**4**	**4**		
Ohio								
Wayne	NF	833,094	159,401	2,483	671,210	673,693	Bedford, Ind.	9
Wayne	NF	216	216	—	—	—	Bedford, Ind.	9
Forest Insect and Disease Lab	EA	248	248	—	—	—	Delaware	9
Other areas		8	8	—	—	—	Bedford, Ind.	9
State total		**833,566**	**159,873**	**2,483**	**671,210**	**673,693**		
Oklahoma								
Ouachita[a]	NF	412,912	244,384	—	168,528	168,528	Hot Springs National Park, Ark.	8
Black Kettle[a]	NG	31,488	31,119	—	369	369	Amarillo, Tex.	3
Rita Blanca[a]	NG	15,639	15,639	—	—	—	Amarillo, Tex.	3
State total		**460,039**	**291,142**	**—**	**168,897**	**168,897**		

Oregon								
Deschutes	NF	1,852,410	—	1,600,559	251,851	251,851	Bend	6
Fremont	NF	1,709,468	880	1,194,710	513,878	514,758	Lakeview	6
Klamath[a]	NF	26,564	—	25,384	1,180	1,180	Yreka, Calif.	5
Malheur	NF	1,540,351	—	1,457,457	82,894	82,894	John Day	6
Mt. Hood	NF	1,108,273	—	1,059,240	49,033	49,033	Portland	6
Ochoco	NF	981,810	—	846,855	134,955	134,955	Prineville	6
Rogue River[a]	NF	633,322	3,847	580,376	49,099	52,946	Medford	6
Siskiyou[a]	NF	1,123,830	854	1,057,260	65,716	66,570	Grants Pass	6
Siuslaw	NF	831,081	94	622,396	208,591	208,685	Corvallis	6
Umatilla[a]	NF	1,189,151	—	1,079,074	110,077	110,077	Pendleton	6
Umpqua	NF	1,033,497	—	987,349	46,148	46,148	Roseburg	6
Wallowa	NF	1,071,608	8,109	982,037	81,462	89,571	Baker	6
Whitman	NF	1,308,347	—	1,264,731	43,616	43,616	Baker	6
Willamette	NF	1,787,821	—	1,667,821	120,000	120,000	Eugene	6
Winema	NF	957,816	—	907,929	49,887	49,887	Klamath Falls	6
Total	NF	**17,155,349**	**13,784**	**15,333,178**	**1,808,387**	**1,822,171**		
Yachats	PU	2,991	—	856	2,135	2,135	Corvallis	6
Crooked River	NG	151,138	—	106,138	45,000	45,000	Prineville	6
State total		**17,309,478**	**13,784**	**15,440,172**	**1,855,522**	**1,869,306**		
Pennsylvania								
Allegheny	NF	742,693	6,615	498,925	237,153	243,768	Warren	9
Office Lab Site	EA	7	—	7	—	—	Radnor	9
Other areas		102	—	102	—	—	Washington, D.C.	9
State total		**742,802**	**6,615**	**499,034**	**237,153**	**243,768**		
Puerto Rico								
Caribbean	NF	55,665	—	27,998	27,667	27,667	Rio Piedras	ITF
Total	NF	**55,665**	**—**	**27,998**	**27,667**	**27,667**		

[a] Unit is in two or more states; total area is on pages 307 and 308.
Abbreviations: EA, experimental area; EF, experimental forest; ER, experimental research area; LU, land utilization project; NF, national forest; NG, national grassland; and PU, purchase unit.

(*Continued*)

301

Table A–2. *(Continued)*

State	Unit	Gross area within unit boundaries (acres)	National forest system lands (acres)	Other lands within unit boundaries			Unit headquarters	Region
				In the process of acquisition (acres)	Other (acres)	Total (acres)		
South Carolina								
Francis Marion	NF	414,700	249,025	3,680	161,995	165,675	Columbia	8
Sumter	NF	959,741	349,441	2,764	607,536	610,300	Columbia	8
Total	NF	**1,374,441**	**598,466**	**6,444**	**769,531**	**775,975**		
Silviculture and Watershed Lab	EA	15	15	—	—	—	Charleston	8
Other areas		6,021	6,021	—	—	—	Columbia	8
State total		**1,380,477**	**604,502**	**6,444**	**769,531**	**775,975**		
South Dakota								
Black Hills	NF	1,327,066	1,048,914	—	278,152	278,152	Custer	2
Custer	NF	77,827	73,489	—	4,338	4,338	Billings, Mont.	1
Total	NF	**1,404,893**	**1,122,403**	—	**282,490**	**282,490**		
Buffalo Gap	NG	591,259	591,259	—	—	—	Chadron, Nebr.	2
Fort Pierre	NG	116,080	116,080	—	—	—	Chadron, Nebr.	2
Grand River	NG	155,210	155,210	—	—	—	Billings, Mont.	1
Total	NG	**862,549**	**862,549**	—	—	—		
State total		**2,267,442**	**1,984,952**	—	**282,490**	**282,490**		
Tennessee								
Cherokee	NF	1,203,789	616,596	436	586,757	587,193	Cleveland	8
Cherokee	PU	8,120	733	—	7,387	7,387	Cleveland	8
Other areas		323	323	—	—	—	Cleveland	8
State total		**1,212,232**	**617,652**	**436**	**594,144**	**594,580**		

Texas								
Angelina	NF	391,300	154,703	605	235,992	236,597	Lufkin	8
Davy Crockett	NF	394,200	161,478	—	232,722	232,722	Lufkin	8
Sabine	NF	439,667	186,689	—	252,978	252,978	Lufkin	8
Sam Houston	NF	491,800	158,410	—	333,390	333,390	Lufkin	8
Total	**NF**	**1,716,967**	**661,280**	**605**	**1,055,082**	**1,055,687**		
Sabine	PU	500	500	—	—	—	Lufkin	8
Black Kettle	NG	576	576	—	—	—	Amarillo	3
Caddo	NG	17,729	17,729	—	—	—	Lufkin	8
Cross Timbers	NG	20,351	20,351	—	—	—	Lufkin	8
McClellan Creek	NG	1,449	1,449	—	—	—	Amarillo	3
Rita Blanca	NG	77,183	77,183	—	—	—	Amarillo	3
Total	**NG**	**117,288**	**117,288**	—				
State total		**1,834,755**	**779,068**	**605**	**1,055,082**	**1,055,687**		
Utah								
Ashley	NF	1,300,636	1,288,150	—	12,486	12,486	Vernal	4
Cache	NF	954,097	415,288	—	538,809	538,809	Logan	4
Caribou	NF	8,940	6,955	—	1,985	1,985	Pocatello, Idaho	4
Dixie	NF	1,967,263	1,885,660	—	81,603	81,603	Cedar City	4
Fishlake	NF	1,530,835	1,429,041	—	101,794	101,794	Richfield	4
Manti–LaSal	NF	1,310,717	1,238,151	—	72,566	72,566	Price	4
Sawtooth	NF	92,404	71,183	—	21,221	21,221	Twin Falls, Idaho	4
Uinta	NF	889,890	812,566	414	76,910	77,324	Provo	4
Wasatch	NF	1,024,320	848,371	—	175,949	175,949	Salt Lake City	4
Total	**NF**	**9,079,102**	**7,995,365**	**414**	**1,083,323**	**1,083,737**		
Desert Range Exp. Station	ER	55,630	55,630	—	—	—	Milford	4
State total		**9,134,732**	**8,050,995**	**414**	**1,083,323**	**1,083,737**		

Abbreviations: EA, experimental area; EF, experimental forest; ER, experimental research area; LU, land utilization project; NF, national forest; NG, national grassland; and PU, purchase unit.

(Continued)

303

Table A-2. (Continued)

State	Unit	Gross area within unit boundaries (acres)	National forest system lands (acres)	In the process of acquisition (acres)	Other (acres)	Total (acres)	Unit headquarters	Region
							Other lands within unit boundaries	
Vermont								
Green Mountain	NF	629,019	245,581	9,614	373,824	383,438	Rutland	9
Green Mountain	PU	499	499	—	—	—	Rutland	9
State total		**629,518**	**246,080**	**9,614**	**373,824**	**383,438**		
Virgin Islands								
Estate Thomas	EF	147	147	—	—	—	St. Croix	ITF
State total		**147**	**147**					
Virginia								
George Washington	NF	1,636,862	933,636	1,064	702,162	703,226	Harrisonburg	8
Jefferson	NF	1,584,960	649,822	1,175	933,963	935,138	Roanoke	8
Total		**3,221,822**	**1,583,458**	**2,239**	**1,636,125**	**1,638,364**		
George Washington	PU	1,911	1,911	—	—	—	Harrisonburg	8
Jefferson	PU	2,629	1,354	—	1,275	1,275	Roanoke	8
Lee Experimental Forest	EF	4,512	2,689	—	1,823	1,823	Enonville	8
State total		**3,230,874**	**1,589,412**	**2,239**	**1,639,223**	**1,641,462**		
Washington								
Colville	NF	1,019,860	943,793	84	75,983	76,067	Colville	1
Gifford Pinchot	NF	1,362,510	1,251,031	—	111,479	111,479	Vancouver	6
Kaniksu	NF	294,617	283,130	—	11,487	11,487	Sandpoint, Idaho	1
Mount Baker	NF	1,312,362	1,282,922	—	29,440	29,440	Bellingham	1

304

Okanogan	NF	1,537,340	1,499,429	—	37,911	37,911	Okanogan	6
Olympic	NF	717,199	651,347	—	65,852	65,852	Olympia	6
Snoqualmie	NF	1,555,916	1,229,754	—	326,162	326,162	Seattle	6
Umatilla	NF	319,419	311,267	—	8,152	8,152	Pendleton, Oreg.	6
Wenatchee	NF	1,902,515	1,614,468	—	288,047	288,047	Wenatchee	6
Total	NF	**10,021,738**	**9,067,141**	**84**	**954,513**	**954,597**		
Northeast Washington WA-2	LU	725	725	—	—	—	Colville and Sandpoint, Idaho	1
State total		**10,022,463**	**9,067,866**	**84**	**954,513**	**954,597**		
West Virginia								
George Washington	NF	157,568	100,422	—	57,146	57,146	Harrisonburg, Va.	8
Jefferson	NF	29,651	18,114	—	11,537	11,537	Roanoke, Va.	8
Monongahela	NF	1,647,146	829,740	5,278	812,128	817,406	Elkins	9
Total	NF	**1,834,365**	**948,276**	**5,278**	**880,811**	**886,089**		
Monongahela	PU	22,561	5,901	—	16,660	16,660	Elkins	9
Jefferson	PU	131	131	—	—	—	Roanoke, Va.	8
Forest Products Marketing Lab	EA	95	95	—	—	—	Princeton	9
State total		**1,857,152**	**954,403**	**5,278**	**897,471**	**902,749**		
Wisconsin								
Chequamegon	NF	1,049,236	839,598	—	209,638	209,638	Park Falls	9
Nicolet	NF	972,879	651,389	80	321,410	321,490	Rhinelander	9
Total	NF	**2,022,115**	**1,490,987**	**80**	**531,048**	**531,128**		
Crandon WI-4	LU	120	120	—	—	—	Rhinelander	9
Wisconsin Isolated Settler WI-21	LU	40	40	—	—	—	Rhinelander	9

Abbreviations: EA, experimental area; EF, experimental forest; ER, experimental research area; LU, land utilization project; NF, national forest; NG, national grassland; and PU, purchase unit.

(*Continued*)

305

Table A-2. (*Continued*)

State	Unit	Gross area within unit boundaries (acres)	National forest system lands (acres)	In the process of acquisition (acres)	Other (acres)	Total (acres)	Unit headquarters	Region
				Other lands within unit boundaries				
Forest Products Lab	EA	39	39	—	—	—	Madison	9
State total		**2,022,314**	**1,491,186**	**80**	**531,048**	**531,128**		
Wyoming								
Ashley	NF	104,701	95,517	—	9,184	9,184	Vernal, Utah	4
Bighorn	NF	1,115,125	1,107,342	—	7,783	7,783	Sheridan	2
Black Hills	NF	201,126	174,738	—	26,388	26,388	Custer, South Dak.	2
Bridger	NF	1,744,724	1,733,098	—	11,626	11,626	Kemmerer	4
Caribou	NF	9,614	7,913	—	1,701	1,701	Pocatello, Idaho	4
Medicine Bow	NF	1,401,944	1,093,155	57	308,732	308,789	Laramie	2
Shoshone	NF	2,464,927	2,431,948	—	32,979	32,979	Cody	2
Targhee	NF	333,204	330,783	—	2,421	2,421	St. Anthony, Idaho	4
Teton	NF	1,718,871	1,690,322	—	28,549	28,549	Jackson	4
Wasatch	NF	47,704	37,762	—	9,942	9,942	Salt Lake City, Utah	4
Total	NF	**9,141,940**	**8,702,578**	**57**	**439,305**	**439,362**		
Thunder Basin	NG	572,319	572,319	—	—	—	Laramie	2
State total		**9,714,259**	**9,274,897**	**57**	**439,305**	**439,362**		

Abbreviations: EA, experimental area; EF, experimental forest; ER, experimental research area; LU, land utilization project; NF, national forest; NG, national grassland; and PU, purchase unit.

Table A-3. Total Area of Units Extending into Two or More States, as of June 30, 1973

Unit	States	Gross area within unit boundaries (acres)	National Forest System lands (acres)	Other lands within unit boundaries		
				In the process of acquisition (acres)	Other (acres)	Total (acres)
National forests						
Ashley	Utah and Wyoming	1,405,337	1,383,667	—	21,670	21,670
Apache	Arizona and New Mexico	1,878,116	1,805,097	—	73,019	73,019
Bitterroot	Idaho and Montana	1,650,503	1,575,895	—	74,608	74,608
Black Hills	South Dakota and Wyoming	1,528,192	1,223,652	—	304,540	304,540
Cache	Idaho and Utah	1,218,539	679,230	—	539,309	539,309
Caribou	Idaho, Utah and Wyoming	1,085,958	987,494	—	98,464	98,464
Cherokee	North Carolina and Tennessee	1,204,116	616,923	436	586,757	587,193
Coronado	Arizona and New Mexico	1,855,984	1,782,079	—	73,905	73,905
Custer	Montana and South Dakota	1,278,227	1,187,200	—	91,027	91,027
Eldorado	California and Nevada	884,877	664,902	533	219,442	219,975
George Washington	Virginia and West Virginia	1,794,430	1,034,058	1,064	759,308	760,372
Inyo	California and Nevada	1,890,834	1,837,500	—	53,334	53,334
Jefferson	Kentucky, Virginia and West Virginia	1,669,225	668,897	1,175	999,153	1,000,328
Kaniksu	Idaho, Montana and Washington	1,846,385	1,622,346	156	223,883	224,039
Klamath	California and Oregon	1,919,022	1,696,457	26	222,539	222,565
Kootenai	Idaho and Montana	2,140,024	1,813,730	13	326,281	326,294

(*Continued*)

Table A-3. (Continued)

Unit	States	Gross area within unit boundaries (acres)	National Forest System lands (acres)	Other lands within unit boundaries		
				In the process of acquisition (acres)	Other (acres)	Total (acres)
Manti-LaSal	Colorado and Utah	1,337,862	1,265,256	—	72,606	72,606
Ouachita	Arkansas and Oklahoma	2,374,187	1,574,123	752	799,312	800,064
Rogue River	California and Oregon	694,353	634,216	3,847	56,290	60,137
Sawtooth	Idaho and Utah	1,874,670	1,792,338	—	82,332	82,332
Siskiyou	California and Oregon	1,163,748	1,090,864	854	72,030	72,884
Targhee	Idaho and Wyoming	1,688,424	1,642,418	—	46,006	46,006
Toiyabe	California and Nevada	3,386,380	3,155,319	536	230,525	231,061
Umatilla	Oregon and Washington	1,508,570	1,390,341	—	118,229	118,229
Wasatch	Utah and Wyoming	1,072,024	886,133	—	185,891	185,891
White Mountain	Maine and New Hampshire	851,866	719,662	86	132,118	132,204
Purchase units						
Jefferson	Virginia and West Virginia	2,760	1,485	—	1,275	1,275
White Mountain	Maine and New Hampshire	34,594	9,536	—	25,058	25,058
National grasslands						
Black Kettle	Oklahoma and Texas	32,064	31,695	—	369	369
Rita Blanca	Oklahoma and Texas	92,822	92,822	—	—	—

Table A–4. Areas of National Game Refuges in National Forests, as of June 30, 1973

Game refuge	National forest	State	Area inside national forests (acres)
Big Levels Game Refuge	George Washington	Virginia	31,725
Cherokee National Game Refuge No. 1	Cherokee	Tennessee	10,900
Francis Marion National Wildlife Preserve	Francis Marion	South Carolina	50,600
Grand Canyon National Game Preserve	Kaibab	Arizona	754,600
National Cataboula Wildlife Preserve	Kisatchie	Louisiana	36,117
National Red Dirt Wildlife Management Preserve	Kisatchie	Louisiana	40,082
Noontootly National Game Refuge	Chattahoochee	Georgia	24,670
Norbeck Wildlife Preserve	Black Hills	South Dakota	44,360
Ocala National Game Refuge	Ocala	Florida	79,396
Ouachita National Wildlife Preserve	Ouachita	Arkansas	78,000
Ouachita National Game Refuges			
No. 1 (Pigeon Creek)	Ouachita	Arkansas	8,440
No. 2 (Oak Mountain)	Ouachita	Arkansas	8,500
No. 4 (Caney Creek)	Ouachita	Arkansas	8,300
Ozark National Game Refuges			
No. 1 (Livingston)	Ozark	Arkansas	8,420
No. 2 (Barkshead)	Ozark	Arkansas	5,300
No. 3 (Moccasin)	Ozark	Arkansas	3,620
No. 4 (Haw Creek)	Ozark	Arkansas	4,160
No. 5 (Black Mountain)	Ozark	Arkansas	19,074
Pisgah National Game Preserve	Pisgah	North Carolina	97,408
Sequoia National Game Refuge	Sequoia	California	15,770
Sheep Mountain Game Refuge	Medicine Bow	Wyoming	28,318

Table A–5. National Recreation Areas in National Forests, as of June 30, 1973

State in which located	National forest(s)	National recreation area name	Areas of National Forest System lands (acres)	Total area of national recreation area (acres)
California	Shasta and Trinity	Whiskeytown–Shasta Trinity[a]	184,771	213,400
Idaho	Boise, Challis, and Sawtooth	Sawtooth	712,670	723,437
Oregon	Siuslaw	Oregon Dunes	21,216	32,348
Utah and Wyoming	Ashley	Flaming Gorge	184,844	196,054
Virginia	Jefferson	Mount Rogers	96,093	154,000
West Virginia	Monogahela	Spruce Knob–Seneca Rocks	47,606	100,000

[a] The National Park Service in the Department of the Interior administers an additional 37,816 acres as a separate (Whiskeytown) unit.

Table A–6. Wilderness Areas in National Forests, as of January 1, 1973

State and wilderness	National forest(s)	National Forest System lands (acres)	Other lands (acres)	Total area (acres)
Arizona				
Chiricahua	Coronado	18,000	—	18,000
Galiuro	Coronado	52,717	—	52,717
Mazatzal	Tonto	205,137	209	205,346
Mount Baldy	Apache	6,975	131	7,106
Pine Mountain	Prescott and Tonto	20,061	—	20,061
Sierra Ancha	Tonto	20,850	—	20,850
Superstition	Tonto	124,117	23	124,140
Sycamore Canyon	Coconino, Prescott, and Kaibab	47,757	5	47,762
State total		**495,614**	**368**	**495,982**
California				
Caribou	Lassen	19,080	—	19,080
Cucamonga	San Bernardino	9,022	—	9,022
Desolation	Eldorado	63,469	—	63,469
Dome Land	Sequoia	62,206	355	62,561
Hoover	Inyo and Toiyabe	47,916	21	47,937
John Muir	Inyo and Sierra	503,478	785	504,263
Marble Mountain	Klamath	213,363	1,180	214,543
Minarets	Inyo and Sierra	109,484	75	109,559
Mokelumne	Eldorado and Stanislaus	50,400	—	50,400
San Gabriel	Angeles	36,137	—	36,137
San Gorgonio	San Bernardino	34,644	74	34,718
San Jacinto	San Bernardino	20,564	1,391	21,955
San Rafael	Los Padres	142,722	196	142,918
South Warner	Modoc	68,507	1,040	69,547
Thousand Lakes	Lassen	15,695	640	16,335
Ventana	Los Padres	95,152	2,450	97,602
Yolla Bolly–Middle Eel	Mendocino, Shasta and Trinity	109,091	2,000	111,091
State total		**1,600,930**	**10,207**	**1,611,137**
Colorado				
La Garita	Gunnison and Rio Grande	48,486	—	48,486
Maroon Bells– Snowmass	White River	71,060	269	71,329
Mt. Zirkel	Routt	72,472	—	72,472
Rawah	Roosevelt	26,674	790	27,464
West Elk	Gunnison	61,412	—	61,412
State total		**280,104**	**1,059**	**281,163**

(*Continued*)

State and wilderness	National forest(s)	National Forest System lands (acres)	Other lands (acres)	Total area (acres)
Idaho				
Sawtooth	Sawtooth	216,383	—	216,383
Selway–Bitterroot[a]	Bitterroot, Clearwater, and Nezperce	988,688	491	989,179
State total		**1,205,071**	**491**	**1,205,562**
Minnesota				
Boundary Waters Canoe Area	Superior	**747,840**	**281,850**	**1,029,690**
Montana				
Anaconda–Pintlar	Beaverhead, Deer-lodge, and Bitter-root	157,803	1,283	159,086
Bob Marshall	Flathead and Lewis and Clark	950,000	—	950,000
Cabinet Mountains	Kaniksu and Kootenai	94,272	—	94,272
Gates of the Mountains	Helena	28,562	—	28,562
Scapegoat	Helena, Lewis and Clark, and Lolo	239,295	641	239,936
Selway–Bitterroot[b]	Bitterroot and Lolo	251,930	2,550	254,480
State total		**1,721,862**	**4,474**	**1,726,336**
Nevada				
Jarbidge	Humboldt	**64,667**	**160**	**64,827**
New Hampshire				
Great Gulf	White Mountain	**5,552**	—	**5,552**
New Mexico				
Gila	Gila	433,690	226	433,916
Pecos	Carson and Santa Fe	167,416	—	167,416
San Pedro Parks	Santa Fe	41,132	—	41,132
Wheeler Peak	Carson	6,027	2	6,029
White Mountain	Lincoln	31,171	112	31,283
State total		**679,436**	**340**	**679,776**

[a] Also in Montana.
[b] Also in Idaho

(*Continued*)

State and wilderness	National forest(s)	National Forest System lands (acres)	Other lands (acres)	Total area (acres)
North Carolina				
Linville Gorge	Pisgah	7,575	—	7,575
Shining Rock	Pisgah	13,350	—	13,350
State total		20,925	—	20,925
Oregon				
Diamond Peak	Deschutes and Willamette	36,637	—	36,637
Eagle Gap	Wallowa and Whitman	293,476	299	293,775
Gearhart Mountain	Fremont	18,709	—	18,709
Kalmiopsis	Siskiyou	76,900	—	76,900
Mountain Lakes	Winema	23,071	—	23,071
Mt. Hood	Mt. Hood	14,160	—	14,160
Mt. Jefferson	Deschutes and Willamette and Mt. Hood	100,208	—	100,208
Mt. Washington	Deschutes and Willamette	46,116	—	46,116
Strawberry Mountain	Malheur	33,003	650	33,653
Three Sisters	Deschutes and Willamette	199,902	—	199,902
State total		842,182	949	843,131
Washington				
Glacier Peak	Mt. Baker and Wenatchee	464,258	483	464,741
Goat Rocks	Gifford Pinchot and Snoqualmie	82,680	—	82,680
Mount Adams	Gifford Pinchot	32,356	10,055	42,411
Pasayten	Mt. Baker and Okanogan	505,524	—	505,524
State total		1,084,818	10,538	1,095,356
Wyoming				
Bridger	Bridger	392,160	—	392,160
North Absaroka	Shoshone	351,104	—	351,104
Teton	Teton	557,311	—	557,311
Washakie	Shoshone	691,130	548	691,678
State total		1,991,705	548	1,992,253
Total area of national forest wilderness (66 areas)		10,740,706	310,984	11,051,690

Table A–7. Primitive Areas in National Forests, as of January 1, 1973

State and primitive area	National forest(s)	National Forest System lands (acres)	Other lands (acres)	Total area (acres)
Arizona				
Blue Range[a]	Apache	173,712	1,400	175,112
California				
Aqua Tibia	Cleveland	25,995	765	26,760
Emigrant Basin	Stanislaus	97,020	1,023	98,043
High Sierra	Sequoia and Sierra	10,247	—	10,247
Salmon Trinity Alps	Klamath, Shasta, and Trinity	223,980	61,776	285,756
State total		**357,242**	**63,564**	**420,806**
Colorado				
Flat Tops	Routt and White River	102,124	—	102,124
Gore Range–Eagle Nest	Arapaho and White River	61,942	183	62,125
San Juan	San Juan	226,656	743	227,399
Uncompahgre	Uncompahgre	53,252	16,001	69,253
Upper Rio Grande	Rio Grande	58,014	—	58,014
Wilson Mountains	San Juan and Uncompahgre	30,104	771	30,875
State total		**532,092**	**17,698**	**549,790**
Idaho				
Idaho	Boise, Challis, Payette, and Salmon	1,224,793	7,951	1,232,744
Salmon River Breaks	Bitterroot and Nezperce	216,870	315	217,185
State total		**1,441,663**	**8,266**	**1,449,929**
Montana				
Absaroka	Gallatin	64,000	—	64,000
Beartooth	Custer and Gallatin	230,000	—	230,000
Mission Mountains	Flathead	73,945	—	73,945
Spanish Peaks	Gallatin	50,516	180	50,696
State total		**418,461**	**180**	**418,641**

[a] Area is also in New Mexico.
[b] Area is also in Arizona.

(*Continued*)

313

State and primitive area	National forest(s)	National Forest System lands (acres)	Other lands (acres)	Total area (acres)
New Mexico				
Gila	Gila	130,637	2,151	132,788
Black Range	Gila	169,336	648	169,984
Blue Range[b]	Apache	36,598	—	36,598
State total		**336,571**	**2,799**	**339,370**
Utah				
High Uintas	Ashley and Wasatch	**237,177**	—	**237,177**
Wyoming				
Cloud Peak	Bighorn	136,905	—	136,905
Glacier	Shoshone	176,303	—	176,303
Popo Agie	Shoshone	71,320	—	71,320
State total		**384,528**	—	**384,528**
Total of primitive areas in national forests (23 areas)		**3,881,446**	**93,907**	**3,975,353**

Appendix **B**

**FOREST
SERVICE
APPROPRIATIONS
FOR
FISCAL
YEAR
1975**

Table B–1. Appropriations, 1975

Appropriation item and projects	Appropriation ($)

APPROPRIATED FUNDS

FOREST PROTECTION AND UTILIZATION

FOREST LAND MANAGEMENT:
National forest protection and management
Timber resource management:

(a) Sales administration and management	83,950,000
(b) Reforestation and stand improvement	50,079,000
Recreation use	46,828,000
Wildlife and fish habitat management	9,190,000
Rangeland management	17,391,000
Soil and water management	16,051,000
Minerals management	3,601,000
Forest fire protection	36,257,000
General land management activities	26,337,000
Total, National forest protection and management	**$289,684,000**
Deduct from *Rangeland management* above *Cooperative range improvements*—permanent (receipts) appropriation	700,000
National forest protection and management appropriated in the Appropriation Act	288,984,000
Fighting forest fires	4,275,000
Forest insect and disease control	11,242,000
	1,618,000
Cooperative law enforcement	
TOTAL, FOREST LAND MANAGEMENT	**$306,119,000**

FOREST RESEARCH:
Forest and range management research

Trees and timber management research	14,089,000
Forest watershed management research	8,294,000
Wildlife, range, and fish habitat research	5,071,000
Forest recreation research	1,218,000
	2,200,000
Surface environment and mining	
Total, Forest and range management research	**$30,872,000**
Forest protection research	
Fire and atmospheric sciences research	8,046,000
	17,346,000
Forest insects and disease research	
Total, Forest protection research	**$25,392,000**
Forest products and engineering research	
Forest products utilization research	9,981,000
	1,590,000
Forest engineering research	
Total, Forest products and engineering research	**$11,571,000**

(*Continued*)

Appropriation item and projects	Appropriation ($)
Forest resource economics research	
Forest resources evaluation	3,804,000
	3,763,000
Forest economics and marketing research	
	$7,567,000
Total, Forest resource economics research	
TOTAL, FOREST RESEARCH	**$75,402,000**
STATE AND PRIVATE FORESTRY COOPERATION:	
Cooperation in forest fire control	25,088,000
Cooperation in forest tree planting	333,000
Cooperation in forest management and processing	5,568,000
	3,649,000
General forestry assistance	
TOTAL, STATE AND PRIVATE FORESTRY CO-OPERATION	**$34,638,000**
TOTAL, FOREST PROTECTION AND UTILIZATION	**$416,159,000**
CONSTRUCTION AND LAND ACQUISITION:	
Development of recreation–public use areas	4,832,000
Water resource development construction	2,194,000
Construction for fire, administration, and other purposes	1,718,000
Research construction	3,939,000
Pollution abatement	16,648,000
	1,577,000
Land acquisition, Weeks Act	
TOTAL, CONSTRUCTION AND LAND ACQUISITION	**$30,908,000**
FOREST ROADS AND TRAILS:	
Construction	122,383,000
	38,981,000
Maintenance	
Total	**$161,364,000**
Transfer from *Roads and Trails for States* (10% Fund) — permanent appropriation	40,500,000
FOREST ROADS AND TRAILS appropriated in the Appropriation Act	120,864,000
ACQUISITION OF LANDS FOR NATIONAL FORESTS, SPECIAL ACTS	161,000
ACQUISITION OF LANDS TO COMPLETE LAND EXCHANGES	39,310
ACQUISITION OF LANDS, KLAMATH INDIANS	49,000,000
COOPERATIVE RANGE IMPROVEMENTS	700,000
ASSISTANCE TO STATES FOR TREE PLANTING	1,344,000
CONSTRUCTION AND OPERATION OF RECREATION FACILITIES	1,260,000
	10,240,000
YOUTH CONSERVATION CORPS	
TOTAL, APPROPRIATED FUNDS	**$630,675,310**

Source: U.S. Department of Agriculture/Forest Service.

317

Appendix C

FOREST
SERVICE
APPROPRIATIONS,
1962–71

Table C-1. Timber Resource Management—Sales Administration and Management
(in thousands of dollars)

	Prior fiscal year appropriation act (a)	Base adjusted due to Pay Act, supplement, etc. (b)	Adjusted base (a + b) (c)	Forest Service proposed increase (d)	Department increase allowed (e)	Bureau of Budget increase allowed (f)	Congressional increase allowed (g)	Appropriation Act (c + g) (h)
1962	21,595		21,595	+2,067	+1,300	+700	+1,185	22,780
1963	22,780	+590	23,370	+1,408	+1,408	+400	+220	23,590
1964	23,590	+27	23,617	+3,061	+5,000	+5,912	+5,171	28,788
1965	28,788	+1,129	29,917	+737	+817	+526	+526	30,443
1966	30,443	+201	30,644	+2,000	+2,914	+165	+165	30,809
1967	30,809	+2,828	33,637	+4,738	+4,100	+826	+826	34,463
1968	34,463	+757	35,220	+6,438	+3,268	+1,437	+1,437	36,657
1969	36,657	+1,394	38,051	+3,025	+2,930	+1,416	+1,300	39,351
1970	39,351	+3,380	42,731	+2,507	+3,573	+5,760	+5,760	48,491
1971	48,491	+1,784	50,275	+12,929	+13,671	+5,260	+5,260	55,535
TIMBER RESOURCE MANAGEMENT—REFORESTATION AND STAND IMPROVEMENT								
1962	4,451		4,451	13,213	+8,850	+5,100	+8,299	12,750
1963	12,750	+238	12,988	+4,876	+4,876	+2,500	+2,380	15,368
1964	15,368	+2	15,370	+10,551	+7,600	+275	+275	15,645
1965	15,645	+267	15,912	+11,639	+11,639	+1,064	+964	16,876
1966	16,876	+184	17,060	+11,100	+5,187	+615	+300	17,360
1967	17,360	+210	17,570	+11,724	+686	+70	+70	17,640
1968	17,640	+1,850	15,790	+7,017	+610			15,790
1969	15,790	+223	16,013	+5,235	+1,875	+94		16,013
1970	16,013	+1,157	17,170	+3,616	−101			17,170
1971	17,170	+212	17,382	+15,987	+15,987	+2,877	+2,877	20,259

Source: U.S. Congress, Senate Public Lands Subcommittee of the Committee on Interior and Insular Affairs, Hearings on "Clear-Cutting" Practices on National Timberlands, 92 Cong., 1 sess., 1971, pp. 859–863.

Table C-1. (Continued)

	Prior fiscal year appropriation act (a)	Base adjusted due to Pay Act, supplement, etc. (b)	Adjusted base (a + b) (c)	Forest Service proposed increase (d)	Department increase allowed (e)	Bureau of Budget increase allowed (f)	Congressional increase allowed (g)	Appropriation Act (c + g) (h)
RECREATION—PUBLIC USE								
1962	15,180		15,180	8,626	+6,000	+3,400	+5,320	20,500
1963	20,500	+392	20,892	9,937	9,937	5,620	5,420	26,312
1964	26,312	+120	26,432	+16,294	+15,700	+463	−1,381	25,051
1965	25,051	+1,113	26,164	+12,283	+12,259	+959	+1,154	27,318
1966	27,318	−1,519	25,799	+20,975	+9,803	+2,100	+2,805	28,604
1967	28,604	+369	28,973	+31,785	+4,339	+1,272	+2,166	31,139
1968	31,139	+539	31,678	+19,001	+10,881	+3,499	+3,429	35,107
1969	35,107	+660	35,767	+19,362	+18,470	+2,434	+1,000	36,767
1970	36,767	+1,459	38,226	+8,734	+8,435	+314	+1,226	39,452
1971	39,452	−5,794	33,658	+3,407	+3,407	+3,598	+3,648	37,306
WILDLIFE HABITAT MANAGEMENT								
1962	1,718		1,718	+2,966	+2,000	+1,150	+1,502	3,220
1963	3,220	+80	3,300	+464	+464	+200	+180	3,480
1964	3,480	+2	3,482	+1,060	+1,000	+89	+89	3,571
1965	3,571	+219	3,790	+680	+683	+53	+53	3,843
1966	3,843	+29	3,872	+2,012	+1,089			3,872
1967	3,872	+74	3,946	+1,692				3,971
1968	3,971	+83	4,054	+958	+330	+25	+25	4,284
1969	4,284	+99	4,383	+399	+260	+330	+230	4,403
1970	4,403	+328	4,731	+684	+25	+162	+20	4,731
1971	4,731	+203	4,934	+501	+239			4,934

(Continued)

RANGE MANAGEMENT

Year								
1962	3,859		3,859	+1,653	+900	+500	+751	4,610
1963	4,610	+153	4,763	+18	+100	+100	+70	4,833
1964	4,833	+8	4,841	+294	+294	+167	+167	5,008
1965	5,008	+146	5,154	+237	+250	+100	+100	5,254
1966	5,254	+108	5,362	+998	+866			5,362
1967	5,362	+123	5,485	+1,046		+42	+42	5,527
1968	5,527	+149	5,676	+1,115	+295	+155	+155	5,831
1969	5,831	+170	6,001	+318		+61		6,001
1970	6,001	+783	6,784	+438	+109			6,784
1971	6,784	+321	7,105		+570			7,105

RANGE REVEGETATION

Year								
1962	1,911		1,911	+787	+810	+550	+629	2,540
1963	2,540	+34	2,574	+126	+120	+120	+100	2,674
1964	2,674	+2	2,676	+181	+181	+38	+38	2,714
1965	2,714	+43	2,757	+23	+23	+23	+23	2,780
1966	2,780	+30	2,810	+514	+12			2,810
1967	2,810	+34	2,844	+320		+10	+10	2,854
1968	2,854	+41	2,895	+138				2,895
1969	2,895	+43	2,938	+296		+229	+10	2,948
1970	2,948	+143	3,091	+86	+63		+200	3,291
1971	3,291	+93	3,384	+552	+314			3,384

RANGE IMPROVEMENTS (INCLUDES COOPERATIVE RANGE IMPROVEMENTS)

Year								
1962	2,388		2,388	+1,492	+950	+550	+792	3,180
1963	3,180	+43	3,223	+175	+100		−20	3,203
1964	3,203	+2	3,205	+612	+612	+47	+47	3,252
1965	3,252	+103	3,355	+320	+328	+28	+28	3,383
1966	3,383	−4	3,379	+1,508	+836			3,379
1967	3,379	+47	3,426	+961		+16	+16	3,442
1968	3,442	+554	3,996	+548				3,996

(Continued)

321

Table C–1. (*Continued*)

Year	Prior fiscal year appropriation act (a)	Base adjusted due to Pay Act, supplement, etc. (b)	Adjusted base (a + b) (c)	Forest Service proposed increase (d)	Department increase allowed (e)	Bureau of Budget increase allowed (f)	Congressional increase allowed (g)	Appropriation Act (c + g) (h)
1969	3,996	−442	3,554	+408		+872	+10	3,564
1970	3,564	+333	3,897	+142	+79			3,897
1971	3,897	+36	3,933	+2,136	+1,004	+650	+650	4,583
SOIL AND WATER MANAGEMENT								
1962	3,201		3,201	+3,282	+2,200	+1,200	+1,939	5,140
1963	5,140	+108	5,248	+836	+836	+400	+370	5,618
1964	5,618	+4	5,622	+2,321	+2,240	+124	−347	5,275
1965	5,275	+3,875	9,150	+1,931	+1,930	+70	+70	9,220
1966	9,220	−3,998	5,222	+5,250	+2,398	+1,000	+500	5,722
1967	5,722	+100	5,822	+5,054	+2,000	+539	+539	6,361
1968	6,361	−491	5,870	+2,492	+1,018			5,870
1969	5,870	+124	5,994	+939		+45		5,994
1970	5,994	+752	6,746	+3,805	+183			6,746
1971	6,746	−25	6,721	+2,306	+323			6,721
MINERAL CLAIMS, LEASES, AND SPECIAL USES								
1962	3,335	−1,589	1,746	+3,249	+2,200	+1,200	+1,618	3,364
1963	3,364	−82	3,282	+936	+936	+400	+340	3,622
1964	3,622	+3	3,625	+371	+360	+106	+106	3,731
1965	3,731	+110	3,841	+200	+203	+63	+63	3,904
1966	3,904	+72	3,976	+490	+342			3,976
1967	3,976	+93	4,069	+496		+28	+28	4,097
1968	4,097	+94	4,191	+206				4,191
1969	4,191	+69	4,260	+173		+39	+39	4,299
1970	4,299	+459	4,758	+330	+162			4,758
1971	4,758	+391	5,149	+2,101	+334			5,149

LAND CLASSIFICATION, ADJUSTMENTS, AND SURVEYS

Year								
1962	1,847	+1,589	3,436					3,436
1963	3,436	+272	3,708					3,708
1964	3,708	+4	3,712	+1,529	+1,480	+117	+117	3,829
1965	3,829	+113	3,942	+1,070	+1,148	+70	+70	4,012
1966	4,012	+83	4,095	+3,020	+1,695	+500	+250	4,345
1967	4,345	+120	4,465	+4,538	+1,800	+1,460	+1,260	5,725
1968	5,725	−139	5,586	+3,264	+1,525	+624	+624	6,210
1969	6,210	+143	6,353	+956				6,353
1970	6,353	+619	6,972	+1,476	+119	+324	+150	7,122
1971	7,122	+259	7,381	+1,447	+416	−150	−150	7,231

FOREST FIRE PROTECTION

Year								
1962	16,051		16,051	+5,576	+4,500	+3,100	+4,339	20,390
1963	20,390	+375	20,765	+1,897	+1,897	+1,400	+1,210	21,975
1964	21,975	+13	21,988	+3,743	+3,572	+450	+750	22,788
1965	22,738	+823	23,561	+3,934	+3,938	+273	+273	23,834
1966	23,834	+120	23,954	+7,009	+3,254		+500	24,454
1967	24,454	+367	24,821	+5,736	+1,400	+666	+666	25,487
1968	25,487	+471	25,958	+3,906	+1,017	+685	+685	26,643
1969	26,643	+498	27,141	+3,328	+392	+946	+825	27,966
1970	27,966	+1,689	29,655	+3,796	+489			29,655
1971	29,655	+1,270	30,925	+4,634	+1,317			30,925

MAINTENANCE OF IMPROVEMENTS FOR FIRE AND GENERAL PURPOSES

Year								
1962	9,802	−359	9,443	+5,369	+3,549	+1,927	+2,338	11,781
1963	11,781	−235	11,546	+1,180	+1,179	+359	+269	11,815
1964	11,815	+230	12,045	+2,143	+2,100	+154	−896	11,149
1965	11,149	−9	11,140	+2,532	+2,739	+322	+322	11,462
1966	11,462	−597	10,865	+4,927	+2,902			10,865
1967	10,865	+131	10,996	+4,748	+95	+44	+44	11,040
1968	11,040	−1,352	9,688	+2,071	+1,017		+50	9,738

(Continued)

Table C–1. (Continued)

Fiscal year	Prior fiscal year appropriation act (a)	Base adjusted due to Pay Act, supplement, etc. (b)	Adjusted base (a + b) (c)	Forest Service proposed increase (d)	Department increase allowed (e)	Bureau of Budget increase allowed (f)	Congressional increase allowed (g)	Appropriation Act (c + g) (h)
1969	9,738	+98	9,836	+1,760	-4,509	+1,056	-1,486	8,350
1970	8,350	+345	8,695	+6,207	+1,336	+779	+779	9,474
1971	9,474	-2,085	7,389	+1,745				7,389
WATER RESOURCE DEVELOPMENT RELATED ACTIVITIES								
1963								
1964								
1965								
1966				+16,000	+9,202	+4,532	+4,770	4,770
1967	4,770		4,770	+11,268	+4,957	+1,646	+1,946	6,716
1968	6,716	+149	6,865	+8,725	+2,855	+542	+1,394	8,259
1969	8,259	+94	8,353	+11,840	+11,840	+40		8,353
1970	8,353	-1,367	6,986	+3,301	+1,773	-1,325	-583	6,403
1971	6,403	-2,628	3,775	+1,187				3,775
INSECT AND DISEASE CONTROL								
1962	7,252		7,252	+2,629	+2,400	+2,150	+2,098	9,350
1963	9,350	+3,160	12,510	+2,153	+2,153	+1,400	+1,020	13,530
1964	13,530	-2,987	10,543	+380	+380	+193	+193	10,736
1965	10,736	+173	10,909	+2,137	+2,116	+116	-134	10,775
1966	10,775		10,775	+2,789	+2,091	+1,800	+1,400	12,175
1967	12,175	-8	12,167	+1,135	+350	+196	+196	12,363
1968	12,363	-287	12,076	+405		-800	-800	11,276
1969	11,276	+707	11,983	+800	+98	+193		11,983
1970	11,983	+17	12,000	-2,069	-1,496	-2,410	-2,410	9,590
1971	9,590	+662	10,252	+3,252	+1,773	+1,500	+1,500	11,752

CONSTRUCTION AND LAND ACQUISITION

Year							
1963							
1964							
1965							
1966							
1967							
1968							
1969							
1970							
1971	12,474	22,020	−4,875	−466	+3,460	15,934	

ACQUISITION OF LANDS, WEEKS ACT

Year								
1962			100	+1,625	+1,625		200	300
1963			300	+3,000	+1,000	+200	+200	500
1964			500	+4,038	+4,038	−462	+462	962
1965		+1,000	1,962	+4,457	+1,000		−282	1,680
1966		−1,000	680	+2,950	+1,800			680
1967			680	+3,729	+250	+1,800	+1,800	2,480
1968		−680	1,800	+480	−680			1,800
1969			1,800	+680	+500		−500	1,300
1970			1,300					1,300

FOREST RESEARCH—EXCLUDES CONSTRUCTION

Year								
1962	17,703		17,703	+9,600	+4,103	+3,470	+3,470	21,173
1963	21,173	+695	21,868	+8,022	+8,022	+1,227	+1,112	22,980
1964	22,980	+35	23,005	+10,315	+3,224	+743	+2,203	25,218
1965	25,218	+3,775	28,993	+4,814	+4,594	+926	+2,516	31,509
1966	31,509	−617	30,892	+10,410	+5,765	+952	+2,297	33,189
1967	33,189	+638	33,827	+15,694	+990	+1,246	+1,347	35,174
1968	35,174	+315	35,489	+13,413	+6,311	+2,580	+2,395	37,884
1969	37,884	+1,180	39,064	+9,100	+4,607	+2,243	+982	40,046
1970	40,046	+1,783	41,829	+10,981	+3,508	+937	+1,160	45,355
1971	45,355	+1,780	47,135	+18,455	+5,845	+1,146	+1,742	48,877

(Continued)

Table C–1. (Continued)

	Prior fiscal year appropriation act (a)	Base adjusted due to Pay Act, supplement, etc. (b)	Adjusted base (a + b) (c)	Forest Service proposed increase (d)	Department increase allowed (e)	Bureau of Budget increase allowed (f)	Congressional increase allowed (g)	Appropriation Act (c + g) (h)
			FOREST RESEARCH—CONSTRUCTION ONLY					
1962	1,075		1,075	+5,700	+5,040	+1,030	+4,120	5,105
1963	5,195		5,195	+2,910	+1,805	−4,445	−2,645	2,550
1964	2,550		2,550	−2,550	−2,550	−2,550	−1,915	635
1965	635	+50	685	+4,287	+4,287	+3,165	+3,316	4,001
1966	4,001	+75	4,076	+1,180		−2,683	+107	4,183
1967	4,183		4,183	−301	−4,108	−4,183	−898	3,285
1968	3,285	−660	2,625	+5,145	+823	−1,007	+803	3,428
1969	3,428		3,428	+13,409	−2,278	−3,428	−3,428	
1970				+20,627	+2,236		+931	931
			STATE AND PRIVATE FORESTRY COOPERATION					
1962	12,409		12,409	+7,603	+5,046	+3,600	+3,391	15,800
1963	15,800	+23	15,823	+5,160	+2,600		+30	15,853
1964	15,853	−1	15,852	+9,525	+3,200	+65	+65	15,917
1965	15,917	+408	16,325	+6,357	+6,357	+1,038	+1,038	17,363
1966	17,363	−305	17,058	+6,300	+5,036	+500	+500	17,558
1967	17,558	+254	17,812	+6,772	+5,000	+339	+339	18,151
1968	18,151	+67	18,218	+5,727	+5,276	+100	+1,600	19,818
1969	19,818	+96	19,914	+6,582	+2,300	+29	+15	19,929
1970	19,929	+210	20,139	+13,693	+580	+600	+2,800	22,910
1971	22,910	+253	23,163	+12,092	+3,154	−1,000	+1,000	24,163
			FOREST ROADS AND TRAILS (INCLUDING 10 PERCENT FUND)—CASH ONLY					
1962	45,166	−4,142	41,024	+14,700	+12,000	+8,000	+6,000	47,024
1963	47,024	+6,996	54,020	+22,180	+4,080	+4,080	+3,380	+57,400

326

Year							
1964	57,400	−1,999	55,401	+26,300	+25,300	+23,000	+19,800	75,201
1965	75,201	+6,412	81,613	+20,400	+20,400	+9,200	+7,500	89,113
1966	89,113	+19,768	108,881	+13,500	+13,387	+7,459	+7,459	116,340
1967	116,340	+2,078	118,418	+25,700	+27,615	+890	−410	118,003
1968	118,008	−5,779	112,229	+32,092	+28,952	+10,152	+9,152	121,381
1969	121,381	+8,316	129,697	+21,790	+25,140	−16,796	−17,766	111,931
1970	111,931	+5,875	117,806	+9,435	+10,630	+17,470	+13,970	131,776
1971	131,776	−311	131,465	+50,130	+33,722	+17,516	+17,516	148,981

FOREST ROADS AND TRAILS (INCLUDING 10 PERCENT FUND)—PROGRAM LEVEL

Year							
1962	45,166	−5,449	39,717	+10,000	+10,000	+9,807	+9,807	49,524
1963	49,524	+8,389	57,913	+9,000	+10,000	+2,487	+2,487	60,400
1964	60,400	+3,213	63,613	+15,500	+15,500	+13,938	+13,938	77,551
1965	77,551	+20,502	98,053	+22,500	+22,038	+7,438	+7,438	105,491
1966	105,491	+10,949	116,440	+14,800	+6,663	+2,763	+2,763	119,203
1967	119,203	+9,463	128,666	−8,370	−8,359	−10,752	−10,752	117,914
1968	117,914	+6,460	124,374	+44,574	+44,574	+14,574	−426	123,948
1969	123,948	+3,486	127,434	+30,000	+30,207	−11,912	−11,912	115,522
1970	115,522	+40,771	156,293	+22,928	+6,653	+10,175	−825	155,468
1971	115,468	+5,438	160,906	+40,032	+34,392	+10,980	+10,980	171,886

INDEX

329